THE ALPHA-TEXT OF ESTHER
*Its Character and Relationship
to the Masoretic Text*

SOCIETY OF BIBLICAL LITERATURE

DISSERTATION SERIES

Michael Fox, Old Testament Editor
Pheme Perkins, New Testament Editor

Number 153

THE ALPHA-TEXT OF ESTHER
*Its Character and Relationship
to the Masoretic Text*
by
Karen H. Jobes

Karen H. Jobes

THE ALPHA-TEXT OF ESTHER
Its Character and Relationship to the Masoretic Text

Scholars Press
Atlanta, Georgia

THE ALPHA-TEXT OF ESTHER
Its Character and Relationship to the Masoretic Text

Karen H. Jobes

Ph.D., 1995
Westminster Theological Seminary

Advisor:
Dr. Moisés Silva

© 1996
The Society of Biblical Literature

Library of Congress Cataloging in Publication Data
Jobes, Karen.
 The alpha-text of Esther : its character and relationship to the
Masoretic text / Karen H. Jobes.
  p. cm. — (Dissertation series : no. 153)
 Includes bibliographical references and indexes.
 ISBN 0-7885-0202-6 (alk. paper). — ISBN 0-7885-0203-4 (pbk. :
alk. paper)
 1. Bible. O.T. Esther—Criticism, Textual. 2. Bible. O.T.
Esther. Greek—Versions—Alpha-text. 3. Bible. O.T. Esther.
Hebrew—Versions. I. Bible. O.T. Esther. Greek. Alpha-text.
1996. II. Title. III. Series: Dissertation series (Society of Biblical
Literature) ; no. 153.
BS1375.2.J63 1996
222'.9048—dc20   95-52130
                               CIP

Printed in the United States of America
on acid-free paper
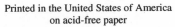

To the memory of Raymond B. Dillard, Ph.D.
who first introduced me to the Alpha-text of Esther

and

To the memory of Pamela Williams,
whose dissertation will never be written

and

To Michael F. Carey, Ed.D.
who first taught me the love of learning

TABLE OF CONTENTS

Appendices

LIST OF TABLES AND GRAPHS

Graphs   Page

LIST OF ABBREVIATIONS

AT	Alpha–text of Esther
AVA	*Authorized Version of the Apocrypha*
BDBG	*Brown–Driver–Briggs–Gesenius Hebrew–English Lexicon*
BHS	Biblia Hebraica Stuttgartensia
BS	*Biblische Studien*
CBQ	*Catholic Biblical Quarterly*
Encycl. Brit.	*Encyclopedia Britannica*
ES	*Even–Shoshan Concordance of the OT*
Harv Th R	*Harvard Theological Review*
HR	*Hatch & Redpath Concordance of the Septuagint*
HUCA	*Hebrew Union College Annual*
JBL	*Journal of Biblical Literature*
J Near East St	*Journal of Near Eastern Studies*
JR	*Journal of Religion*
J St OT	*Journal for the Study of the Old Testament*
LCL	*Loeb Classics Library*
LS	*Liddell & Scott Greek–English Lexicon*
MT	Hebrew text of Esther, *BHS 3*
NASB	*New American Standard Bible*
OG	Old Greek
OL	Old Latin
OT	Old Testament
OTP	*Old Testament Pseudepigraha* , J. Charlesworth, ed. (Garden City: Doubleday, 1983)
PAAJR	*Proceedings of the American Academy for Jewish Research*
R Qumran	*Revue de Qumran*
Z Altt W	*Zeitschrift für die Alttestamentliche Wissenschaft*
Z Rel Gg	*Zeitschrift für Religenis—und Geistesgeschicte*
θ	Theodotion

ACKNOWLEDGMENTS

Because my husband, Dr. Forrest (Buzz) Jobes, has wholeheartedly supported and amply provided for me during these long years of study, I have been free to pursue this dissertation unfettered. In the truest spirit of Ephesians 5:25, he has sacrificed much to make my achievement possible. Buzz, thank you for patiently loving me through this dissertation. It would not have been possible without you.

The late Prof. Raymond B. Dillard first incited my interest in the alpha–text of Esther. How I wish he had lived to see the completion of this work. Ray, your willingness to face the hard questions of biblical scholarship has challenged me to a higher standard of intellectual integrity. We all miss you very much.

As with any project that takes as much time as a doctoral dissertation, life goes on, bringing inevitable joys and sorrows. Carol Kane has prayed for me daily throughout these years. Carol, thank you for lifting your shield of faith over my work. Patty Comber has encouraged me with her prayers and friendship, especially through troubled times. Patty, thank you for walking with me through the days of this dissertation and constantly reminding me how great is our God.

Tracey (Jolly) Taylor provided assistance in proof–reading and correcting the parallel texts. Tracey, your keen eye for detail greatly improved the texts. Many thanks!

The staff of the library at Westminster Theological Seminary cheerfully provided the resources required by my work. Special thanks to Grace Mullen and Dr. Darryl Hart. You have each been most helpful in the preparation of this dissertation.

Prof. Michael V. Fox served as my external reader. Prof. Fox, I thank you for your kind and generous critique of my work. Although we have reached different conclusions about the AT of Esther, your previous work on this topic opened the way and invited me to follow. I thank you also for your encouragement and assistance that brought this work to press in SBLDS.

Prof. C. A. Moore read the dissertation in consideration for SBLDS. Thank you, Prof. Moore, for judging my work worthy of publication. Your fine work over the last thirty years has provided the foundation of all the studies of Esther that have followed.

Prof. Tremper Longman, III served as my second faculty reader at Westminster Theological Seminary. Tremper, thank you for your encouragement and for the many things you have taught me over these last several years. The Bible is more precious and exciting to me because of your teaching and scholarship.

Prof. Moisés Silva introduced me to the Septuagint and has supervised this dissertation. Moisés, your commitment to the ministry of teaching has motivated me, the excellence of your scholarship has inspired me, and your friendship has brought joy to my work. Thank you, Moisés, for being the "wind beneath my wings."

INTRODUCTION

> Why is there no Greek translation of the Hebrew text [of Esther]?
> Every other book of the Hebrew Bible, whatever its nature, has its
> faithful rendering (at least one, often several) in Greek. For the
> canonical Esther, on the contrary, no such version is extant, nor is
> there evidence that one ever existed, ... (Torrey 1944, 1)

Torrey's statement is striking because there are in fact two
distinct Greek versions of Esther. (There are three, if the Esther story
recounted by Josephus is considered to be a distinct version.) However,
both of the two extant Greek versions are so dissimilar to the canonical
Hebrew Esther that Torrey believed neither of them to be a translation
of the Masoretic text (MT). Although he has probably overstated his
point, the nature and extent of the differences between the versions of
Esther does raise intriguing questions about their origin and
relationship to one another.

The two distinct Greek versions of Esther have been known since
J. Ussher published the Esther texts found in a 13th century codex (ms.
93) in his *De Graeca Septuaginta interpretum versione syntagma cum
libri Estherae editione Origenica et vetere Graeca altera* in 1655. The
manuscript he published, now catalogued in the British Library as
Royal I.D.2, contains two separate Greek versions of Esther. The
second text of Esther in this codex is the same version found in the
majority of Greek manuscripts of Esther. This text is preserved in the
great uncials, such as Vaticanus, and is referred to as the B–text or
LXX–text of Esther. The first text of Esther preserved in ms. 93,
Royal I.D.2, is a rare version found only in four extant manuscripts.

– 1 –

Both Greek texts were again published in de Lagarde's *Librorum V.T. canonicorum pars prior Graece* in 1883. He also used ms. 93, Royal I.D.2, as his base text but departed from it when, in his opinion, one of the other manuscripts preserved a preferred reading. He labeled the rarer of the two Greek versions the alpha–text of Esther and identified it as a Lucianic recension of the majority text. Since de Lagarde's edition of the Greek texts of Esther, the alpha–text has been referred to variously as the AT, the A–text (not to be confused with codex Alexandrinus) or the L–text (L standing for "Lucianic").

In this study, the Greek version of Esther represented by the majority of manuscripts is called the LXX text; the alpha–text, preserved in only four manuscripts, is referred to as the AT.

THE EXTANT MANUSCRIPTS OF THE GREEK ESTHER

The LXX text of Esther survives in thirty–six manuscripts. The oldest complete manuscripts of Esther are found in the uncials of the third/fourth century of this era. The oldest manuscript preserving extensive fragments of the text is the Chester Beatty papyrus no. 967 (2nd/3rd century A.D.). A complete listing of the extant manuscripts of the LXX text of Esther can be found in the preface to Hanhart's Göttingen edition.

In comparison, the alpha–text of Esther is preserved only in four medieval manuscripts:

Siglum		Manuscript	Date	Current
G.	C.[1]			Location
19	b	Chigi R.vi. 38	12th cent.	Vatican Library, Rome
93	e$_2$	Royal I.D.2	13th cent.	British Library, London
108	*b*	Vat. Gr. 330	13th cent.	Vatican Library, Rome
319	y	Vatop. 600	1021 A.D.	Mt. Athos, Greece

A more detailed description of the features of these manuscripts is found in Appendix 2.

---

[1] G. = Göttingen notation; C. = Cambridge notation

THE PRINTED EDITIONS OF THE ALPHA–TEXT

In addition to Ussher's publication of ms. 93 in 1655 and de Lagarde's eclectic edition of 1883, the two Greek versions of Esther were printed on facing pages with critical apparatus in the 1871 edition of Otto Fritzsche's *Libri Apocryphi Veteris Testamenti Graece* (Lipsiae: F. A. Brockhaus, 1848). The Cambridge Septuagint merely reprints the eclectic text of the AT published by de Lagarde in 1883 (Brooke, McLean and Thackeray, 1940).

The critically reconstructed texts of both the LXX and AT of Esther used in this study are those published in *Septuaginta: Vetus Testamentum Graecum* (Göttingen: Vandenhoeck & Ruprecht, 1983) edited by Robert Hanhart. The Hebrew text of Esther used in this study is that published in *Biblia Hebraica Stuttgartensia* (BHS 3), a diplomatic text based on the Leningrad codex dating from 1008/9 A.D.

The only English translation of the AT has been made by D. J. A. Clines and is printed as an appendix in Clines (1984).

VERSIFICATION

Unfortunately, there is no standard numbering for the versification of the AT. The versification of the AT used in the Cambridge edition is different from that in the Göttingen edition and both are different from that used in the LXX and MT versions of Esther. Because this study uses the Göttingen edition as its textual base, the Göttingen versification is followed. The reader must be cautioned, however, that this system of versification has some anomalies. Verse numbering does not always proceed in sequence. For instance, in chapter 1 verse numbers proceed from verse 14 to 16; there is no verse 1:15. Even more confusing, in chapter 3, the verse numbered 10 follows the verse numbered 11! In the AT there are only seven chapter divisions. In the AT, chapter 7:1–59 comprises what is numbered as chapters 7–10 in the MT and 7–F in the LXX. As imperfect as the Göttingen scheme may be, it seemed preferable to use the versification of one of the printed editions rather than to invent yet another scheme for the purposes of this study.

In order to minimize the confusion and to allow the reader to accurately locate a citation, this study uses notation to specify the version being cited. For instance, a reference to 1:10 in the MT will be noted as MT:1:10, using BHS versification. A reference to the verse numbered 1:10 in the LXX text, which may or may not be the same verse as 1:10 in the MT, will be noted as LXX:1:10, using Göttingen versification. Similarly, references to the AT will be noted as AT:1:10, also using Göttingen versification, which may or may not be the same verse so numbered in the LXX or the MT. In long lists of citations with no prefix, the AT should be assumed, unless otherwise noted.

In the parallel texts found in Appendix 1, the versification for each of the three versions is specified only where they differ. Because the LXX more closely follows the MT than does the AT, the versification of the LXX and MT should be assumed the same unless the MT versification is explicitly given.

DEFINING THE SCOPE OF THIS STUDY

Scholarly interests attending the versions of Esther are many and varied. Therefore it seems wise to delimit the scope of this work by stating what this study is not attempting to address. This work is not a commentary on the Greek versions of Esther, similar for instance to Wevers' *Notes on the Greek Text of Exodus* (Wevers 1990), although such a work for Esther is needed. This study does not address the issue of literary sources from which the biblical text of Esther may have developed (e.g., the Mordecai source, the Esther source and possibly the third Vashti source). Even if such sources were used, the Greek versions clearly correspond to the Esther story after they were redacted together. And although this work is concerned with the minutiae of the texts, this study does not attempt to establish the original text of either Greek version or to reconstruct the *Vorlage* of the AT. It is assumed that Göttingen has produced the best available critical text of the Greek versions of Esther. This study also does not attempt to reconstruct the *Vorlage* of the AT. It may offer information which would be helpful to textual critics reconstructing the Hebrew text of Esther, but that is not primarily its goal.

This study focuses on the issue of the relationship of the AT to its parent text and the relationship of that parent text to the MT of Esther. The methodology employed is accordingly toward that end. The three versions of Esther are printed in parallel columns in Appendix 1, which highlight at a glance where and to what extent the texts correspond. To determine if the AT is a translation of a Semitic version of Esther, R. Martin's criteria for identifying syntactical evidence in Greek texts of Semitic sources is applied to both of the Greek versions of Esther in their entirety (Martin 1974). Chapter 1 answers the question, Was the AT of Esther originally a translation of a Semitic source?

The character of the AT in relation to the MT is profiled using E. Tov's criteria for determining how closely a Greek text follows its Hebrew *Vorlage* (Tov 1981). The results of this analysis are discussed in chapters 2 and 3. Chapter 2 discusses the question, How is the AT similar to the MT? Chapter 3 discusses the question, How is the AT different from the MT?

The character of the AT is then compared to the LXX in chapter 4 with special attention given to the differences between the six major additions in the two Greek versions. It addresses the question, To what extent does the AT depend on the LXX? and advances the discussion on the origin and relationship of the six major additions.

Chapter 5 compares the results of this study to work on the AT previously published by C. A. Moore, E. Tov, D. J. A. Clines, and M. V. Fox. The conclusion of this work proposes an answer to the question, What is the AT and its relationship to the MT? At the end of this work an excursus compares the AT of Esther to the Old Greek of Daniel, using data published in the doctoral dissertations of D. Wenthe (1991) and S. Jeansonne (1988).

A PREVIEW OF THE CONCLUSIONS

The major conclusions of this study are: (1) The AT was originally produced as a translation of a Semitic source, not as a recension of a Greek parent text. (2) The AT, excluding the six major additions, originally translated a Semitic *Vorlage* which was similar in its extent and content to the extant MT and which was in many places throughout identical to the MT. (3) The AT preserves the older form of five of the six additions: A, B, C, E and F. (4) There are more redactional similarities among the additions in the AT than has been previously noted. (5) The AT was probably the first Greek translation to be made of the Esther story, possibly in Ptolemaic Egypt, and was later replaced by the LXX translation of Esther produced in Jerusalem.

CHAPTER 1: IS THE ALPHA–TEXT A TRANSLATION OF A SEMITIC SOURCE?

There are three possible origins of the Greek alpha–text of Esther (AT). It may be (1) a fresh translation made directly from a Semitic source, or (2) a recension of a Greek text that had previously been translated from a Semitic source, or (3) a new telling of the Esther story composed in Greek with no genetic relationship to a previously existing text.[1] Because of the extent and the nature of the similarities between the AT and the Masoretic text (MT) and between the AT and the LXX of Esther, it is almost certain that the AT, with the exception perhaps of one or more of the additions, is either a translation made from a Semitic *Vorlage* of Esther or a subsequent recension of such a translation. It is therefore appropriate to examine the AT to determine whether or not a Semitic source can be detected.

SYNTACTICAL EVIDENCE OF SEMITIC SOURCES IN THE ALPHA–TEXT OF ESTHER

Raymond A. Martin has demonstrated that a Greek translation made directly from a Hebrew *Vorlage* will bear distinctive patterns of

---

[1] I will use "translation" to refer to a Greek text produced directly from a Semitic source, "recension" to refer to subsequent revisions of a Greek parent text, and "composition" to refer to a Greek text which has no *Vorlage*, either Semitic or Greek. A genetic relationship is that which exists between a translation and the Semitic *Vorlage* from which it was made, or between a recension and the Greek text from which it was produced.

syntax that arise from the influence of the Hebrew syntax of the *Vorlage*. He has formulated seventeen criteria that differentiate translation Greek from original Greek composition (Martin 1974). Martin's methodology involves counting the number of times each of the seventeen syntactical constructions occur in the Greek text in question. The relative frequency of the occurrence of the given syntax with respect to other elements of the syntax is expressed as a mathematical ratio. Martin has examined texts known to be Greek translations and texts known to be Greek compositions and has calculated ratios characteristic of each group for each of the seventeen criteria. By calculating the ratios for the Greek text in question and comparing them to the ranges published by Martin for translation Greek and composition Greek, the syntax of the Greek text in question can be deemed one or the other.

For the first eight of the seventeen criteria, which are based on the frequency of occurrence of prepositions, Martin used the Greek Old Testament to determine the ratios characteristic of translation Greek. To the extent that any of these texts have interpolated pericopes which were composed in Greek, Martin's ratios characterizing "translation" Greek will be somewhat skewed. To determine ratios characteristic of composition Greek for criteria 1–8, Martin used 2, 3 and 4 Maccabees, selected Greek papyri, Polybius, Herodotus, Thucydides, Xenophon, Diodorus, Dionysius, and Josephus.

To determine characteristic ratios for criteria 9–17, Martin used Rahlfs' text of Gen 1–4, 6, 39; 1 Sam 3, 4, 22; 1 Kgs 13; Daniel (both OG and Theodotion) and Ezra (both OG and Theodotion) as texts representative of translation Greek. For texts representing composition Greek he examined Plutarch's *Lives*, Polybius Bks. I, II, Epictetus Bks. III, IV, Josephus' *Contra Apionem* and *Antiquities*, and selected papyri. Martin has subsequently expanded his textual base by an additional 2270 lines of translation Greek and 1630 lines of composition Greek. These additional controls "basically confirm the results of the original study" and result in only "a slight, modification of some of the ranges established in the original study" (Martin 1987, 138–39).

I have analyzed the Göttingen text of both the LXX and AT versions of Esther in their entirety using Martin's methodology to determine if, according to his seventeen criteria, the overall character of the syntax of the AT tends toward translation Greek or toward composition Greek and how it compares to the syntax of the LXX version of Esther. Because the six additions, A–F, found only in the Greek versions, were almost certainly added after the text was first produced, I have analyzed separately the syntax of both the total AT (including the additions) and the so-called "proto–AT" (the AT minus the six additions). An analysis of each of the six major additions in both the LXX and AT was also done, but they are too short for syntax criticism to indicate their original language with any certainty.

Martin has applied his methodology to the additions to Esther (Martin 1975) and M. V. Fox has analyzed a selected fifty–seven lines of both the AT and LXX (Fox 1991, 33–4). A comparison of their results to mine is discussed below.

The voluminous data collected from my examination of both the AT and LXX texts of Esther is displayed in two series of tables in Appendix 3. Tables a–j display the frequency of occurrence and the ratios calculated for each of the seventeen criteria. Table 1 summarizes all seventeen criteria for each text. To make the results of this study more easily grasped, I have statistically analyzed the data to determine the central tendency and variability of the syntax of the texts. The S–number ("S" for "syntax") expresses the central tendency of the syntax of the entire text in one number. The standard deviation of the S–number indicates the spread of the syntax of the text between the poles of translation and composition Greek. The results of this analysis are presented in three graphs at the end of this chapter.

Graph 1 displays the syntactic profiles of the LXX and AT as a histogram of the frequency distribution of the ratios of the criteria. The syntactic profiles of the Greek versions of Esther can be compared to those of Polybius, Josephus and selected papyri, which are displayed in Graph 2. A comparison of the S–numbers of the AT and LXX of Esther with their deviations compared to other texts known to be composition and translation Greek is displayed in Graph 3.

Since Martin used the LXX text of Esther when he determined characteristic ratios of translation Greek for criteria 1–8, my ratios for criteria 1–8 of the LXX of Esther can be compared directly with his as a check on my work. A comparison of LXX:Table a to Martin's published data (Martin 1974, 7) shows that my ratios for criteria 1–8 are almost exactly the same as Martin's, even though he used Rahlfs' text and I have used the Göttingen edition.

A comparison of Rahlfs' text of Esther to the Göttingen text shows thirty–two differences, most of which are insignificant. (For instance, fifteen of the differences are simply the presence or absence of the moveable-ν.) Only three of the differences would affect the syntactical criteria that involve genitive constructions. In these three instances the Göttingen text does not have a genitive personal pronoun where Rahlfs does (4:1, 7:3, F:9). These differences are too few to change perceptibly the ratios of the entire text.

For a full discussion of the rationale behind each of Martin's seventeen criteria, I refer the reader to Martin (1974); however, the following brief statement of the criteria is given to help understand the nature of syntax criticism and to make the tables displaying the data more useful.

Criteria 1–8. The first eight of Martin's criteria are the relative frequencies of occurrence of eight Greek prepositions, each with respect to the frequency of occurrence of the preposition ἐν. By comparing the syntax of texts known to be composition Greek to that of texts known to be translation Greek, Martin has determined that a Greek translation of a Semitic text uses the preposition ἐν disproportionately more often than other Greek prepositions. According to Martin, this is because Greek translators tended to translate consistently the oft–occurring Hebrew preposition בְּ with ἐν. Therefore, Martin uses the relative frequency of occurrence of the following eight prepositions with respect to ἐν to help distinguish between Greek translated from a Semitic source and composition Greek: (1) διά with the genitive case, (2) διά with all cases, (3) εἰς, (4) κατά with the accusative case, (5) κατά with all cases, (6) περί, (7) πρός with the dative case, and (8) ὑπό with the genitive.

Criterion 9. The ninth criterion is the number of times the copulative καί is used to coordinate independent clauses compared to the postpositive δέ. A comparison of the Greek versions to the Hebrew Bible shows that the Hebrew waw–consecutive is often translated using καί, preserving Hebrew word order, instead of a postpositive conjunction, which would not.

Criterion 10 counts the number of times the Greek definite article is separated from its substantive by an adjective, prepositional phrase, postpositive conjunction, etc. In composition Greek the definite article is often separated from its substantive by modifiers, particles, etc. In contrast, the definite article in Hebrew is a morpheme prefixed directly to its substantive with any modifiers following the substantive. Martin reasons that translation Greek would tend to follow the word order of its Hebrew *Vorlage* and therefore have a lower occurrence of articles separated from their substantives than would be found in composition Greek.

Criterion 11 is based on the premise that in translation Greek dependent genitives infrequently precede the word on which they depend because in Hebrew or Aramaic the genitive relationship is expressed either by the construct state, the particle **דִּי** or a pronominal suffix. In each of these constructions, the genitive follows the substantive. Martin observes that in composition Greek the genitive frequently precedes the word it qualifies. Martin gives the example that the phrase "the father's house" would be expressed as ἡ τοῦ πατρὸς οἰκία in composition Greek but by ἡ οἰκία τοῦ πατρός if translated from Hebrew. Therefore, a more frequent occurrence of genitives following their substantives is characteristic of translation Greek.

Criterion 12 is similar to criterion 11. The genitive personal pronoun in Hebrew and Aramaic is expressed by a pronominal suffix and therefore follows the substantive it possesses. Furthermore, the pronominal suffix is repeated for each noun in a series. In composition Greek, the genitive personal pronoun is used only once in a series or a possessive adjective is used instead. Therefore, a greater number of dependent genitive personal pronouns indicates Greek translated from a Semitic language.

Criterion 13 is similar to criteria 11 and 12. In Semitic languages a noun with the pronominal suffix does not also take a definite article. Therefore in translation Greek Martin expects to find a greater number of genitive personal pronouns dependent on anarthrous substantives.

Criterion 14 is based on the observation that in Hebrew or Aramaic an attributive adjective generally follows the word it modifies. Since the translator often preserves the word order of his *Vorlage*, translation Greek will therefore exhibit fewer occurrences of an attributive adjective preceding the word it modifies.

Criterion 15 is similar to criterion 14. Martin observes that Hebrew and Aramaic use fewer attributive adjectives than are used in composition Greek and therefore the number of lines of text per attributive adjective is higher for translation Greek than for composition Greek.

Criterion 16 is based on the rationale that Greek uses the adverbial participle in subordinate clauses but that the Semitic languages do not generally subordinate clauses. Martin observes that the adverbial participle therefore occurs more frequently in composition Greek than in translation Greek.

Criterion 17 is based on the frequency of use of the dative case. In Hebrew and Aramaic the locative and the instrumental concepts, expressed in Greek by the dative case, are expressed by using the preposition בְּ. As previously mentioned, בְּ is usually translated into Greek using a prepositional phrase introduced by ἐν with the dative case. In composition Greek, however, the dative case is more frequently used without the preposition ἐν. Therefore, a more frequent use of the dative case without the preposition is more characteristic of composition Greek than of translation.

Martin calculated an expected range of ratios for each of the seventeen criteria by counting the occurrence of each construction in texts known to be translations and in texts known to be compositions. To determine the character of a given Greek text whose origin is unknown, one first counts the number of times each of these seventeen syntactical criteria occur in the text, and then calculates the ratio of the relative frequencies.[2] A comparison of the calculated ratios of each criterion to Martin's published ranges indicates whether the use of the given syntactical feature in the Greek text is characteristic of translation Greek or composition Greek.

The overall character of the syntax of the text is determined by observing whether there are more translation traits exhibited by the text or more composition traits. If a text is found to have more criteria indicating translation Greek than composition Greek, Martin takes the arithmetic difference to compute "net translation Greek frequencies." If there are more criteria indicating composition Greek than translation Greek, the resulting difference is called "net original Greek frequencies." In other words, the value of each of the seventeen criteria

---

[2] Martin gives step–by–step directions for counting and calculating the ratios in appendix 1 of Martin (1987).

votes for either translation or composition Greek, and the majority vote indicates the probable origin of the text.

AT:Table 1 and LXX:Table 1 in Appendix 3 display a summary of the ratios of the seventeen criteria calculated for the Greek texts of Esther. For the AT, nine of the seventeen criteria indicate translation Greek, two indicate composition Greek and six are inconclusive because the ratios fall in between the ranges determined by Martin. Excluding the inconclusive criteria and subtracting the composition traits from the translation yields seven net translation frequencies for the AT. For the LXX, nine of the seventeen criteria indicate translation Greek, five indicate composition Greek and three are inconclusive, yielding four net translation frequencies. The conclusion based on net frequencies is that the syntax of both the AT and LXX texts of Esther indicate they are translations of Semitic sources. This suggests that the AT was originally produced as a translation of a Semitic text and not as a recension of the LXX, unless, as a recension, it somehow retained its Semitic character or, as E. Tov has suggested, was revised toward a Hebrew text (Tov 1982). The likelihood of a recension retaining the Semitic influence of its parent text is discussed further in chapter 4; Tov's theory is critiqued in chapter 5. In any case, the syntax of the AT is not markedly different from that of the LXX.

When the ratios of Martin's seventeen criteria are calculated in the Greek versions of Esther, a large number of them (six for the AT and three for the LXX) produce ratios that are inconclusive because they fall in between the control values for translation vs. composition Greek published by Martin. Because Martin has not calculated the average and standard deviation of his ranges, there is no way to determine accurately whether a ratio that falls outside of his ranges is actually closer to the values for translation or composition Greek. Moreover, a measure of the central tendency of the syntax of a text and its variability from the norm of translation or composition is lacking in Martin's treatment of the ratios.

I have applied simple statistical methods to the ratios that not only overcome this problem but that also reveal more detailed information about the syntactic character of the texts and make a direct comparison of the overall syntax of the AT and the LXX texts possible. A critique of Martin's methodology and the modifications and extensions I have made while using it for this study are presented in the excursus at the end of this chapter.

THE RESULTS OF SYNTAX CRITICISM
OF THE GREEK TEXTS OF ESTHER

Syntax criticism indicates that both the AT and LXX of Esther are translations of Semitic sources and that there is no discernible difference in their syntax. Graph 1, located at the end of this chapter, shows a comparison of the profiles of the syntax of the Greek versions of Esther. The ratio of each of the valid sixteen criteria has been normalized to fall between −1 (=composition Greek) and +1 (=translation Greek). (See the excursus at the end of this chapter for the reason why normalization is necessary and the formula used to normalize the ratios.) Then, the ratio for each criterion is "binned" in increments of 0.1. The number of criteria that fall in each "bin" is counted. Graph 1 shows a histogram indicating this frequency distribution of the normalized ratios for both the AT and LXX of Esther, both including and excluding the secondary major additions.

Graph 1 shows that the central tendency of these texts is towards translation Greek because most of the normalized ratios fall between 0 and +1. Note from Graph 1 that although the central tendency of the LXX is towards translation Greek, the syntax of the LXX of Esther is more mixed than is the syntax of the AT.

The syntactical tendencies of the Greek versions of Esther can be compared to those of Polybius, Josephus and selected papyri, displayed in Graph 2. Graph 2 shows the normalized values for the ratios of those texts as published by Martin (1974, *passim*). Graph 2 shows that most of the normalized ratios for Polybius and Josephus are less than zero, indicating composition Greek. The syntax of the selected papyri shows a surprisingly split character, with half the criteria clustering in the range of composition Greek and half in translation Greek. Since the papyri are known to have been composed in Greek, this finding raises the question that Martin's criteria may in fact be differentiating between different styles of Greek, for instance the literary Attic style as compared to the koine of the papyri, rather than translation vs. composition *per se*.

Graph 1 further shows that the central tendencies of both the AT and the LXX of Esther were shifted somewhat towards composition Greek when the six additions were added. This corroborates the hypothesis that at least some of the additions were original Greek compositions and that the entire text was edited when the additions were included. The origin of the additions is discussed in more detail below and in chapter 4.

Graph 3 displays the S–number for each text (i.e., the average and standard deviation of the normalized ratios) and shows that the central tendency of the AT of Esther is somewhat closer to translation Greek than is the central tendency of the LXX of Esther. This could be construed as evidence congenial to the hypothesis that the AT of Esther stands closer to its Semitic *Vorlage* than does the LXX of Esther and, furthermore, as evidence that the AT cannot therefore be a recension of the LXX. However, it is not at all clear that the difference between the syntax of the LXX and the AT has anything to do with the source(s) from which they were originally translated. There are at least three other scenarios that could also possibly account for the evidence.

Firstly, in view of the relative paucity of extant manuscripts of the AT of Esther compared to the LXX of Esther (four medieval manuscripts compared to at least thirty–six manuscripts of the LXX, the oldest dating to the fifth–century), the AT may have had a much more limited circulation than the LXX of Esther. If the LXX of Esther was copied more frequently over time than the AT, then scribes would have had more opportunities to introduce changes that could tend to make the syntax more idiomatic. The overall effect of these many small changes in syntax could shift the syntax of the LXX in the direction of composition Greek. The AT would of course experience the same effect as it was copied, but if it was exposed to fewer scribes the net effect would be proportionately smaller.

A second scenario that could account for the somewhat stronger translation tendency of the syntax of the AT is that the original translator adopted, either deliberately or unconsciously, a more literal style than did the original translator of the LXX. In this scenario the original texts of both the AT and the LXX stood equally close to their respective *Vorlagen*, but from the very beginning the AT was written in a style that possessed the characteristics Martin has identified as "translation" Greek.

A third possibility is that the AT, regardless of whether it was originally a new translation or a recension of the LXX, was at some time in its history deliberately "corrected" toward a Hebrew text of Esther, which moved its syntax in the direction of "translation" Greek. E. Tov has proposed this hypothesis to explain the differences between the LXX and the AT (Tov 1982). Tov's theory is critiqued in light of this study in chapter 5.

Although certain elements of syntax may be used differently in the AT compared to the LXX, there is no *overall* difference in syntax between them. The overlap of the standard deviations of the S-numbers for the LXX and the AT displayed in Graph 3 at the end of this chapter shows that, statistically speaking, no difference between the syntax of the LXX and that of the AT of Esther can be distinguished using Martin's criteria. In comparison, the big difference between the S– numbers shows that there is a sharp distinction between the syntax of the Greek texts of Esther and that of Polybius, who wrote in a modified Attic style that came into use about 300 B.C. (Graph 3).

The overlap of the deviations of the S–numbers displayed on Graph 3 between the Greek versions of Esther and the papyri shows that their syntax is significantly similar in many respects. This raises the question whether Martin's criteria can be confidently used to distinguish composition Greek from translation Greek, or whether the criteria are really indicating different styles of Greek in use during the Hellenistic period. Graph 3 suggests that, if one assumes that both of the Greek versions of Esther are independently made translations of a Hebrew *Vorlage*, both translators used a vernacular style of Greek similar to that found in the papyri.

A CHARACTERIZATION OF THE SYNTAX OF THE AT

Given the profiles of the syntax of the AT and the proto–AT shown in Graph 1, the occurrence of each of Martin's criteria can be summarized for the AT of Esther. As discussed in the excursus at the end of this chapter, only sixteen of Martin's criteria are valid for the Greek versions of Esther. The following table lists the normalized ratio for each of the sixteen valid criteria for the Greek texts of Esther in ascending order from –1 (composition) to +1 (translation):

Normalized Ratios for the Syntax of the Alpha–text of Esther
in Ascending Order from Composition Traits to Translation Traits

Alpha–Text			Proto–Alpha–Text		
	Criterion	Ratio		Criterion	Ratio
9	# of καί for each δέ	−0.93	9	# of καί for each δέ	−0.91
16	frequency of adverbial participles	−0.80	16	frequency of adverbial participles	−0.67
15	relative infrequency of attributive adjectives	−0.72	15	relative infrequency of attributive adjectives	−0.20
11	infrequency of dependent genitives preceding the word on which they depend	−0.60	5	κατά in all its occurrences	0.66
10	separation of article from substantive	0.31	10	separation of article from substantive	0.71
5	κατά in all occurrences	0.63	6	περί in all occurrences	0.73
2	διά in all occurrences	0.67	17	frequency of the dative case	0.74
8	ὑπό with genitive	0.69	4	κατά with accusative case	0.76
6	περί in all occurrences	0.69	3	occurrences of εἰς	0.92
4	κατά with accusative case	0.71	14	attributive adjectives preceding word they qualify	1.02
17	frequency of dative case	0.71	8	ὑπό with genitive	1.02
14	attributive adjectives preceding word they qualify	0.79	12	greater frequency of dependent genitive personal pronouns	1.04
7	πρός with dative	0.81	2	διά in all occurrences	1.09
3	occurrences of εἰς	0.95	13	greater frequency of genitive personal pronouns with anarthrous substantives	1.13
13	greater frequency of genitive personal pronouns with anarthrous substantives	1.21	11	infrequency of dependent genitives preceding the word on which they depend	2.79
12	greater frequency of dependent genitive personal pronouns	1.06	7	πρός with dative	not appl.
average & std. dev. of alpha–text		0.39 ± .71	average & std. dev. of proto–alpha–text		0.49 ± .89

This table shows that the syntactical features that most strongly tend toward composition Greek in both the AT and the proto–AT are (1) the relative frequency of the copulative καί with respect to the postpositive δέ, (2) the relative frequency of adverbial participles, and (3) the relative infrequency of attributive adjectives.

The syntactical feature that is most strongly characteristic of translation Greek involves, for both the AT and the proto–AT, the use of the genitive case. For the AT, it is criterion #12, the relative frequency of dependent genitive personal pronouns, which is the criterion in that text most characteristic of translation Greek; for the proto–AT it is criterion #11, the infrequency of dependent genitives preceding the word on which they depend.

The relative frequency of occurrence of seven of the eight prepositions with respect to the frequency of occurrence of ἐν as found in both the AT and proto–AT of Esther is highly characteristic of translation Greek. (Criterion #1, the relative frequency of διά with the genitive case with respect to ἐν, does not appear in the table because it has been found to be statistically invalid for the AT of Esther, as discussed in the excursus at the end of this chapter.) For every preposition except εἰς, the syntax of the six additions shifted the use of these prepositions in the direction of composition Greek, but in every case their use nevertheless remained characteristic of translation Greek. As for εἰς, the additions shifted the use of this preposition slightly more toward translation Greek.

The article is found separated from its substantive (criterion #10) in the proto–AT of Esther with such relative infrequency as to suggest translation Greek. However, when the additions are added, this syntactical feature shifts prominently in the direction of composition Greek. An examination of AT:Table c (see Appendix 3) shows that it is addition E, with its thirty–three articles separated from their substantives, which almost single–handedly produces this shift.

The frequency of dependent genitives preceding the word on which they depend (criterion #11) is the syntactical feature that changes most drastically between the proto–AT and AT. In the proto–AT the use of dependent genitives is the syntactical feature most characteristic of translation Greek. When the additions are included, the use of the dependent genitive shifts to the opposite end of the spectrum and indicates composition Greek. Again, it is addition E that contributes the most to this shift in syntax (see AT:Table d in Appendix 3).

The relative frequency of dependent genitive personal pronouns (criterion #12) is virtually the same in both the proto–AT and AT of

Esther. In both texts the use of the genitive personal pronoun is ideally characteristic, statistically speaking, of translation Greek.

Similarly, the frequency of genitive personal pronouns dependent upon anarthrous substantives (criterion #13) is characteristic of translation Greek in both the proto–AT and the AT. The additions cause a slight shift of this syntactical feature in the direction of translation Greek.

The position of attributive adjectives in relation to the words they qualify (criterion #14) is found in both the proto–AT and AT to be characteristic of translation Greek. The additions cause a slight shift in the use of the attributive adjective in the direction of composition Greek. AT:Table g (Appendix 3) shows that this shift is caused almost completely by the use of the attributive adjective in addition E.

Martin observes that translation Greek exhibits relatively few attributive adjectives compared to composition Greek (criterion #15). However, the proto–AT of Esther, thought to be a translation, possesses a sufficiently high number of attributive adjectives to indicate composition Greek; the additions, especially addition E, contribute even more attributive adjectives (see AT:Table h in Appendix 3) making this syntactical feature of the AT a strong indicator of composition Greek.

The relative infrequency of adverbial participles (criterion #16) is also thought by Martin to indicate translation Greek. Again, however, both the proto–AT and AT of Esther possess sufficient numbers of adverbial participles to indicate composition Greek.

Martin observes that composition Greek typically has three times as many datives used without the preposition $\dot{\epsilon}\nu$ as are used with $\dot{\epsilon}\nu$, compared to translation Greek (criterion #17). The use of the dative case in both the proto–AT and the AT indicates translation Greek. When the additions are included, the proportion of the number of occurrences of the dative case without $\dot{\epsilon}\nu$ to the number of occurrences with $\dot{\epsilon}\nu$ does not change even though twice as many datives are found in the AT as in the proto–AT (see AT:Table j in Appendix 3).

An examination of the ratios for the AT shows that although some criteria indicate translation Greek, not all of them do so with equal strength. Similarly, although a few of the criteria very strongly indicate composition Greek, the overall character of the syntax of the AT indicates it is a translation. The average of all the criteria, not the net frequencies, is the relevant number.

A CRITIQUE OF FOX'S SYNTAX ANALYSIS
OF THE GREEK VERSIONS OF ESTHER

Michael V. Fox applied Martin's criteria to a selection of fifty–seven lines from the AT of Esther and to the corresponding lines of the LXX of Esther (Fox 1991, 30–34). He has used inferences from his analysis of syntax to support his hypothesis that the AT could not be a recension of the LXX and that it is a translation of a Hebrew text of Esther which is older than that preserved in the MT.

Having analyzed both the AT and the LXX texts of Esther in their entirety and then comparing the ratios I computed with those calculated by Fox, it is clear that the fifty–seven lines chosen by Fox do not represent the overall character of the syntax of the texts as a whole. (The AT in the printed Göttingen edition is comprised of 472 lines.) Fox's decision to analyze only fifty–seven lines may have been based on Martin's claim that the criteria can be used with confidence on very short texts. As I show in the excursus at the end of this chapter, the size of a statistically valid sample of text is not determined by the number of lines, but by the presence of the minimally sufficient number of occurrences of syntactical features, a number that is different for each of the seventeen criteria. (A table listing the minimum number of needed occurrences for each criterion is found in the excursus.)

This is why for some of the criteria, Fox's analysis of fifty–seven lines was more or less true to the overall character of the text, but for many of the criteria, his ratios were not. Fox's ratios are displayed next to mine in Tables a–j for both the LXX and the AT in Appendix 3. An examination of those tables shows that his selection of fifty–seven lines of the AT do produce ratios for five criteria (#2, 9, 12, 14, and 17) which are characteristic of the syntax of the text as a whole. But for the remaining twelve criteria, his ratios do not reflect the overall character of the AT. For the LXX text, his selection of fifty–seven lines was not true to the overall character of the syntax for *any* of the criteria. In fact, the ratios he published for his analysis of the LXX of Esther indicate that the LXX of Esther possesses ten traits of composition and six of translation, yielding four net composition frequencies (Fox 1991, 32–33). This characterization of the LXX of Esther as composition Greek does not stand when one analyzes the entire text.

Even though Fox's analysis of fifty–seven lines of the LXX text of Esther showed it to have more composition traits than translation traits, no one, including Fox, would care to argue on that basis that the LXX text is not a translation. Fox parenthetically comments that

> this surprising finding does not undermine Martin's methodology, since the latter figure [4 net composition traits] is well below the net count of 15–17 original–Greek traits that Martin found in the original–Greek texts he studied (Fox 1991, 34).

Fox concludes that the LXX of Esther is a translation, even though his analysis of the syntax shows the selected text to have more composition traits than translation. His conclusion seems to be based on Martin's statement that while translated texts may have composition traits, "in no case does a known original Greek document have any frequencies characteristic of translation Greek" (Martin 1974, 38, emphasis original).

Although it is true that Martin's range of ratios for composition Greek do not overlap the ratios for translated texts, this is somewhat misleading because some of ratios do deviate far enough from the norm for composition Greek to tend toward translation syntax. His statement seems to be true only for the Attic style of Polybius and for addition E of Esther. Graph 2 shows that even composition Greek, albeit not literary Greek, may have certain criteria that tend toward translation Greek. In the selected papyri the syntax represented by criteria #2, 3, 4, 5, 6, 8, 12, and 14 is closer to the norm for translation Greek than for composition Greek; in Josephus the syntax represented by criteria #3 and 12 is closer to the norm for translation than for composition. Note however that Polybius (203?–120? B.C.) shows no criteria tending toward translation Greek. Since the papyri and Josephus are also in fact Greek compositions, the tendency of some of their syntax toward translation Greek shows that Martin's claim that texts composed in Greek show *no* translation traits is not statistically true and cannot be taken as absolute and unqualified. The fact that literary texts show no "translation" traits while non–literary texts composed in Greek do, strongly suggests that Martin's criteria are actually differentiating different styles of Greek and not "translation" vs. "composition" *per se*.

In addition to the problem that the selected fifty–seven lines of text misrepresent the character of the syntax of the texts as a whole, Fox follows Martin in basing his conclusions on using the "net differences" method which I critique in the excursus at the end of this chapter. As discussed there, this method of allowing each criterion to vote for the character of the text is inadequate because some of the ratios computed by Fox, like those I computed, fall between Martin's published values for translation and composition Greek, and Fox had to guess which way to construe them without the benefit of a statistical measure of variability. Furthermore, the "net frequencies" method is inadequate because a criterion that only weakly indicates translation Greek will cancel out a criterion that strongly indicates composition Greek, or *vice versa*. As discussed in the excursus, the simple arithmetic difference of the number of traits used by Fox following Martin is inadequate to characterize the syntax of the text as a whole.

A specific example of this problem is seen with Fox's unnormalized ratio for criterion #4, κατά with the accusative case, 0.28, which falls outside of Martin's range 0.01–0.18 for translation Greek, but is barely within the range 0.25–1.8 for composition Greek. Nevertheless, criterion #4 is counted by Fox to be a composition trait when he computes the net difference between translation traits and composition traits. However, Martin's range of ratios cannot indicate how far a ratio must deviate from the norm for translation Greek to be counted with confidence as a composition trait, or *vice versa*. An examination of Martin's published data shows that the unnormalized ratios for criterion #4 for the translated texts of Exodus (0.20), Numbers (0.58), Joshua (0.29), and 1 Chronicles (0.22) *all* fall outside of the range for translation Greek (0.01–0.18) (Martin 1974, 7). Furthermore, Xenophon, a text composed in Greek, has a ratio of 0.25 for criterion #4, which is less than the ratio Martin calculated for Numbers and Joshua! Xenophon is the reason Martin defines the lower limit of the range indicating composition Greek where he does. Here is an example of a text composed in Greek behaving for this particular criterion very much like some texts translated into Greek. With no measure of deviation from a norm, how can Fox say with any confidence whether a ratio of 0.28 for criterion #4 should be construed as indicating translation or composition?

Graph 1 shows the normalized value of criterion 4, κατά with the accusative, for the AT of Esther. A glance at this frequency distribution shows that on the scale of −1 (composition) to +1 (translation), criterion #4 in the AT falls at 0.7 and is clearly indicating translation Greek, contra Fox. Therefore, Fox's computation, following Martin, of net traits based on the "raw," unnormalized ratios distorts the conclusion.

Based on the ratios he computes for fifty–seven lines of the AT and LXX of Esther, Fox concludes

> These statistics leave little doubt that the proto–AT is a translation from a Semitic language — in this case Hebrew — and not a recension of the LXX... Now there is no dispute that the proto–AT is a translation at *some* remove; somewhere behind its version of the Esther story obviously lies a Semitic text. The issue is whether the proto–AT is a translation or a *recension* of a translation, in particular, of the LXX. The above statistics provide strong evidence that the proto–AT as we have it is close to the original translation...
>
> It is doubtful that a recensor of a Greek text would or could vary the content of that text extensively while maintaining a strongly "Semitic" character. A recension that moved as far from its base text as the proto–AT is from the LXX would certainly have taken on a stronger *original–Greek* character (Fox 1991, 31–33, emphasis his).

I agree with Fox that the AT is not a recension of the LXX (see chapter 4), but I would not care to argue that case on the basis of the differences of syntax. Graph 3 shows that though the overall syntax of the LXX of Esther tends slightly more toward composition Greek, it is not significantly different from the syntax of the AT. The difference between the syntax of the LXX and AT of Esther is not as pronounced as, say, the difference between the syntax of the AT of Esther and that of Josephus.

Furthermore, Fox's assumption that a recension *must* move the syntax of the recension in the direction of composition Greek, though it sounds reasonable, must be questioned. Fox believes that a Greek translation of a Hebrew *Vorlage* will bear strongly the influence of its Semitic source, while a recension of a Greek translation will move the syntax toward "composition" Greek (Fox 1991, 33). The assumption that a recension of a Greek translation will lose the influence of its original Semitic source is reasonable only if the recension was made without reference to a Semitic text. If, for instance, the purpose of the recension was to make the Greek syntax more faithful to the syntax of a Hebrew version, it could be argued that such a recension might be as much or even more strongly influenced by Hebrew syntax, as Fox himself apparently would agree (ibid., 34).

For instance, Origen chose ἐν ἡμέραις ἑκατὸν ὀγδοήκοντα as the reading of Esth 1:4 where other manuscripts of this verse read ἐπὶ ἡμέρας πολλάς (Field 1875, 793). While I am not arguing from this example that Origen was "Semitizing" his recension, in this case he does choose, for whatever reason, ἐν over ἐπί. Recall Martin's assumption that translators of a Semitic *Vorlage* show a preference for ἐν and Fox's argument that recensions become less "Semitic" the farther they are in time from the original translation. The point is simply that a recensor may, even centuries after the original translation was made, in some cases move the syntax, deliberately or otherwise, toward what Martin has identified as "translation" Greek. Furthermore, if, as the papyri indicate, some of Martin's criteria are indicating differences in style rather than source, those criteria cannot be used to distinguish a translation from a recension, nor to measure how far a "recension" stands from its presumed Semitic source.

Fox summarizes his conclusion about the AT:

> ... it is hardly conceivable that a recension of the LXX produced the proto–AT. While a harmonizing recension (like the hexaplaric) would enhance a text's Semitic character, the proto-AT is *farther* from the MT than the LXX is. A recension creating a text like the proto–AT could hardly produce such a highly translational character. The proto–AT must be fairly close to its Hebrew vorlage, which was quite different from the MT (Fox 1991, 34).

Because Fox bases his analysis on such a limited selection of text, and because Martin's methodology cannot sharply differentiate between the syntax of the LXX and the syntax of the AT of Esther, Fox's conclusion about the relationship of the AT and the LXX is undermined. Because Martin's criteria may be distinguishing style rather than source and because Fox's selected fifty–seven lines do not characterize the syntax of the AT as a whole, it is questionable whether

Fox can use syntax analysis to argue that the AT stands much closer to its Hebrew *Vorlage* than does the LXX. And certainly there is nothing about the character of the overall syntax of the AT that allows one to conclude whether or not it is the text of the MT that stands behind it.

THE SYNTAX OF THE ADDITIONS

Because the six major additions were almost certainly introduced into the AT after it was originally produced, the syntax of these sections may be quite different from that of the AT as it stood before the additions were included. Furthermore, since it cannot be assumed that all six of the additions had the same origin, or were introduced into the AT at the same time, some may have been composed in Greek and others may have been translated from a Semitic source.

Martin himself has applied his criteria for syntax criticism to the six secondary additions, A–F, of the LXX of Esther to determine the original language of each addition (Martin 1975). He concludes that two of the additions, B and E, were originally Greek compositions, that three of them, A, C, and D, were translated from a Semitic source and that addition F was either an original Greek composition or a very free translation of a Semitic source.

Martin's conclusions about the original language of the six additions more or less corroborate those previously drawn by C. A. Moore that additions B and E were originally composed in Greek, additions A, C, and F probably are translations of Semitic sources and that the original language of D could not be conclusively determined (Moore 1973). Subsequently, Moore has accepted Martin's syntactical analysis as conclusive (Moore 1977, 155).

My analysis of the six additions to the LXX and AT texts of Esther concurs with Martin that addition E was unquestionably composed in Greek (see Graph 3 at the end of this chapter). On the normalized scale of −1 (composition) to +1 (translation), the syntax of addition E stands at −0.87 ± 0.88. All of the valid criteria for addition E indicate it was composed in Greek. However, the additions taken as individual units of text do not possess the minimally sufficient number of occurrences that would be necessary to make all seventeen criteria valid. For addition E of the AT just six of the seventeen criteria were valid (#3, 10, 14, 15, 16, 17). (See the discussion of how to determine valid criteria in the excursus at the end of this chapter.)

The following table displays the average normalized value and standard deviation, and the criteria on which they are based, for each of the six additions of both the AT and LXX texts of Esther:

S-numbers of the Additions to Esther

AT Esther			LXX Esther		
Add	Ave. ± std. dev.	Valid Criteria	Add	Ave. ± std. dev.	Valid Criteria
A	−0.26 ± 0.66	9, 10, 11, 12, 13,14,15,16,17	A	−1.71 ± 1.68	9,10,11,12,13,14, 15,16,17
B	−0.48 ± 0.88	3, 10, 15, 16, 17	B	−0.85 ± 1.25	3, 15, 16, 17
C	0.22 ± 0.83	2, 3, 4, 5, 10, 12, 15, 16, 17	C	0.46 ± 0.76	2, 4, 5, 12, 15, 16, 17
D	0.72 ± 0.51	3, 5, 10, 15, 16	D	−0.62 ± 1.36	3, 15, 16
E	−0.87 ± 0.88	3, 10, 14, 15, 16, 17	E	−3.47 ± 5.55	3, 10, 14, 15, 16, 17
F	1.11 ± 0	3	F	−0.20 ± 1.4	3, 15

For the additions as they stand in the AT of Esther, this study shows that A and B tend toward composition Greek; additions C, D, and F tend toward translation Greek. Since additions A and F function together in the Greek versions of Esther to frame the story within an apocalyptic dream (A) and its interpretation (F), it seems likely that additions A and F were either both composed in Greek or both translated from a Semitic source, in spite of the indications of syntax criticism.

For the additions as they stand in the LXX of Esther, addition A tends toward composition Greek (contra Martin), C towards translation Greek. Although the average values of B, D, and F tend toward composition Greek, their standard deviations are all greater than 1, which means their origin must remain undetermined. There are simply too few valid criteria in operation for each addition to make the results of syntax criticism reliable.

One of the surprising findings of this syntax analysis of the additions is that the syntax of the additions is *not* identical in the AT and the LXX. Usually the additions are treated as if they are identical because obviously they were copied from one Greek version to the other. In spite of the extensive similarities between the additions as they stand in the AT and the additions as they stand in the LXX, there are differences in content implied by the differences in syntax. Perhaps the additions were not simply copied verbatim from the LXX to the AT (or *vice versa*) but were carefully edited into the target text, changing the content and syntax of the additions to merge with that of the receptor text. Or perhaps the additions were originally copied verbatim and the differences in syntax were introduced subsequently during transmission. Chapter 4 discusses in detail the differences between the AT and LXX version of the additions. What is relevant here is that for both the AT and the LXX of Esther, the overall effect of the additions was to move the syntax in the direction of composition Greek.

Addition E is the major contributor to that shift in syntax. Addition E in both the AT and the LXX tends so strongly toward composition Greek by every criterion that there is no doubt that it was composed in Greek. Addition E therefore introduces a small error into Martin's computed range of ratios for translation Greek, because Martin used the LXX text of Esther, which includes addition E, as a text known to have been translated into Greek. To the extent that the other Greek texts of the OT contain pericopes originally composed in Greek, Martin's ratios for translation Greek are proportionately skewed.

Although I counted the frequency of occurrence for each of the criteria in each of the chapters in both the LXX and AT of Esther, the results of syntax criticism on a chapter by chapter basis are not useful because the text is too short to contain the minimum number of occurrences to make the criteria valid. At best, the results of syntax criticism of individual chapters presented by this study should be used only as corroborating evidence if (1) *all* valid criteria indicate either translation or composition, and (2) the conclusion of syntax criticism agrees with those of form criticism, literary analysis and historical information. Because of the statistical uncertainty involved in the analysis of such small units of texts, syntax criticism should not be used independently to argue against conclusions reached by other means.

CONCLUSIONS

• There is no statistically significant difference between the syntax of the AT and the syntax of the LXX of Esther.
• The syntax of the AT and the LXX of Esther indicate that both are translations of a Semitic source.
• Fox's syntax analysis of fifty–seven lines of the Greek texts of Esther does not accurately represent the character of the syntax as a whole for either the AT or the LXX. His conclusion that the AT has a radically more pronounced translation syntax than does the LXX is not corroborated by a statistical treatment of the analysis of the syntax of both texts in their entirety.
• Not all of Martin's seventeen criteria are valid for any given text. A minimum number of occurrences of certain syntactical features is required. (See the excursus that follows.)
• Generally speaking, very little can be inferred from syntax criticism about the origin of the six additions because each is so short that only a few of the seventeen syntactical criteria are valid for any addition.
• However, the syntax of addition E in both the AT and LXX texts of Esther strongly and consistently indicates that it was composed in Greek.
• Syntax criticism reveals that the additions as they stand in the AT are not identical in either syntax or content to the additions as they stand in the LXX. (See further discussion of the differences between the additions in chapter 4.)
• If the computed ratios are normalized, the central tendency of the text and its deviation from the norm for translation or composition Greek can be easily viewed. Furthermore, the use of normalized ratios reveals more information about the syntax of a given text and allows it to be directly compared to the syntax of other texts. (See the excursus that follows.)

EXCURSUS: A STATISTICAL EXTENSION OF MARTIN'S METHODOLOGY

In order to formulate the seventeen criteria that are used to distinguish translation Greek from composition Greek, Martin examined 3400 lines of translated Greek and 1500 lines of original Greek (Martin 1974, vi). He has subsequently expanded his textual base by an additional 2270 lines of translation Greek and 1630 lines of original Greek. These additional controls "basically confirm the results of the original study" (Martin 1987, 138–39). When one recalls that Martin did much of his work before computer searching of texts was possible, his already prodigious effort becomes all the more impressive. Certainly Martin has made a significant contribution by providing a methodology that reaches toward some objective measure of the syntax of a text and moves beyond an intuitive search for "Semitisms," mistranslations and general impressions. He has provided the necessary groundwork for further advances toward characterizing the syntax of translation Greek. In a spirit of appreciation for Martin's work, I offer a critique of his methodology based on my experience using it with the Greek texts of Esther and an extension of it that overcomes some of its weaknesses and limitations. I extend his technique by introducing a simple statistical analysis of the ratios and by attempting to define more rigorously the limits within which Martin's criteria are statistically significant.

A CRITIQUE OF THE CRITERIA

The confidence we can place in any conclusion we reach about the character of the syntax of a text using Martin's criteria depends entirely on how well those criteria actually do the job they set out to do. We can use Martin's criteria to distinguish translation Greek from composition Greek only if (1) the syntax identified by Martin does in fact occur distinctively and differently in translation Greek as compared to composition Greek and (2) if the differences in the ratios used to measure this distinction are in fact statistically significant.

Others have recognized this problem with using the criteria but have not offered a way to determine when a given criterion is valid for a given text. For instance, while reviewing Martin's syntax criticism of the Synoptic Gospels, Maloney has suggested that criterion #7, the use of the preposition πρός with the dative, should be dropped as a criterion because it occurs too infrequently in "nontranslated Hellenistic Greek" (Maloney 1989, 379). I have quantified "too infrequent" for each of the seventeen criteria to indicate when they may be validly used for a given text (see the table below). If the text in question does not contain the necessary minimum number of occurrences for a given criterion to be statistically valid, that criterion must not be applied to the text. A criterion that is not statistically significant for one text may be fine when applied to another.

A second weakness of Martin's methodology noted by S. Farris is that the cut–off point of the ranges for distinguishing composition Greek from translation Greek is arbitrary (Martin 1989, 169). This is because Martin does not calculate average, normative values and standard deviations for each of the criteria. Instead he believes that what he calls the "gap" (i.e., the arithmetic difference) between the ratios of original Greek texts and the ratios of translation Greek text is sufficient to indicate "sharp differences" between the two. As shown above, the ratios for criterion #4 for the Greek translations of Exodus, Numbers, Joshua and 1 Chronicles fall within the range Martin gives for composition Greek, and the ratio for Xenophon, a text composed in Greek, is closer to translation Greek than those four biblical books. Martin nevertheless uses the ratio for Xenophon to define the lower limit on composition Greek anyway. My statistical treatment of the ratios provides a quantitative measure of when a criterion is valid for a given text and also a measure of how close a ratio must be to the norm for translation or composition to be deemed one or the other.

Based on my experience of applying his criteria to the syntax of the Greek texts of Esther, I suggest that there is for each criterion a minimal number of occurrences of the syntactical feature upon which it is based that must occur in any given text in order for that criterion to be valid. For the Greek texts of Esther I have found that criterion #1, the frequency of occurrence of διά with the genitive case, is not valid for the Greek texts of Esther. I will use this example from the text of Esther to illustrate a problem that could occur with any of the seventeen criteria depending on the text in question.

If for any criterion the difference between the average value Martin has calculated for composition Greek and the average value for translation Greek is very small, then a very large number of occurrences of that syntactical construction is needed within the text to discern any difference at all between translation and composition using his published ranges. The average value for translation Greek of Martin's ratio for criterion #1, the frequency of occurrence of διά with the genitive case relative to the frequency of occurrence of ἐν, is 0.0375. This value is simply the sum of the ratios for criterion #1 as published by Martin for all books of the Greek OT divided by the number of books (1974, 7). The corresponding average value for composition Greek is 0.0323, calculated similarly from Martin's ratios for texts composed in Greek (ibid., 7). The difference between these two values is a very small 0.0052. Such a tiny difference between the average value for translation Greek vs. composition Greek suggests this criterion would seldom, if ever, be valid. To quantify this, consider that the difference between translation and composition Greek for criterion #1 is based on counting the number of times διά occurs with the genitive. Because there is no such thing as a fraction of a διά, the minimum difference in a count indicating translation Greek from composition Greek is 1. Therefore, as the following equation shows, to see *any* difference between translation and composition Greek using Martin's ranges when the difference of the average ratios is only 0.0052, one needs at least about 200 occurrences of ἐν:

$$\frac{1 \ \deltaι\acute{\alpha}}{min.\# \ \grave{\epsilon}\nu} = \left| T_{ave} - C_{ave} \right|$$

$$\text{or, } \frac{1 \; \delta\iota\acute{\alpha}}{\left|T_{ave} - C_{ave}\right|} = \text{min. } \# \; \dot{\epsilon}\nu$$

where,

T_{ave} = average of ratios for criterion #1 for translation Greek
C_{ave} = average of ratios for criterion #1 for composition Greek

However, if $\left|T_{ave} - C_{ave}\right| > 1$, then the inverse of the equation yields the minimum number required, e.g., for criterion #9,

$$\frac{\left|T_{ave} - C_{ave}\right|}{1 \; \delta\acute{\epsilon}} = \text{min. } \# \; \kappa\alpha\acute{\iota}$$

For criterion #1 the minimum number of $\dot{\epsilon}\nu$'s is therefore:

$$\frac{1}{0.0052} = 192.3 = 200 \; \dot{\epsilon}\nu\text{'s}$$

Even given 200 occurrences of $\dot{\epsilon}\nu$, it would be difficult to see *any* distinction between translation Greek and composition Greek because the difference would depend on a count of just *one* more $\delta\iota\acute{\alpha}$ with the genitive case. In other words, the ratio resulting from x occurrences of $\delta\iota\acute{\alpha}$ with the genitive would indicate translation Greek, but the ratio resulting from $x+1$ occurrences would indicate composition Greek! Although 200 occurrences of $\dot{\epsilon}\nu$ within the text is the minimum required to see differentiation between translation and composition for criteria #1, multiple times that (i.e., 400 or more) are needed to increase the criterion's validity. With even 400 occurrences of $\dot{\epsilon}\nu$ the difference between translation Greek and composition would depend on just two more occurrences of $\delta\iota\acute{\alpha}$ with the genitive. A simple counting mistake of 1 or 2 occurrences could flip the ratio from the range of translation to composition or vice versa.

To generalize this example, there must be a minimally sufficient number of occurrences of the given syntax represented by the denominator of Martin's ratio to assure that the numerator of the ratio will be at least unity (i.e., 1). Otherwise, the resulting ratio represents a fractional number of occurrences (for instance, 1/2 of a $\delta\iota\acute{\alpha}$ with the genitive), which is meaningless. There is, therefore, a minimum number of occurrences needed to assure that Martin's ratios at least have a meaningful correspondence to the real nature of texts. Multiples of that minimum number of occurrences are needed to clearly discern translation from composition Greek. If the actual number of occurrences in a given text is less than the minimum required for a given criterion, that criterion must not be used for that text. If the actual number of occurrences in a given text is equal to or only a little greater than the minimum required, then that criterion is a very weak indicator of the nature of the syntax.

Martin senses this problem when he uses a dash to indicate that there are no occurrences of a given criterion in a given text (i.e., the numerator of the ratio would be zero) or when there are "too few" ἐν's in the text (i.e., the denominator approaches zero) (Martin 1974, 45–47). Because he does not quantify "too few" one is left to guess whether or not a given criterion will be valid for a given text.

The following table lists the average values for translation Greek (T_{ave}) and composition Greek (C_{ave}) for each of the seventeen criteria, the absolute value of the difference between them ($|T_{ave} - C_{ave}|$) and the minimum number of occurrences of each syntactical item that a text must possess in order for the criteria to begin to function meaningfully. If the text being analyzed does not possess the minimum number of occurrences indicated, that criterion should not be used in deciding whether the text is translation or composition.

Minimum Occurrences Needed for Criteria to be Valid

Criterion No.	Ave. Value for Translation (T_{ave})	Ave. Value for Composition (C_{ave})	Difference between translation & composition $\|T_{ave} - C_{ave}\|$	Minimum Occurrences Needed
1	0.037	0.032	0.005	200 ἐν
2	0.915	0.788	0.127	10 ἐν
3	0.513	2.679	2.166	2 ἐν
4	0.119	0.876	0.757	10 ἐν
5	0.133	0.987	0.859	7 ἐν
6	0.056	0.604	0.548	20 ἐν
7	0.014	0.079	0.065	100 ἐν
8	0.023	0.323	0.300	50 ἐν
9	95.98	0.298	95.68	95 καί
10	0.024	0.274	0.250	50 articles
11	80.87	1.5	79.37	80 gen follow

Minimum Occurrences Needed ... cont.			
12	3.46	30.46	27.0	27 lines
13	34.57	216	181.43	182 lines
14	0.132	3.56	3.428	4 lines
15	17.67	4.88	12.79	17 lines
16	25.62	3.96	21.66	25 lines
17	1.04	6.88	5.84	7 dat w/o ἐν

Since by my count ἐν occurs in the AT of Esther only 83 times and in the LXX of Esther only 116 times, Martin's criterion #1 cannot be used meaningfully to distinguish between translation or composition Greek for these particular texts, because at least 200 are needed, even though διά with the genitive occurs six times in the AT and 13 in the LXX. Therefore, I have excluded criterion #1 from my analysis, reducing the number of valid criteria to sixteen. Although those sixteen are valid for the Esther texts, not all are equally strong indicators .

Although not every criterion is an equally strong indicator for any given text, Martin's use of "net frequencies" does not take this into consideration. Martin's use of "net" frequencies of occurrence implicitly assigns equal weight to each of the criteria and allows a statistically weak criterion to cancel out a statistically strong criterion. For instance, though the majority of criteria may indicate translation Greek, they may do so only weakly; whereas the fewer number of criteria indicating composition Greek may be statistically stronger. A simple subtraction of one from the other is inadequate because it yields a misleading conclusion. This problem, and my solution to it, are presented below.

These limitations also imply that the smallest portion of a Greek text to which the criteria can be meaningfully applied is that amount of text that possesses the minimum number of occurrences for the maximum number of criteria, regardless of the length of the text. In other words, if the text being analyzed possesses the minimum number of occurrences needed for only a few of the seventeen criteria, then we could have only very low confidence in a conclusion based on so few criteria.

Martin recognizes that "As the unit of text which is being analyzed becomes smaller, syntactical variations due to content and style [as opposed to the influence of a Semitic source] become more pronounced" (Martin 1974, 45). Nevertheless he claims that

> the differences between the original Greek and the translated Greek is
> sufficient in all units of 31–50 lines in length, in most units of 16–30
> lines in length and in many units of 4–15 lines in length to indicate that
> they are indeed translation rather than original Greek (ibid., 45).

I would argue that the number of lines of text is in itself irrelevant, except for those criteria which use that number in the denominator of their ratio (criteria #13–16). Rather, it is the minimal number of occurrences of the denominator value that determines the validity of a criterion in a given text. Martin has been misled here because he is depending on arithmetic differences in "net" frequencies. It is true, as Martin claims, that even in units of text 4–15 lines in length, there will be an arithmetic difference in net frequencies. One can always subtract two numbers and get a difference. But is the resulting value meaningful? Martin believes that even one "net translation Greek frequency" is sufficient for concluding that the text is translation Greek (ibid., 52). However, Martin fails to see that what he has observed as "considerable overlapping for such units [i.e., units of text 4–15 lines in length] in the area of 0 to 4 net original Greek frequencies" is an indication that statistically his methodology has run into trouble. He doesn't take into account that an arithmetic difference in net frequencies does not imply a statistically significant distinction *if* there is not a minimally sufficient number of occurrences of the expected syntax to begin with. It is most unlikely that any text 4–15 lines in length will possess anywhere near the minimum number of occurrences needed for *any* of the criteria to operate meaningfully.

Therefore, one cannot simply state that Martin's criteria are valid for 10 lines of text, or 50, or even 100 lines of text. Instead one must say that the smallest number of lines of text for which Martin's criteria are valid is that number of lines of text which possesses the minimum number of occurrences for the maximum number (preferably all seventeen) of criteria.

The results of this study also question whether Martin's criteria are really differentiating translation Greek from composition Greek, or just different styles or genres of Greek text. This concern arose particularly with using criterion #9, the relative frequency of occurrence of the copulative καί, to indicate a Semitic source. This criterion is based on the observation that the Greek translator will often preserve the Hebrew word order of the waw-consecutive by using καί instead of a postpositive conjunction. When the Hebrew of the OT is compared to its Greek translation it does seem that translators often did use καί to translate the waw–consecutive. However, within a given text the translator also sometimes uses the postpositive δέ or completely rephrases the Greek in such a way that does not preserve Hebrew word order. An examination of how 260 waw–consecutives in the Hebrew text of Esther were handled by the translator who produced the LXX (Göttingen o´) text shows this inconsistency. Sixty–two percent of the waws were translated by καί, preserving the Hebrew word order. However, 23% of the waws were rendered by a postpositive δέ, and another 15% were rendered by either a postpositive γαρ, no conjunction at all, or by a rephrasing that rendered the waw– consecutive as a subordinate clause using a participle or infinitive. Thirty–eight percent of the waws were translated without preserving the Hebrew word order. This diversity calls into question the premise that Martin so heavily relies upon, that the word order of a Semitic *Vorlage* will be preserved often enough in translation to make it *characteristic* of translation Greek.

Even if the waw–consecutive were consistently translated by καί, one cannot infer the converse is also true, that frequent occurrence of καί indicates a Semitic source. This is because the frequent use of the copulative καί may not have been truly distinctive of translation Greek; it may simply have been the natural Greek syntax used to relate sequential events. A. Deissmann noticed that the copulative καί is frequently found in Egyptian Greek papyri that narrate a sequence of events (Deissmann 1927, 131–145). Deissmann cites as examples four papyri, dating from 160 B.C. to the 4th–century A.D., which make frequent use of the copulative καί while narrating events in a popular style. Deissmann gives a further example of an inscription from a temple of Asclepius near Rome dating from some time after A.D. 138 which, by Martin's standard would be deemed even more "Semitic" than most biblical texts (ibid., 134–136)! These documentary papyri and inscriptions are autographs not subject to subsequent modification.

Moreover, they are texts that have not been translated from any source, Semitic or otherwise.

Some may wish to argue that the papyri exhibiting this feature were written by Jews using some Semitic dialect of Greek. It is, in my opinion, unlikely that all of such papyri and inscriptions were written by Jews. Even if they were, it is far from certain that Jews in the Diaspora spoke a Semiticized dialect of Greek. Moreover, the influence of the Semitic languages on Hellenistic Greek is a complex and highly debated issue. Even if this feature in Greek resulted from contact with a Semitic language originally, the papyri and inscriptions present strong evidence that the relatively frequent use of the copulative καί with respect to δέ was not a *distinctively* Semitic idiom during the Hellenistic period, much less an indication of a Semitic literary source. For a fuller discussion of the various sources of Semitic influence on Greek see Maloney (1981).

Graph 2 shows that eight of Martin's ratios for the papyri he himself analyzed indicate composition Greek and eight translation Greek. (I excluded criterion #1 for the reason discussed above.) The papyri analyzed by Martin show equal traits of both composition and translation Greek. Because Martin states that "in no case does a known original Greek document have any frequencies characteristic of translation Greek," on the basis of this methodology one would have to conclude that the papyri are translations of Semitic sources (Martin 1974, 8, emphasis original). But since the papyri are clearly not translations of any source, Semitic or otherwise, they raise the question of whether Martin's criteria might be characterizing different styles of Greek, perhaps even changes in the Greek language over time, and therefore do not distinctively differentiate translation and composition Greek. Graph 2 suggests that perhaps Martin's criteria show that the translators of the Hebrew scripture used a Greek style more like the vernacular of the papyri than like the style used by Polybius.

Because two of the seventeen ratios computed from Josephus and eight of the ratios computed from the papyri tend toward translation Greek, I suspect that some of Martin's criteria do not in fact always *distinctively* differentiate translation from composition Greek. In other words, some of the syntactical characteristics Martin has observed occur in both composition Greek and translation Greek with frequencies that cannot be used decisively to distinguish one from the other. More texts must be examined and their ratios statistically analyzed to investigate further this important question of whether Martin's criteria truly represent traits of translation Greek or rather variations in Hellenistic Greek style.

A CRITIQUE OF MARTIN'S TREATMENT OF THE RATIOS

Beyond these cautions concerning the criteria, Martin's arithmetic treatment of the data using "net frequencies" poses some serious limitations as mentioned above. After the occurrences of a given element of syntax have been counted and the ratio of relative frequency for the given criterion has been calculated, a comparison of that ratio to Martin's ranges often fails to yield a conclusive indication of translation or composition Greek. For the Greek texts of Esther I found that the ratio for any given criterion often fell neither in the range of values indicating translation Greek nor in the range indicating composition Greek, but somewhere in between. This left me in a quandary, because Martin gives no statistical measure of variability for his numbers. This meant that there was no way to make an informed decision about whether to count the ratio as indicating translation or composition. Martin's technique of calculating the "net frequency," which is the arithmetic difference between the number of criteria indicating translation and the number indicating composition, demands that each criterion count for one or the other. Without a statistical measure of variability, it is almost an arbitrary decision how to count those ratios that fall between. Intuition might suggest that the ratio should be counted with whichever range its value is closest. But intuition can mislead if one doesn't know how close a ratio must be to either range in order to construe it with confidence. In other words, since Martin gives no statistical measure of variability for his computed ranges, any ratio that falls between his ranges should be excluded as inconclusive.

A look at the summaries in AT:Table 1 and LXX:Table 1 shows that for the Greek texts of Esther this is a serious problem, because too many of the ratios produced inconclusive indications by falling between the ranges of translation and composition Greek. For the total text of the AT, including the additions, the ratios of six of the sixteen criteria produced inconclusive results (that is, 35% of the data could not have been used). For the total text of the LXX, including the additions, the ratios of three of the sixteen criteria (18%) did not decisively indicate either translation or composition Greek. Although it is tempting to make an intuitive decision and count these indecisive ratios for one or the other, some statistical measure of variability is needed before one can make that decision with confidence.

In addition to lacking a measure of variability, Martin's technique of determining the character of the syntax by taking the arithmetic difference of the translation frequencies and composition frequencies is inadequate for two other reasons. A consequence of having no statistical measure of variability is that once one makes the (arbitrary) decision to count an indecisive criterion as indicating either translation or composition Greek, each criterion is implicitly given an equally weighted vote. This means that a criterion that only weakly indicates translation Greek will cancel out a criterion that strongly indicates composition Greek, and vice versa. We have noted above that for frequencies of occurrence that are close to the minimums needed, the resulting ratios are extremely sensitive to small variations in counting. For instance, for criterion #7, πρός with the dative case, if a text has the minimum number of 100 ἐν's and three occurrences of πρός with the dative, the resulting ratio is 0.03, which falls within Martin's range indicating composition Greek. If however there are only two occurrences of πρός with the dative, the ratio becomes 0.02, which moves it into the range of translation Greek. For small numbers of occurrences, which is typical, the ratios are so sensitive that a simple counting error can change the "vote" of a criterion. Here again, more statistical awareness is needed to judge the strength of each criterion as it represents a given text and to interpret the data more accurately.

A third problem with Martin's handling of the data is that the net frequency method of interpreting the data is insufficient for determining the overall character of the text because it does not reveal the central tendency of the text. Looking at Table 1 in Appendix 3 (for either the AT or the LXX) it is impossible to decide with confidence whether the syntax of the AT really tends toward translation Greek or toward composition Greek. Furthermore, a count of net frequencies is insufficient for answering important questions, such as whether the syntactical differences between the LXX of Esther and the AT of Esther are necessarily significant.

The usefulness of Martin's methodology can be improved and the data for a given text interpreted with more confidence if some simple descriptive statistics are applied. This improvement provides some measure of the central tendency of a text and its variability from the computed norm for translation and composition Greek, and allows the syntax of two or more texts to be more easily compared.

The first step is to normalize the ratios for each statistically valid criterion. A glance at the unnormalized ratios shows them to have greatly varying magnitudes. For instance, translation Greek is indicated by criterion #3 by a ratio in the range of 0.01–0.49. Criterion #13 indicates translation Greek if its ratio is ≤77. It is impossible to understand the relative strength of the ratios when they cannot be directly compared. It is therefore necessary to normalize them so that all which indicate translation Greek tend toward the same number (e.g., +1) and all which indicate composition Greek tend toward another (e.g., –1), regardless of the magnitude of the "raw" ratios.

It is easy to normalize the ratios so their values can be directly compared. Using a standard formula for normalizing measurements which tend toward two expected values, I have scaled the ratios, both for Martin's data and for the Greek texts of Esther, so that they all fall on a scale where a value of –1 will indicate composition Greek and a value of +1 will indicate translation Greek. The formula I used for normalizing the ratios is:[3]

$$S_i = \frac{N_i - 0.5\,(T_i + C_i)}{0.5\,(T_i - C_i)}$$

where, S_i is the resulting normalized ratio, on a scale of –1 to +1
N_i is the ratio of the relative frequency of criterion i
T_i is the average ratio for criterion i in translation Greek
C_i is the average ratio for criterion i in composition Greek

---

[3] I gratefully acknowledge advice on how to normalize data with two expected values from Dr. Forrest C. Jobes, Senior Research Physicist, Princeton University. Of course, any mistakes in the application of the formula or the computation of the results are mine alone.

$i = 1$ to n, where n is the number of valid criteria (16 for the Greek texts of Esther)

Note that if the ratio, N_i, of a given criterion, i, equals the average for translation Greek, T_i, then the normalized value, S_i, will equal $+1.0$. Alternatively, if a ratio, N_i, equals the average for composition Greek, C_i, then the normalized value, S_i, will equal -1.0. Language being what it is, it would be very rare for a normalized ratio to equal precisely either -1.0 or $+1.0$. Moreover, the actual normalized ratio for any criterion in a given text can, and probably will, deviate greatly from the norm in either direction. The values of -1 and $+1$ are not limits which a normalized ratio cannot exceed; they are markers of where the two normative (i.e., average) values of the ratios for composition and translation Greek lie respectively. These norms are calculated from the control texts previously analyzed. Individual normalized ratios may have values less than -1 or greater than $+1$. This means that a comparison of the normalized ratios to -1 and $+1$ gives an indication of both the central tendency of the syntax of the text and a measure of its variability from the norm.

In other words, if the normalized ratios for all valid criteria cluster around -1.0, the central tendency of the syntax of the text is toward that previously observed in texts composed in Greek; if they cluster around $+1.0$, the central tendency is toward that previously observed for texts translated into Greek. The extent to which the normalized values spread out over the scale of -1.0 to $+1.0$ shows how strongly the criteria collectively indicate translation or composition. The average of the normalized values for the text in question is a single number that characterizes on a scale of -1.0 to 1.0 the nature of the syntax of the text as a whole:

$$\text{S-number} = S_{ave} = \frac{\Sigma\, S_i}{n} \qquad i = 1, n$$

The standard deviation offers some measure of the spread of the normalized ratios and is useful for determining whether syntactical differences between two or more texts is statistically significant:

$$\text{std dev} = \sqrt{\frac{\Sigma\, dev_i{}^2}{n-1}} \qquad \text{where, } i = 1, n;\ dev_i = S_i - S_{ave}$$

This treatment of the ratios yields one number, the S–number, that represents the syntax of the entire text. A comparison of the S–numbers of two or more texts provides a quick measure of where the texts stand in relation to one another along the continuum of "translation" to "composition" Greek. Furthermore, this treatment of the ratios is congenial to graphic representation, which is visually easier to comprehend than tabular format and that allows the syntax of two or more texts to be compared at a glance. (See Graph 3 at the end of this chapter.)

The following table lists in order from composition to translation the S–number and standard deviation for each of the texts Martin has examined and for the two Greek texts of Esther:

A Comparison of the S–numbers of Examined Texts

Composition = –1	
Text	**S–number and std. dev.**
Polybius	–1.68 ± 0.97
Josephus	–1.38 ± 1.1
selected papyri	–0.25 ± 0.67
LXX Esther — Fox's data	–0.19 ± 1.2
LXX Esther — Jobes' data	0.33 ± 0.74
LXX proto–Esther — Jobes' data	0.36 ± 0.62
AT Esther — Jobes' data	0.39 ± 0.71
AT proto–Esther — Jobes' data	0.49 ± 0.89
AT Esther — Fox's data	0.55 ± 0.70
LXX Esther — Martin's data (8 criteria)	0.81 ± 0.16
Translation = +1	

Although this statistical treatment improves Martin's methodology by extracting more information from the ratios, it is only fair to point out some of the limitations and liabilities of my approach. Although I am confident that the S–numbers and deviations accurately represent *relative* relationships between the texts, the magnitude of the values must not be pressed with the mathematical rigor usually implied when such statistical methods are brought to bear on problems in, for instance, the physical sciences. For one reason, there are no normative values that are *independently* known and to which these computed values can be compared. The "normative" values for translation and composition Greek used in this analysis are just the average of those values previously calculated by Martin.

For instance, on an exam the perfect score is a fixed number that is known independently of whatever score individuals may achieve. Language being what it is, there is no value corresponding to a "perfect score" for either translation or composition Greek against which any given text can be evaluated. The normative value for translation Greek is by definition the average of the ratios of texts known (assumed?) to have been translated; likewise the normative value for composition Greek is by definition the average of the ratios of the texts known to have been composed in Greek. Theoretically, the most precise normative value for each group could be determined only by tabulating and including in the calculation of the average *all* texts of translation Greek and *all* texts of composition Greek. Even then any given text could (and probably would) deviate significantly from that norm. Therefore, given the very nature of language and texts, these ratios and their standard deviations are based on the texts themselves and not on an independently known value.

Furthermore, a glance at the standard deviations shows them to be quite large. This probably indicates that the nature of language is such that there is considerable spread in the way Greek syntax is used in both compositions and translations. These large deviations imply that Martin's criteria must be used with caution; they should not be too rigorously pressed into the service of drawing hard conclusions. Instead, the results of syntax analysis should be taken as important evidence that must be considered with other historical, textual and literary evidence before drawing conclusions about a given text.

For instance, in the case of the Greek versions of Esther, a look at Graph 3 shows that it is difficult to conclude with certainty that there is *any* statistically significant syntactical difference between the syntax of the LXX of Esther and that of the AT because, although their S–numbers differ (0.2047 ± 0.794 and 0.3853 ± 0.713, respectively), their standard deviations overlap. An overlap of the deviations indicates that the ratios do not statistically indicate any difference between the syntax of the AT and that of the LXX.

Graph 1: A Profile of the Syntax of the Greek Versions of Esther

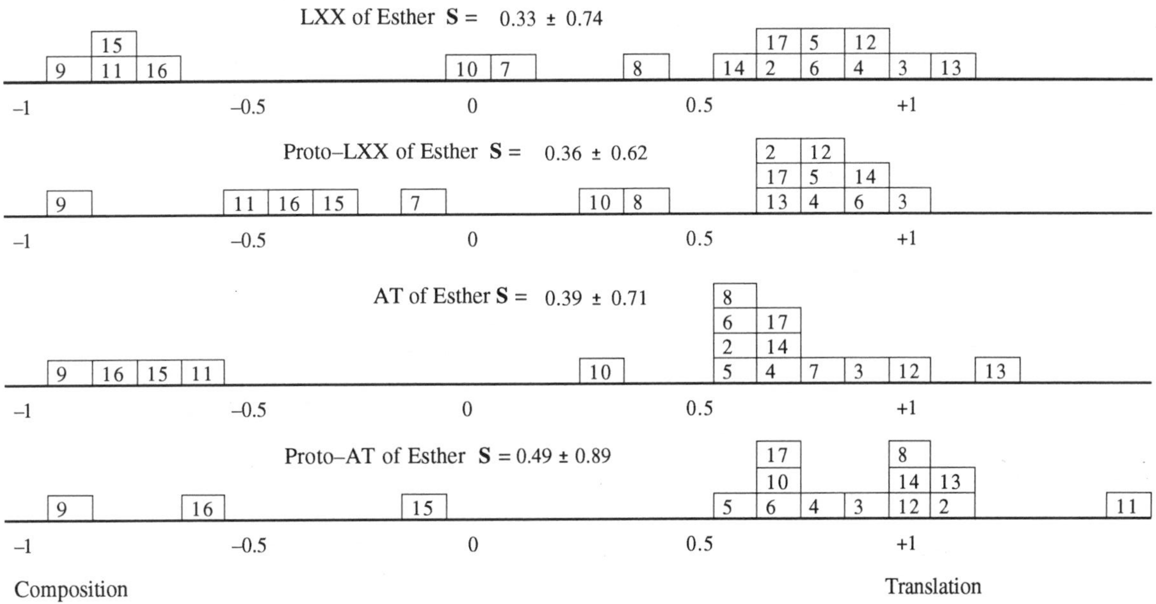

LXX of Esther **S** = 0.33 ± 0.74

Proto–LXX of Esther **S** = 0.36 ± 0.62

AT of Esther **S** = 0.39 ± 0.71

Proto–AT of Esther **S** = 0.49 ± 0.89

Composition

Translation

The numbers in the boxes refer to the criterion number. For instance, the normalized ratio of criterion #10 is 0.3 for the AT, 0.7 for the proto–AT, 0.1 for the LXX and 0.4 for the proto–LXX. If the ratio of every criterion equaled the norm for translation Greek, all of the boxes would pile up over +1; if the ratio of every criterion equaled the norm for composition Greek, all of the boxes would pile up over -1.

Graph 2: A Profile of the Syntax of Texts Composed in Greek

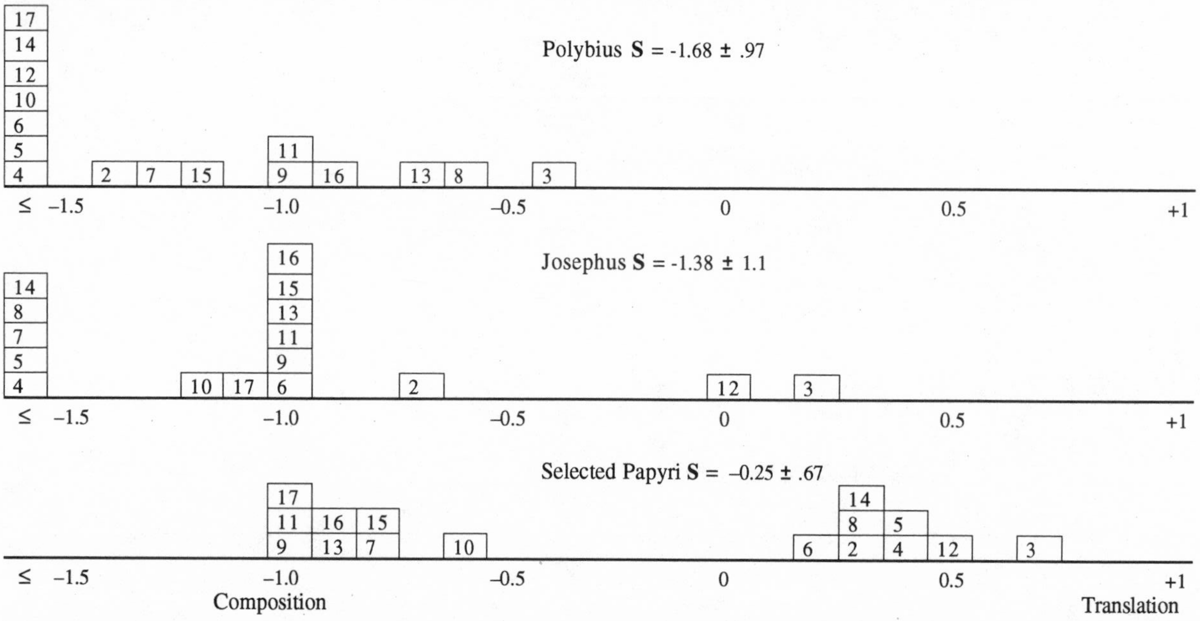

Polybius S = -1.68 ± .97

Criterion boxes (Polybius): 17, 14, 12, 10, 6, 5, 4 | 2, 7, 15 | 11 | 9, 16 | 13, 8 | 3

Axis: ≤ -1.5   -1.0   -0.5   0   0.5   +1

Josephus S = -1.38 ± 1.1

Criterion boxes (Josephus): 14, 8, 7, 5, 4 | 10, 17, 6 | 9 | 16, 15, 13, 11 | 2 | 12 | 3

Axis: ≤ -1.5   -1.0   -0.5   0   0.5   +1

Selected Papyri S = -0.25 ± .67

Composition: 17, 11, 16, 15 | 9, 13, 7 | 10 | 14, 8, 5 | 6, 2, 4, 12 | 3

Axis: ≤ -1.5   -1.0   -0.5   0   0.5   +1

Composition   Translation

The numbers in the boxes refer to the criterion number. For instance, the normalized ratio of criterion #10 is < -1.5 for Polybius, -1.2 for Josephus and -0.6 for the selected papyri. If the ratio of every criterion equaled the norm for composition Greek, all of the boxes for these texts would pile up over -1. (Data from R. Martin, *Syntactical Evidence of Semitic Sources in Greek Documents* [Cambridge, MA: Society of Biblical Literature, 1974].)

Graph 3: S-Numbers with Standard Deviations

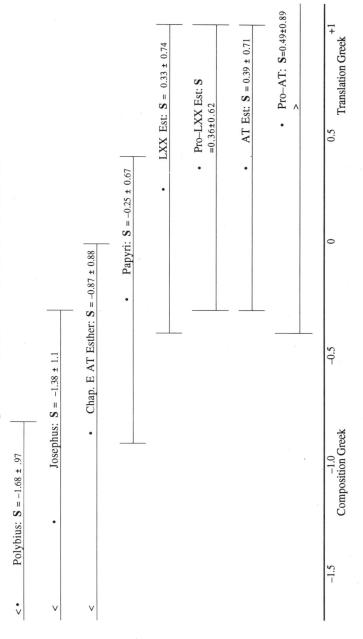

Polybius: **S** = –1.68 ± .97

Josephus: **S** = –1.38 ± 1.1

Chap. E AT Esther: **S** = –0.87 ± 0.88

Papyri: **S** = –0.25 ± 0.67

LXX Est: **S** = 0.33 ± 0.74

Pro–LXX Est: **S** = 0.36±0.62

AT Est: **S** = 0.39 ± 0.71

Pro–AT: **S**=0.49±0.89

| –1.5 | –1.0 Composition Greek | –0.5 | 0 | 0.5 | +1 Translation Greek |

(Normalized ratios for Polybius, Josephus and papyri computed from the ratios published by R. Martin in *Syntactical Evidence of Semitic Sources in Greek Documents* [Cambridge, MA: Society of Biblical Literature, 1974].)

CHAPTER 2: HOW IS THE ALPHA–TEXT SIMILAR TO THE MASORETIC TEXT?

As discussed in chapter 1, the syntax of the AT indicates it is a translation of a Semitic source. How similar was the *Vorlage* of the AT to the extant MT? Do the many differences between the AT and MT reflect a different Hebrew version of Esther? E. Tov, D. J. A. Clines and M. V. Fox have each discussed these questions with differing conclusions. Their work is compared to the results of this study in chapter 5.

Any theory about the relationship of the AT of Esther to the MT (and LXX text) of Esther must be based on the character of the AT as a whole with respect to the MT (and LXX). It is easy to find individual examples within the AT that suggest that the AT is a translation of the MT and examples that suggest that its *Vorlage* was quite different from the MT. All such examples must be evaluated in light of the character of the AT as a whole. Different readings between the AT and MT that might suggest that the AT translates a different Hebrew *Vorlage* may find a different explanation when examined in light of the differences between the texts in their entirety, especially if that reading is part of a group of differences that share some common aspect. In this study the textual character of the AT as a whole and the extent of its similarities with the MT (and LXX) is first determined in order to provide the context in which the many differences between the texts can then be most properly evaluated.

This chapter first describes the methodology used to determine the overall character of the AT of Esther. It then discussses the character of the AT in comparison to the MT of Esther, highlighting the similarities of the AT to the MT; the distinctive differences are discussed in the following chapter. The relationship of the AT to the LXX of Esther is the topic of chapter 4.

DETERMINING THE CHARACTER OF THE AT

To determine the overall character of the AT, the entire text must be thoroughly examined and carefully compared to the MT and LXX texts of Esther. To facilitate a fine-scale comparison, the three texts of Esther have been aligned and printed in three parallel columns (see Appendix 1). The texts have been divided into small syntactic units suitable for fine-scale comparison. For instance, one syntactic unit might consist of the explicit subject of a verb and its article. Another unit might consist of a prepositional phrase, or of a subordinate relative clause, etc. The intent was to break the text of each verse into the smallest sensible units for comparison, so that even the smallest difference between the texts could be identified and noted.

The overall character of the AT was determined by comparing each syntactic unit of the AT, all 1728 of them, with the corresponding units of the other two texts. This fine-scale comparison determines precisely where the texts agree and disagree and precisely how they disagree. Only then can the textual nature of the AT with respect to the other texts be characterized. By its very nature the decision of whether two units of text "agree" or "disagree" is very subjective. If the units are not identical, how similar must they be to be deemed in "agreement"? Furthermore, agreement may be *semantic*, where the corresponding units convey the same thought but in different words, or *formal*, where the same vocabulary and syntax are used.

Determining whether two units of text agree or not is, of course, most straightforward when comparing the two Greek texts. The judgment of whether a unit of Greek text agrees or disagrees with a unit of Hebrew text involves a different kind of comparison, which is by its nature more subjective. Moreover, the conclusion of whether the AT is translating the MT or a different *Vorlage* in any given unit rests on precisely this judgment of whether or not, and to what extent, the AT agrees with the MT. The subjective element can never be completely eliminated in studies of this kind. When two scholars make the same comparison, one may conclude that the Greek is a reasonable translation of the corresponding Hebrew; the other may disagree and see a different Hebrew *Vorlage* behind the Greek. Well-defined criteria must be introduced in order to make the comparison as objective as possible, but the subjective element can never be eliminated completely.

I have attempted to introduce objective controls and to minimize the subjectivity that attends studies of this type by (1) using small units of text for comparison, and (2) consistently using well–defined criteria as the basis of comparison. If one compares a whole Greek verse to its corresponding Hebrew verse, there is much more room for debate over whether the Greek text "agrees" or not with the Hebrew. But by comparing small units of text, the judgment of whether the Greek unit agrees or disagrees with the Hebrew is so narrowly focused that the subjective element is minimized, though not eliminated entirely. Comparing the 1728 syntactic units of the AT to the other two texts one unit at a time is extremely tedious, but the overall character of the AT cannot be adequately determined in any faster way. The texts must be compared in fine–grain detail consistently using well-defined criteria throughout to determine both semantic and formal agreement.

In this analysis I distinguish between semantic agreement and formal agreement of small syntactic units of text. I deem two units of text to agree semantically if they both convey the same thought even if they use very different expressions to do it. Consider the following:

LXX	MT	AT
2:4 a καὶ ἡ γυνή,	וְהַנַּעֲרָה	καὶ ἡ παῖς,
b ἣ ἂν ἀρέσῃ	אֲשֶׁר תִּיטַב	ἣ ἐὰν ἀρέσῃ
c τῷ βασιλεῖ	בְּעֵינֵי הַמֶּלֶךְ	τῷ βασιλεῖ

Unit c of the AT was deemed to be in semantic agreement with the MT, but not in formal agreement, because it uses the dative case of the referent (τῷ βασιλεῖ) instead of preserving the idiomatic expression "in the eyes of the king."

Formal agreement requires word order, syntax and vocabulary to be the "same." For example, consider:

LXX	*MT*	*AT*
2:5g ἐκ φυλῆς Βενιαμιν	אִישׁ יְמִינִי	τῆς φυλῆς Βενιαμιν

A comparison of the AT to the MT shows that Mordecai is described as "a man of Benjamin" in the MT and "of the tribe of Benjamin" in the AT. These units are deemed to agree semantically, but not formally. A comparison of the AT to the LXX shows semantic agreement, and near formal agreement. Because the AT uses the genitive of source and the LXX the preposition ἐκ, the two units do not agree formally.

It may sound simple to decide if the word order, syntax and vocabulary of two small units of text are the same or not. However, defining "same" when dealing with the variations of language is easier said than done. For instance, if the unit of Greek text in the AT uses a verbal form and the corresponding unit of Greek text in the LXX uses a compound of that verbal form that does not change the meaning, do they formally agree or not? Although others may disagree with my judgment, in the interest of catching even the smallest differences I deemed them not to agree and noted the nature of their disagreement.

Should the presence or absence of the definite article constitute formal disagreement? I decided that it does, again in the interest of making the sieve of my analysis fine enough to catch the smallest differences, even if they are subsequently ignored as irrelevant for my further purposes.

The three texts of Esther as I have formatted them in parallel columns are comprised of a total of 2814 syntactic units (including the six major additions in the Greek texts), and they require an equal number of judgments to make concerning agreement. I do not pretend that all of my judgments are right, but I have tried to err on the side of noting even minute differences and I have tried to judge consistently throughout the texts. Nevertheless, I recognize that others might disagree with good reason with the calls I have made on whether any two units of text agree or disagree; the subjective element cannot be completely eliminated.

The more straightforward Greek–to–Greek comparison of the AT compared to the LXX is discussed in chapter 4. Because of the differences between the Greek and Hebrew languages, the decision whether a syntactic unit of the AT "agrees" with the MT is not made as easily. The basis of "agreement" must be more carefully defined when comparing two languages.

The Criteria of the Comparison of Greek to Hebrew

As a basis for comparing the Greek of the AT to the Hebrew of the MT, I used the criteria formulated by E. Tov for determining the translation character of a Greek text (Tov 1981, 54-60). These criteria are (1) lexical *consistency*, defined as whether a given Hebrew word is consistently translated by the same Greek word, (2) *equivalence* between units of Hebrew and units of Greek, (3) the preservation of Hebrew *word order* in the Greek, (4) the extent of *correspondence* between individual elements of the Hebrew unit with elements of the Greek unit, and (5) the *linguistic adequacy* of the corresponding Greek expression.

Tov developed these criteria in order to characterize a Greek translation of a Hebrew source as literal or free. His methodology therefore presupposes that the Greek text under study *is* a translation of the Hebrew text, though the results of the comparison can then be used to confirm or refute the assumption. The MT is the only extant Hebrew text of Esther with which the AT can be compared, but that does not necessarily mean that the MT was the Hebrew *Vorlage* from which the AT was translated. Since the identity of the *Vorlage* of the AT is precisely the issue addressed in this study, Tov's methodology as originally conceived is not strictly appropriate to this problem. If the AT is not translating the MT, either because it is a recension of a previously existing Greek text or because it is translating a Semitic *Vorlage* quite different from the MT, one would expect *a priori* that the application of Tov's criteria in comparing these two texts could lead only to the conclusion that the AT is a very free rendering in comparison to the MT.

However, because the MT is the only Hebrew text of Esther available for comparison with the AT, I believe it is both necessary and appropriate to use Tov's criteria to determine the precise location and nature of the disagreement between the AT and the MT. This information is essential when trying to reconstruct the *Vorlage* of the AT and to determine its relationship to the MT. Although Tov's criteria cannot lead to the definitive answer about the relationship between the MT and the AT, they will assist the analysis by identifying all syntactic units of the AT that are sufficiently different from the MT as to suggest a different *Vorlage*. I therefore use Tov's criteria as functional categories of comparison, without assuming that the MT is in fact the *Vorlage* of the AT.

A brief explanation of each of the five criteria of comparison as they were applied to the AT will clarify how the character of the AT has been determined. The first of the five criteria is lexical *consistency*. This criterion is used to examine how repeated occurrences of a given Hebrew word within a text are translated in the Greek target text. Some translators will translate a given Hebrew word by the same Greek word every time it occurs, apparently insensitive to the linguistic phenomenon of polysemy, where one word may have very different senses depending on context. Others may use a number of different Greek words to translate a given Hebrew word. If a comparison of the MT to a Greek version shows that a given Hebrew word is translated consistently throughout the text by the same Greek word, and then suddenly a different, unexpected Greek word is used, it may suggest that a Hebrew word differing from the MT was found at that place in the *Vorlage*.

I have slightly redefined Tov's second criterion, which I call *equivalence,* to measure how well the syntactic units of the Greek correspond to the syntactic units of the Hebrew. In Tov's formulation of the criterion, there seemed to be too little difference for my purposes between his second category, "the representation of the constituents of Hebrew words by individual Greek equivalents," and his fourth category, "quantitative representation" of each individual element in the MT by one equivalent element in the Greek (Tov 1981, 57–8). For the purposes of this study, I consider equivalence a measure of how well a unit of Greek as a whole corresponds to its parallel unit of Hebrew. A very literal translation will represent each unit of Hebrew with an easily identified corresponding unit of Greek; the text of a paraphrastic translation, while preserving the sense of the Hebrew, cannot be so easily aligned. The comparison between the AT and MT based on this criterion is effectively accomplished by breaking them into syntactic units and aligning them in parallel columns. For instance, the following selection of text shows a high degree of Hebrew–Greek equivalence because there is a Greek unit for almost every unit of Hebrew:

	MT		AT	
3:1	אַחַר הַדְּבָרִים הָאֵלֶּה	3:1	Καὶ ἐγένετο	a
	גִּדַּל		μετὰ τοὺς λόγους τούτους,	b
	הַמֶּלֶךְ		ἐμεγάλυνεν	c
	אֲחַשְׁוֵרוֹשׁ		ὁ βασιλεὺς	d
			Ασσυῆρος	e
	אֶת־הָמָן בֶּן־הַמְּדָתָא		Αμαν Αμαδάθου	f
	הָאֲגָגִי		Βουγαῖον	g
	וַיְנַשְּׂאֵהוּ		καὶ ἐπῆρεν αὐτὸν	h
	וַיָּשֶׂם אֶת־כִּסְאוֹ		καὶ ἔθηκε τὸν θρόνον αὐτοῦ	i
	מֵעַל		ὑπεράνω	j
	כָּל־			k
	הַשָּׂרִים אֲשֶׁר אִתּוֹ		τῶν φίλων αὐτοῦ	l

Of the twelve syntactic units which comprise this passage, ten have Hebrew–Greek equivalents. Greek units AT:3:1b–j and l each have an easily identified corresponding unit of Hebrew. Furthermore, except for unit g, the Greek is an arguably good translation of the corresponding Hebrew unit. These units would therefore be deemed equivalent. Though Hebrew unit MT:3:1g (הָאֲגָגִי) has a corresponding Greek unit (Βουγαῖον), the Greek does not appear to be a faithful translation of the Hebrew. Therefore AT unit g would be deemed not equivalent. Because Greek unit k has no corresponding Hebrew unit, it would be noted as a minus in the AT.

Compare AT:3:1 to a passage that shows much less equivalence between the Hebrew and Greek:

	MT		AT	
5:1	וַיְהִי	5(D):1	Καὶ ἐγενήθη	a
	בַּיּוֹם הַשְּׁלִישִׁי		ἐν τῇ ἡμέρᾳ τῇ τρίτῃ,	b
			ὡς ἐπαύσατο	c
			Εσθηρ	d
			προσευχομένη,	e
			ἐξεδύσατο	f
			τὰ ἱμάτια τῆς θεραπείας	g

וַתִּלְבַּשׁ	καὶ περιεβάλετο	h
אֶסְתֵּר		i
מַלְכוּת	τὰ ἱμάτια	j
	τῆς δόξης	k

Greek units a and b are faithful equivalents of the corresponding Hebrew, but Greek units c–g have no equivalent in the Hebrew text.

One more example will serve to illustrate another way equivalence can fail:

MT	AT	
2:3 אֶת־כָּל־נַעֲרָה־בְתוּלָה	παρθένους	k
טוֹבַת מַרְאֶה	καλὰς τῷ εἴδει	l

In this example, the Greek of unit l seems to translate quite faithfully the corresponding Hebrew unit. But is the Greek of unit k equivalent to the corresponding Hebrew? Though the referent is generally the same, the Hebrew phrase כָּל־נַעֲרָה seems to be untranslated. This unit would be designated as somewhat, but not completely, equivalent.

By using this modified definition of Tov's criterion of equivalence, units of Greek text that are not equivalent to the Hebrew can be identified. These readings in the AT suggest that its *Vorlage* may have been different from the MT in these places.

The criterion of *word order* indicates to what extent the translator follows the word order of the Hebrew *Vorlage*. Because Greek word order is relatively free, the translator is usually able, if he chooses, to follow the Hebrew word order. If the Greek of the AT is faithfully following the Hebrew word order found in the MT and then suddenly deviates from it, this may suggest that the AT is actually faithfully following the Hebrew word order in a *Vorlage* which differs in that place from the MT. Consider for instance,

	MT		AT	
6:10	וַיֹּאמֶר הַמֶּלֶךְ	6:12	καὶ εἶπεν ὁ βασιλεὺς	a
	לְהָמָן		τῷ Αμαν	b
	מַהֵר		Ταχὺ	c
			δράμε καὶ	d

קַח	λάβε	e
אֶת־הַלְּבוּשׁ וְאֶת־הַסּוּס	τὸν ἵππον καὶ στολὴν	f
כַּאֲשֶׁר דִּבַּרְתָּ	ὡς εἴρηκας	g
וַעֲשֵׂה־כֵן	καὶ ποίησον	h
לְמָרְדֳּכַי הַיְּהוּדִי	Μαρδοχαίῳ τῷ Ἰουδαίῳ	i

Greek units AT:6:12a–c, e, and g–i faithfully follow the word order of the corresponding Hebrew unit. However, in Greek unit AT:6:12f, the two nouns found in the Hebrew אֶת־הַלְּבוּשׁ וְאֶת־הַסּוּס ("the robe and the horse") are rendered in the opposite order in the Greek τὸν ἵππον καὶ στολήν ("the horse and robe"). Because the Hebrew word order is followed in the immediately surrounding units, unit f may represent a Hebrew *Vorlage* where "horse" precedes "robe."

The fourth of Tov's criteria, *correspondence*, examines whether the translator provides a Greek element for every Hebrew element in the corresponding unit. For instance, the following example shows almost exact one–to–one correspondence between the Hebrew and Greek elements:

	MT	*AT*	
1:3	וְשָׂרֵי	καὶ οἱ ἄρχοντες	m
	הַמְּדִינוֹת	τῶν χωρῶν	n
	לְפָנָיו	κατὰ πρόσωπον αὐτοῦ	o

The Hebrew text is comprised of seven discrete elements, each of which is represented by a discrete element in the Greek (the definite article implied by the Hebrew construct state in unit m is rendered explicitly by the Greek definite article). Here there is a one–to–one correspondence between the Greek and the Hebrew it translates. Contrast 1:3 to an example in which the Greek faithfully renders the Hebrew, but without one–to–one correspondence:

	MT	*AT*	
1:5	עָשָׂה הַמֶּלֶךְ	ἐποίησεν ὁ βασιλεὺς	f
	(LXX plus)		g
	לְכָל־	πᾶσι	h
	הָעָם		i

הַנִּמְצָאִים	τοῖς εὑρεθεῖσιν	j
בְּשׁוּשָׁן	ἐν Σούσοις	k
הַבִּירָה	τῇ πόλει	l

The Greek of units AT:1:5h–j uses a substantive participle, τοῖς εὑρεθεῖσιν, and does not translate the Hebrew noun הָעָם. Here the Greek phrase πᾶσι τοῖς εὑρεθεῖσιν accurately translates the Hebrew לְכָל־הָעָם הַנִּמְצָאִים, but without one–to–one correspondence between the elements of the Hebrew and the elements of the Greek.

The fifth and final of Tov's criteria is the *linguistic adequacy* of the lexical choices made by the translator. For instance, the following example shows complete linguistic adequacy between the Hebrew and Greek units, because each Hebrew word is rendered by the expected Greek word:

	MT	*AT*	
1:2	עַל כִּסֵּא	ἐπὶ τοῦ θρόνου	e
	מַלְכוּתוֹ	τῆς βασιλείας αὐτοῦ	f

Compare this to 1:6, where the Greek is not linguistically adequate:

	MT	*AT*	
1:6	וְאַרְגָּמָן	καὶ πορφυροῖς	h
	עַל־גְּלִילֵי	ἐπὶ κύβοις	i
	(LXX plus)		j
	כֶּסֶף	ἀργυροῖς	k

In unit i, the Hebrew word גְּלִילֵי ("rings") is unexpectedly rendered, in both the AT and the LXX, by the Greek word κύβοις ("cubes"), a completely inadequate lexical choice. Does this mean that the Greek translates a Hebrew *Vorlage* that had the Hebrew noun for "cubes" where the MT has גְּלִילֵי ("rings")? (The only other occurrence of גְּלִילֵי is in Song 5:14, יָדָיו גְּלִילֵי זָהָב, "his hands are rings of gold," which is rendered in Rahlfs' Greek edition as χεῖρες αὐτοῦ τορευταὶ χρυσαῖ, "his hands are as gold turned on a lathe," another unexpected and probably inadequate lexical choice!) Because the Hebrew word גְּלִילֵי occurs only twice in the Hebrew Bible, perhaps the meaning of the word was unknown to the translator of

Esther. Or perhaps a different Hebrew word did stand at this place in the *Vorlage* of one or both of the Greek texts. In either case, it is an example where the criterion of linguistic adequacy fails.

In 1:20, the AT and LXX also agree against the MT in another instance of inadequate lexical choice:

	LXX	MT	AT
1:20m	ἀπὸ πτωχοῦ	לְמִגָּדוֹל	ἀπὸ πτωχῶν
	ἕως πλουσίου	וְעַד־קָטָן	ἕως πλουσίων

We find in both the AT and the LXX texts a Greek phrase that is equivalent in syntactical structure to the corresponding Hebrew. However, the Greek words chosen ἀπὸ πτωχῶν ἕως πλουσίων ("from the poor to the rich") are not what one would expect to find rendering the Hebrew לְמִגָּדוֹל וְעַד־קָטָן ("from the greatest to the least"). This anomaly is all the more surprising since the same Hebrew phrase also occurs in 1:5, where the AT translates it as expected, ἀπὸ μεγάλου ἕως μικροῦ. Outside of Esther, this Hebrew phrase is translated as expected in six other places (2 Chron 31:15, 34:30, 36:18; Ps 115:13 [LXX:133:21], Jer 31:34 [LXX:38:34] and Jonah 3:5). Clearly this Hebrew phrase was not a difficult one for the Greek translators to understand.

Furthermore, according to HR, the Greek word πτωχός is never used elsewhere in the LXX to translate קָטָן, nor is the Greek word πλούσιος used elsewhere to translate גָּדוֹל, so it is unlikely the Greek phrase was ever intended to translate the Hebrew phrase found in the MT. Because it is difficult to see how the Greek letters ἀπὸ μεγάλου ἕως μικροῦ could be corrupted into ἀπὸ πτωχῶν ἕως πλουσίων, it seems unlikely that this difference was introduced in the subsequent transmission of the Greek text. Furthermore, although the lexical form of the Greek words is the same in both the AT and the LXX, the inflection is singular in the LXX and plural in the AT, which means it is unlikely that one Greek text was used to "correct" the other. In this instance it is more likely that the Hebrew *Vorlage* of the AT did indeed have a different phrase in 1:20 than now stands in the MT.

As this brief discussion of the criteria has demonstrated, it is completely inadequate to judge a syntactic unit of Greek as simply agreeing or disagreeing with the corresponding Hebrew unit, because it is usually neither identical nor completely different, but most often lies somewhere in between. Therefore, for each syntactic unit an indication of the extent of agreement between the Greek unit and the corresponding Hebrew unit for four of the five criteria was noted on a scale of 1 to 5, where 1 indicates the Greek unit is for all intents and purposes the same as the Hebrew, and 5 indicates it is completely different. (The criterion of lexical consistency does not lend itself to the same type of value assignments as the other four criteria and is treated separately.)

For instance, if a comparison of an entire Greek text to a Hebrew text turned up all 1's in every category for every syntactic unit, which is highly unlikely, then the Greek text would be an extremely literal translation of the Hebrew. If the comparison turned up all 5's in every category for every syntactic unit, then one would probably conclude that the Greek text in question was a translation of a completely different Hebrew text (e.g., comparing the Greek of Esther to the Hebrew of Ruth!).

Because a comparison of most syntactic units warrants neither a 1 nor a 5, but a value in between, it is not sufficient to use only two values. Furthermore, because the in-between range needs to have some differentiation, three values were allowed, 2, 3, and 4. This dynamic range allows sufficient differentiation between units of text that are neither identically the same nor completely different.

For instance, in unit 1:11e, the Hebrew reads בְּכֶתֶר and is translated by the AT with ἐν τῷ διαδήματι. The Greek AT unit includes the definite article τῷ where there is no article in the Hebrew unit, but otherwise the Greek unit is equivalent, preserves the Hebrew word order, and is linguistically adequate; in other words, the Greek is the "same" as the Hebrew. This comparison was assigned 1's in the categories of consistency, equivalence, word order and linguistic adequacy. The category of correspondence between individual elements of the Hebrew with individual elements of the Greek was assigned a value of 2 because the Greek has a definite article where none is found in the Hebrew.

This is an example of a kind of difference between the texts which is due to a difference between Hebrew and Greek syntax. Hebrew nouns in the construct state never take the definite article, but Greek syntax permits the inclusion or omission of the definite article.

If the Greek translates a Hebrew noun in construct state using a Greek definite article, a formal difference between the units of text has been introduced. Such differences have no value for understanding the technique of the translator or in discerning a Hebrew *Vorlage* different from the MT.

Formal differences due to Hebrew and Greek grammar and syntax were assigned a value of 2 in this study so they could be distinguished from more significant differences. This assignment acknowledges that the difference between the texts exists but allows all such differences to be easily eliminated from further consideration in subsequent analysis. For the purposes of this study, only differences assigned a value of 3 or greater are considered as potential evidence for either a difference intentionally introduced by the translator or for an underlying *Vorlage* different from the MT.

This fine–grain comparison of the AT to the MT yields a huge amount of data. Many kinds of questions could be researched with the data accumulated from this comparison. However, the focus of this work is to identify if and where and how the AT is *distinctively* different from the MT in order to shed light on the nature of the relationship between the AT and the MT. A syntactic unit of the AT is considered to be *distinctively* different from the MT if one or more of the four criteria (equivalence, word order, correspondence and linguistic adequacy) is assigned a value of 3, 4 or 5 *and* if the reading of the AT is not identical to the LXX. (If the reading is identical to that of the LXX it may have been copied from one Greek version to the other and, therefore, cannot be used as decisive evidence of a distinctive *Vorlage*.)

Each syntactic unit of the AT for which there is corresponding Hebrew was compared to the MT and judged to either agree or disagree both semantically and formally with the Hebrew. Each unit was further assigned a value of 1–5 (1 = same, 5 = completely different) for each of the four criteria of equivalence, word order, correspondence, and linguistic adequacy. Pluses or minuses in the AT for which there are no corresponding Hebrew and Greek text were noted and counted.

SO HOW SIMILAR IS THE AT TO THE MT OF ESTHER?

A notable characteristic of the AT is that it is significantly shorter than both the MT and the LXX. Although the Greek AT of Esther includes the six major additions not found in the Hebrew MT, so much of the canonical Hebrew text is missing that the total AT is, in spite of the additions, shorter than the MT by about 20%. The MT contains about 7400 Hebrew words; the AT, *including* the six major additions, contains about 6100 Greek words, of which only about 3800 correspond to the Hebrew. If the AT was at its beginning a faithful translation of a Hebrew *Vorlage* different from the MT of Esther, that *Vorlage* must have been shorter than the version found in the MT by approximately 50%!

The issue in question is the same as that for the Greek versions of other books. Does the shorter Greek version reflect a shorter Semitic text from which the MT developed or a deliberate literary redaction of the Greek version? In the case of Jeremiah, the Qumran material has provided manuscript evidence that the Greek version does reflect a Hebrew text different from the MT. In the absence of such manuscript evidence, the problem is complex. Experienced scholars are often divided in their conclusion about any given text. An interesting example of this is the cooperative research venture of D. Barthélemy, D. W. Gooding, J. Lust, and E. Tov, who each independently considered the relationship of the Greek version of the David and Goliath story to the MT (Barthélemy et al. 1986). E. Tov and D. Barthélemy see the differences between the texts as primarily reflecting the *Vorlage*, while J. Lust and D. W. Gooding see them as evidence of literary art. The same debate attends the Greek versions of Esther.

The AT is similarly shorter than the LXX of Esther, because the LXX translates many of the Hebrew units that are not translated in the AT. If the AT is a later recension of the LXX text, it substantially shortens the story. The relationship of the AT to the LXX is discussed in chapter 4.

The AT has been described as midrashic because it expands upon many of the scenes of the narrative by including additional details. The AT also includes the prayers of Mordecai and Esther and the content of two royal memos that are only mentioned in the MT. Despite the midrashic quality of the version, the AT is not expansionistic. To illustrate, consider the following passage:

LXX	MT	AT	
		7:8(6) καὶ θαρσήσασα	a
7:6 a εἶπεν δὲ Εσθηρ	וַתֹּאמֶר־אֶסְתֵּר	ἡ Εσθηρ εἶπεν	b
b ”Ανθρωπος ἐχθρός·	אִישׁ צַר וְאוֹיֵב		c
c Αμαν	הָמָן	Αμαν	d
d		ὁ φίλος σου	
		ὁ ψευδὴς οὑτοσί,	e
e ὁ πονηρὸς οὗτος.	הָרָע הַזֶּה	ὁ πονηρὸς ἄνθρωπος	
		οὗτος.	f
f Αμαν δὲ ἐταράχθη	וְהָמָן נִבְעַת		g
g ἀπὸ τοῦ βασιλέως	מִלִּפְנֵי הַמֶּלֶךְ		h
h καὶ τῆς βασιλίσσης.	וְהַמַּלְכָּה׃		
i			

Although the passage is comprised of nine syntactic units, the AT and MT have only three units in common for which there is corresponding Hebrew and Greek text (b, d and f). In comparison the LXX has seven of the nine units in common with the MT. Although the AT includes two units, a and e, not found in either the MT or the LXX, the AT is still the shortest text of the three. Note however, that for the three units the AT and MT do have in common, the AT agrees with the MT. This passage is characteristic of the AT throughout. Where the AT has text corresponding to the MT, it is arguably close to the MT. When we speak of the great differences between the AT and the MT, we are speaking primarily of pluses and minuses.

Because redactors tend to add and excise material subsequent to the original production of the text, the study of the AT with respect to the MT must compare the texts with each other in two stages: (1) as they now stand with all of the pluses and minuses, *and* (2) only those passages where they have material in common. This study is attempting to distinguish the relationship of the original AT to the MT as well as to identify later redactions of the AT. Therefore it is necessary to consider separately both the agreement of the AT in its final form (however, excluding the six major additions) with the MT and the agreement of the AT with the MT when the many small pluses and minuses are excluded, because they may represent redactional activity in either text after the translation was made.

Although overall agreement between the AT in its final form and the MT is low, agreement between them where they have corresponding text is high. Excluding the six major additions that were almost certainly not originally a part of the AT, the AT agrees semantically with the MT in only 28% of the text; it agrees formally with MT in only 18% of the text. However, most of this disagreement is due to the many small pluses and minuses that are found virtually in every sentence of the AT. Only 33% of the AT corresponds to Hebrew text in the MT. Out of a total of 1803 syntactic units between them, there are only 590 (33%) that have corresponding Hebrew and Greek text. When just those 590 units are considered, the extent of agreement rises sharply to 84% semantic agreement and 54% formal agreement. This shows that where the AT has text in common with the MT, the Greek agrees more with the MT than it disagrees.

When the LXX of Esther is similarly compared to the MT, excluding the six major additions, there are a total of 1773 syntactic units between them, of which 61% are in semantic agreement and 45% in formal agreement. Although the LXX text also has many small pluses and minuses as compared to the MT, there are many fewer than are found in the AT. Of the 1773 total units there are 1236 units, or 70%, for which there is corresponding Hebrew and Greek text. When only these units of the LXX for which there is corresponding Hebrew text are considered, semantic agreement between the LXX and the MT rises to 88% and formal agreement to 64%.

These percentages show that where the AT has text corresponding to the MT, the AT agrees with the Hebrew about as often as does the LXX of Esther. The AT semantically agrees with the MT in 84% of its units compared to 88% semantic agreement of the LXX with the MT. The AT agrees formally with the MT in 54% of its units compared to 64% formal agreement between the LXX and the MT. Clearly the reason the LXX is closer to the MT is primarily that it has a greater number of units corresponding to the Hebrew than does the AT.

The following graphs compare the percentage of semantic and formal agreement of both the AT and the LXX with the MT. Graphs 1a and 1b show the extent of agreement when the many small pluses and minuses, but not the six major additions, of the Greek texts are counted in the total number of syntactic units:

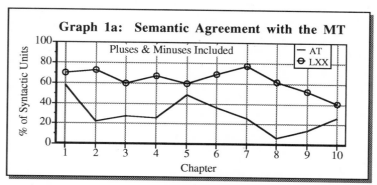

Graph 1a. When the many small pluses and minuses are included, the LXX is everywhere semantically closer to the MT than is the AT.

	Percentage of Semantic Agreement with MT when Pluses and Minuses Included									
chapter:	1	2	3	4	5	6	7	8	9	10
AT	58%	22%	27%	25%	49%	36%	25%	6%	14%	26%
LXX	70%	73%	60%	67%	60%	69%	77%	62%	53%	41%

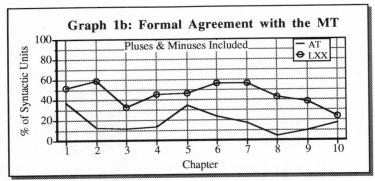

Graph 1b. When the many small pluses and minuses are included, the LXX is everywhere formally closer to the MT than is the AT.

	Percentage of Formal Agreement with MT when Pluses and Minuses Included									
chapter:	1	2	3	4	5	6	7	8	9	10
AT	37%	13%	12%	14%	35%	24%	17%	4.5%	10%	17%
LXX	52%	59%	33%	45%	46%	56%	56%	43%	38%	24%

(Line graphs, as opposed to bar charts, were chosen to represent the agreement of the texts because the shape of the curves more clearly reveals relationships between the agreement of the AT with the MT and the agreement of the LXX with the MT. The use of line graphs is not, of course, meant to imply that textual agreement is a continuous mathematical function, since the units of the x–axis are discrete and not continuous. For instance, looking at Graph 1b, there is no such thing as chapter 4.5 in the AT that agrees semantically with the MT 28%!)

When the many small pluses and minuses are excluded from the calculation, the agreement profiles change sharply. Graphs 1c and 1d show that where there is corresponding Greek and Hebrew text, the agreement of the AT with the MT approaches that of the LXX with the MT:

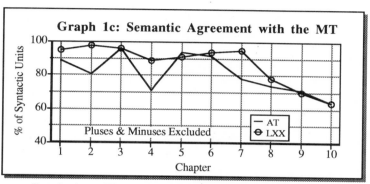

Graph 1c. When only the units for which there is corresponding Greek and Hebrew text are considered, semantic agreement of the AT with the MT approaches that of the LXX.

Percentage of Semantic Agreement with MT when Pluses and Minuses Excluded										
chapter:	1	2	3	4	5	6	7	8	9	10
AT	89%	81%	96%	71%	94%	92%	78%	74%	71%	64%
LXX	95%	98%	96%	89%	91%	94%	95%	78%	70%	64%

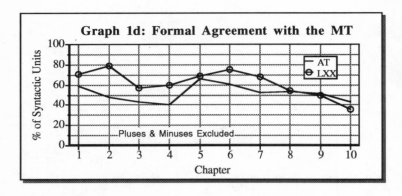

Graph 1d. When only the units for which there is corresponding Greek and Hebrew text are considered, formal agreement of the AT with the MT approaches that of the LXX.

	Percentage of Formal Agreement with MT when Pluses and Minuses Excluded									
chapter:	1	2	3	4	5	6	7	8	9	10
AT	59%	48%	43%	40%	66%	61%	52%	53%	51%	43%
LXX	71%	79%	57%	60%	69%	75%	68%	54%	50%	36%

A comparison of Graphs 1a and b to graphs 1c and d indicates that most of the difference between the AT and MT is due to pluses and minuses but that where the AT and MT have corresponding text, the *Vorlage* of the AT was quite similar to the MT.

HOW DO TOV'S CRITERIA CHARACTERIZE THE AT?

Tov's criteria of comparison can, of course, be applied only to those units for which there is corresponding Greek and Hebrew text. The AT has only 590 units of text that correspond to the MT. The Greek of each of those 590 units was compared to the Hebrew and assigned a value of 1 to 5 for each of the four criteria of equivalence, word order, correspondence and linguistic adequacy. Tov's first criterion of consistency does not lend itself to arithmetical quantification and is treated separately below. The following table shows the average values of each of these four criteria for each chapter and for the text as a whole and also displays the number of pluses and minuses:

					The Average Values of the Criteria for the AT of Esther		
Chap.	Equiv.	Word Order	Corresp.	Linguistic Adequacy	Ave. of Criteria	No. of Minuses	No. of Pluses
1	1.22	1.41	1.88	1.51	1.51	52	31
2	1.50	1.59	2.19	1.93	1.84	150	13
3	1.36	1.93	2.75	1.69	1.93	81	55
4	1.95	1.74	2.44	2.53	2.17	82	37
5	1.30	1.40	1.80	1.52	1.51	51	113
6	1.61	1.63	1.99	1.85	1.77	53	66
7	2.11	2.01	2.67	2.38	2.29	42	61
8	2.21	1.63	2.16	2.53	2.13	149	58
9	2.13	2.06	2.50	2.29	2.25	96	13
10	2.07	1.50	1.86	2.5	1.98	11	10
Total Text	1.75 ± .39	1.69 ± .24	2.22 ± .30	2.07 ± .42	1.93 ± .29	767	457

↑ Average for entire AT

This table shows that where the AT and MT have corresponding text, the AT is most like the MT in chapters 1–6; chapters 7–10 show consistently higher values indicating a larger difference between the Hebrew and Greek. Interestingly, chapters 8 and 9 also have the highest percentage of material found in the MT but missing from the AT. This raises the question of whether there is a correlation in these chapters between the "missing" material and the nature of the changes to the Greek text that causes it to deviate the greatest from the Hebrew. This question is examined more closely in chapter 3.

The average value for all four criteria for the entire text represents, in one number, how closely the Greek of the AT can be considered to render the Hebrew of the MT. An average value close to 1 means that the Greek quite literally renders the Hebrew; an average value close to 5 means that the Greek is so different from the Hebrew that it could not be considered a rendering of it at all. Recall that the value of 2 designates differences that are due only to the differences required by the syntax and grammar of the Hebrew and Greek languages. For the AT of Esther the average of the criteria is 1.93 ± 0.29 (i.e., 1.64–2.22). This shows that where there is corresponding Hebrew and Greek text, most of the many differences between the AT and the MT are due to inherent differences between the Hebrew and Greek languages.

The values of these criteria for the AT can be better understood in comparison to those of other biblical texts. To provide a comparison to the values of the criteria for the AT of Esther, selected text from Genesis 17, 1 Samuel 15 and both the OG and θ' texts of Daniel 8 were similarly analyzed. The syntactic units of the Greek of these passages were compared to the corresponding Hebrew using Tov's criteria and values from 1 to 5 were assigned. The following table compares the values of these texts to the values for the entire AT of Esther and for chapters 6 and 8, which are the chapters of the AT with the most and least material, respectively, corresponding to the MT. The texts are listed in the order from most literal agreement with the MT to least literal agreement.

The Average Values of the Criteria for Other Biblical Texts (1=same as MT; 5=completely different)					
Text	Equiv.	Word order	Corresp.	Linguistic adequacy	Overall Average
Gen 17	1.0	1.2	1.7	1.2	1.3
1 Sam 15	1.0	1.1	1.6	1.6	1.3
θ':Dan 8	1.3	1.2	1.5	1.6	1.4
OG:Dan 8	1.4	1.3	1.9	2.0	1.6
AT Esth 6	1.6	1.6	2.0	1.9	1.8
AT – all	1.8	1.7	2.2	2.0	1.9
AT Esth 8	2.2	1.6	2.2	2.5	2.1

Consistent with what is generally known about the Greek version of the Pentateuch, the selection from Genesis is most literal compared to the MT. Note that "Theodotion's" recension (θ ') of Daniel 8 stands closer to the MT than does the OG of Daniel 8. The OG of Daniel 8 is closest to the AT's chapter 6, which has the most material corresponding to the MT. These figures show that of the texts examined, the AT is furthest from the MT. However, so is the LXX of Esther, as the following values for chapters 6 and 8 of the LXX text of Esther show:

Text	Equiv.	Word order	Corresp.	Linguistic adequacy	Overall Average
LXX Esth 6	1.3	1.5	2.1	2.0	1.7
LXX Esth 8	1.6	2.0	2.4	2.4	2.1

The overall average of chapter 6 is 1.8 for the AT and 1.7 for the LXX; for chapter 8, it is 2.1 for the AT and 2.1 for the LXX. These values mean that in these chapters the rendering of the MT is quite similar in character in both the AT and the LXX. This advances the results of syntax criticism, which found no significant difference in the syntax of the AT compared to LXX Esther (see chapter 1). This indicates that not only is the syntax of the AT and LXX quite similar, but the overall character of the translation, at least in chapters 6 and 8, is also quite similar.

The following graph shows the values of the average of the four criteria for each chapter of the AT of Esther:

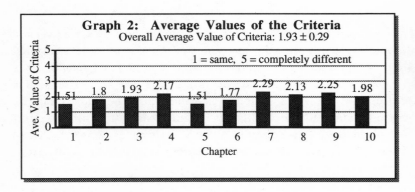

Graph 2. Where there is both Hebrew and Greek text, most of the differences between the AT and MT are due to differences between the Hebrew and Greek languages.

Lexical Consistency: How Consistent is the AT in Its Lexical Choices?

The consistency with which a given Greek word is found in the AT corresponding to a given Hebrew word was studied by examining occurrences of twenty verbs and sixteen Hebrew nouns (listed in the table at the end of this chapter).

Even a glance at the table shows that the AT of Esther displays much lexical diversity. The twenty Hebrew verbs examined were represented in the AT by fifty–three different Greek expressions. However, the table also shows that the AT, though lexically diverse, is less so than the LXX of Esther. For almost every Hebrew word, the list of Greek words translating it is longer for the LXX than for the AT. The LXX of Esther represents those same twenty Hebrew verbs with seventy–eight different Greek expressions.

The translation of nouns inherently tends toward less diversity because they name objects and therefore have less semantic range. For instance, the verb אָמַר can be construed in more than one way depending on its context and appropriately translated by λέγω, λαλέω, καλέω, κηρύσσω, ἐντέλλομαι, etc. In comparison, nouns, particularly those with concrete referents (e.g., מֶלֶךְ, עַם, מִשְׁתֶּה, etc.), show less diversity when translated. Nevertheless, the AT shows a considerable amount of lexical diversity in the sixteen nouns examined. The sixteen Hebrew nouns were represented in the AT by forty-eight different Greek words. The diversity in the LXX for those same nouns was greater, with sixty Greek terms representing the sixteen Hebrew nouns.

Similar studies of the Old Greek of Daniel compared to the later recension labeled "Theodotion" show that the Old Greek displays the greater lexical diversity of the two. (For Daniel 1–6 see D.O. Wenthe [1991, 247, 251–57]; for Daniel 7–12 see S. Jeansonne [1988, 60–69].) The lexical diversity found in the LXX of Esther makes it more like the OG version of Daniel than is the AT. A comparison of the Greek of the AT of Esther to the Greek versions of Daniel is discussed in the excursus at the conclusion of this work.

The particle **גַּם**, which is so distinctively translated by Theodotion's καίγε, appears eight times in the MT of Esther. In both the LXX and AT it is represented in four of its occurrences by καί; the other four occurrences of the particle are not represented in either Greek text.

There is a close relationship between the criterion of lexical consistency and that of linguistic adequacy. The lexically distinctive features of the AT are discussed below in relation to linguistic adequacy.

Equivalence: Is the Greek of the AT Equivalent to the Hebrew of the MT?

Eighty–five percent of the syntactic units of the AT for which there is corresponding Hebrew text (500 units out of 590) are Greek equivalents of the MT. Only ninety units of text were found where, based on a comparison of the equivalence between the Hebrew and Greek, one could argue for a different *Vorlage*. These distinctive differences are discussed in the next chapter. The following graph shows the average values of equivalence between the Greek of the AT and the Hebrew of the MT:

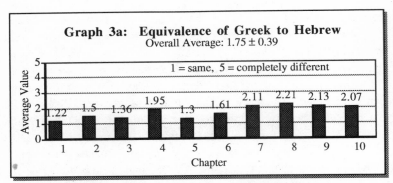

Graph 3a. The Greek of the AT is most equivalent to the MT in chapter 1 and least equivalent in chapter 8.

In terms of equivalence, the Greek of the AT most closely follows the Hebrew of the MT in chapter 1 and most deviates from it in chapter 8. There are only a few units in chapter 8 that have Hebrew text corresponding to the Greek of the AT. Addition E is embedded in chapter 8 of both the AT and the LXX. Excluding that major block of text, there remain 441 syntactic units in the parallel texts of chapter 8. Of these, there are only nineteen units where the Greek of the AT has a corresponding unit of Hebrew text and six of the these nineteen units have values ≥3.

Word Order: Does the AT Follow the Word Order of the MT?

Since the Greek language allows for very free word order, any deviation from the Hebrew word order (i.e., a value of 2 or greater) was counted as potentially significant. The only exception to this was where the waw-consecutive was translated by a post–positive δέ or γάρ. This occurs in only ten units in the entire AT. Those ten units were assigned a value of 2 and counted as formally different, but were eliminated from further study.

The following graph shows the average values of word order for the AT:

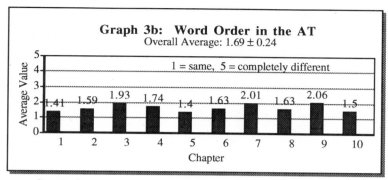

Graph 3b. More often than not, the AT follows the word order of the MT.

Graph 3b shows that the word order of the AT most faithfully follows the MT in chapters 1 and 5 and most deviates from it in chapters 7 and 9.

There are only 130 other units out of 590 (22%) where the word order in the AT did not follow the MT. Where there is corresponding Hebrew text, the AT agrees in word order with the MT 78% of the time. The percentage of the AT that follows the word of the MT can be compared to similar statistics reported by G. Marquis for the Greek versions of other biblical books (1986, 64) and are listed here in ascending order:

Job 1-30	53.8%
Isaiah 1-30	66.4%
AT Esther	78%
Jeremiah	89.8%
Ezekiel	90.1%
1 Samuel	92.2%
Psalms 1-78	96.2%
2 Kings	97.3%

Word order is integrally related to two other criteria, Hebrew–Greek equivalence and one–to–one correspondence, because word order is necessarily disrupted if the Greek phrase is quite different from the Hebrew or if elements are added or omitted. Therefore, the units where word order has been assigned a value ≥ 3 also have other significant differences from the corresponding Hebrew. Those differences are discussed in the next chapter.

There are but three units in the AT where the *only* difference between the Hebrew and Greek unit is word order:

LXX		MT	AT
1:1k	ἑκατὸν εἴκοσι ἑπτὰ	שֶׁבַע וְעֶשְׂרִים וּמֵאָה	ἑκατὸν εἴκοσι ἑπτὰ
6:10f		אֶת־הַלְּבוּשׁ וְאֶת־הַסּוּס 6:12f	τὸν ἵππον καὶ στολὴν
9:20j	τοῖς ἐγγὺς	הַקְּרוֹבִים 7:47j	τοῖς μακρὰν
	καὶ τοῖς μακράν,	וְהָרְחוֹקִים:	καὶ τοῖς ἐγγύς

In each case, elements which otherwise faithfully represent the Hebrew have been transposed. (One of the three units, 1:1k, may be due to the AT being corrected by the LXX, or vice versa, since the Greek is identical in both. However, note that this unit is a numeral. A selective examination of the word order of similar numerals elsewhere shows that the Greek preserves the Hebrew word order [cf. Num 7:13; Ezra 2:18, 21, 23; 1 Chr 15:10; Dan 6:1]. However, the word order of numerals may not be a good indicator of the translator's literalness because the Greek form of numerals may have been fixed.)

Hanhart does not list any textual variants in his apparatus that would indicate that the reversals in these three instances are due to scribal error. These three likely represent a word order in the *Vorlage* different from the MT, since the MT word order is faithfully followed in the surrounding units.

Subject–Verb Order

Of special interest under the rubric of word order is subject–verb order. There are three patterns that frequently occur in the MT of Esther: (1) verb–subject (V–S), (2) verb only (V), with implied subject, (3) subject–verb (S–V).

The V–S pattern occurs seventy-two times in the Hebrew and the AT follows the order of the MT in all but twenty–one units. Of those twenty–one units, the AT reverses the pattern to S–V six times, a tendency also observed by Marquis in the Greek of Ezekiel (Marquis 1986, 75). Fifteen times the AT omits the explicit subject found in the Hebrew and uses a verb only.

The V–only pattern occurs in the Hebrew forty–six times and the AT follows the MT in all but seven units. In every one of those seven units, the AT supplies an explicit subject, usually in the V–S pattern but once in the S–V pattern.

The S–V pattern occurs thirty–three times in the Hebrew text and the AT follows the MT in all but eight units. In those eight units, the AT reverses the pattern to V–S in four units and in the other four the AT omits the explicit subject and uses a verb alone.

Out of a total of 151 units, the AT follows the subject–verb order of the MT in all but thirty–six units, or 76% of the time. In the thirty–six units where the AT deviates from the subject–verb pattern of the MT, it agrees with the LXX against the MT in sixteen units.[1] Of these sixteen units, the AT and LXX are in identical agreement in six units; in another six units either the verb or the subject is identical; in three units the subject and verb are synonyms. The fact that in fifteen out of sixteen places where the AT subject–verb order deviates from the MT it also substantially agrees with the LXX, suggests a literary dependence between the AT and LXX in those fifteen units.

Most of the time the AT follows the subject–verb order of the MT. In the relatively few units where it does not, half of those instances agree with the LXX and probably reflect later corrections of one Greek version to the other.

One–to–One Correspondence: Do the Greek Elements of the AT Correspond to the MT?

Seventy-four percent of the syntactic units of the AT (439 out of 590) show correspondence between a given element of Greek and an element of Hebrew in the corresponding unit. These units were assigned a value of either 1 or 2. The remainder, 151 units of text, show little or no correspondence between the Greek and Hebrew elements (i.e., they were assigned a value ≥ 3).

Of the four criteria, the AT deviates from the MT most in this category of correspondence of Hebrew elements to Greek elements,

---

[1] The 16 units are AT:2:7k, 3:5f, 3:5l, 3:6h, 4:2c, 5:1h, 5:10a, 5:22b, 6:1a, 6:11g, 6:11n, 6:23b, 7:18a, 7:33a, 7:42g, 7:49a.

with an overall average value of 2.22 ± 0.30 (compared to the average values for equivalence: 1.75, word order: 1.69, and linguistic adequacy: 2.07). Nevertheless, as discussed below, most of the differences in correspondence are due to differences in syntax.

Graph 3c shows that correspondence of Hebrew elements to Greek elements is most preserved in chapters 1, 5, and 10 and is most disrupted in chapters 3, 7, and 9.

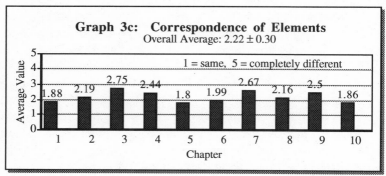

Graph 3c.   The AT deviates from the MT most in its correspondence of Greek to Hebrew elements.

Examples of units where the Greek and Hebrew do correspond (i.e., value = 1, which represent the majority), are:

	MT	*AT*
2:17e	לְפָנָיו	κατὰ πρόσωπον αὐτοῦ,
2:18a	וַיַּעַשׂ הַמֶּלֶךְ	καὶ ἤγαγεν ὁ βασιλεὺς

In these examples each element of the Hebrew phrase is rendered by one corresponding element in the Greek.

Many units of the AT were assigned a value of 2, indicating that although the Greek and Hebrew elements do not correspond exactly, the difference is due to required syntax. There were nine reasons found in the AT where correspondence between the Greek and Hebrew fails due to difference in syntax. The following examples illustrate each type of difference in syntax that breaks the one–to–one correspondence between Hebrew and Greek elements.

1. When Hebrew prepositions are translated by Greek cases, correspondence is not preserved:

> a. The Greek dative case used to translate the Hebrew preposition **בְּ**. For instance, in MT:1:10a (AT:1:10b):

> **בַּיּוֹם הַשְּׁבִיעִי**   τῇ ἡμέρᾳ τῇ ἑβδόμῃ

> b. The Greek genitive case is used to translate the Hebrew preposition **מִן**. For instance, in MT:6:9d (AT:6:11t):

> **מִשָּׂרֵי הַמֶּלֶךְ**   τῶν φίλων τοῦ βασιλέως

> c. The Greek dative case is used to translate the Hebrew **לְ**. For instance, in MT:7:2,a,b (AT:7:2b,c):

> **וַיֹּאמֶר הַמֶּלֶךְ לְאֶסְתֵּר**   εἶπεν ὁ βασιλεὺς τῇ Εσθηρ

2. The Hebrew direct object marker is not translated in the AT. For instance in 1:11b:

> **אֶת־וַשְׁתִּי**   Ουαστιν

3. When the definite article is included in the Greek to translate a definite Hebrew noun in construct state, an element is introduced in the Greek that is not found explicitly in the Hebrew. For instance, in Mt:2:8i (AT:2:8c):

> **אֶל־בֵּית הַמֶּלֶךְ**   εἰς τὸν οἶκον τοῦ βασιλέως

4. Often the Hebrew waw is untranslated in the Greek or the Greek inserts a καί where there is no waw in the Hebrew. Consequently, correspondence is not preserved. For instance, in MT:3:2i and MT:6:10l (AT:6:12l):

> **וּמָרְדֳּכַי**   Μαρδοχαῖος
> **אַל־תַּפֵּל**   καὶ μὴ παραπεσάτω

5. The Hebrew relative pronoun אֲשֶׁר is not translated. For instance, in MT:4:1c:

אֶת־כָּל־אֲשֶׁר נַעֲשָׂה   πάντα τὰ γεγονότα,

6. The Hebrew preposition כְּ not translated. For instance in MT:4:14l (AT:4:10b):

אִם־לְעֵת כָּזֹאת   εἰ εἰς τὸν καιρὸν τοῦτον

7. An implied personal pronoun in the Hebrew is made explicit in the Greek, adding an element not found in the Hebrew. For instance, in MT:5:3h (AT:5:13h):

הַמַּלְכוּת   τῆς βασιλείας μου.

8. The post-positive γάρ is added to the Greek. For instance, in MT:5:8k (AT:5:18p):

וּמָחָר   καὶ αὔριον γὰρ

9. The Hebrew infinitive absolute is translated by a Greek finite verb or vice versa, changing the syntax in a way which does not preserve correspondence. For instance, in MT:6:6c (AT:6:9c) and MT:6:7f (AT:6:11f):

מַה־לַעֲשׂוֹת בָּאִישׁ   Τί ποιήσωεν τῷ ἀνδρὶ
חָפֵץ בִּיקָרוֹ   βούλεται δοξάσαι

After eliminating units that fail correspondence because of required syntax, there still remain about 130 units, which indicate something further is involved. These units are included in the discussion in chapter 3.

Linguistic Adequacy: Does the AT Adequately Represent the Words of the MT?

There is a close relationship between semantic agreement and linguistic adequacy, although they are not the same. A Greek unit may be deemed to agree semantically with the Hebrew, and yet not be linguistically adequate. For instance, the following unit presents an interesting example:

	MT	*AT*
1:12a	וַתְּמָאֵן	καὶ οὐκ ἠθέλησεν

The Hebrew "and [Vashti] refused" agrees semantically with the Greek "and she did not wish." However, the Greek verb θέλω is not lexically equivalent to the Hebrew verb תְּמָאֵן and is therefore deemed linguistically inadequate. On closer examination, the Greek verb was chosen most likely because this form of the verb מאן had been corrupted to or confused with a form of אמן because of metathesis. The verb אמן is also rendered by θέλω in LXX Judg[A] 11:20.

In most units of the AT, the Greek is linguistically adequate to represent the corresponding Hebrew words. In 452 of the 590 syntactic units, or 77%, the Greek words adequately represent the sense of the Hebrew words in the corresponding unit of the MT. Note however, that because there can be semantic agreement without linguistic adequacy, the semantic agreement between the AT and the MT for those 590 units is a higher 84%.

As Graph 3d shows, the AT is most linguistically adequate in chapters 1 and 5; it deviates the most from the Hebrew sense in chapters 4 and 8:

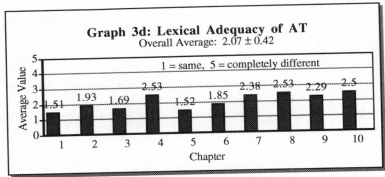

Graph 3d. **Linguistic adequacy of the Greek is most deficient in chapters 4 and 8.**

The following are examples of units that are linguistically adequate and were assigned a value of 1:

	MT	AT
AT:1:16n	וְעַל־כָּל־הָעַמִּים	καὶ εἰς πάντας τοὺς λαοὺς
AT:2:2b	נַעֲרֵי־הַמֶּלֶךְ מְשָׁרְתָיו	οἱ λειτουργοὶ τοῦ βασιλέως
AT:3:1h	וַיְנַשְּׂאֵהוּ	καὶ ἐπῆρεν αὐτὸν
AT:3:1i	וַיָּשֶׂם אֶת־כִּסְאוֹ	καὶ ἔθηκε τὸν θρόνον αὐτοῦ

For these units, each Hebrew element is represented in the AT by the expected Greek word.

Many of the units contained Greek words which arguably render the corresponding Hebrew word accurately, but are not completely synonymous with the sense of the Hebrew word. These units were assigned a value of 2. Examples are:

	MT	AT
AT:1:16a	וַיֹּאמֶר	καὶ παρεκάλεσεν

Although one might expect the Greek to read καὶ εἶπεν, the Greek verb chosen, παρεκάλεσεν, is still within the semantic domain of speaking, as discussed above under lexical consistency. The Greek verb παρακαλέω has a more specific sense than the corresponding Hebrew verb, but is appropriate in the context of 1:16. Units 5:16a and 7:12i provide a similar example of Hebrew verbs being rendered by Greek verbs that have a more specific sense, but are still appropriate in the given context and therefore, linguistically adequate:

	MT	AT
AT:5:16a	וַיָּבֹא	καὶ παραγίνονται
AT:7:12i	אֲשֶׁר־עָשָׂה הָמָן	ὃ ἔκοψεν Αμαν

Unit AT:7:40b is an example of a unit whose linguistic adequacy was also assigned 2, but for a different reason:

	MT	AT
AT:7:40b	וְהָעִיר שׁוּשָׁן	οἱ ἐν Σούσοις

In the context of this unit, the Hebrew noun הָעִיר is a metonymy referring to the people of Susa. The Greek does not translate the noun הָעִיר with πόλις, but accurately expresses the referent of the Hebrew metonymy by using the nominative plural article with a prepositional phrase. Although the metonymy of the Hebrew is not preserved in the Greek, the referent of the metonymy is.

An issue related to metonymy is how the AT expresses Semitic idioms. The issue of how Semitic idioms are translated involves consideration of both linguistic adequacy and lexical consistency. Idioms involving the words פָּנִים ("face"), יָד ("hand"), עֵינַיִם ("eyes"), and לֵב ("heart") are frequent in the MT of Esther. These words often occur in construct state in metonymical or synecdochical expressions such as לִפְנֵי הַמֶּלֶךְ, meaning "before the king."[2] The following examples show that while preserving the sense of the idiom, the AT generally does not render the Hebrew idiom literally. Moreover, the AT and LXX often disagree in the translation of idioms, indicating they are independent translations.

The noun פָּנִים occurs thirty–four times in the MT of Esther in idiomatic expressions. Twenty–three of these occurrences are in sentences that are not found at all in the AT. Of the eleven occurrences that are found in the AT, six are translated with πρόσωπον and five with other expressions. In comparison, the LXX of Esther translates twenty–two of the occurrences of פָּנִים in the MT, but only once

---

[2] *Metonymy* is the use of one word to refer to another object to which it is related; *synecdoche*, a form of metonymy, is the use of a part to refer to the whole.

expresses the idiom literally using πρόσωπον; the other twenty–one times other expressions are used.

The AT does not render this Hebrew idiom literally in about half of its occurrences; the LXX of Esther almost never does.

The word יָד occurs twenty–one times in the MT of Esther. Only six of these twenty–one occurrences are found in the AT, three of that use the word χείρ (1:12, 2:3, 3:13). In the LXX, fourteen of the twenty–one occurrences of יָד are found, with the word χείρ again used only three times (but not at the same three places as in the AT). In the MT of Esther four occurrences the word יָד are found in the idiomatic expression שָׁלְחוּ אֶת־יָדָם (2:21, 9:10, 9:15, 9:16). Where this expression is translated in both the AT and the LXX it is rendered by a form of the verb διαρπάζω ("I plunder"), which preserves the sense of the Hebrew idiom but not its form.

The word עֵינַיִם occurs thirteen times in the MT of Esther but is never rendered literally using the noun ὀφθαλμός in either the AT or the LXX of Esther. The Greek noun does occur twice in the AT (3:6; 7:2), but there is no corresponding Hebrew text for those units and the AT does not agree with the LXX at those places. Again the AT preserves the sense of the idiom but not the form.

The word לֵב occurs four times in the MT of Esther (MT:1:10, 5:9, 6:6, 7:5) and, like עֵינַיִם, is never rendered literally in either the AT or LXX. The Greek word καρδία does occur in the AT in 1:21 where the noun עֵינַי is found in the corresponding Hebrew text. This is a particularly interesting instance, because it is used by Moore as evidence for a *Vorlage* different from the MT (Moore 1967, 353). See chapter 3 for a discussion of this peculiar expression. The noun καρδία appears five more times in the AT in places for which there is no corresponding Hebrew text (AT: A:10, 3:6, 3:9, 4:25, 5:3). In three of these occurrences the AT and LXX agree identically (AT:A:10, 4:25, 5:3).

In 77% of the text, the AT adequately renders the Hebrew. In those cases involving Hebrew idioms, the AT always preserves the sense of the idiom, but most often does not preserve the literal form of the idiom.

Summary

A close comparison of the AT to the MT of Esther reveals that the AT differs from the MT primarily because of the pluses and minuses, not because the Greek text that corresponds to the Hebrew is so different from what one would expect. Using Tov's five criteria as the basis of comparison reveals that of the 590 syntactic units where the AT has text corresponding to the MT, 45% differ from the MT in equivalence, word order, correspondence or linguistic adequacy. Of these, only 179 units (30% of the total) reflect differences that may indicate a variant *Vorlage*. These will be discussed in chapter 3.

CONCLUSIONS

- The AT is shorter than the MT (and the LXX) by about 20%.
- Even excluding the six major additions, the AT has about 1200 units of text that are either pluses or minuses compared to the MT. The pluses and minuses constitute the primary difference between the AT and MT.
- Where the AT has text in common with the MT, it agrees with the MT more than it disagrees (semantic agreement: 84%, formal: 54%).
- The *Vorlage* of the AT was quite similar to the MT in those places where the AT and MT have corresponding text.
- Where the AT has text corresponding to the MT, the AT agrees with the MT about as often as does the LXX of Esther (LXX semantic agreement: 88%, formal: 64%).
- Where there is corresponding Hebrew and Greek text, most of the differences (70%) between the AT and the MT are due to inherent differences between the Hebrew and Greek languages.
- The AT shows much less lexical diversity than does the LXX.
- More often than not (78% of the time), the AT follows the word order of the MT. The AT usually follows the subject-verb order of the MT except where one Greek version has been corrected to agree with the other.
- The AT rendering of the Hebrew idioms involving the words פָּנִים ("face"), יָד ("hand"), עֵינַיִם ("eyes"), and לֵב ("heart") is in every occurrence linguistically adequate but usually does not preserve the form of the idiom.

Words Used to Evaluate the Lexical Consistency of the AT

I. Verbs

Semantic Domain: Say, speak

	MT		AT		LXX	
1.	אמר	(51)	λέγω	(25)	λέγω	(39)
			λαλέω	(3)	λαλέω	(3)
			ἐρωτάω	(1)	ἐντέλλομαι	(1)
			παρακαλέω	(1)	ἐπαγγέλλω	(1)
			ἀποστέλλω	(1)	ἐπιτρέπω	(1)
			καυχάομαι	(1)	ἐξαποστέλλω	(1)
			λογίζομαι	(1)	ἐμφανίζω	(1)
			καλέω	(1)	—	(4)
			—	(17)		
2.	נגד	(13)	ἀπαγγέλλω	(2)	ὑποδείκνυμι	(5)
			λέγω	(1)	ἀπαγγέλλω	(4)
			—	(10)	λαλέω	(1)
					λέγω	(1)
					σημαίνω	(1)
					—	(1)
3.	קרא	(11)	καλέω	(3)	καλέω	(5)
			κηρύσσω	(2)	κηρύσσω	(2)
			ἀναγινώσκω	(1)	ἀναγινώσκω	(1)
			ἄκλητος	(1)	ἄκλητος	(1)
			—	(4)	ἐπικαλέω	(1)
					προσκαλέω	(1)
4.	צוה	(9)	λέγω	(1)	ἐντέλλομαι	(4)
			ἀποστέλλω	(1)	ἀποστέλλω	(1)
			τὸ πρόσταγμα	(1)	πορεύομαι	(1)
			—	(6)	προστάσσω	(1)
					ἐπιτάσσω	(1)
					—	(1)
5.	דבר	(6)	λέγω	(1)	λαλέω	(4)
			λαλέω	(1)	—	(2)
			ὁ λόγος σου	(1)		
			—	(3)		
6.	ענה	(2)	λέγω	(2)	λέγω	(1)
					ἀποκρίνομαι	(1)
7.	זעק	(1)	—	(1)	βοάω	(1)

Total of 7 Hebrew verbs for "say, speak" represented by 13 different Greek terms in AT; cf. to 22 different Greek in LXX.

Semantic Domain: Go, Come

	MT		AT		LXX	
1.	בוא	(36)	εἰσέρχομαι	(8)	εἰσέρχομαι	(15)
			ἐξέρχομαι	(1)	ἔρχομαι	(4)
			ἔρχομαι	(1)	εἰσπορεύομαι	(4)
			ἄγω	(1)	καλέω	(3)
			συνάγω	(1)	προσκαλέω	(1)
			εἰσάγω	(1)	ἐπιδίδωμι	(1)
			ὄρνυμι	(1)	εἰσάγω	(1)
			ποιέω	(1)	εἰσφέρω	(1)
			ἀποστέλλω	(1)	ἐπισπουδάζω	(1)
			καλέω	(1)	ἄντειπον	(1)
			σπουδάζω	(1)	φέρω	(1)
			λαμβάνω	(1)	—	(3)
			—	(17)		
2.	יצא	(9)	ἐξέρχομαι	(1)	ἐξέρχομαι	(3)
			—	(8)	διάγω	(1)
					προστάσσω	(1)
					ἐκπηδάω	(1)
					—	(3)
3.	עבר	(7)	παρακούω	(1)	ἀφαιρέω	(2)
			—	(6)	χράω	(2)
					ἄγω	(1)
					βαδίζω	(1)
					παρακούω	(1)
4.	בהל	(3)	σπεύδω	(2)	σπεύδω	(2)
			—	(1)	ἐπισπεύδω	(1)
5.	דחף	(3)	ἀπέρχομαι	(1)	ὑποστρέφω	(1)
			—	(2)	—	(2)
6.	מהר	(2)	ταχὺ δράμε	(1)	κατασπεύδω	(1)
			κατασπεύδω	(1)	—	(1)
7.	נדר	(1)	ἀφίστημι	(1)	ἀφίστημι	(1)
8.	הלך	(3)	προσπίπτω	(1)	προσπίπτω	(1)
			—	(2)	περιπατέω	(1)
					—	(1)

Total of 8 Hebrew verbs for "go, come" represented by 19 different Greek terms in AT; cf. to 27 different Greek in LXX.

Semantic Domain: Know

	MT		AT		LXX	
1.	ידע (7)	οἶδα	(2)	οἶδα	(1)
		γινώσκω	(1)	γινωσκω	(1)
		ἐπιγινώσκω	(1)	ἐπιγινώσκω	(1)
		—	(3)	μανθάνω	(1)
				δηλόω	(1)
				—	(2)

Total of 1 Hebrew verb for "know" represented by 3 different Greek terms in AT; cf. to 5 different Greek in LXX.

Semantic Domain: Give

	MT		AT		LXX	
1.	נתן (28)	δίδωμι	(5)	δίδωμι	(10)
		ἐπιδίδωμι	(1)	εἰμί	(3)
		ἐκτίθημι	(1)	ἐκτίθημι	(2)
		εἰμί	(1)	παραδίδωμι	(1)
		ἔχω	(1)	περιτίθημι	(1)
		—	(19)	ἐπιτάσσω	(1)
				ἔχω	(1)
				—	(9)

Total of 1 Hebrew verb for "give" represented by 5 different Greek terms in AT; cf. to 7 different Greek in LXX.

Semantic Domain: Do, Make

MT		AT		LXX	
1. עשׂה	(51)	ποιέω	(20)	ποιέω	(20)
		χράω	(2)	ἄγω	(4)
		κόπτω	(2)	ἑτοιμάζω	(3)
		θέλω	(1)	χράω	(3)
		ἄγω	(1)	εἰμί	(2)
		δοξάζω	(1)	λαλέω	(1)
		προσέχω	(1)	κόπτω	(1)
		ἐγένετο	(1)	παρακούω	(1)
		ταπεινόω	(1)	δοξάζω	(1)
		οἱ βασίλικοι γραμματεῖς	(1)	οἱ βασίλικοι γραμματεῖς	(1)
		—	(20)	συντελέω	(1)
				συμβαίνω	(1)
				ἐπιτελέω	(1)
				λέγω	(1)
				—	(10)

Total of 1 Hebrew verb for "do, make" represented by 10 different Greek terms in AT; cf. to 14 different terms in LXX.

MT		AT		LXX	
1. אבד	(12)	ἀπολύω	(1)	ἀπολύω	(5)
		ἀποθνήσκω	(1)	δουλεία	(1)
		ἀπώλεια	(1)	—	(6)
		—	(9)		

Total of 1 Hebrew verb for "destroy" represented by 3 different Greek terms in AT; cf. to 2 different terms in LXX.

MT		AT		LXX	
1. אכל	(1)	—	(1)	ἐσθίω	(1)

II. Nouns

MT		AT		LXX	
1. מלכות	(24)	βασιλεία	(8)	βασιλεία	(9)
		βασίλικος	(3)	βασίλικος	(2)
		βασιλεύς	(2)	βασιλεύω	(2)
		βασίλειος	(1)	βασιλεύς	(1)
		βασιλεύω	(1)	βασίλειος	(1)
		δόξα	(1)	δόξα	(1)
		—	(8)	γυναικεῖος	(1)
				—	(7)

One Hebrew noun "kingdom" represented by 6 different Greek terms in AT; cf. to 7 different terms in LXX.

MT		AT		LXX	
2. מלך	(166)	βασιλεύς	(55)	βασιλεύς	(91)
		αὐτός	(4)	βασιλεία	(8)
		κύριος	(2)	ἐγώ, μου	(4)
		βασιλεία	(1)	αὐτός	(3)
		βασίλικος	(1)	βασίλικος	(2)
		—	(103)	σου, σοι	(2)
				βασίλειος	(1)
				—	(55)

One Hebrew noun "king" represented by 5 different Greek terms in AT; cf. to 7 different terms in LXX.

MT		AT		LXX	
3. נערה	(10)	παῖς	(2)	κορασίον	(3)
		κορασία	(1)	κορασία	(3)
		παρθένος	(1)	ἁβρά	(2)
		—	(5)	γυνή	(1)
				—	(1)

One Hebrew noun "maiden, virgin" represented by 3 different Greek terms in AT; cf. to 4 different terms in LXX.

MT		AT		LXX	
4. שׂרים	(13)	ἄρχοντες	(5)	ἄρχοντες	(7)
		φίλος	(1)	φίλος	(4)
		ἔνδοξος	(1)	ἔνδοξος	(2)
		στρατιά	(1)	—	(1)
		—	(5)		

One Hebrew noun "leaders, princes" represented by 4 different Greek terms in AT; cf. to 3 different terms in LXX.

MT		AT		LXX	
5. עם	(22)	λαός	(3)	ἔθνος	(6)
		ἔθνος	(2)	λαός	(4)
		Ἰουδαῖος	(1)	γένος	(1)
		—	(16)	—	(11)

One Hebrew noun "people" represented by 3 different Greek terms in the AT; cf. to 3 different terms in the LXX.

Semantic Domain: Request, Petition (noun)

MT		AT		LXX	
6. שׁאלה	(6)	αἴτημα	(3)	αἴτημα	(2)
		θέλημα	(1)	τί ἐστιν	(2)
		κίνδυνος	(1)	ἄξιος	(1)
		—	(1)	—	(1)

One Hebrew noun "request" represented by 3 different Greek terms in AT; cf. to 3 different terms in the LXX.

MT		AT		LXX	
7. בקשׁ	(7)	ἀξίωμα	(2)	ἀξίωμα	(3)
		ἀξιός	(1)	ἀξιός	(1)
		αἴτημα	(1)	αἴτημα	(1)
		ἀναγγέλλω	(1)	—	(2)
		—	(2)		

One Hebrew noun "request" represented by 4 different Greek terms in the AT; cf. 3 different terms in the LXX.

	MT		AT		LXX	
8.	מִשְׁתֶּה	(19)	δοχή	(3)	δοχή	(5)
			πότος	(3)	πότος	(4)
			συμπόσιον	(1)	συμπόσιον	(1)
			—	(12)	κώθων	(1)
					χαρᾶς	(1)
					ἡμέραν ἀγαθήν	(1)
					γάμος	(1)
					—	(5)

One Hebrew noun "feast, banquet" represented by 3 different Greek terms in AT; cf. to 7 different terms in the LXX.

Semantic Domain: Garment, clothing

	MT		AT		LXX	
9.	לְבוּשׁ	(6)	στολή	(3)	στολή	(3)
			σάκκος	(1)	σάκκος	(1)
			στολίζω	(1)	στολίζω	(1)
			—	(1)	—	(2)

One Hebrew noun "garment, clothing" represented by 3 different Greek terms in AT; cf. to 3 different terms in the LXX.

	MT		AT		LXX	
10.	בֶּגֶד	(2)	ἱματία	(1)	ἱματία	(1)
			—	(1)	στολίζω	(1)

One Hebrew noun "garment, clothing" represented by 1 Greek noun in the AT; cf. 2 terms in the LXX.

	MT		AT		LXX	
11.	אָב	(3)	πατήρ	(1)	πατήρ	(1)
			—	(2)	γονεύς	(1)
					—	(1)

One Hebrew noun "father" represented by 1 Greek noun in the AT; cf. 2 terms in the LXX.

	MT		AT		LXX	
12.	יָד	(21)	χείρ	(3)	μετά, διά	(4)
			διαρπάζω	(1)	χείρ	(3)
			εἰς	(1)	διαρπάζω	(3)
			ὄν	(1)	ὄν, οὗ	(2)
			—	(15)	ἔνι	(1)
					ἐζήτουν ἀποκ.	(1)
					—	(7)

One Hebrew noun "hand" represented by 4 Greek terms in the AT; cf. 6 terms in the LXX. It is clear that the Greek is representing the sense of the phrase in which יָד occurs and not the noun itself.

	MT		AT		LXX	
13.	לֵב	(4)	βασιλεύς	(1)	ἑαυτός	(1)
			λογίζομαι	(1)	εὐφραίνω	(1)
			τολμάω	(1)	τολμάω	(1)
			—	(1)	—	(1)

One Hebrew noun "heart" represented by 3 Greek terms in the AT; cf. 3 terms in the LXX. It is clear that the Greek is representing the sense of a phrase in which לֵב occurs and not the noun itself.

	MT		AT		LXX	
14.	יַיִן	(6)	οἶνος	(2)	οἶνος	(1)
			συμπόσιον	(1)	συμπόσιον	(1)
			—	(3)	πότος	(1)
					—	(3)

One Hebrew noun "wine" represented by 2 Greek terms in the AT; cf. 3 terms in the LXX. It is clear that sometimes the Greek is representing the sense of a phrase in which יַיִן occurs and not the noun itself.

	MT		AT		LXX	
15.	ראש	(5)	κεφαλή	(1)	κεφαλή	(1)
			τράχηλος	(1)	τράχηλος	(1)
			—	(3)	αὐτός	(1)

One Hebrew noun "head" represented by 2 Greek terms in the AT; cf. 3 terms in the LXX.

	MT		AT		LXX	
16.	ארץ	(2)	γῆ	(1)	γῆ	(1)
			—	(1)		—
	(1)					

III. Particle

	MT		AT		LXX	
1.	גם	(8)	καί	(4)	καί	(4)
			—	(4)	—	(4)

CHAPTER 3: HOW IS THE ALPHA–TEXT DIFFERENT FROM THE MASORETIC TEXT?

Determining the origin of the many differences between the AT and MT is a very complex problem because they almost certainly arose in many different ways, by several different hands, over a long period of time. Some differences probably are the result of the deliberate and creative activity of the translator. Other differences between the AT and MT no doubt arose as scribes and/or redactors introduced changes, deliberate or inadvertent, in both the Hebrew and Greek texts.

Differences between the Hebrew *Vorlage* from which the AT translation was made and the extant MT may account for other discrepancies. The major issue attending the AT is to what extent its *Vorlage* varied from the extant MT. Such differences in the Hebrew *Vorlage* could have arisen from textual corruption in the transmission of the Hebrew or from the deliberate and creative effort of a redactor of the Hebrew text. It is possible that larger and more substantial differences were introduced as the Hebrew text developed over time to address the contemporary issues of a new generation of readers. Is the AT a key to understanding and even reconstructing the history of the Hebrew text of Esther?

Although it is simply a matter of much tedious work to locate and catalog the many differences between the AT and the MT, it is quite another task to reconstruct accurately the redactional history of the text in any detail or to explain adequately each and every difference. Such a project requires expertise in widely ranging skills of textual criticism, retroversion of Greek into Hebrew and/or Aramaic, sophisticated knowledge of the fine points of Hebrew and Greek syntax and style, a sense of what translators generally did, and the art of literary criticism. Even those who have command of these skills do not agree on what we can learn about the Hebrew *Vorlage* from the Greek versions.

Scholars such as I. Seeligmann, E. Tov, and E. Ulrich, among others, have spent a lifetime contributing to the vast literature on the relationship of the Greek versions to the Hebrew text. The differences between the AT and MT must be judged not only within the context of the character of the AT, but also in light of the more general issues in Septuagint research. For a good survey of the state of the issues see Seeligmann (1990).

This study does not attempt to ascertain the origin of each difference between the AT and MT or to reconstruct the *Vorlage* of the AT in any detail. It attempts to contribute to the discussion of two related questions: How different was the *Vorlage* of the AT from the MT? and, Was this *Vorlage* a genetic ancestor of the MT or a completely independent version of the Esther story? Fortunately, even without exhaustively explaining the origin of every identified difference, the voluminous data generated by this study can be queried for evidence that supports or refutes particular beliefs about the AT. D. J. A. Clines and M. V. Fox have argued independently that the *Vorlage* of the AT was radically different from the extant MT, especially in its ending (Clines 1984; Fox 1991). Clines argues that the *Vorlage* of the AT captures an earlier stage in the development of the MT. Fox believes that the AT translates a Hebrew text that is not in the direct lineage of the MT. This study has found evidence that the AT reflects a Hebrew text that was in many respects quite similar to the MT. The conclusions of Clines and Fox will be discussed in light of this study in chapter 5.

To locate evidence relevant to this issue, all syntactic units of the AT with a value of 3 or greater for any one of the four criteria of correspondence, word order (2 or greater), equivalence or linguistic adequacy were scrutinized further. Those units which agree identically with the LXX were eliminated as evidence for a variant *Vorlage,* because of the probability that in such cases one Greek version was corrected to agree with the other. Therefore, this study focused on those units of the AT which are distinctive to that version, agreeing with neither the MT nor the LXX. A list of the units reflecting a distinctive AT reading is included in a table at the end of this chapter. The AT's distinctive readings were catagorized into types of differences as follows (the citations refer to the parallel texts in Appendix 1):

A CATALOG OF THE DIFFERENCES BETWEEN THE AT AND THE MT
(In approximately descending order of frequency of occurrence)

1. *Minuses* — syntactic units present in the MT but not in the AT (MT versification)

a. prepositional phrase

1:2a, 1:3a, b, 1:8h, 1:10f, 1:16d, 2:3g, h, 2:9p, s, 2:16c, 2:17m, 2:18c, d, 3:8i, m, w, 3:11b, 4:10b, 4:11k, 4:14c, 4:15e, 4:16c, 4:17e, 5:1g, h, l, m, 5:2f, 5:6d, 5:12g, l, 5:14m, 5:23u, w, 6:1a, 6:4d, 6:7c, 6:9n, 6:11i, 6:12c, 6:13g, 6:14f, 7:2c, d, 7:3l, 7:4c, d, e, 7:5c, 7:7e, f, 7:8b, 7:11b, 8:1a, 8:15b, 9:4b, 9:12d, 9:21i, j, 9:22a, 10:1d

b. proper names

1:1e, 1:9j, 1:10f, g–l, 1:14c, 1:16q, 1:21i, 2:1c, 2:7d, 2:16c, 3:5b, f, 3:6j, 3:8c, 3:11b, 3:5l, 3:6e, h, 3:8a, 3:7f, 4:16b, c, 5:1d, 5:2f, 5:12c, 6:6a, 6:13c, i, 7:2g, 7:5b, c, 8:1e, 9:8b, c, 9:9a–c, 9:23b, 10:1b, 10:3b

c. subordinate clause

1:2g, 1:9i, 1:11n, 1:16o, 1:17a, 2:7g, 3:2c, 3:3c, 3:5b, 3:6i, 4:11g, 4:7n, 4:17d, 5:2h, 5:12h, 6:4i, 6:8e, i, j, p, 6:9h, 6:14g, 7:7m, n, 9:4a, e, f, 9:13g, 10:2d

d. part of compound phrase

1:3i, 1:6p, s–u, 1:11l, 1:16f, 1:21d, 3:2d, j, 3:8h, 4:9a, 4:10a, 4:17a, 5:2i, 5:3i, 5:10a, 5:14d, 6:13d, 8:15k, 9:6d, 10:2a, c

e. explicit subject

1:12j, 1:21g, 2:9a, 3:5f, 3:6e, 3:8a, 3:13b, 4:11b, c, p, (cf. LXX Esth 8:11a), 5:2f, 5:12c, 5:14p, 6:3d, 6:9a, 7:5a, 7:8j, 7:33a

f. redundant phrases   1:1e, 1:4h, i, 3:5b–d, 4:9a, 4:11s, u, 5:7c,
                         7:3c, 7:4c–e, 7:5c, 7:5f

g. adjective   1:7i, 1:16k, 2:3e, 3:1j, 4:16b, c, 5:2g,
                         5:13a, 8:15e, (cf. 1 Sam 15:6, OG Dan
                         8:5; 9:3a, 9:20f, h (LXX Esth 8:5t)

h. direct object   1:11m, 2:9i, j, 2:17d, 2:18b, 4:8m, 4:15c,
                         4:16b, c, 9:20e, 10:1c

i. indirect object   2:9k, 3:5d, 4:8g, m, 5:2f, 5:3b, 5:4j,
                         6:13g, 7:5c (cf. OG Dan 8:7)

j. noun in apposition   1:2c, 1:12b, 5:3e, 7:2g, 7:5c, 8:1i, 9:6a,
                         9:12c

k. possessive noun   2:3n, 4:11b, 6:12k

l. conjunction   4:16k, 5:1f

m. demonstrative pronoun   1:5c

n. adverb   6:10h

o. unclassified   1:19f, 2:3p, 2:4e, 2:9q, 2:17s, 3:8v,
                         4:11c, g, m, 4:13a, 4:17a, 5:4g, 5:6g,
                         5:13e, 6:1e, 6:9a, b, e, 6:11c, 6:12g,
                         7:2h, n, 7:4j, 7:5e, 7:6b, 8:1b, 9:13c, e,
                         9:16j, 10:1b

2. *Pluses* — syntactic units present in the AT but not in the MT (AT versification, with the MT chapter numbers given in parentheses)

a. prepositional phrase   2:8h, 4:7h, 4:9b, 5:21v, 5:23q, z, 7:4i,
                         7:12g, (9)7:43b, (9)7:47c, m, n,
                         (10)7:51g, (10)7:52g

b. part of compound phrase   1:6m, 1:20j, 2:9b, 3:5m, 4:4m,
                                4:9a, b, 5:21e, 6:22f, 7:4h, i, 7:11h, i,
                                (8)7:40a

c. adjective   1:1g, 1:9e, f, 1:13c, 2:7m, 2:9aa, 2:18h,
                         6:9d, 6:11 l, hh, 6:19h, 7:52i

d. conjunction   1:6n, 1:14h, 2:5a, 2:9h, 6:23a, (9)7:44q

e. pleonastic participle   1:16c, 3:10d, 4:7c, 5:21r, 6:10c, 7:8a

f. adverb   1:21f, 2:4g, 2:7a, 2:18f, 4:12b, 5:18o

g. noun in apposition   2:8e, 5:14f, 5:16e, 5:17c, 6:5f, 7:8e

h. indirect object   2:1d, 3:2k, 6:5b
                   (cf. 1 Sam 15:28; Dan 8:19; LXX Esth 8:8k)

i. explicit subject of verb   1:3e, 1:10e, 2:9a, 4:12b, 6:2b

(cf. 1 Sam 15:27, 29; 15:30, 31)

j. proper name 1:16m, 2:9a, 4:12b, (9)7:43b, (9)7:44s

k. clarifying verb 2:2 o, p, 2:9e, (10)7:52g

l. implied genitive personal pronoun 1:4h, 1:11f, k, 1:18c

m. genitive noun 1:3j, 1:16m, 7:3k, (9)7:44s

n. introductory formula 1:10a, 3:1a, 4:3m, 7:1a

o. adds redundant phrase 6:1e, 7:9b

p. implied noun 7:8f

q. relative pronoun 1:5e

r. unclassified 1:5s, 2:17b, 3:5g, 3:7g, k, 3:8g, 4:3p,
4:4e, 4:7u, 5:22h, 6:6k, 6:22r, 7:5a, i, j,
7:11p, 7:12a, (8)7:15g, (8)7:41d,
(9)7:45j, (9)7:46j, (10)7:50e

3. *Substitutions* — syntactic units in the AT that correspond to the MT, but with some significant difference (AT versification unless otherwise noted):

a. unexpected lexical choice 1:5i, 1:11d, j, 1:12c, d, 1:16b, s, t,
1:20a, 2:9k, 2:18g, 3:5a, 3:9e, 4:2c,
4:6c, 4:9h, 4:11a, g, j, p, s, 5:13f, 5:14j,
5:18r, 5:21w, z, 5:22a, 6:7a, 6:20a, b, f,
7:3h, j, 7:4g, 7:5g, h, 7:10c, d, 7:11o,
7:12d, (8)7:4lb, c, (9)7:42e, (9)7:43a,
(9)7:45k, (9)7:46i, (10)7:50a

b. idiomatic rendering 1:7d, 1:8j, 1:9h, 1:18a, 2:2b, 3:8h,
3:9a, 4:2n, r, 5:21s, 6:2g, 6:18b, 7:3f,
7:11c, (8)7:41f, (9)7:44v

c. replaces proper name(s) 1:10f, 1:21h, 2:8b, 3:2e, 3:5n, 4:6b,
with noun or pronoun 4:7b, 4:9c, 4:11b, 5:23r, 6:2g, 6:23b,
(8)7:15h, (8)7:41f

d. changes subject of verb 1:1h, 2:9y, 3:13b, 6:2a, 6:11g, i, s, v,
6:23b, (9)7:43a, (9)7:45 l, (9)7:48a,
(10)7:51c

e. clause structure

  i. independent clause instead of relative clause, 1:20c, 2:5c, 4:4a,
    or vice versa 5:23v, 6:18b

  ii. independent clause instead of prepositional phrase 6:11aa

  iii. relative clause instead of prepositional phrase 1:7k, 3:11f

  iv. adjective instead of relative clause 4:7o

f. AT eliminates synecdoche or metonymy   1:10d, 1:21c, 2:8g, 3:11f, 5:18g, 6:2g, 6:11s, 7:12e

g. changes 3rd person to 2nd   3:8k, 4:3n, 4:4d, 4:7d, g, 5:14e

h. substitution for verbal expressions
    i.   finite verb for Hebrew infinitive   2:9h, 4:9c, 7:8m
    ii.   infinitive for Hebrew jussive   6:8b
    iii.   relative clause for infinitive   7:46h
    iv.   prepositional phrase for infinitive   1:11i

i. different proper name   2:2r, 2:8d, 7;12c, (8)7:44m

j. sense of the Hebrew reversed   2:1a, b, (9)7:44v, w

k. passive verbal form instead of active   1:12i, 6:2a, 6:11g (cf. LXX Esth 8:10a, c)

l. different numeral   (9)7:44f, (9)7:46 l (cf. 1 Sam 15:4)

m. negative expression, same meaning   4:7r–u, 7:4k

n. active verbal form instead of passive   3:13b

o. direct object made subject of passive verb   6:2d

p. noun with adverb   5:24d

q. participle instead of prepositional phrase   5:23p

r. personal pronoun instead of relative clause   6:12m

4. *Other*
    a. possible scribal errors
      1. inner–Hebrew   1:12a, 2:8d, 3:5a, 4:2c, 4:7a, 6:6j, (8)7:40g
      2. inner–Greek   1:12c, (9)7:44h
    b. unclassified   1:6a, 3:8f, 4:2f, 4:8d, 4:11t, 5:1j, 6:23d, 7:9a, 7:11m, (9)7:42e, (9)7:47i, (10)7:52d, (10)7:52i

5. *Displaced Text* — corresponding syntactic units found in different places in the AT and MT:

    AT:2:14a, b   // MT:2:14a, b   AT:6:20e   // MT:6:12a, b
    AT:3:5o   // MT:3:13j   AT:6:20f   // MT:6:12c
    AT:3:10a–d   // MT:3:10a–c   AT:6:22f   // MT:6:13h

AT:4:10b   // MT:4:14c   AT:6:23c // MT:6:14f
AT:5:13f   // MT:5:3i   AT:7:10c // MT:7:8d
AT:5:17g, h   // MT:5:6g   AT:7:10f // MT:7:8e, f
AT:5:23m–o   // MT5:14i, j, k (??) AT:7:12h // MT:7:9m
AT:6:11bb   // MT:6:9n

6. *Pluses of More than One Syntactic Unit* (AT versification):
1:6c–f, 1:12f–h, 1:13h–j, 1:18d, e, 2:14a–c, 3:1m–o, 3:3a–d, l, 3:4d, e, 3:6a–f, 3:8m–q, 3:9b–d, 3:10a–i, 3:7a–k, 4:1d–h, 4:2a, b, 4:4o–v, 4:5a–e, 5:1c–g, 5:14b, c, 5:19a, b, 5:20a–d, 5:23e–j, m–o, 6:3 all, 6:4 all, 6:5l–o, 6:6a, b, 6:13 all, 6:14c–e, 6:15 all, 6:16 all, 6:17 all, 6:19a–c, 6:22g–j, 6:23h–j, 7:2 all, 7:4m–o, 7:6 all, 7:7 all, 7:11k l, 7:12a, o, p, 7:13c–g, 7:14 all, (8)7:16 all, (8)7:17 all, (8)7:18b–e, (8)7:19 all, (8)7:20 all, (8)7:21 all, (8)7:33d–g, (8)7:34 all, (8)7:35 all, (8)7:36 all, (8)7:37 all, (8)7:38 all, (8)7:41c, d, (9)7:43d, e, (9)7:49e–g, (10)7:50m, n, (10)7:52k, l, n

7. *Minuses of More than One Syntactic Unit* (MT versification):
1:13e, f, 1:15 all, 1:16o–q, 1:18 all, 1:19h–m, 1:22 all, 2:1a–c, 2:2d–f, 2:3a–d, 2:6 all, 2:7o–p, 2:8a–f, 2:10all, 2:11 all, 2:12 all, 2:13 all, 2:14 all, 2:15 all, 2:16e–h, 2:18b–d, i–k, 2:19all, 2:20 all, 2:21 all, 2:22 all, 2:23 all, 3:4a–e, 3:5b–d, 3:6a–d, 3:7 all, 3:9d–f, 3:10 all, 3:12 all, 3:13d–n, 3:14 all, 3:15 a, b, e–g, 4:1o–r, 4:3 all, 4:4a–j, 4:5 all, 4:6 all, 4:7 all, 4:8a–e, 4:10a, b, 4:12 all, 4:14g–h, 4:16e–h, 4:17d, e, 5:2a–d, 5:9 all, 5:11 all, 5:14i–k, 6:3f–k, 6:5a–e, 6:12a–c, 6:13h–i, 7:3d, e, 7:6f–h, 7:7m–o, 7:8d–f, q, r, 7:10 all, 8:1k–p, 8:2 all, 8:3 all, 8:4 all, 8:5f–t, 8:6 all, 8:7 all, 8:8 all, 8:9 all, 8:10 all, 8:11 all, 8:12 all, 8:13 all, 8:14a–e, 8:17a–g, 9:1 all, 9:2 all, 9:5 all, 9:11 all, 9:12c–i, m–o, 9:13 l, m, 9:14 all, 9:15 all, 9:16a–f, 9:17 all, 9:18 all, 9:19 all, 9:22a–k, 9:23 all, 9:24 all, 9:25 all, 9:26i–m, 9:27 all, 9:28 all, 9:29 all, 9:30 all, 9:31 all, 9:32 all, 10:3o, p

8. *Substitutions of More than One Syntactic Unit:*

AT:1:16s–v for MT:1:17	AT:6:22f–r	for MT:6:13p–v
AT:4:3a, b for MT:4:4a, b	AT:6:23i, j	for MT:7:1
AT:4:9a, b, c for MT:4:13	AT:(8)7:15	for MT:8:1

cont...

AT:5:4f	for MT:5:1g, h	AT:(8)7:16	for MT:8:3
AT:D	for MT:5:2a–d	AT(8)7:34–38	for MT:8:11,12
AT:6:3, 6:4	for MT:6:2		

The large number of differences identified between the AT and MT make it impossible to discuss even each type of difference in any detail. Furthermore, it is difficult to decide if the types of differences found are best explained as reflecting a different *Vorlage* or the technique of the translator or the work of a later redactor. Most likely, all three factors have introduced these many differences into the Greek text. Examination of these differences have led in most cases to inconclusive results.

Some of the types of differences are more likely to reflect a different *Vorlage* than other types. For instance, pluses and minuses involving compound or redundant phrases and readings that include unexpected lexical choices more strongly suggest a different *Vorlage* than do differences involving the addition of introductory formulas, pleonastic participles, variations in clause structure due to differences in the languages and the elimination of Semitic idioms. Differences between the AT and MT that are also observed in other books of the Hebrew Bible must be evaluated in that larger context. Any one of the many features of the AT listed above invites substantial further study.

If one's goal is to reconstruct the *Vorlage* of the AT in detail, then each difference must be examined and decided individually. As worthy as that goal may be, it is beyond the scope of this work. This study aspires to a more modest goal: (1) to characterize the AT as a whole, providing a context in which individual readings can be judged; and (2) to use information produced by this study to further the discussion of the relationship of the AT to the MT.

The discussion that follows highlights selected features that are distinctive of the AT and that suggest something about its relationship to the MT.

THE EXTENT AND LOCATION OF THE DIFFERENCES

It is informative to see where in the AT the differences with the MT are located. The distribution of syntactic units in the AT that disagree with the corresponding units of the MT is displayed in Graph 4:

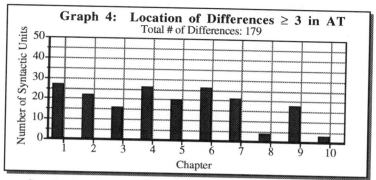

Graph 4. **This graph shows where the differences between text common to the AT and MT are located. Note that the fewest number of differences are in chapters 8 and 10.**

The distribution of the differences between the AT and MT where there is corresponding text demonstrates a surprising and interesting fact: chapters 8 and 10 contain the fewest differences between the AT and the MT. This is surprising because in fact the AT is most different from the MT in chapters 8–10. Although these two statements sound contradictory, further consideration of the data resolves the contradiction. As shown below in Graph 5b, the reason the AT is so different overall from the MT in chapters 8–10 is that the AT "omits" so much of the text found in those chapters in the MT. The reason Graph 4 shows the fewest differences in chapters 8 and 10 is that where the AT and MT do have text in common in chapters 8 and 10, there is a fairly high percentage of agreement:

The Extent of Agreement Between the AT and MT in Chapters 7–10
(considering only units of text in common)

Chapter	No. of Units in Common	Semantic Agreement	Formal Agreement
7	46	78%	52%
8	19	74%	53%
9	51	71%	51%
10	14	64%	43%

Although they are few in number, these units should not be summarily dismissed because they may be traces of the original ending of the AT. Any theory that attempts to explain the relationship of the MT to the *Vorlage* of the AT must therefore account for *both* the large amount of canonical material not found in chapters 8–10 *and* the high percentage of agreement with the MT where there is text in common. The implications of this evidence for the relationship of the endings of the versions is discussed below in this chapter under the sub–heading *LITERARY DIFFERENCES BETWEEN THE AT AND MT* and, in relation to the works of Clines and Fox, in chapter 5.

THE EXTENT AND LOCATION OF THE PLUSES AND MINUSES

The extent and location of the many pluses and minuses is shown in Graph 5a, where the minuses clearly outnumber the pluses. Most of the minuses are in chapters 2, 8 and 9, but every chapter exhibits a significant number.

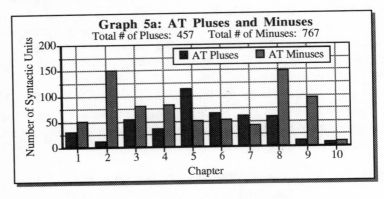

Graph 5a. Much of the material in the canonical Hebrew text is not found in the AT. The AT is shorter than the MT, even though it includes much material not found in the Hebrew.

It is interesting to consider what percentage of the Hebrew text these minuses represent. Graph 5b shows that more than half of the Hebrew text is missing from the AT in five of the ten chapters! Chapters 8 and

9 have the least material in common with the MT; chapters 5 and 6, have the most.

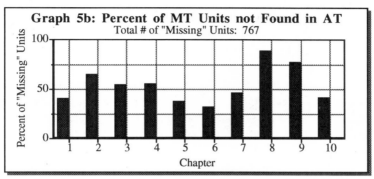

Graph 5b. **Most of the material in chapters 8 and 9 of the Hebrew text is not found in the AT.**

Percent of Hebrew Material Not in AT									
chap.	1	2	3	4	5	6	7	8	9	10
%	41	65	55	56	38	33	47	89	78	42

These graphs show that most minuses are in chapters 2, 8 and 9. It is widely recognized that both Greek versions of Esther deviate the most from the MT in chapters 8–10. Clines (1984) and Fox (1991) argue that the difference between the AT and MT in these chapters indicates that the Hebrew *Vorlage* of the AT ended somewhere in chapter 8 and that chapters 9 and 10 in the MT developed after the AT was produced. An evaluation of their arguments in light of this study is included in chapter 5.

Most of the difference between the AT and the MT (even excluding the six major additions) is due to the more than 450 pluses and more than 750 minuses that range in size from one syntactic unit to two or three sentences. As the above catalog shows, there are many pluses, minuses and substitutions that involve more than one syntactic unit. If we wish to postulate a *Vorlage* of the AT that is substantially different from the MT, we must decide which of these units of text were in fact present in the Hebrew *Vorlage* of the AT. We must explain how what appear as pluses in the AT dropped out of the Hebrew text after the AT was produced. It must be further shown that what appear as minuses in the AT were additions made in the Hebrew text after the translation was made.

Some of the pluses and minuses were clearly the work of the redactor(s) made at the time the six large additions were introduced. Generally, however, it is very difficult (impossible?) to determine if any individual unit was added or omitted from the Greek or if it reflects a variant *Vorlage*. This is, of course, the major question relevant to all Greek versions of the Hebrew Bible and it is answered differently by different scholars looking at the same evidence.

Paton has made an interesting observation about the many small pluses and minuses in the Greek versions of Esther. He notes that the short "additions" probably do not reflect the original Hebrew *Vorlage* because few of them are found in "more than one of the recensions" (Paton 1908, 46). His logic is valid only on the assumption that all Greek texts of Esther must have originated from the same Hebrew *Vorlage*, which is of course the point in question. On the other hand, Paton notes a different situation with regard to the "omissions," which he observes "are found in all the recensions with a uniformity that is not true of the additions" (ibid., 47). In his opinion the many small pluses are glosses that entered the Greek versions independently after the insertion of the six major additions, but the many small minuses may or may not indicate a shorter Hebrew *Vorlage* from which the AT was made. He leaves the question open.

Lacking Hebrew manuscripts that attest the pluses and minuses, there seems to be no criterion or method that can decisively indicate whether the pluses and minuses originated in the Hebrew *Vorlage* or in the Greek translation. Because the Qumran materials have now provided manuscript evidence that some of the pluses and minuses in the books of Samuel and Jeremiah did originate in a Hebrew text different from the MT, there is good reason to believe that other readings attested only in the Greek manuscripts also reflect a different Hebrew *Vorlage*. On the other hand, it is too easy to rush in that direction when development of the Greek text during or after translation may be an equally probable explanation. The origin of the many pluses and minuses in the AT is a problem that promises to resist certain resolution unless new manuscripts are discovered.

The question of the origin of the minuses and pluses in the AT of Esther is particularly acute compared to the Greek versions of other OT books, because about *half* the text of the MT has no corresponding text in the AT. No other Greek text of a book of the Hebrew Bible omits as much as does the AT. In spite of the many syntactic units found in the AT that are not in the MT, the AT (even with the six major additions A–F) is still significantly shorter, by about 20%, than the MT. If the material missing from the AT was originally present in the Hebrew *Vorlage* from which it was translated, it seems difficult to imagine the motivation for a translator to deliberately omit almost half the *Vorlage* before him.

But the alternative is equally difficult. If the AT accurately reflects a Hebrew *Vorlage* much shorter than the extant MT, a whole new Pandora's box of difficult questions is opened. For instance, if the material was not in the Hebrew text at the time the AT was translated, was the material subsequently added to the Hebrew text that has reached us in the extant MT, or were there two Hebrew versions of Esther simultaneously in circulation, one which included the material found in the MT and another, shorter by half, that did not? Given the relatively late date assigned to the original Hebrew text of Esther, and the relatively short lapse of time between the autograph of the Hebrew and the production of the Greek translation, does either (1) the existence of more than one Hebrew version, or (2) a literary development that doubles the size of the book, make sense in this particular case? Such intriguing questions will continue to attract study until either new manuscripts are found or until the AT can be associated with other books whose origin and history are better understood.

DIFFERENCES ALSO FOUND IN GREEK VERSIONS OF OTHER BOOKS OF THE HEBREW BIBLE

An examination of the types of differences identified shows that many of them are not unique to the AT of Esther. Many of the differences found between the AT and the MT of Esther are typical of the differences found between the MT and the Greek version(s) of other books of the Hebrew Bible. Many of the types of differences between the AT and MT are also found between the LXX of Esther and the MT.

For instance, the inclusion or omission of the explicit subject of a verb occurs twenty–three times in the AT but is not unique to it. To cite but one example, the Greek text of 1 Sam 15 adds an explicit subject several times where none appears in the MT (15:27, 29, 30, 31). The situation is similar for the presence or absence of objects, which accounts for another twenty–three differences between the AT and MT. The implied indirect object of the Hebrew verb is made explicit in the Greek in 1 Sam 15:28, Dan 8:19 and LXX Esth 8:8. Likewise, the Hebrew adjective כָּל ("all") is missing from the AT in five readings (1:16 l, 3:1k, [9]7:42a, [9]7:47f, and [9]7:47h). This adjective also does not appear where expected in 1 Sam 15:6, OG Dan 8:5 and LXX Esth 8:5.

The many differences between the AT and MT that are also found in other books of the Greek versions are best evaluated in the larger context of work done on those books by other scholars. Such differences between the Greek and Hebrew in more than one book may suggest a common point in the textual history of the Greek versions which share those traits. The comparison of the character of the AT to other Greek texts of the Hebrew Bible is limited in this study to a brief comparison of the AT with the OG of Daniel, as discussed in the excursus at the end of this work. An initial comparison of the AT to the OG Daniel shows sufficient affinity to warrant further investigation of the similarities between them. Much more work remains to be done to determine if the character of the AT has affinity with Greek versions of other books of the Hebrew Bible.

MECHANICAL ERRORS THAT INDICATE THE NATURE OF THE HEBREW VORLAGE

The AT of Esther includes a number of deviations from the corresponding MT that most probably arose from mechanical errors during translation or textual transmission. The AT, like other ancient texts, has suffered the vicissitudes of scribal copying. The types of mechanical errors attested by the AT apparently were made (1) by a scribe while copying the Hebrew text, and consequently the errors were already in the *Vorlage* from which the Greek translator read; or (2) by the translator, who, for instance, mentally transposed two Hebrew characters or mistook one Hebrew letter for another, etc., so that no Hebrew text ever actually existed that corresponds to the errant Greek reading; or (3) by a scribe while copying the Greek text subsequent to its original translation.

There are several distinctive readings in the AT that are best explained as the result of such mechanical errors and that provide information about the *Vorlage* of the AT. In the absence of Hebrew manuscripts attesting the AT's distinctive readings, it is difficult (impossible?) to determine whether such errors were made only in the mind of the translator or were already present in his *Vorlage*. Tov writes about the interchange of consonants between the MT and LXX, "There are hardly any criteria for distinguishing between retroverted variants that existed in writing and those that existed only in the translator's mind" (Tov 1992, 257).

Although one wishes that such criteria could be discovered, the problem is not crippling to this study, because it is not our purpose to reconstruct the *Vorlage* of the AT. Several differences involving small pluses and minuses and unexpected lexical choices can be explained as a misreading of the MT. Whether the translator found these readings in his *Vorlage* or created them by his own misreading of the Hebrew, they all reflect misreadings *of the MT*. This indicates that if the translator introduced the readings, his *Vorlage* was at those places virtually identical to the extant MT. If he found them in his *Vorlage*, it must have descended from a text virtually identical to the MT at those places.

The following are examples of differences between the AT and MT that may be explained, with varying degrees of certainty, as various types of mechanical error. Because these errors can be explained with reference to the MT reading, they indicate that at these particular places the *Vorlage* of the AT was virtually identical to the extant MT.

Haplography

The difference in AT:1:1d could have resulted from haplography during transmission of the Hebrew text or at the time the translation was made:

	LXX	*MT*	*AT*
1:1d	’Αρταξέρξου —	אֲחַשְׁוֵרוֹשׁ	Ασσυήρου
e	οὗτος ὁ ’Αρταξέρξης	הוּא אֲחַשְׁוֵרוֹשׁ	
f		הַמֶּלֶךְ	τοῦ βασιλέως

The MT and the LXX present two occurrences of the king's name, but the AT omits the second occurrence. The eye of either a Hebrew scribe or the translator likely skipped from the first occurrence of the king's name in the Hebrew text to the second, inadvertently omitting unit e. Alternatively, two occurrences of the name in such a short span of text may have seemed just too redundant for the translator. In either case, the AT reading can be explained if the MT reading was its *Vorlage*. Because line e is absent from the AT but present in the LXX, it may have been added to the Hebrew after the AT was produced, but before the LXX was. If so, the AT represents a *Vorlage* that is different from the MT, but genetically related to it.

If homoioteleuton in the Greek explains the minus found at 1:6p, the error suggests that the MT reading stood in the *Vorlage* of the AT:

	LXX	*MT*	*AT*
1:6o	κλῖναι χρυσαῖ	מִטּוֹת זָהָב	κλῖναι χρυσαῖ
p	καὶ ἀργυραῖ	וָכֶסֶף	
q	ἐπὶ λιθοστρώτου	עַל רִצְפַת	ἐπὶ λιθόστρωτον

Unit p may have dropped out of the AT during transmission of the Greek text because the words χρυσαῖ and ἀργυραῖ have identical endings as well as two other letters in common. The scribe wrote χρυσαῖ and then continued with ἐπὶ λιθόστρωτον, inadvertently omitting unit p, which had originally stood in the AT.

Two close occurrences of הַמֶּלֶךְ in the MT (or τοῦ βασιλέως in the Greek) resulted in AT: 3:3g being dropped out either by the translator or by a subsequent scribe:

	LXX	*MT*	*AT*	
3:3 a	καὶ ἐλάλησαν	וַיֹּאמְרוּ	καὶ εἶπον	e
b		עַבְדֵי הַמֶּלֶךְ	οἱ παῖδες τοῦ βασιλέως	f
c	οἱ ἐν τῇ αὐλῇ	אֲשֶׁר בְּשַׁעַר		g

τοῦ βασιλέως	הַמֶּלֶךְ	
d τῷ Μαρδοχαίῳ	לְמָרְדֳּכָי	πρὸς τὸν Μαρδοχαῖον h

The translator may have introduced the difference between the AT and MT by skipping the words between two close occurrences of הַמֶּלֶךְ in the Hebrew text. A scribe subsequently copying the Greek may have introduced the difference by skipping the words between the resulting two close occurrences of τοῦ βασιλέως.

AT unit 3:8d is missing from both the AT and the LXX:

	LXX	*MT*	*AT*	
3:8f	Ὑπάρχει ἔθνος	יֶשְׁנוֹ עַם־אֶחָד	Ἔστι λαὸς	b
g	διεσπαρμένον	מְפֻזָּר	διεσπαρμένος	c
h		וּמְפֹרָד		d
i	ἐν τοῖς ἔθνεσιν	בֵּין הָעַמִּים		e
j	ἐν πάσῃ	בְּכֹל	ἐν πάσαις	f
	τῇ βασιλείᾳ σου	מְדִינוֹת מַלְכוּתֶךָ	ταῖς βασιλείαις	

The similar Hebrew forms מְפֻזָּר ("scattered") and מְפֹרָד ("dispersed") following one after the other could have been easily confused, suggesting that haplography in the Hebrew may explain the omission in the AT. However, both the LXX and AT omit this unit. Since it is unlikely (or is it?) that the same mistake would have been made at the same place by two different translators or scribes, this evidence suggests that וּמְפֹרָד was not present in the *Vorlage* of either the AT or the LXX. If the omission of the unit in the Greek versions is the result of haplography in the *Vorlage*, וּמְפֹרָד dropped out of the Hebrew before either translation was made, or was added to the Hebrew after both translations were made. Alternatively, the unit may indeed have been present in the Hebrew from which both the LXX and AT were made, but both translators thought the compound expression מְפֻזָּר וּמְפֹרָד redundant and chose to translate it with only one word. It is unlikely that the AT and LXX have corrected one another here, because none of the units in the rest of the verse agree between them.

Even fairly large minuses in the AT may be explained by haplography. AT units 4:2g–j form a large clause that may have dropped out during transmission of the Greek if the MT was the *Vorlage* of the original AT reading:

	LXX	*MT*		*AT*	
4:1 n	καὶ κατεπάσατο σποδὸν	וָאֵפֶר	4:2	καὶ σποδωθεὶς	f
o	καὶ ἐκπηδήσας	וַיֵּצֵא		[ἐξῆλθεν]	g
p	διὰ τῆς πλατείας	בְּתוֹךְ			h
q	τῆς πόλεως	הָעִיר			i
r	ἐβόα	וַיִּזְעַק			j
	φωνῇ μεγάλῃ	זְעָקָה גְדֹלָה וּמָרָה׃			
s	Αἴρεται ἔθνος				k
t	μηδὲν ἠδικηκός.				l
4:2 a	καὶ ἦλθεν	וַיָּבוֹא		ἐξῆλθεν	m

The omission in the AT of units g–l can be explained if the Hebrew verbs in MT:4:1o (וַיֵּצֵא) and MT:4:2a (וַיָּבוֹא) were both once translated in the AT as ἐξῆλθεν. This seems probable since HR shows that ἐξέρχομαι was most often used to translate יָצָא. Elsewhere in Esther ἐξέρχομαι translates יָצָא (LXX:8:14,15; AT:8:15). (The LXX reading of ἐκπηδάω for יָצָא in this example is interesting because it is unique in the Greek OT, but that is a separate issue.) The omission in the AT could have occurred when the eye of a scribe copying the Greek skipped from the first to the second occurrence of ἐξῆλθεν. If so, this suggests that the MT reading was the *Vorlage* of the original AT reading.

One small plus, AT:5:18o, is possibly due to haplography in the Hebrew where a word dropped out after the AT translation was made:

	LXX	*MT*		*AT*	
5:8 i	ἣν ποιήσω	אֲשֶׁר אֶעֱשֶׂה	5:18	ἣν ποιήσω	n
	αὐτοῖς·	לָהֶם		αὐτοῖς	
j				καὶ τῇ αὔριον·	o
k	καὶ αὔριον	וּמָחָר		καὶ αὔριον γὰρ	p

The two occurrences of αὔριον in the AT, units o and p, suggest that מָחָר dropped out of the Hebrew on line j after the AT translation was made but before the LXX was produced. The retroverted Hebrew would have read in translation, "come to the banquet which I shall prepare for them tomorrow, and tomorrow I will do as the king says." K. H. Wynn also reconstructs the *Vorlage* of the AT here in this way (Wynn 1990, 285).

Confusion of Hebrew Consonants

In addition to various forms of haplography, another type of difference between the AT and MT can be explained as a misreading of the MT which resulted in what appear as unexpected lexical choices in the Greek. These differences can be explained if a transposition of consonants in the MT reading occurred. In his recent work on the frequency of occurrence of consonantal interchanges, Tov lists none for the book of Esther, but he was examining the LXX version and not the AT (Tov 1992, 262). Tov has found the *daleth/resh* and the *yod/waw* interchanges to be the most frequently occurring in the texts of the Hebrew Bible (ibid., 265). This study finds that the confusion of consonants has possibly generated three variant readings in the Greek of Esther.

By interchanging a *daleth* for a *resh*, the translator or scribe mistook וַיְּרָא the imperfect, 3ms form of יִרְאָ for a form of the verb יָרַע:

LXX	MT	AT	
3:5a καὶ ἐπιγνοὺς Αμαν	וַיְּרָא הָמָן	ὡς δὲ ἤκουσεν Αμαν	a

Because ἐπιγινώσκω is frequently used as the translation equivalent of יָרַע, the LXX reading clearly resulted from mistaking the *resh* for a *daleth* and the *aleph* for an *ayin*, reading a form of יָרַע instead of the imperfect 3ms form וַיְּרָא. The confusion of these letters, because of morphological and/or phonetic similarity, is known to have been a common source of mechanical error in the Hebrew scripts of the Second Temple period (see Cross 1961, 137, especially scripts 1 and 2 which date from the Persian and early Hellenistic periods). The AT reading, ἤκουσεν, possibly came from the same confusion, because the Greek infinitive of ἀκούω is found in the place of the qal infinitive construct of יָרַע in Isa 32:4. Alternatively, perhaps the AT translator correctly read the Hebrew verb יִרְאָ but used ἀκούω as the substitution of one verb of sense ("hearing") for another ("seeing"). In either case, the AT reading can be explained with reference to the MT reading.

The confusion of Hebrew characters probably resulted in the reading of AT:4:7a:

LXX	MT	AT	
4:10c Πορεύθητι	וַתְּצַוֵּהוּ	4:7 καὶ ἀπέστειλεν	a
d πρὸς Μαρδοχαῖον	אֶל־מָרְדֳּכָי	αὐτῷ	b

In MT unit 4:10c, the Hebrew piel imperfect, 3fs, of צָוָה with a 3ms pronominal suffix, תְּצַוֵּהוּ ("she [Esther] ordered him") is rendered in both Greek versions by verbs of movement, an imperative of πορεύομαι in the LXX and an aorist indicative of ἀποστέλλω in the AT. Since both Greek versions use verbs of movement, it is likely that the *Vorlage* of both was different from the MT in this place. The transposition of consonants in the Hebrew verb form would result in a form of יָצָא, a verb of motion, explaining the Greek readings. The transposition of the *tzade* and the *waw* in תְּצַוֵּהוּ ("she ordered him") would result in the first three consonants of תּוֹצִיא ("she caused to go"), which is the hiphil imperfect, 3fs of יָצָא. The explanation of the confusion of the ־הוּ for a ־יא is not as clear but may have resulted because all four consonants are quiescent. Furthermore, the written forms of *aleph* and *he* were graphically similar, as were *waw* and *yod* (Cross 1961, 137, especially script 1 from the Persian period). Although the multiple confusion this explanation requires may seem improbable, another factor weighs in its favor. This corruption also explains why the Greek readings both lack the direct object found in the MT reading. The 3ms pronominal suffix וּ, which expresses the direct object of תְּצַוֵּהוּ, was confused with the yod construed as part of the verbal stem of תּוֹצִיא. Since it is unlikely that two different translators made exactly the same mistake at exactly the same place (or is it?), there probably was a Hebrew manuscript that contained the hiphil imperfect of יָצָא. The decision of which Hebrew reading was original will be left to the text critic of the Hebrew Bible.

AT:6:6j reads as follows:

LXX	*MT*	*A T*	
6:4h Τίς ἐν τῇ αὐλῇ;	6:4b מִי בֶחָצֵר	6:6j Τίς ἐστιν ἔξω;	j

The AT reading probably resulted when the MT reading בֶחָצֵר ("in the courtyard") was mistakenly read as בַחוּץ ("outside"), which is translated at least ten times elsewhere in the Greek OT with the expected adverb ἔξω.

Substituting Passive for Active Voice

One of the distinctive types of differences between the AT and MT, which at first seems to involve a misreading of the Hebrew, should be mentioned here. There are two, or possibly three, readings which are passive voice in the AT but active in the MT (6:2a, 6:11g and possibly 1:12i) and one AT reading that is active voice where the MT is passive (3:13b). Although one's first thought might be that such errors could arise from incorrectly pointing the Hebrew, none of these readings can be explained solely as a misreading of the Hebrew stem. The reading in AT:6:11g is the one most likely to have resulted from such a misreading of the Hebrew:

LXX	*MT*	*A T*	
6:8 a ἐνεγκάτωσαν οἱ παῖδες	יָבִיאוּ	6:11 ληφθήτω	g
b τοῦ βασιλέως			
c στολὴν βυσσίνην	לְבוּשׁ	στολὴ	i
d	מַלְכוּת	βασιλικὴ	j

If the 3s aorist passive verb ληφθήτω in the AT reading resulted from a misreading of the Hebrew stem, the translator must have read the 3ms hophal imperfect יוּבָא ("let it be brought") instead of the 3mp hiphil imperfect (jussive) יָבִיאוּ ("let them bring"). This misreading would require an interchange of *beth* and *yod*, which is not generally attested elsewhere, a further confusion of the *yod* and *waw* and finally the omission of the final *waw*.

Explaining the other two readings in the AT that deviate in voice from the MT as a misreading of the Hebrew would require even more compounding of errors. The more complicated an explanation, the less likely it is to be correct. Therefore, these readings of passive voice in the AT likely require an entirely different kind of explanation and may contribute no evidence for a Hebrew *Vorlage* different from the MT.

Moreover, this peculiar trait is also found in the OG Daniel (e.g., 6:17, 8:10) and is not distinctive to the AT (see the excursus at the end of this work). The fact that OG Daniel has this same characteristic suggests that the answer may not be in the *Vorlage* of the AT but requires a broader explanation.

All of these readings are found only in the AT and not in LXX Esther. The AT and LXX do not agree in any of these readings involving errors that could arise only from a misreading of Hebrew. Therefore, the AT did not copy its reading from the LXX in these places. These readings indicate that the Greek of the AT, at least in these places, is the result of following a Hebrew *Vorlage*.

Moreover it is noteworthy that all of the errors in the AT identified by this study that arose from a misreading of the Hebrew can be explained in reference to the readings *of the MT*. These AT readings involve pluses, minuses and unexpected lexical choices, differences that at first glance may suggest a variant *Vorlage*. However, if these differences resulted from a misreading of the Hebrew, they actually show that the Hebrew *Vorlage* of the AT was in those places virtually the same as the extant MT. What appears at first glance as evidence that the AT was not translating the MT turns out to confirm that it was!

OTHER DISTINCTIVE FEATURES OF THE AT IN RELATION TO THE MT

The way the AT handles Persian loan–words, proper names, numerals, synecdoche and metonymy, and changes verbal person from 3rd to 2nd are further differences between the AT and MT that characterize the AT. Though these differences present no direct evidence of the relationship of the AT to its *Vorlage* the following discussion of these features is included because they do contribute to the distinctive character of the AT. Moreover, they provide a larger context in which to evaluate individual readings that have been offered as evidence for a *Vorlage* of the AT that differs from the MT.

Persian Loan-words

Paton has identified ten Persian loan–words, excluding personal names, in the Hebrew text of Esther (Paton 1908, 65).[1] The following table shows how each occurrence is handled in the Greek versions:

The Translation of Persian Loan–Words in the Greek Esther

1. Hebrew: **אֲחַשְׁדַּרְפְּנִים** Persian: *khshatrapavan*   English: satraps

MT	LXX	AT
3:12g	στρατηγοῖς	omits verse
8:9k	οἰκονόμοις	omits verse
9:3c	τύραννοι	τύραννοι

2. Hebrew: **אֲחַשְׁתְּרָנִים**   Persian: *khshatra*   English: royal horses

MT	LXX	AT
8:10h	omits unit	omits verse
8:14b	omits unit	omits verse

3. Hebrew: **בִּיתָן**   Persian: *apadana*[2]   English: palace or gazebo

MT	LXX	AT
1:5q	οἴκου	omits word
7:7f	omits word	omits unit
7:8b	omits word	omits unit

4. Hebrew: **גְּנָזִים**   Persian: *kanja*   English: treasury

MT	LXX	AT
3:9f	γαζοφυλάκιον	γαζοφυλάκιον (displaced)
4:7g	γάζαν	omits verse

---

[1] For a discussion of the Persian origin of proper names in the book of Esther see Paton (1908, 66–71), Gehman (1924, 321–8), Duchesne–Guillemin (1953, 105–8) and Gordis (1976, 43–58).

[2] The etymology of this word is debated. Paton thinks the Persian word *apadana* is a doubtful equivalent of **בִּיתָן**. For a fuller discussion of the origin of this word see Oppenheim (1965, 328–333).

5. Hebrew: דָּת

	Persian: *data*	English: law
MT	*LXX*	*AT*
1:8b	νόμον	νόμον
1:19h	νόμους	omits unit

6. Hebrew: כַּרְפַּס

	Persian: *karpasa/karpas*	English: cotton
MT	*LXX*	*AT*
1:6a	βυσσίνοις	βύσσινα

7. Hebrew: כֶּתֶר

	Persian: uncertain	English: turban
MT	*LXX*	*AT*
1:11e	omits unit	διαδήματι
2:17p	διάδημα	διάδημα
6:8j	omits unit	omits unit

8. Hebrew: פַּרְתְּמִים

	Persian: *fratama*	English: nobles
MT	*LXX*	*AT*
1:3 1	ἐνδόξοις	omits word
6:9e	ἐνδόξων	omits unit

9. Hebrew: פִּתְגָם

	Persian: *patigama*	English: decree
MT	*LXX*	*AT*
1:20b	νόμος	φωνῆς

10. Hebrew: פַּרְשֶׁגֶן ˏ פַּתְשֶׁגֶן

	Persian: *paticayan*	English: copy
MT	*LXX*	*AT*
3:14a	ἀντίγραφα	omits verse
4:8a	ἀντίγραφον	omits verse
8:13a	ἀντίγραφα	omits verse

The ten Persian loan–words occur twenty–two times in the Hebrew text. The LXX translates sixteen of these occurrences; the AT only seven. Where the AT does not translate the Persian loan–word, more than just the word in question is omitted; either the entire verse or the entire syntactic unit in which the word occurs is missing. Therefore the data showing how the AT handles Persian loan–words is sparse.

It is notable that in five of the six places where both the LXX and the AT translate a Persian loan-word, the AT and LXX have the same reading. This may indicate a literary dependence between the two versions at these places. Or, it may indicate that both translators independently used the same Greek equivalent simply because there was no other choice.

In only one instance do the LXX and AT both translate the loan-word but with a different Greek word. In 1:20b the AT renders the loan-word פִּתְגָם with a much more general noun, φωνῆς, than the LXX reading νόμος. This would be expected if the translator were construing the sense of the Persian loan-word only from its context and not from familiarity with the word itself. The reading in 1:20b would be unlikely if the AT were following the LXX here. This one reading suggests that the AT is attempting to translate the Persian loan-word independently of the LXX. This slim evidence must be considered alongside the six other places where the AT and LXX agree in the translation of the loan-word and the fifteen places where the AT does not render the loan-word at all. The evidence of how the AT handles Persian loan-words is therefore inconclusive *vis-à-vis* the relationship of the texts.

Proper Names

It is well known that the Greek versions of Esther exhibit many differences in the rendering of proper names compared to the MT and to each other. Of the thirty-eight proper names found in MT Esther, the only names spelled the same in both Greek versions are those of Esther (Εσθηρ),[3] Mordecai (Μαρδοχαῖος), and Haman (Αμαν). There has been much discussion about the significance of the proper names in the book of Esther, including their Persian etymology and reasons for the differences in the Greek morphology. (See J. Duchesne-Guillemin, 1953; H.S. Gehman, 1924; J. Hoschander, 1923; A.R. Millard, 1977; R. Zadok, 1986; also the commentaries by L.B. Paton and C.A. Moore.)

Compared to the MT, the AT exhibits some distinctive features with respect to proper names. The omission of proper names is the second most frequently occurring category of syntactic units not found in the AT. Thirty-eight times a proper name is simply not found in the

---

[3] In ms. 93, Esther is spelled ΑΙΣΘΗΡ in the title, but εσθηρ within the text.

AT where one is found in the MT. In fourteen other places, a proper name in the MT is replaced with a noun or pronoun in the AT. It would be interesting to compare this characteristic of the AT with the Greek versions of other books of the Hebrew Bible.

The following table shows the frequency of occurrence of other proper names in each version of the book:

Frequency of Occurrence of Proper Names

	MT	*LXX*	*LXX+Add.*	*AT*	*AT+Add.*
Esther	55	41	46	23	26
Mordecai	52	46	54	35	45
Haman	49	43	52	36	44
Ahasuerus	26	18	30	5	10
Vashti	10	6	6	6	6
Susa	19	10	13	12	14
Jew(s)	50	17	21	38	45
Israel	0	0	7	1	6
Abraham	0	0	2	0	1
Egypt	0	0	1	0	1
Nebuchadnezzar	1	1	2	0	1
Babylon	1	1	2	0	1
Jerusalem	1	1	2	0	0
Judah	1	0	1	0	1
Jeconiah	1	0	1	0	1

Of the four major characters (Esther, Mordecai, Haman and Ahasuerus), Esther is most frequently mentioned by name in the MT, but in the AT, with or without the additions, she is the least frequently named of the four. Furthermore, Hadassah, her Hebrew name, is found in neither the LXX nor the AT text. Mordecai, who ranks a close second to Esther for frequency of mention by name in the MT, assumes a greater relative prominence in the AT in comparison to Esther. In the final redaction of the AT, including the six major additions, Mordecai is mentioned by name almost twice as many times as Esther. This accords with the apparent esteem given to Mordecai's memory in the Hellenistic period, presumably the period in which both Greek versions originated and developed. In 2 Macc 15:36 the thirteenth day of Adar is referred to as "Mordecai's day," indicating that for at least some Jews of that period, Mordecai over–shadowed Esther as the figure associated with that great deliverance. (On the Jewish calendar of our time, Adar 13 is called the Fast of Esther.)

It is interesting to note that in the additions to both the LXX and AT the covenant name "Israel" is found several times, the patriarch Abraham is mentioned and the exodus from Egypt is recalled. None of these is mentioned in the MT, although the reference to Nebuchadnezzar's destruction of Jerusalem, to Judah's King Jeconiah and to the Agagites implies these themes. The additions apparently make explicit what is only hinted in the MT — that the Jews of Persia were continuing the pre–exilic relationship that Israel enjoyed with God. This allowed the Jews of the Diaspora to experience a continuity with their national and religious heritage in spite of the circumstances in which they found themselves politically and culturally.

Numerals
Two occurrences of large numerals in the AT are distinctive readings:

	LXX	*MT*	*AT*
AT:7:44f	500	500	700
AT:7:46l	15,000	75,000	70,100

Since the numerals in the Greek OT most often disagree with those in the corresponding MT, these discrepancies in the AT readings must be considered in light of this larger issue.

Synecdoche and Metonymy

In five places, and possibly six, the AT eliminates Semitic synecdoche or metonymy found in the MT.[4] Since the LXX also eliminates the same occurrence of synecdoche or metonymy, even where it otherwise follows the MT closely, these particular Semitic idioms apparently would have been unnatural in Greek and were deliberately changed by the translator:

	LXX	*MT*	*AT*
1:10d	——	לֵב־הַמֶּלֶךְ	τὸν βασιλέα
		the heart of the king	the king
2:9a	καὶ ἤρεσεν αὐτῷ	וַתִּיטַב ... בְּעֵינָיו	καὶ ἤρεσεν αὐτῷ
	pleased him	was good in his eyes	pleased him
3:11f	ὡς βούλει	כַּטּוֹב בְּעֵינֶיךָ	ὡς ἄν σοι ἀρεστὸν ᾖ
	as he wishes	as good in your eyes	as is pleasing to you
5:8b	ἐνώπιον τοῦ βασιλέως	בְּעֵינֵי הַמֶּלֶךְ	ἐναντίον σου, βασιλεῦ
	before the king	in the eyes of the king	before you, O King
6:9c	ἑνὶ	עַל־יַד־אִישׁ	καὶ εἰς τῶν ἐνδόξων
	to one	into the hand of a man	one of the nobles

and possibly,

7:9d	πρὸς τὸν βασιλέα	לִפְנֵי הַמֶּלֶךְ	αὐτοῦ
	to the king	to the face of the king	him

A notable reading deserving further discussion is found in 1:21a–c:

---

[4] Synecdoche is a figure of speech where a part is used for the whole or vice versa (e.g., "it seemed good in the eyes of the king" for "it seemed good to the king"). Metonymy is a figure of speech where the name of one object or concept is used in place of another with which it is closely associated (e.g., "scepter" for "sovereignty").

LXX	MT	AT
1:21a καὶ ἤρεσεν	וַיִּיטַב	καὶ ἀγαθὸς
b ὁ λόγος	הַדָּבָר	ὁ λόγος
c τῷ βασιλεῖ	בְּעֵינֵי הַמֶּלֶךְ	ἐν καρδίᾳ τοῦ βασιλέως

Here the LXX eliminates the Semitic synecdoche, but the AT replaces the original synecdoche, "in the eyes of the king" (בְּעֵינֵי) with another, "in the heart of the king" (ἐν καρδίᾳ). This reading is especially interesting because C. A. Moore cites it as evidence for an AT *Vorlage* different from the MT, presumably by retroverting the Greek ἐν καρδίᾳ to the Hebrew בְּלֵב (Moore 1967, 353). The Hebrew expression וַיִּיטַב הַדָּבָר בְּעֵינֵי הַמֶּלֶךְ found at 1:21 in the MT of Esther also occurs four other times in the Hebrew Bible (Gen 41:37, Josh 22:33, 1 Kgs 3:10 and Esth 2:4). The very similar expression יִיטַב בְּעֵינֵי occurs eight times (Gen 45:16, Lev 10:20, Deut 1:23, Josh 22:30, 1 Sam 18:5, 24:5, 2 Sam 3:36, 18:4). *Not once* is this idiom translated into Greek with the expression found in the AT using καρδίᾳ. This may indicate that the *Vorlage* of the AT may indeed have had a different Hebrew phrase at this place, as Moore suggests.

On the other hand, it must also be noted that the retroverted Hebrew phrase demanded by this Greek expression,

וַיִּיטַב בְּלֵב or וַיִּיטַב הַדָּבָר בְּלֵב,

does not occur *even once* in the entire Hebrew corpus. This makes Moore's retroversion highly improbable. If a different Hebrew *Vorlage* stands behind the Greek reading, it involves more than a simple substitution of לֵב for עֵינֵי. Given the inclination of the AT to eliminate Semitic synecdoche and metonymy elsewhere, and given that the retroversion demanded by the Greek does not occur elsewhere in the Hebrew Bible, the AT reading most probably reflects a translation decision and not a variant Hebrew *Vorlage*, contra Moore.

This is a good example of a Greek reading that when viewed in isolation seems almost certainly to reflect a *Vorlage* different from the MT. However, when that reading is considered in the light of the character of the Greek text as a whole, the probability of its being a translation decision, consistent with the technique used in the rest of the text, becomes the more likely explanation.

Change in Verbal Person

The reading in AT:5:18g illustrates another interesting difference between the MT and AT that is characteristic of the AT. A change from third person in the Hebrew to second person in the Greek, often in the vocative case, occurs five times in the AT (3:8k, 4:3n, 4:4d, 4:7d, 5:14e). For example:

	LXX	*MT*	*AT*	
3:8n	τῶν δὲ νόμων	וְאֶת־דָּתֵי	τοῖς δὲ νομίμοις	j
o	τοῦ βασιλέως	הַמֶּלֶךְ	σοῦ, βασιλεῦ	k

The MT and LXX read "the laws of the king" where the AT has "your laws, O King." Readings 3:8k, 4:7d and 5:14e each occur within a discourse, and make a 3rd person circumlocution into a more direct statement. Unit 4:4d effectively changes 3rd person narrative into discourse, which disrupts the text even more than the change in person. The reading at 4:3n is almost certainly due to an inner–Greek problem, where the resulting 2nd person plural form περιέλεσθε is a misreading or alternate spelling of the expected infinitive form περιέλεσθαι. The LXX text of Esther also renders 3rd person in the Hebrew with 2nd in the Greek, but not in the same places. For instance the LXX Esth 6:5g renders the qal jussive 3ms, יָבוֹא, as the 2nd plural imperative καλέσατε. These types of differences are related to a change in sub-genre, from narrative to discourse, and should be studied further by comparing these readings to those found in discourse in the Greek texts of other books of the Hebrew Bible.

BOUGAIOS: A CLUE TO THE TEXTUAL HISTORY OF THE AT?

In AT:(9)7:44s the patronymic name βουγαίου is given to Haman in both the AT and LXX versions. This small addition harmonizes with Haman's introduction in 3:1, where the Hebrew הָאֲגָגִי ("the Agagite") is replaced in both the AT and LXX by βουγαῖον.

Clines suggests that a variant reading of the name, γωγαιον, found only in manuscript 93, connects the name with Gog of Ezek. 38–39 and implies an interpretative rendering of the Hebrew הָאֲגָגִי (Clines 1984, 197n7).

J. Lewy argues that βουγαῖος actually reflects an original reading in the source text that preceded "Agagite." He believes the term βουγαῖος is derived from the West–Iranian term *baga* ("god"), which in the Babylonian Marduk–Istar mythology denoted a "worshipper of Mithra" (Lewy 1939, 134–35). He argues that a Jewish redactor used the Babylonian myth as a source for the biblical Esther story, and changed the identity of the villain, Haman, from a "worshipper of Mithra" to an "Agagite," the perennial enemy of the Jews. His theory does not adequately explain the evidence, because the term βουγαῖος occurs in what is clearly a Greek version of the Jewish *biblical form* of the Esther story, and not a version of some earlier literary stage where Babylonian mythology was prominent (if such a stage ever existed in the origins of the book of Esther).[5]

Haman is identified as both a "Bougaion" and a "Macedonian" in both the AT and LXX texts:

	LXX	*AT*
A:17f	βουγαῖος	Μακεδόνα
3:1f	βουγαῖον	βουγαῖον
E:10d	Μακεδών	ὁ βουγαῖος
9:10c	βουγαίου	τοῦ βουγαίου

According to LS, βουγάϊος is a vocative adjective used in Homer as a term of reproach meaning "bully" (*Il.* 13.824, *Od.* 18.79). Plutarch mentions that Homer used the word to mean "loud–mouthed" (*Moralia*, The Greek Questions, 299). Certainly that characterization fits Haman's demeanor as one who would commit genocide to avenge a personal affront. "Haman, the bully" is an apt literary ascription.

LS lists βαγώας as a Persian loan–word meaning "eunuch." In AT:1:16b, the eunuch who makes a political incident out of Vashti's refusal to come to the king is referred to as βουγαῖος, as is the eunuch who guards the virgins in 2:8d. This may suggest either an etymological relationship or a phonetic word play between βαγώας and βουγαῖος. Admittedly I cannot prove the etymological relationship of these two terms. However, I suggest that βουγαῖος and βαγώας are

---

5 For a discussion of possible sources for the Esther story see Cazelles (1961, reprinted in Moore 1982, 424–36), Bardtke (1963), Dommershausen (1968), Clines (1984, 115–138).

variant spellings of the Persian word. The substitution of βουγαῖος in the Greek text for "Agagite" in the Hebrew was probably motivated by an identifiable historical person and event.

Bagoas (βαγώας) was the name of the commander in chief of the Persian forces under Artaxerxes III who led a campaign into Egypt in 343 B.C. He made his mark in history (as a bully) by looting sacred books from the Egyptian temples and then selling them back to the priests at exorbitant prices (*Encycl. Brit.*, 1963 ed., s.v. Bagoas).

Immediately after recounting the Esther story, Josephus tells of a general of the Persian army who played a role in the history of the post–exilic Jews of Jerusalem. Although Josephus gives his name as Bagoses (βαγώσης), this is almost certainly the same general. A textual variant in the manuscripts of Josephus indicates that Bagoas is a variant of Bagoses (LCL: *Ant.* 11.297, note f).

Josephus describes Bagoses (or Bagoas) as an enemy of the Jews who was involved in the intrigue surrounding the office of high priest. He intended to procure the office of high priest for his friend, Jesus, in the place of Jesus' brother, John. When John murdered Jesus, Bagoses took revenge by defiling the temple in Jerusalem, imposing a tax on the daily sacrifices and oppressing the Jews for seven years (*Ant.* xi, vii, 1). Bagoses became so politically powerful that in 338 B.C. he led a coup and assassinated Artaxerxes III and all of his sons except one.

If βουγαῖος and βαγώας are variant spellings or closely related names, Haman could anachronistically be labeled a "Bougaion" to characterize both his political ambitions and his hostility toward the Jews by alluding to the notorious assassin who killed Artaxerxes III. This would be analogous today to calling a potential assassin an "Oswald," which Americans would immediately recognize as a reference to the assassin of President John F. Kennedy.

The association of Haman with the assassin Bagoas is consistent with the *Tendenz* of the AT, which amplifies the theme of political assassination only suggested by the MT version. According to addition A, the conflict between Haman and Mordecai began, not because Mordecai refused to bow to Haman, but when Mordecai foiled an assassination plot against the Persian king. The AT, but not the MT, implies that Haman at least favored the plot, although the text does not involve him personally in it. According to the AT, it was because

Mordecai foiled this assassination attempt that Haman became an enemy of the Jews.

Moreover, addition E of the AT accuses Haman of conspiring to give the Persian empire over to the Macedonians (AT:7:27), an element entirely missing from the MT. (Chapter 4 of this work includes a discussion of the implications of this detail for the redactional relationship between additions A and E.) It is most likely that the term "Bougaion" would be used pejoratively to label Haman soon after the historical Bagoses became infamous as an assassin in 338 B.C. By referring anachronistically to Haman as a Bougaion, the AT characterizes him politically as plotting to overthrow and assassinate the Persian king. This implies a date for this redaction of the AT late in the Persian period or quite early in the Hellenistic period.

The characterization of Haman as a "Bougaion" in the Greek versions also goes far in explaining why the LXX text gives the name of the king as Artaxerxes. The translator or a subsequent redactor who read "Bougaios" as an appellation for Haman knew that it was Artaxerxes III, not Xerxes, who was assassinated by a close advisor named Bagoas, and accordingly "corrected" the name of the king. This suggests that the AT reading of the king's name, which agrees with the MT, preserves the original reading.

The AT and the LXX also refer to Haman as a Macedonian, but not at the same places. This is also a political, not ethnic, appellation. The appellation "Macedonian" was in use in the Greek language at least from the 5th century B.C. (e.g., in Herodotus) through the 1st century A.D. In the historical context of the Persian–Graeco wars, the "Macedonians" were the enemy of the Persians; after Alexander the Great the term the "Macedonian" often referred to him personally. The fact that "Bougaion" appears in addition E in the AT where the LXX reads "Macedonian" suggests that the AT reading was a more parochial reading that arose early in the Hellenistic period while the infamy of Bagoas, assassin of Artaxerxes, was still a living memory. The more general appellation "Macedonian" would have functioned pejoratively where the memory of Bagoas' assassination of the Persian king had faded or was unknown. Since the term "Macedonian" could function pejoratively in both the Persian and Hellenistic periods, it is difficult to decide which was the original reading in the Greek Esther.

The use of the term "Bougaion" as an appellation was probably limited specifically to the late Persian period if it is an allusion to the Persian general. This raises the interesting question of whether the redaction that identifies Haman as a "Bougaion" was produced during that time. If the Jews were "bullied" by Bagoses, as Josephus describes, the Greek text(s) of Esther may have been a political message intended to encourage the Jews by condemning their current enemy to the same fate as Haman, the Persian bully and enemy of a previous generation of Jews. His changing identity as an Agagite, Bougaion and Macedonian, represents a succession of political crises experienced by the Jews. The Greek Esther story addressed each political crisis as it arose, reassuring the Jews of their ultimate survival under God's covenantal protection.[6]

LITERARY DIFFERENCES BETWEEN THE AT AND MT

The literary differences are primarily represented by pluses and minuses in the text of the AT compared to the MT. The greatest and most obvious difference between the AT and MT is that the AT includes six large blocks of material, labeled additions A–F, which are not found in the Hebrew. The inclusion of these major additions motivated other changes throughout the text of the AT. (See the discussion of the secondary nature of the additions and their relationship to one another in chapter 4.)

In spite of these six large additions, the AT is nonetheless 20% shorter than the MT because it omits so much of the material found there. As shown above in Graph 5b, five of the ten chapters have only

---

[6] The political situation recorded in 3 Maccabees and its affinity with the Greek Esther is well recognized. 3 Macc 3:26–7:23 tells of Ptolemy Philopator decreeing the arrest of all Jews in Egypt, who were then assembled in the hippodrome in Alexandria to be trampled by frenzied elephants. At the last moment, God changed the heart of the king, who ordered the Jews released. They then celebrated a great feast of deliverance reminiscent of the Esther story. For a discussion of the relationship between 3 Maccabees and the Greek Esther see Motzo (1934). His argument, originally published in Italian, has been briefly summarized in English (Nickelsburg 1984).

In our times, the book of Esther was forbidden in the concentration camps of Nazi Germany because it reassured the Jews of their ultimate survival as a people.

50% or less of the material found in the Hebrew text. It has been argued that the AT is faithfully following its Hebrew *Vorlage*, and that most of the material "missing" from the AT was actually added to the Hebrew text that has come to us as the MT. I would agree that some of the minuses of the AT actually reflect material added to the Hebrew version after the AT was produced. However, this study has found that because of the nature of much of the "missing" material, it is easier to understand why it would be omitted by the translator (or subsequent redactor) of the Greek than added later in the Hebrew.

This discussion will focus on chapters 2, 8 and 9, which, as Graph 5b shows, are the chapters in the AT with the highest percentage of "missing" material. Clines identifies four discrete scenes that comprise the twentythree verses in chapter 2 of the Hebrew text (Clines 1984, 9):

1. the king's decision to seek a new wife (2:1–4)
2. Esther's entrance to the court (2:5–11)
3. Esther ascends to the throne (2:12–18)
4. Mordecai's discovery of the eunuch's plot (2:19–23)

Based on principles of literary criticism, Clines judges these four scenes to be "progressively indispensable prerequisites for the plot of the main section of the book" (ibid., 9). That is, the unrewarded service of Mordecai in verses 2:19–23 is the essential component that gives rise to his power, and consequently the deliverance of the Jews, later in the story. In Clines' opinion, Esther's accession to the throne and her admission to the court "rank as marginally less significant for the ultimate purposes of the plot" (ibid., 10). The king's decision to seek a new wife, and the circumstances that precipitate it in chapter 1, are viewed by Clines as increasingly less pivotal to the development of the plot. In his opinion, the significance of these scenes is not for plot development but to paint a picture of the power struggles and intrigue characteristic of the Persian court.

It is interesting to note how much of each of these four scenes is preserved in the AT (the corresponding data for the LXX is also given for completeness and for comparison):

Number of Units Comprising the Four Scenes of Chapter 2

# of Syntactic Units in:	MT	AT	LXX [7]
scene 1, MT:2:1–4	32	19	33
scene 2, MT:2:5–11	60	31	58
scene 3, MT:2:12–18	80	18	70
scene 4, MT:2:19–23	30	0	31

Scene 4 in the MT, which Clines judges to be most indispensable for the development of the plot, is completely missing from chapter 2 of the AT. This is because it was relocated from chapter 2 when addition A was included in the text (regardless of whether addition A was first introduced into the Hebrew text or the Greek text). The story of Mordecai's discovery of the plot against the king is found in addition A of the Greek Esther where it is also given greater prominence. In the AT it both introduces and justifies the hostility between Mordecai and Haman. A motivation for the omission (or relocation) of the scene is clear within the redaction of the Greek text.

Scene 3, Esther's accession to the throne, is detailed in the MT with the twelve–month beauty program and how she pleased the king more than any of the other virgins. The AT omits almost all of this, substituting the less sensual, "And when Esther was taken to the king, she pleased him greatly ... And when the king had examined all the maidens, Esther proved the most outstanding." As discussed above, the AT mentions Esther only half as often as it does Mordecai. It is characteristic of the AT to minimize Esther's role in the story and to highlight Mordecai's. Therefore, the omission of this material from scene 3 is consistent with the *Tendenz* of the AT as a whole.

The omission of this material by the translator or a later redactor seems more probable than its later addition to the Hebrew because, as Clines observes, this scene ranks "as marginally less significant for the ultimate purposes of the plot" (ibid., 10). Since the material missing

---

[7] In some cases the LXX text has more syntactic units than the corresponding MT because of pluses found in the LXX text. Overall the LXX is much more faithful to the MT in chapter 2 than is the AT.

from this scene in the AT adds nothing of importance to the development of the story, it could be omitted without significant consequence. It is more difficult to explain why the details of this scene would be added to the Hebrew text much later.

Scenes 1 and 2 are similarly shortened by about 50% in the AT. If Clines is correct that the literary function of the detail of these scenes is to paint a picture of the sensuality and intrigue of the Persian court (ibid., 10), it is more likely that they were originally present in the *Vorlage* and omitted much later when the Greek version was produced during the Hellenistic period. It is more difficult to explain why such details would be added to the Hebrew text a few centuries after interest in life at the Persian court had expired.

The relationship between the AT and MT in chapters 8 and 9 is much more complex. Within these chapters the AT and MT are most different, primarily because 89% and 78% of the material in MT chapters 8 and 9, respectively, is missing from the AT. The substantial differences between the AT and MT in chapters 8–9 have given rise to the reigning hypothesis defended in greatest detail by Clines (1984) and Fox (1991), that the AT attests to a Semitic *Vorlage* much shorter than the MT, which ended somewhere within chapter 8. This shorter Hebrew version was, for Clines, an ancestor of the MT translated into Greek before the Esther story reached its final extant form. For Fox, its relationship to the development of the MT is less direct. The work of each these scholars on the relationship of the AT to the MT is discussed in chapter 5.

The hypothesis that the MT and AT have no direct relationship as *Vorlage* and translation, respectively, in chapters 8–10 has been persuasively argued by both Clines on Fox on the basis of the many and significant differences between the endings of the two versions. The extent and nature of the differences would be compelling were it not for the fact that, despite the many significant differences, there is a degree of agreement between the AT and MT even in chapters 8 and 9 that is difficult to explain if they developed independently.

As shown above in Graphs 5a and b, when we speak of the differences between the AT and MT in chapters 8–10 we are speaking almost entirely of pluses and minuses. Even so, almost lost within these many pluses and minuses are points of agreement between the AT and MT that are admittedly easy to overlook. This study found similarity between the AT and MT in chapters 8–10 to be of two types: similarities in content and similarities in text.

Although the AT does not include most of the material of the MT in chapters 8–10, it nevertheless contains all of the major events and points found in the MT in those chapters, albeit often in a truncated and less eloquent form. From AT:7:13 (MT:7:9) to the end of the book the following events are found in both the AT and MT in the same order of occurrence:

1. The king orders Haman to be hanged on the gallows prepared for Mordecai.
2. The king disposes of Haman's property.
3. A request is made for Haman's decree to be revoked.
4. The king gives Mordecai permission to write in his name.
5. Mordecai sends letters to the Jews, sealed with the king's ring.
6. Mordecai goes out into the city in royal robes, Susa rejoices, the Jews celebrate.
7. The fear of Mordecai falls upon the officials of the empire.
8. Mordecai writes to the Jews to celebrate hereafter the 14th and 15th of Adar as days for rejoicing instead of for grief.
9. Gifts are sent to the poor.
10. These days are called Purim ("Phourdaia" in AT).
11. The king's wealth and might (with Mordecai as his close advisor) is described.
12. These things are written in the chronicles of the Persians and Medes.
13. Mordecai is beloved by the Jews and they benefit from his position.

The differences between the AT and MT in how each event is reported are numerous and sometimes contradictory. For instance, in the MT the king disposes of Haman's property by giving it to Esther, who in turn puts Mordecai in charge of it. In the AT the king gives Haman's property to Mordecai directly. However, this is consistent with the overall character of the AT that minimizes Esther's role and magnifies Mordecai's.

Clines analyzes such differences from a literary perspective and concludes that the MT and AT are unrelated in their endings (Clines 1984, chs. 7, 8). The numerous differences that Clines identifies in how each event is reported is indisputable; nevertheless, his analysis of the details must not obscure the overarching fact that the same events are reported in the same order of occurrence in both versions. This would be an extraordinary coincidence if the ending of each version had developed independently.

Perhaps the similarity of the sequence of events in chapters 8–10 of the AT and MT could be explained apart from a direct relationship. For instance, perhaps an oral tradition developed after the AT was first produced and was later incorporated independently into both the Hebrew and Greek versions. If the similarities were only in content such a hypothesis might be plausible.

However, the similarities between the AT and MT in chapters 8–10 extend even to the textual level. As shown above, because of the large number of pluses and minuses in these chapters the AT and MT have few units of text in common. However, when those few common units of text are examined, there is a significant extent of agreement which is difficult to explain if the endings of the AT and MT developed independently:

The Extent of Agreement Between the AT and MT in Chapters 7–10
(considering only units of text in common)

Chapter	No. of Units in Common	Semantic Agreement	Formal Agreement
7	46	78%	52%
8	19	74%	53%
9	51	71%	51%
10	14	64%	43%

An examination of the parallel texts in Appendix 1 shows that the units in the AT are in the same place and sequence with the units in the MT with which they agree. In other words, the agreement between the AT and MT in chapters 8–10 cannot be explained as two independent texts generally using the same vocabulary because they are both telling the same story.

Nor can the evidence be explained as resulting from the dependence of the AT on the LXX, or *vice-versa*, because the ending of the two Greek versions does not show a literary relationship except in addition E and a few verses immediately following it (see chapter 4).

The evidence also cannot adequately be explained by the AT being "corrected" toward the MT. If chapters 8–10 of the AT had been "corrected" toward the MT, it is most difficult to explain why only these particular units, and so few of them, were brought into agreement with the MT.

This evidence is best explained if the AT originally translated a Hebrew text very similar to the MT in chapters 8–10 but was subsequently revised almost beyond recognition, probably when addition E was added. Almost lost in the midst of the many pluses and minuses there is some common core of text (not just content) between the *Vorlage* of the AT and the MT in chapters 8–10. The hypothesis that the *Vorlage* of the AT ended somewhere in chapter 8 must be reconsidered in light of this data (see chapter 5). If chapters 9 and 10 of the Hebrew text are, as Clines argues, appendices which were added to the original Hebrew text, the AT must have been produced after those chapters were added. Agreement of this nature would not occur if the endings of the AT and MT developed independently.

When the pluses and minuses in chapters 8–10 are examined, a *Tendenz* becomes apparent. The interests of the AT translator/redactor are considerably different than those of the author/redactor of the Hebrew text. Firstly, much of the material present in chapters 8–10 of the MT but not found in the AT involves Esther. This pattern is also observed in the material missing from chapter 2 and in the drastically fewer times her name is mentioned all throughout the AT. The first two verses of chapter 8 in the MT have the king giving Haman's property to Esther, who in turn puts Mordecai in charge of it. In the AT the king gives Haman's property directly to Mordecai, with no mention of Esther. Verses MT:8:3–8 depict Esther's role in the reversal of Haman's decree that brought deliverance to the Jews. These verses are entirely omitted in the AT, where it is Mordecai who asks the king to revoke Haman's decree. MT:9:29–32 shows Esther's role in establishing Purim as a permanent tradition for the Jews. This is omitted in the AT, where Mordecai alone decrees the 14th and 15th of Adar for celebration. Clearly this a *Tendenz* that intends to emphasize Mordecai's role in Jewish history and minimizing (if not eliminating)

Esther's.[8] Because this same *Tendenz* is present in some of the major additions (as discussed in chapter 4), the omission of material involving Esther in chapters 8 and 9 was probably made when certain of the additions were included.

Although one could argue that this *Tendenz* was already present in the *Vorlage* of the AT, it is difficult to identify a reason the Esther material would have been added to the Hebrew text during the Hellenistic period. There is some evidence to suggest why it would have been removed. The prominence of Mordecai as a hero during the Hellenistic period is attested in 2 Macc 15:36 where Purim is referred to as "Mordecai's Day." The *Tendenz* of these particular omissions in the AT can therefore be historically located in the Hellenistic period, when Mordecai attained legendary stature. This is the same period in which the Greek version of the Esther story would have been originally produced. The translator (or a later redactor of the Greek text) was simply more interested in Mordecai's role than in Esther's.

The second major difference between the AT compared to the MT in the material missing from chapters 8–10 is that the AT shows much less interest in a detailed etiology of Purim. The MT devotes thirteen verses to a discussion of the origin of Purim (MT:9:20–32) where the AT limits its discussion to just three verses:

> And Mordecai wrote these matters in a book, and sent it to the Jews who were in the kingdom of Ahasuerus, to those far and near, to keep these days for hymns and rejoicing instead of pain and mourning, the fourteenth and fifteenth. And he sent portions to the poor and they received them. Because of this these days are called Phourdaia, because of the lots which fell on these days as a memorial.

In spite of its brevity, the AT includes all the major points about the origin of Purim found in the MT. The AT mentions its origin in Persia during the reign of Ahasuerus, its celebration of rejoicing on a day which might have brought mourning, the practice of sending portions, the name of the feast, and an explanation of the name. The AT does not include the explanation that the rural Jews celebrated on a

---

[8] For an interesting analysis of how Esther is portrayed in each of the three versions of the story see Day (1995).

different day than the Jews in Susa. The brevity of the account may be appropriate to explain the holiday to an audience who know that the Jews of Persia celebrate Purim but, because neither they nor their ancestors personally experienced that deliverance, have less interest in the holiday (e.g., Jews in other parts of the Diaspora, such as Egypt).

Having shown that the material missing from the ending of the AT can be explained as redactional *Tendenz*, the material added to the ending also shows a special interest. Much of the additional material found in chapters 8–10 is related to addition E and displays a distinct interest in showing that the Persian king and empire (not just the Jews) were delivered through Mordecai. Beginning with addition A and throughout the text, the theme of assassination is more prominent in the AT than in the MT. Haman is portrayed in the AT as giving approval to the assassination plot which Mordecai foils and which is the reason for the hostility between them. Addition E in the AT portrays Haman as a traitor who attempted by deceit to give the Persian kingdom to the Macedonians. In comparison, in the MT Haman is an enemy of the Jews, but not of the king. The role of Haman as a political assassin and conspirator is not found at all in the MT. In the MT the assassination plot foiled by Mordecai provides only the motivation for his later reward. (See the discussion of addition E in chapter 4.)

The material added to the ending of the AT is consistent with other additions throughout the text that highlight the political intrigue endangering not only the Jews but the king and the whole empire as well. In the AT Mordecai is cast not just as the deliverer of the Jews from destruction, but the savior of the Persian king and kingdom. The political message of the AT is clear: it is good for the king and the empire to have a Jew in high positions of political power. Addition E and the additions throughout which amplify the political intrigue likely arose within a Diaspora community that advocated Jewish cooperation and participation within a pagan empire for the good of both the Jews and the empire. This attitude would be most likely to occur in Ptolemaic Egypt while it exercised hegemony over Jerusalem.

Although an Egyptian provenance for the Greek versions is most often associated with Alexandria in the Hellenistic period, there was a prominent Jewish presence in Egypt much earlier during the Persian period at Elephantine. If the autograph of Esther dates from the late Persian period, it is plausible that the Semitic *Vorlage* of the AT entered Egypt soon after its production and that it was subsequently translated into Greek in Egypt. The same Semitic text traveled to Jerusalem with the returning exiles and was later translated into the Greek version known as LXX Esther. This scenario is presented in more detail in the conclusion of this work.

Summary

The literary differences between the AT and MT are represented primarily by the many pluses and minuses. An examination of the material missing from the AT shows that much of it reflects two interests: (1) Esther's role in the AT is minimized while Mordecai's is magnified, and (2) the AT shows less interest in the origin and celebration of Purim. An examination of the pluses show an interest in highlighting the role of the Jews, as represented by Mordecai, in the political intrigue of the pagan court, with a particular focus on the theme of royal assassination. While these three interests converge in the ending of the AT, they are found throughout the text.

CONCLUSIONS

• Many of the types of differences between the AT and MT are also found between the Greek and Hebrew versions of other books of the OT, such as 1 Samuel, Daniel and LXX Esther.
• The differences between the AT and MT that can be explained as inner–Hebrew haplography or a misreading of the Hebrew show that the AT is a translation of a Hebrew *Vorlage*, not a recension of a Greek parent text. Moreover, such differences can be explained with reference to the MT, indicating that the *Vorlage* of the AT was virtually identical to the MT at those places.
• Although chapters 8–10 are very different in the AT compared to the MT, they both record at least thirteen of the same events in the same sequence. Furthermore, there is a high degree of agreement between those few units of text that the AT and MT do have in common in chapters 8–10. This indicates that the AT originally translated a text very similar to what is now chapters 8–10 of the MT.
• Most of the differences between the AT and MT in chapters 8–10 are due to pluses and, to an even greater extent, minuses. An examination

of these reveals three special interests of the AT: (1) Esther's role is minimized while Mordecai's is magnified; (2) the origin and celebration of Purim is of less interest; (3) the AT highlights the role of the Jews in the political intrigue of the pagan court with a special focus on the theme of political assassination.

• The *Tendenz* most apparent in chapters 8–10 is found throughout the AT and is consistent with a pre–Maccabean, Ptolemaic setting.

• Both the degree of similarity between the AT and MT (discussed in chapter 2 of this work) and the nature of the differences between the AT and MT (as discussed in this chapter) indicate that the *Vorlage* originally translated by the AT was in most respects quite similar to the extant MT.

Distinctive Differences Between the AT and MT
Values ≥3 and AT ≠ LXX

Unit (AT versification)	Equivalence	Word Order (≥2)	Correspondence	Linguistic Adequacy
1:4g	x			
1:6a			x	x
1:6b	x		x	
1:7d			x	x
1:7k	x		x	
1:8j			x	
1:9h			x	
1:10d			x	
1:10f			x	
1:11d			x	x
1:11f			x	
1:11i				x
1:11j				x
1:12a				x
1:12c				x
1:12d				x
1:12l			x	
1:14e			x	x
1:17b			x	x
1:17c	x		x	x
1:18a			x	
1:18b				x
1:20a	x		x	x
1:20b				x
1:20c				x
1:21c				x
1:21h			x	
— MT ch 2				
2:1b				x
2:2b			x	
2:2k	x		x	
2:2r			x	x
2:4g			x	
2:5c			x	
2:7a			x	
2:7b			x	
2:7k				
2:8b	x			x
2:8d	x		x	x
2:8f	x		x	x
2:8g		x	x	x

Unit (AT versification)	Equivalence	Word Order (≥2)	Correspondence	Linquistic Adequacy
2:9a			x	
2:9h	x		x	x
2:9k			x	x
2:9s			x	x
2:9y	x		x	x
2:9z	x		x	
2:18f	x		x	x
2:18g	x		x	x
2:18h			x	
— MT ch 3				
3:2d				x
3:2e				
3:2g			x	
3:3k			x	
3:5a				
3:5f	x		x	
3:5l			x	
3:5n		x	x	x
3:6h			x	
3:8f			x	
3:8h			x	
3:8k	x		x	x
3:9a			x	x
3:9d	x		x	x
3:11f			x	
— MT ch 4				
4:2c				x
4:2f				x
4:2n			x	x
4:2r				x
4:3b				
4:3n	x		x	x
4:4a				x
4:4d	x			x
4:6b				x
4:6c	x			
4:7a				x
4:7b			x	x
4:7d	x		x	x
4:7g	x			x
4:7r	x		x	x
4:8d			x	
4:9c			x	x
4:9h	x		x	x

Unit	Equivalence	Word Order (≥2)	Correspondence	Linquistic Adequacy
(AT versification)				
4:11a	x			x
4:11b	x			x
4:11g	x			x
4:11j	x		x	x
4:11p				x
4:11q	x		x	
4:11s	x		x	x
4:11t	x		x	x
— MT ch 5				
5:1j			x	x
5:4c			x	
5:10c	x		x	x
5:13f	x		x	x
5:14e				x
5:14i	x			
5:18g			x	
5:18r	x		x	x
5:21a	x		x	
5:21c	x		x	x
5:21r	x		x	x
5:21s				x
5:21w			x	x
5:21z			x	x
5:21aa			x	
5:22a	x		x	x
5:23p			x	
5:23r				x
5:23v	x		x	x
5:24d			x	x
— MT ch 6				
6:2a				x
6:2e			x	
6:2g				
6:6j			x	x
6:7a	x	x		x
6:8b			x	
6:9a			x	x
6:11g	x			x
6:11l	x		x	
6:11s	x		x	x
6:11w				x
6:11aa	x		x	x
6:11hh	x		x	x
6:12h			x	
6:12k			x	

Unit (AT versification)	Equivalence	Word Order (≥2)	Correspondence	Linquistic Adequacy
6:12m	x		x	x
6:18b			x	x
6:19h			x	x
6:20a				x
6:20b	x			x
6:21c	x		x	x
6:22a				x
6:23a			x	x
6:23b	x		x	x
6:23d	x		x	x
— MT ch 7				
7:3f	x		x	x
7:3h	x		x	x
7:3j			x	
7:4g	x		x	x
7:4k	x		x	x
7:4l	x		x	x
7:5b	x		x	x
7:5g			x	x
7:5h	x		x	x
7:8f			x	
7:9a	x		x	x
7:10c	x		x	x
7:10d			x	x
7:11c	x		x	x
7:11m			x	x
7:11o	x		x	x
7:12c				x
7:12d				x
7:12e	x		x	x
— MT ch 8				
7:15h				x
7:40g	x		x	
7:41b	x		x	x
7:41f	x		x	x
— MT ch 9				
7:42a		x		
7:42e	x			
7:43a	x			
7:44b			x	
7:44f	x		x	x
7:44h	x		x	x
7:44m	x			x
7:44q			x	x
7:44v	x			
7:45k	x		x	x

Unit	Equivalence	Word Order (≥2)	Correspondence	Linquistic Adequacy
(AT versification)				
7:45l	x		x	x
7:46h	x		x	x
7:46i	x		x	x
7:46l	x		x	x
7:47f			x	x
7:47h		x		x
7:47i				x
7:48a				x
— MT ch 10				
7:51c	x		x	x
7:52d			x	x
7:52i			x	x

(179 total)

Units with Values ≥3 but also AT = LXX

Unit (AT versification)	Equivalence	Word Order (≥2)	Correspondence	Linquistic Adequacy
1:5c	x			
1:7b			x	
— MT ch 2				
2:4c			x	
2:5g			x	
2:7e			x	
2:8g			x	
— MT ch 3				
3:1f			x	
3:1l				x
3:11d			x	
3:11e			x	
— MT ch 4				
4:7o	x		x	
4:10c			x	
— MT ch 5				
5:10f	x		x	
5:14d			x	
5:14i			x	
5:15c	x			
5:16b			x	
5:17i			x	
5:21bb			x	x
5:22b			x	
5:23k			x	
5:23l			x	
5:24c			x	
— MT ch 6				
6:1b	x	x	x	
6:2g			x	
6:10b			x	
6:10e	x		x	
6:10f			x	
6:11n			x	
— MT ch 7				
7:1f	x		x	
7:1n			x	
— MT ch 8				
7:33a	x			
7:33c	x		x	
7:40d	x			
— MT ch 9				
7:42a			x	
7:42e			x	
7:42g		x		
7:43a			x	

Unit	Equivalence	Word Order (≥2)	Correspondence	Linquistic Adequacy
(AT versification)				
7:44v			x	
7:47h	x			
7:47l	x		x	
7:47p	x		x	
7:47r	x		x	
7:49d	x		x	
— MT ch 10				
7:50g	x			
7:52c	x			
7:52m	x			

CHAPTER 4: HOW DOES THE THE ALPHA–TEXT COMPARE TO LXX ESTHER?

Any discussion of the AT of Esther must include a discussion of its character compared to the LXX of Esther. The LXX text of Esther, found in the 4th–century uncials, is the majority text of the Greek version of Esther. Before 1965 the AT was thought to be the Lucianic recension of the LXX of Esther, primarily because the AT was found in codices that contain the Lucianic recension of Samuel–Kings. In his classic commentary on Esther written at the beginning of this century, L. B. Paton describes the AT as "a recension, not a version; nevertheless, it is the most widely variant recension that is found in the whole Greek OT" (Paton 1908, 38). Nevertheless, he argues that the AT preserves in places a translation different from that of the LXX, which "presupposes a different Hebrew text" at those places (ibid., 38).

In 1965 Carey A. Moore convinced the scholarly world that, whatever the AT was, it was not a Lucianic recension of the LXX (Moore 1965). Since that time it has been suggested that the AT is an independent translation of a Semitic source, perhaps quite different from the *Vorlage* from which the LXX translation of Esther was made. Any verbatim agreement between the AT and the LXX, especially in the six major additions, is explained as the direct influence of one Greek text upon the other subsequent to their original production.

The most prominent characteristic of the AT compared to the LXX text is that it is shorter than the LXX by about 20%. As discussed in chapter 2, the AT is also about 20% shorter than the MT. (M. V. Fox finds the AT about 29% shorter than the LXX [Fox 1991, 11]. His count is based on the number of words, mine on the number of syntactic units.) Careful examination of the texts shows that it is by and large the same 20%. That is, most (83%) of the material "missing" from the AT is present both in the LXX and MT. The LXX of Esther is more like the MT than is the AT, primarily because the LXX translates more of the MT material than does the AT (the LXX translates about 80% of the MT; the AT, about half). Therefore, generally speaking, the puzzle of the relationship of the AT to the LXX is very similar to the puzzle of the relationship of the AT to the MT. How can the material "missing" from the AT be best explained? Was it omitted at some point in the textual history of the Greek Esther or was it not present in the *Vorlage* of the AT to begin with?

The LXX is comprised of 2178 syntactic units; the AT, 1728. However, because the AT has material not found in the LXX, and *vice versa*, the two texts have only 1227 units in common. If the texts are compared as they both stand, with all the pluses and minuses, the AT agrees semantically with the LXX in 40% of the text (1033 out of 2571 units); it agrees formally with the LXX in 22% of the units (552 out of 2571 units). These low values seem to corroborate the reigning hypothesis that the AT is not a recension of the LXX; if it were, one would expect a much higher percentage of at least semantic, if not formal agreement.

However, if only the material in common to both versions is considered, the agreement between the AT and LXX rises to 84% semantic agreement (1033 out of 1227 units) and 46% formal agreement (564 out of 1227 units). This common core can be explained in two ways: (1) the material common to the AT and LXX came from the *Vorlage(n)* from which each was translated, or (2) one Greek text is a very early recension of the other, after which both versions independently developed.

The extent of the agreement between the AT and the LXX is shown in the following graphs, which display the distribution of semantic and formal agreement between these two Greek versions chapter-by-chapter:

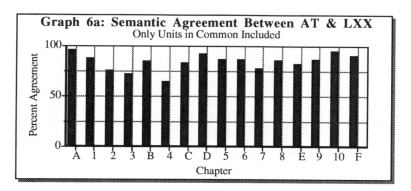

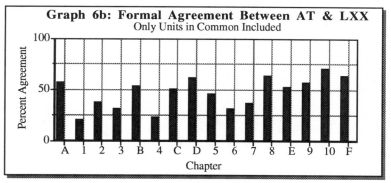

Graphs 6a, b. The AT exhibits high semantic and formal agreement with the LXX when only the text they have in common is compared.

chapter	A	1	2	3	B	4	C	D	5	6	7	8	E	9	10	F	Ave
Semantic	96	88	76	72	85	65	83	93	87	87	78	86	82	87	95	91	84
Formal	57	21	38	32	54	24	51	62	46	32	37	64	53	57	71	64	48

Percentage Agreement of AT with LXX (only units in common included)

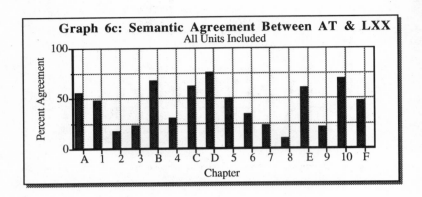

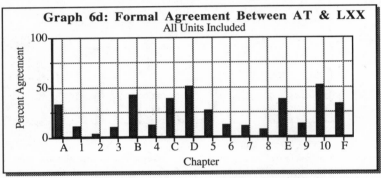

Graphs 6c, d. When all syntactic units are included, the percentage of semantic and formal agreement falls sharply. As the texts now stand, there is greatest agreement in the additions, but even there it is surprisingly low.

chapter	A	1	2	3	B	4	C	D	5	6	7	8	E	9	10	F	Ave
Semantic	56	48	18	23	68	31	62	76	50	34	23	10	60	21	69	47	44
Formal	33	11	4	10	43	12	39	51	27	12	11	7	38	13	52	33	25

Percentage Agreement of AT with LXX (all units included)

To interpret these graphs correctly, consider chapter 8, which, when all syntactic units are counted (Graphs 6c and d), exhibits a very low percentage of agreement between the LXX and AT. This is because out of the 204 syntactic units that comprise chapter 8, there are only 23 which are found in both the LXX and the AT! Yet Graphs 6a and b show 86% semantic and 64% formal agreement between the AT and LXX in chapter 8. This means that although almost none of the syntactic units in chapter 8 appear in both the AT and LXX, those few which do exhibit a high percentage of agreement. A possible explanation for this is offered below in the discussion of addition E and in the conclusion to this work.

Graphs 6c and d show that when the AT is compared to the LXX the six additions have the most material in common and exhibit prominent formal agreement (Graph 6d) compared to the canonical chapters. This evidence is consistent with the hypothesis that (1) these chapters are secondary material not present in the *Vorlage(n)* of the Greek texts and (2) they were copied from one Greek version to the other. If the additions had been a part of the Semitic *Vorlage* from which the original translation was made, one would expect the translator to use the same technique in translating the "additions" as elsewhere, since the "additions" would not be distinguished from other chapters. This would result in greater uniformity of (dis–)agreement across all chapters than is actually present.

What is surprising, however, is that even within these secondary additions, which were copied from one Greek version to the other, the AT exhibits such disagreement with the LXX. For instance, chapter D, which is the most similar between the AT and the LXX, nevertheless agrees only 76% semantically and 51% formally. Assuming that at the time an addition was copied from one Greek version to the other it would have had virtually 100% agreement with its exemplar, these percentages of agreement are surprisingly low. This evidence shows that even the additions have experienced considerable editing after being copied from one version to the other. The nature and extent of the differences between the additions is discussed further below.

HOW DOES THE AT DISAGREE WITH THE LXX?

The differences between the AT and the LXX are of two general types: (1) pluses and minuses and (2) differences where the AT and LXX have text in common. There are many syntactic units distributed throughout both Greek versions that are not found in the other. For discussion, units present in the AT but not in the LXX are identified as pluses; units in the LXX not present in the AT, as minuses. A small number of units that have fallen out of each text due to haplography during transmission of the Greek are discussed below. However, even where the AT and LXX have corresponding syntactic units of text, there are differences of various types that have been identified and counted. These are listed in Table 1 below in descending order of frequency. Table 1 clearly shows that pluses and minuses far outnumber the differences where there is corresponding text. This is the same pattern observed in the relationship between the AT and MT (see chapters 2 and 3).

A List of the Differences Between the AT and LXX

Rank	Difference	# Syntactic Units
1.	AT omits a clause	550
2.	AT omits a word(s)	318
3.	AT adds a word(s)	275
4.	AT adds a clause	272
5.	AT uses a synonym	112
6.	AT rephrases a thought	89
7.	AT has a different thought	86
8.	AT uses a different word (not a synonym)	67
9.	AT has different word order	41
10.	AT displaces text	37
11.	AT same word, different case	33
12.	AT same verb, different mood	29
13.	AT has different compound verb	26
14.	AT different proper noun	24
15.	AT same verb, different tense	22
16.	AT same verb, different number	21
17.	AT has καί instead of δέ	13
18.	AT same verb, different person	8
19.	AT same verb, different voice	5
20.	AT has δέ instead of καί	2
	Total	2030 units

Of the 2030 syntactic units where the AT and LXX disagree, 70% of them (1415 out of 2030 units) are due to pluses and minuses. In the 1227 units that the AT and LXX have in common, 52% of the text formally disagrees for other reasons.

In spite of this, where the AT and LXX have text in common there is a high rate of semantic agreement. This is because so many of the types of formal disagreement exhibited by the AT are such that they do not change the meaning. When compared to the LXX, the AT uses a synonym in 112 units; in eighty–nine units it rephrases a thought, preserving the meaning; in forty–one units the AT has a different word order; twenty–six units use a compound of the same verb; twenty–two units have the same verb in different tense; fifteen units use καί instead of δέ or *vice versa*. These types of differences account for half of the units that disagree. If one includes differences in verbal voice and mood and units of text that agree but are displaced, about 60% of the differences between the AT and LXX where there is text in common do not reflect redactional *Tendenz* or a different *Vorlage*. Many of the types of differences between the AT and the LXX, such as the use of synonyms, different word order, rephrasing of a thought and changes in verbal aspect, voice and mood, are consistent with the nature of the relationship between a recension and the base text from which it was produced. However, the nature of these types of differences could also reflect an independent translation *of the same Vorlage*.

About 25% of the units where there is corresponding text disagree between the AT and LXX to the extent that the meaning is changed, possibly reflecting either redactional *Tendenz* or a different *Vorlage*. Only those differences where the AT has a completely different word or thought not synonymous with the corresponding LXX reading (and which cannot be explained due to haplography) can be considered as possible evidence of redactional *Tendenz* or of a different *Vorlage*. Of the approximately 600 differences between the AT and LXX where they have text in common, about 240 (40%) are of this nature.

THE ENDING OF THE VERSIONS

The endings (chapters 8–10) of the three versions exhibit such substantial differences that most of the discussion of a different and shorter *Vorlage* has been focused there. Evidence for a *Vorlage* of the AT that ended somewhere in chapter 8 will be evaluated in chapter 5. Here it should be noted that although the three versions do differ substantially in their endings, there is nevertheless a surprising degree of agreement, suggesting that all three share a common core that was extensively edited as much material was subsequently added and deleted independently to the Greek versions.

The common core is evident in the fifty–nine units in chapters 8–10 (out of a total of 475) where AT = MT = LXX. All but two of these units exhibit both semantic and formal agreement among all three texts. There are an additional forty–five units where AT = LXX ≠ MT. The agreement of the AT with the MT might be explained as coming *via* the LXX, making these readings in the AT dependent on the LXX. However, the endings in the AT and LXX (excluding addition E) do not show sufficient agreement overall to suggest that one is directly dependent on the other except in scattered readings.

I suggest that the reason for agreement of the AT with both the MT and LXX is that both Greek versions independently translated what was essentially the same *Vorlage*. The ending of the AT developed independently and substantial changes were made, especially when addition E was included. After this, only a vestige of its *Vorlage* remained in the ending of the AT. Later, when addition E was present in both Greek versions, an attempt was made to correct the ending of the AT to the LXX. However, because the endings were by that time so different, only a few corresponding units could be made to agree. This scenario is discussed further in chapter 5 and in the conclusion to this work.

EVIDENCE THAT THE AT IS NOT A RECENSION OF THE LXX

In his doctoral dissertation, C. A. Moore argued convincingly that the AT is not a Lucianic recension of the LXX (Moore 1965). More recently, M. V. Fox presented the most rigorous and convincing argument that the AT is not a recension of LXX Esther (Fox 1991). He concludes, "the AT is composed of two levels — the proto–AT and a redactional level, the latter comprising mostly supplementary material taken from the LXX" (Fox 1991, 17). Fox has found that the relationship between the AT and the LXX in the "additions" is of a quite different nature than that between them in the canonical sections (which he calls the "proto–AT").

From his study of the "frequency–range" of vocabulary correspondences Fox shows that there is a statistically significant higher frequency of vocabulary matches between the AT and LXX in the additions than elsewhere. This is the primary evidence that the additions were copied from one Greek version to the other. The comparatively low frequency of vocabulary matches between the AT and LXX in the canonical sections suggests no such literary dependency. Fox concludes that "the AT was not produced by one person reworking the LXX, but rather by *two different acts of literary creativity* of two fundamentally different types" (ibid., 24, emphasis original). The first creative act originally produced the AT without the additions; the second act introduced the additions into the text.

This study agrees with Fox that the "additions" are aptly named as secondary material introduced subsequent to the original production of the AT. However, the fact that there are two distinct types of material in the AT, the "proto–AT" and the "additions," does not imply that the AT as it comes to us was produced in only two stages. The additions may or may not have been introduced into the text all at the same time. Whether they were or not, this study shows that even after the additions were introduced, the entire text was edited (perhaps more than once), producing changes of a similar nature both in the additions and in the "proto–AT." In the simplest scenario, there must have been at least three redactional stages which produced the text as it now stands: (1) the original production of the AT, (2) the introduction of the additions, (3) at least one redaction after the additions were introduced. No doubt the text's history is even more complicated. [1]

---

[1] For instance, the recent work of K. Wynn proposes seventeen distinct redactional strata for the Esther texts and attempts to identify the socio–historical motivation for

As Fox recognizes, the fact that the major additions were later introduced to both the AT and the LXX does not say anything about whether or not the proto–AT was originally a recension of the LXX produced before any of the additions were introduced in it. To show that the proto–AT is an independent translation of a Hebrew *Vorlage* Fox relies heavily on the application of Martin's seventeen syntactical criteria to a small sample, just fifty–seven lines, of text. This study has applied Martin's criteria to all of the text of both the AT and the LXX of Esther. A comparison of Fox's syntactical analysis is compared to the results of this study in chapter 1. Fox's conclusion that the proto–AT has a "radically more pronounced translational character than LXX–Esther" may have been true for the fifty–seven lines he examined, but it does not stand when the entire texts are examined (ibid., 34). To the extent that Martin's criteria in fact differentiate translation Greek from composition Greek (as opposed to simply different styles of Greek regardless of origin), this study agrees with Fox that the AT is clearly "translation" Greek. However, as demonstrated in chapter 1, the syntax of the texts of the AT and the LXX are overall about the same, certainly within statistical error. Based on the statistics of syntactical evidence, neither can be said to stand closer to a Semitic *Vorlage*.

Fox's analysis of fifty–seven lines of the AT led him to believe that the AT has a radically more pronounced translational character than the LXX. Therefore, he reasoned that if the AT were a recension of the LXX, its syntax would move away from that of translation Greek.[2] This inference seems sound in general but may not always hold. It would almost certainly not hold if the redactor was intending to make the Greek follow the Hebrew more closely. For instance, if Theodotion Daniel is a recension of OG Daniel (see the excursus at the end of this work), then it is an example of a recension moving toward "translation" Greek, perhaps because it was revised toward the MT. Furthermore, any Hexaplaric reading will probably shift the syntax of the text towards "translation" Greek, even though the influence of the

---

each. Although his hypothesis certainly exceeds the evidence, his work shows the complicated nature of the problem (Wynn 1990).

[2] As noted in chapter 1, the syntax of the additions does shift the overall syntax of both the AT and LXX toward composition Greek.

Semitic *Vorlage* is indirect. Fox dismisses this in the case of the AT with the claim that the AT is further from the MT than is the LXX. As this study shows, that is simply because the LXX translates more of the text of the MT than does the AT; where the AT and MT have text in common, the AT often agrees with it (see chapter 2). For the reasons cited, the "translational" character of the syntax of the AT cannot be used to prove it was not originally a recension of the LXX.

Fox presents more convincing evidence that the AT was originally produced as an independent translation of a Semitic *Vorlage* by citing the many individual readings in the "proto–AT" where the AT agrees with the MT against the LXX, evidence which this study also observed. Furthermore, this study found only three readings outside of the additions where the AT and LXX clearly agree against the MT (AT:3:1g, AT:6:14b, AT:7:51f). If the AT were a recension of the LXX, one would expect that where the LXX disagrees with the MT, the AT would more frequently follow.

To add to the evidence presented by Fox, this study has found some distinctive AT readings that can be best explained as mechanical errors that could have arisen only from a misreading of a Hebrew *Vorlage* (see the more detailed discussion of this in chapter 3). This evidence indicates that, at least at these places, the language of the parent text of the AT was Hebrew and not Greek.

This study also concludes that the AT was not originally produced as a recension of the LXX (nor *vice versa*). Both the extent of the agreement and the nature of the differences between them where they have text in common can be best explained as resulting from two independent translations (hence the differences) of a very similar *Vorlage* (hence the agreement).

DID THE AT COPY THE ADDITIONS FROM THE LXX OR VICE VERSA?

Although the origin of the AT is not found in the LXX, much of the secondary material is found in both versions. Fox argues that the "redactional level," i.e., the additions and whatever changes were made in the "proto–AT" when they were introduced, is comprised of "mostly supplementary material *taken from the LXX*" (ibid., 17, emphasis mine). The simplest scenario, that all the secondary material was copied from one Greek version to the other at one point in time, may or may not be correct. Theoretically, some of the additions could have been copied from the LXX to the AT; others, in the opposite direction. Even if all six major additions were copied at one time from one Greek version to the other, the nature of the differences between the texts of the additions in the AT and LXX is evidence of further redactional activity (see discussion below). The evidence suggests that the direction of the copy of each unit of secondary material must be considered individually. It is nevertheless legitimate to consider if there is evidence that a significant amount of secondary material was copied from one Greek version to the other at one time and, if so, in which direction the copy went.

Fox argues for the direction of the copy of the secondary material from the LXX to the AT for four reasons (ibid., 36). Firstly, he argues that the redactor of the AT used the "cut–and–splice" technique, which condenses the text of its exemplar by omitting words to create new sentences from those that remain. He writes that this technique "can only be explained as a deliberate reduction [not "redaction"] of the LXX, not as an expansion of the AT" (ibid., 36). What he cites as the best example of this technique in AT:7:49 // LXX:9:26, 27 is not convincing because the AT reading involves more than just a cut–and–splice. Other words were added and the words common to the LXX and AT that might indicate a cut–and–splice are in different grammatical cases. I agree with Fox that the LXX reading here does not appear to be an expansion of the AT. But that is because the LXX so closely follows the MT here that it was surely originally a translation of the Hebrew and not an expansion of the AT. The AT has either re–written the LXX here in condensed form or it has translated a shorter *Vorlage*. The other examples of "cut–and–splice" he cites are even less convincing *vis–à–vis* the direction of the copy.

Fox's second argument is based on two textual variants at C:28, where the LXX reads Αμαν compared to the AT's ἅμα, and at 9:7, where the LXX reads Δελφων compared to the AT's ἀδελφόν. Even if the LXX preserves the original reading, this does not argue for the direction of the original copy, or even that this unit of text was copied from one Greek version to the other. In the case of 9:7 direct LXX–AT influence is not necessarily implied. Both the LXX and AT readings could have originally and independently translated the corresponding

Hebrew, וְאֵת דַּלְפוֹן, and later the AT reading was corrupted during transmission. The corruption in both C:28 and 9:7 certainly appears to be inner–Greek, but it could have occurred at any time during the transmission of the text, without the direct influence of one Greek text on the other.

Fox's third argument is that addition E is better integrated into the text of the LXX than it is in the AT. Paton also argued along these same lines that E was added first to the LXX because it appears to be in a different location, after 8:6 in the LXX but after 8:12 in the AT (Paton 1908, 44). Verses 8:7–12 in the LXX, which are omitted in the AT, make a better introduction to addition E. In addition to noting the inferior introduction of addition E in the AT compared to the LXX, Fox identifies several contradictions and difficulties in the AT that are not present in the LXX (9:26, 8:47, 8:44, 8:12–13). All of them are in the ending following addition E, but they do not all seem to be related to addition E. Fox argues that the redactor is focusing on the material he is importing from the LXX while taking the proto–AT for granted (ibid., 91). While these difficulties do exist, most of them are independent of addition E and could have been in the text even before E was added. The complicated differences between the ending of the AT and LXX begin as early as 7:10 and continue through chapter 10. The question of the relationship between the "proto–AT" and addition E is a difficult one but surely only a part of the larger question about the relationship of the endings of all three versions. The problems Fox cites in the AT ending are symptoms of this larger issue. Inferences about the direction of the copy (if there is in fact a literary relationship between the endings of AT and LXX) cannot be made until the larger issue is better understood. (See chapter 5 and the conclusion of this work.)

Fox's fourth argument, that scattered LXX verses appear in the AT, but no proto–AT material appears in the LXX, is a convincing argument for the direction of the copying *of those particular verses*, but does not strongly argue that most of the secondary material came into the AT from the LXX.

As discussed below, this study and other recent work have found evidence that the AT preserves the older form of all the additions except D. Although this does not necessarily imply that the additions were introduced first to the AT and later copied to the LXX, it is consistent with that scenario. An examination of Fox's arguments for the direction of the copy and the evidence of this study shows that the direction of the copy of most of the secondary material, i.e., the additions and changes made to the canonical sections when the additions were introduced, must remain an open question.

DIFFERENCES BETWEEN THE AT AND LXX
DUE TO MECHANICAL ERROR

Not all of the differences between the AT and LXX indicate the *Tendenz* of a redactor or evidence of a different *Vorlage*. Some are almost certainly due to scribal errors during transmission of the Greek texts. Such differences due to inner-Greek textual corruption must be identified and eliminated, as they have no bearing on determining redactional *Tendenz* or a different *Vorlage*.

The omission of the description of Mordecai when he is first introduced in AT:A:1 units l and m as "a Jew living in the city of Susa" is almost certainly due to haplography and not to some redactional *Tendenz* or a different *Vorlage*:

LXX		AT	
A:2a ἄνθρωπος	A:1l ἄνθρωπος		m
b Ἰουδαῖος οἰκῶν ἐν Σούσοις τῇ πόλει,			
c ἄνθρωπος μέγας		μέγας	n

The repetition of ἄνθρωπος in the first and third lines has caused a scribe to drop out the intervening words Ἰουδαῖος οἰκῶν ἐν Σούσοις τῇ πόλει. In a recent literary study of the texts of Esther, C. Dorothy identifies this not as a scribal error but as a *Tendenz* of the LXX that "stresses the ethnicity of Mor[decai] as Jewish in a foreign surrounding" (Dorothy 1989, 55). However, where the text is ripe for haplography, scribal error is the more probable explanation. In the absence of compelling evidence to the contrary, literary *Tendenz* must be reserved for those instances where no principle of haplography adequately explains the variant text.

In the apocalyptic dream of addition A, in AT:A:8d the subject of the sentence is οἱ ποταμοί ("the rivers") but in the LXX it is οἱ ταπεινοί ("the lowly"):

	LXX		*AT*	
A:10d	καὶ οἱ ταπεινοὶ ὑψώθησαν	A:8	καὶ οἱ ποταμοὶ ὑψώθησαν	d
e	καὶ κατέφαγον τοὺς ἐνδόξους.		καὶ κατέπιον τοὺς ἐνδόξους.	e

This variant reading is explained as a confusion of the Greek words involving metathesis of the τ and π and misreading μ for ν, since both words occur elsewhere in the text and either makes sense in the immediate context. The original reading is probably preserved in the LXX, because (1) every other occurrence of the river symbol occurs in the singular number and, (2) in the interpretation of the symbol in addition F in the AT the river is identified as the nations gathered to destroy the Jews, but in a reversal the Jews are exalted over their enemies. Since the apocalyptic dream symbolizes this victory, the "lowly" (i.e., the Jews) not the "rivers" (i.e., the nations) are exalted and swallow up the powerful. Again, instead of recognizing this as probable haplography, C. Dorothy construes the variant as redactional tension that shows "slippage in the river symbology" (ibid., 331).

What appears to be a plus in the AT at (C)4:25c is no doubt haplography in the LXX:

	LXX		*AT*	
C:24b	εἰς τὸ στόμα μου	4:25	εἰς τὸ στόμα μου	b
c			καὶ χαρίτωσον τὰ ῥήματά μου	c
d	ἐνώπιον τοῦ λέοντος		ἐνώπιον τοῦ βασιλέως	d

The repetition of μου in lines b and c caused the rest of line c to be dropped from the LXX.

The secondary material in chapter 5 of the Greek Esther gives many additional details about Esther's uninvited appearance before the king. In AT:5:11g, Esther tells the king that her heart was troubled ἀπὸ τῆς δόξης τοῦ θυμοῦ σου ("from the glory of your rage"); in the LXX the corresponding phrase (D:13g) reads, ἀπὸ φόβου τῆς δόξης σου ("from the fear of your glory"). The AT reading can be explained if φόβου was mistaken for θυμοῦ, resulting in the difficult reading "from the rage of your glory," which was then transposed to read more smoothly "from the glory of your rage."

In AT:7:23ii (addition E) a word may have dropped out due to homoiarchton with two consecutive words beginning with παραλογισ–; or, it may been a stylistic change to avoid repetition of the syllable:

LXX		*AT*	
E:6 a τῷ τῆς κακοηθείας		7:23 τῷ τῆς κακοποιΐας	hh
ψευδεῖ		ψεύδει	
b παραλογισμῷ			ii
c παραλογισαμένων		παραλογισάμενοι	jj

A COMPARISON OF THE AT TO THE LXX
IN THE SIX MAJOR ADDITIONS

The origin of the six major additions and their relationship to one another is one of the great puzzles attending the Greek versions of Esther. All of the extant manuscripts of the Greek versions of Esther include all six major additions. The simplest scenario is that the additions accrued over a period of time in one version and were then all copied at some point from one version to the other. It is surprising that there are no surviving manuscripts, in either Hebrew or Greek, which preserve any hint about the development of the additions. (If one assumes the more complicated scenario, that each addition was copied from one Greek version to the other at different times, and perhaps in different directions, this lack of manuscript evidence is even more surprising.)

None of the texts which stand in the Semitic tradition, the Talmud, the targums of Esther or the Syriac version, include any hint of any of the six additions. Although there is internal syntactical evidence that additions A, C, D and F may be translations of Semitic sources, this lack of any manuscript evidence must be given its due consideration. In contrast, the Old Latin, Coptic and Ethiopic versions, which derive from the Greek texts, all include the additions (although the Old Latin is lacking a few verses of addition C). The OL version has readings that agree with the AT against the LXX (see text notes in Moore 1977). This external evidence strongly suggests that all of the additions originated and were transmitted solely within the Greek textual tradition.

On the other hand, because Esther has not been found at Qumran,[3] the oldest Hebrew manuscript of Esther dates to A.D. 1000 (Codex Leningradensis) and the oldest Greek manuscript to the 3rd century A.D. (Chester Beatty $\mathfrak{P}$967, the LXX version). Given that the autograph may date as early as the mid–5th century B.C. and the oldest manuscript in any language is 3rd century A.D., the Esther story was extant during many centuries for which there is no manuscript evidence at all. The pluriformity of Hebrew texts of other OT books, which had been reflected only by the Greek versions until recently confirmed by the Qumran texts, suggests that there may have been more than one Semitic version of Esther, one of which may have included at least some of the additions.

Lacking external manuscript evidence for the origin and relationship of the additions, whatever is to be said of their history must be inferred from internal evidence. Such inference is by its nature most tentative. Furthermore, the available internal evidence is sufficiently ambiguous that it may be construed in many ways, giving rise to a plethora of complicated theories about the development of the additions and the historical impulse from which they came.

The original language of the additions has been discussed since the 16th century when Cardinal Bellarmin (died 1605) proposed that all of the additions were translations of a Hebrew Esther that has not survived. (Bellarminus, *de verbo Dei* I c. VII,10). Early in this century, scholars recognized that additions B and E were almost certainly composed in Greek (Roiron 1916).

The work of C. A. Moore remains the most thorough treatment of the additions to date (Moore 1973 and 1977). Moore believes that additions A, C, D, and F exhibit syntactic evidence of having been

---

[3] In 1992 Milik published six Aramaic fragments from Qumran with the unfortunate sigla 4QprEsth[a], ... 4QprEsth[f] (Milik 1992). It is far from certain that these fragments are from a literary source of Esther. In any case, the text does not correspond to the biblical form of the Esther story. The statement that there are no texts of Esther yet identified from Qumran still stands.

translated from a Semitic source, while additions B and E are "unquestionably Greek compositions" (ibid., 155). Using syntax criticism, R. A. Martin confirmed that A, C and D are translations of a Semitic *Vorlage*, that B and E were originally composed in Greek and that addition F is either a very free translation or original Greek (Martin 1975). As this study argues in chapter 1, many of Martin's seventeen criteria are invalid here because the additions are too short. Furthermore, it is questionable whether the criteria he identifies really differentiate translation Greek from composition, or just different styles of Greek regardless of origin (see especially the syntactic profile for papyri on Graph 2, chapter 1). Unless the criteria of syntax criticism unanimously indicate translation or composition Greek (as they do for additions B and E), syntax criticism alone cannot reliably determine the original language. If A, C, D and F are translations of Semitic sources, they apparently were not present in the *Vorlage* of either the AT or the LXX. This means they either circulated separately in the Semitic tradition (which seems somewhat doubtful given their nature and their absence from all Semitic texts) or they were found in a now lost Semitic text of Esther from which they were subsequently translated into one of the existing Greek versions.

If A, C, D and F had Semitic sources, not only have these sources been lost to our time, but apparently none were extant even at the time of Origen. In his *Epistle of Africanus*, iii, Origen comments that neither the prayers of Esther and Mordecai (addition C) nor the decrees of Haman and Mordecai (additions B and E) were found in any Hebrew text known to him (Swete 1914, 257). One wonders if his comment implies that additions A, F and D, thought possibly to have Semitic sources, *were* found in Hebrew texts known to Origen. However, Origen's meticulous system of marking Greek text in the Hexapla for which no Hebrew was extant suggests that he would have so indicated a Greek reading if he knew of *any* Hebrew text with which it agreed. Origen's work suggests that the only Hebrew text he knew was the MT, and there is no evidence to suggest that the MT ever included any of the six additions.

The Hexapla offers no evidence that Origen knew of the AT. Field's edition of the Hexapla shows that Origen's text agrees only with the LXX of Esther. In a few instances the Hexapla reading does agree with the AT, but only in readings where the AT also agrees with the

LXX. There is no instance where the Hexapla agrees with the AT against the LXX.

Whatever their origin, a comparison of the additions in the AT with the additions in the LXX shows that they are surprisingly different. The six additions can be ranked based on the percentage of agreement between the AT and LXX:

Ranking of the Additions by Percentage of Agreement
Between the AT and the LXX
(all units included)

Semantic Agreement			*Formal Agreement*	
1.	D	76%	D	51%
2.	B	68%	B	43%
3.	C	62%	C	49%
4.	E	60%	E	38%
5.	A	56%	A	33%
6.	F	47%	F	33%

As the additions now stand, addition D is the one most alike in the AT and LXX; addition F shows the most disagreement. Assuming that the additions were copied from one Greek version to the other, at that point they would have been identical. Therefore, the extent of the differences that now stand between them must have resulted from redactional activity either at the time the addition was copied or subsequently during transmission of the Greek texts. It is not possible to infer from the extent of disagreement which text, the AT or LXX, was subsequently changed. Most likely, both experienced a long history of redaction after the additions were introduced. Because each addition agreed virtually 100% with its exemplar at the time it was copied, the extent of this subsequent redactional activity for each addition is inversely indicated by the percentage of agreement as the texts now stand. That is, the more a given addition agrees between the AT and LXX, the less editing it has experienced since it was copied from one version to the other.

Table 2 shows that addition D has experienced the least redactional activity since the time it was copied from one Greek version to the other. Addition F has experienced the greatest redaction since being copied. Does this data suggest that the additions were not all copied at the same time? Although it may be tempting to infer from their ranking that addition F must have been copied first and addition D must have been copied most recently, such a chronological correlation cannot be justified from this evidence alone. Although the evidence is consistent with the idea that the addition which has experienced the most redaction may be the oldest, it does not prove it. The data shows only that since the time it was copied, whenever that was, every addition has experienced some degree of editing.

The following discussion of the text of each addition will proceed more or less in the order of their ranking of agreement between the AT and the LXX.

Addition D — Esther's Uninvited Approach to the King

Addition D has been inserted into chapter 5 where Esther appears uninvited before the king. This addition provides an expanded account of Esther's anxious approach to the king and the dialogue between them. Of the six additions, addition D is the one that is most alike between the AT and the LXX. It is also the addition which is most interwoven with the immediately surrounding text. In the MT, the scene opens in MT:5:1 with, "And it came about on the third day / that Esther put on her royal robes / and stood in the inner court ..." In both the AT and the LXX, the sentence is split in three parts and the beginning of addition D is inserted at exactly the same places in both Greek versions as indicated by the virgules (/). The first words of addition D, "when Esther ceased praying and took off the garments of worship," are inserted after the introductory formula "And it came about on the third day" and before "she put on her royal robes." Then four more verses of addition D, describing Esther's approach, are inserted before "and she stood..."

The outcome of Esther's uninvited approach to the king is summarized succinctly in the MT in one verse (MT:5:2), "And it happened when the king saw Esther the queen standing in the court, she obtained favor in his sight; and the king extended to Esther the golden scepter which was in his hand" (NASB). The first half of this verse is replaced in both Greek versions by the continuation of addition D, which describes the fearsome appearance of the king, the swooning of Esther and the tender comment that the king "took her in his arms and comforted her." The second half of the MT verse, "and the king extended the scepter," is reported in the Greek versions, followed by the several concluding verses of addition D.

The fact that addition D is interwoven exactly the same way with the canonical text in exactly the same places in both the AT and the LXX shows conclusively that addition D was copied from one Greek text to the other. For if addition D came into the LXX and AT independently from a third source, it is highly improbable that it would have been interwoven at identically the same places, splitting sentences apart at precisely the same point. This also indicates that the Greek texts of chapter 5 in the LXX and AT were either virtually identical to allow addition D to be positioned identically in both or that the canonical text immediately surrounding addition D was also copied from one Greek text to the other.

An examination of the distribution of formal agreement between the AT and LXX within chapter 5 shows that the latter scenario is the most probable. The first eighteen verses of chapter 5 of the AT, which include both addition D (AT:5:1–12) and the canonical text in and immediately following those verses (AT:5:13–18), show a much greater formal agreement with the corresponding LXX verses (49%) than do verses 19ff. (23%). Apparently this entire section, AT:5:1–18, including both addition D and some canonical verses, were copied from one Greek text to the other.

The differences that now exist between the AT and LXX in these first eighteen verses are small differences of style, synonymous vocabulary and small pluses that clarify the sense. For instance, in AT:5:2a, the middle deponent form, $\gamma\epsilon\nu o\mu\acute{\epsilon}\nu\eta$, is found where the LXX:D:2a uses the passive deponent form, $\gamma\epsilon\nu\eta\theta\epsilon\hat{\iota}\sigma\alpha$. In AT:5:4c, the verb is $\acute{\epsilon}\sigma\tau\eta$ where the compound form $\kappa\alpha\tau\acute{\epsilon}\sigma\tau\eta$ is found at that place in the LXX. Some dative phrases differ between the texts only because of the presence or absence of the preposition $\acute{\epsilon}\nu$ (e.g., AT:5:5c). The implied subject is sometimes made explicit in one text (e.g., AT:5:8b). The definite article may or may not be present (e.g., AT:5:2i). These types of differences show no deliberate *Tendenz*, reflect no variant *Vorlage* and probably originated with scribes during the transmission of the Greek texts after addition D was copied from one version to the other.

However, within this section of addition D there are two interesting differences that violate the verbatim relationship in the surrounding verses. These may be the creative work of a redactor or indicate a *Vorlage* different from the MT. Where the LXX reads that Esther put on τὴν δόξαν αὐτῆς ("her glory") AT:5:1j,k has the distinctive reading τὰ ἱμάτια τῆς δόξης ("the garments of glory"). M. V. Fox takes the AT reading here to be a deliberate clarification of the LXX reading (Fox 1991, 60). This phrase does not occur elsewhere in the Greek OT, but is found in the pseudepigraphal Psalm of Solomon (1st century B.C.) at 11:7, "Jerusalem, put on *the garments of your glory*, Prepare the robes of your holiness." In the AT it may, therefore, have been intended not as a clarification of the LXX reading but as an allusion.

A second distinctive reading is found in the AT at 5:5d, where the king is said to look upon Esther ὡς ταῦρος ἐν ἀκμῇ θυμοῦ ("as a bull in fierce anger"). Although the LXX does not have this reference to a bull, the Old Latin (OL) version of Esther also describes the king at this point in the text as an enraged bull (Moore 1977, 216).

Other than these two exceptions, addition D is virtually identical in both the AT and LXX through D:13 (AT:5:11). A significant difference is found in the concluding sentences of addition D, after the king extends the scepter to Esther:

LXX	*AT*
D:14a ὅτι θαυμαστὸς εἶ, κύριε,	
b καὶ τὸ πρόσωπόν σου 5:12a καὶ ἐπὶ τὸ πρόσωπον αὐτῆς	
χαρίτων μεστόν.	μέτρον ἱδρῶτος
D:15a ἐν δὲ τῷ διαλέγεσθαι αὐτὴν	
b ἔπεσεν ἀπὸ ἐκλύσεως	

The LXX reads, "For you are wonderful, lord, and your face is full of grace. While she was speaking, she fainted and fell." The AT reads, "And on her face was a measure of sweat." Because the text on both sides of these verses in both the LXX and AT is identically the same, this wildly variant reading is most peculiar. Moreover the noun translated "sweat," ἱδρώς, is a rare word occurring in only one other place in the LXX (Gen 3:19) and twice in the texts of Maccabees.

C.C. Torrey regards this as evidence that addition D was translated from an Aramaic source. He claims that the translator of the AT confused the Aramaic word דְּעֲתָא ("sweat") with רְעָתָא ("good will"), misreading a daleth instead of a *resh* (Torrey 1944, 8). Attempts to make some sense of the thought once this confusion occurred resulted in two completely different Greek readings.

Whether or not Torrey is correct, there does seem to be a striking allusion to this peculiar AT reading in 2 Macc 2:26, 27. In discussing the arduous task of abridging Jason's five–volume story of the Maccabean revolt into one volume, the labor is described thus:

> Therefore to us, that have taken upon us this painful labor of abridging, it was not easy, but a matter of *sweat* [ἱδρῶτος] and *watching* [ἀγρυπνίας]; even as it is no ease unto him *that prepareth a banquet*, and seeketh the benefit of others. (AVA, emphasis mine).

Perhaps it is just a coincidence, but after the AT describes sweat on Esther's face, her next statement is, "you and Haman come to the banquet I will prepare." To further the coincidence, the verb form of the word translated "watching" [ἀγρυπνίας] in 2 Macc 2:26 is found in another distinctive reading in the AT at 6:1e, "And the Mighty One took away the king's sleep that night and he was *wakeful* [ἀγρυπνῶν]." The king's wakeful night was, of course, the turning point that brought Mordecai to power. And the banquet Esther prepared was the setting for Haman's downfall which resulted in benefit to the Jews.

It seems plausible that this is a deliberate allusion to the Esther tradition because the author of 2 Macc 2:26 uses two words that occur distinctively in the AT of Esther (neither of them in LXX Esther) and in the same sentence refers to a banquet, a major motif in Esther. The author of 2 Macc definitely had the Esther story in mind later when in 15:36 he refers to Purim as "Mordecai's day." If the author of 2 Macc was making a deliberate allusion to the Esther story in 2:26 it was to the textual tradition preserved in the AT version, not the LXX, of the Esther story.

The book of 2 Maccabees is believed to have been written in Jerusalem to the Hellenized Diaspora Jews in Ptolemaic Egypt during the Hasmonean period. This apparently was a time when the Jews in Jerusalem were attempting to standardize the practices (and texts?) of the Diaspora Jews to those of Palestine. If 2 Macc 2:2 is a deliberate allusion to the distinctive AT readings in 5:12 and 6:1, the Greek of addition D *of the AT* was known to the writer of 2 Maccabees, a Jew in Jerusalem about 100 B.C. If the allusion was expected to be understood by the original readers, we can infer that the Jews in Ptolemaic Egypt were also familiar with the distinctive reading of addition D as it stands in the AT.

Addition B — Haman's Decree Against the Jews

In chapter 3 of the MT, when Haman gets the king's permission to destroy the Jews, the text says that the scribes were gathered, that Haman dictated a decree in the king's name to annihilate all the Jews and that the letters were sent by couriers to all the king's provinces. In both the LXX and AT, the decree itself, addition B, is inserted between 3:13 and 3:14. It is inserted as a whole and is not integrated into the immediately surrounding text.

Of the six additions, B is the second highest ranking in agreement between the LXX and AT. A comparison of addition B in both texts shows that the only differences that have developed between them are differences of style consistent with an updating of the vocabulary and syntax as the Greek text was copied. The differences between the AT and LXX in addition B are for the most part the substitution of a synonymous word, a stylistic change in syntax and the addition of an occasional pronoun or relative clause for clarification.

For instance, the AT uses σατράπαις ("satraps") at 3:14i where the LXX (B:1i) reads τοπάρχαις ("rulers of places").[4] In AT:3:15l, the kingdom is described as ἀταράχους ("untroubled") but in the LXX (B:2l) as ἀκυμάτους ("serene"). In the AT at 3:15p, the preposition ἄχρι is found where μέχρι stands in the LXX (B:2p). In AT:3:16y, the noun προστάγματα ("order") is found where the LXX (B:4l) reads διατάγματα ("commandment"). A change in syntax for stylistic purposes is found at AT:3:16g, which reads εὐνοίᾳ where the LXX (B:3g) reads ἐν τῇ εὐνοίᾳ.

---

[4] C.A. Moore notes that the word τόπαρχος may have been specific to an Egyptian provenance. (Moore 1977, 191)

There are very few syntactic units added to addition B in the AT. The few that occur seem to be for clarification, not for additional content. For instance the explicit ὑμῖν found at AT:3:18b is only implied in the LXX (B:6:b). An interesting subordinate clause added for clarification is found at AT:3:18s: ὅς ἐστι Δύστρος ("which is Dustros"). This clause gives the Macedonian month name that corresponds to the Jewish month of Adar. (See the discussion of the Macedonian month names and their implications for dating the AT in the conclusion to this work.)

Syntax criticism indicates that addition B was probably composed in Greek (see chapter 1). The nature of the relationship between the texts of addition B in the AT compared to the LXX indicates that this addition was copied directly from one to the other and that addition B has experienced virtually no redaction in either the AT or LXX since being copied from one Greek version to the other.

Because additions B and E are the same genre (both are royal decrees) and exhibit the same syntax and vocabulary, addition E will be discussed next.

Addition E —The Royal Decree

Addition E, which is the royal decree permitting the Jews to defend themselves if attacked, is found within chapter 8 of the Greek Esther. It is almost certain that additions B and E were both originally written in Greek, probably by the same author. Both additions are royal decrees which were inserted without integration into the LXX and AT between the Greek verses corresponding to MT:8:12 and 8:13.

Torrey believes that Lysimachus, the translator named in the colophon of the LXX Esther, both translated Esther (from Aramaic) and composed additions B and E in 114 B.C. (Torrey 1944, 28). L. Soubigou believes Lysimachus inserted, but did not compose, these royal decrees (Soubigou 1952, 588). C.A. Moore accepts that B and E were composed by the same author, but does not believe it could have been the translator Lysimachus because the style of the translation is so different from the style of these two additions, the former being characterized as "simple" and "unpretentious," the later as "flowery rhetoric" (Moore 1977, 166). A. E. Gardner agrees that Lysimachus could not have written these additions, and suggests that Dositheus and his son Ptolemaus, who are also named in the LXX colophon, not only carried the book from Jerusalem to Egypt, but also made the insertions in 78/77 B.C. (Gardner 1984, 4).

Another theory of origin identifies Alexandria, not Jerusalem, as the provenance of these additions (Moore 1977, 166). According to Motzo (1934, 275–80) and Moore (1977, 195) additions B and E exhibit some strong parallels with 3 Maccabees, which is believed to have been written in Greek in Alexandria between 100 and 30 B.C. (Moore 1977, 195; OTP, 512). Moore has shown similarities both in content and structure between addition B and Ptolemy's letter in 3 Macc 3:14–26. He interprets this as evidence that the composition of 3 Maccabees was shaped by the Greek Esther (Moore 1977, 198–99). Using similar evidence, Motzo argues for a dependency in the other direction, that the Greek Esther is dependent upon 3 Maccabees.

K. H. Wynn proposes that additions B and E were added in Alexandria after the Roman emperor Claudius wrote to the Alexandrians in A.D. 41 (Wynn 1990, 239). This is the latest possible date for additions B and E, since Josephus refers to them in *Ant.*, xi, 6. Wynn's argument is based on the identification of Haman as a "Macedonian" in addition E (apparently overlooking the term "Bougaion" in the same text) and on the dating of 3 Maccabees to the Roman period. The term "Macedonian" is not specific to the Roman period, being found in the text of the 5th century B.C. historian Herodotus (which is itself, of course, also subject to the vicissitudes of textual transmission). Since the parallels between the Greek additions to Esther and 3 Maccabees do not indicate the chronological relationship of the texts, and since the date of 3 Maccabees is uncertain, Wynn's argument is not convincing.

The evidence found in this study confirms that additions B and E were composed by the same author and added to the AT at the same time, though not necessarily in either 77 or 114 B.C. I would further argue that additions B and E in the AT are closer to their autographs than are the additions in the LXX. This conclusion is based on the high incidence of certain words found *only in the AT* text in *both* additions B and E.

The appearance of certain distinctive words in both addition B and addition E, but not elsewhere in the text, reinforces the conclusion based on syntax and style that B and E were composed by the same author. Furthermore, since the texts of additions B and E must have been virtually identical at the time one was copied from one Greek text to the other, these words must have at one time appeared at the same places in additions B and E in both the AT and the LXX. By listing the expected occurrence of each word and observing whether the AT or the LXX preserves that occurrence, one can determine in which text, the AT or the LXX, most of the expected occurrences of these words have been preserved. The text that preserves most of the expected occurrences is the text that has changed the least since additions B and E were copied from one Greek version to the other.

The following Greek words, in various inflected forms, occur only in both additions B and E. If this list had been made at the time these additions were originally copied from one Greek text to the other, the list of the occurrences of these words in both texts would be identical:

Occurrences of Words Common Only to B and E

	AT		*LXX*	
1. ἀτάραχος	(B)3:15l		——	
	——		(B)3:13j	
	(E)7:24q	=	E:8c	
2. ἐπιεικής	(B)3:15g	=	B:2g	
	(E)7:24z	≈	E:9e	
3. ἐπικρατέω	(B)3:15b	=	B:2b	
	(E)7:23kk	=	E:6d	
	(E)7:26u	≈	E:14e	
	——		E:18j	
4. κατευθυνομένη	——		B:4n	
	(B)3:17q		——	
	(E)7:27n	=	E:16e	
5. καταστῆσαι	(B)3:15m	=	B:2m (also occurs in AT:2:4d)	
	(E)7:23ff	≈	E:5j	
6. μετέπειτα	(B)3:18dd	=	B:7g	
	(E)7:24p		——	
7. σατράπαις	(B)3:14i		—— (also occurs in AT:[9]7:42)	
	(E)7:22h	≈	E:1h	

8. ὑποτεταγμένην (B)3:14b   ——

                 ——   B:1j

                 (B)3:15k   =   B:2k

                 (E)7:22b   ——

                 (E)7:23f   =   E:3b

The symbol ≈ ("approximately equal to") indicates that although the reading of the LXX is not identical to the AT, it is too similar to count as disagreeing. "——" means the reading is entirely different or is missing.

Because this vocabulary originally (i.e., at the time the additions were copied) must have occurred in *both* B and E, there are twenty–two possible occurrences where the AT and LXX once had the same reading. The AT preserves this vocabulary in eighteen out of the possible twenty–two readings. In contrast, the LXX preserves only thirteen occurrences of this vocabulary. This shows that additions B and E in the AT more closely reflect the form of the additions when they were copied than does the LXX text of these additions.

The conclusion that the AT preserves the earlier form of additions B and E has been independently reached by C. Dorothy, who has recently analyzed the texts of Esther from a literary approach. He too concludes, but for literary reasons, that "... both length and complexity point toward L [AT] as preserving an earlier form of both B and E" (Dorothy 1989, 440).

It may be tempting to infer from this that additions B and E must therefore have originated in the AT and were copied to the LXX. However, the fact that the AT preserves the earlier form of additions B and E does *not* prove the direction of the copy. It means only that since the time when additions B and E were copied, in whichever direction, they have experienced fewer changes in the AT than they have in the LXX. Though this data is consistent with the chronological priority of additions B and E in the AT, it does not prove it. Given that the LXX text is the majority text and was apparently in wider circulation than the AT, it is reasonable that it would have had the greater opportunity for both deliberate and inadvertent textual changes.

Within addition E, up to E:20 (AT:7:29) the AT exactly agrees with the LXX except for the same kind of minor stylistic and syntactical differences observed in addition B. For instance, explicit pronouns have been added to the AT text of addition E in AT:7:24f, 25b, and 27d. The particle τε is found in the LXX reading at E:16e but not in the corresponding AT reading (AT:7:27n). In that same unit, the participle is in the aorist tense in the AT but the present in the LXX. Different compounds of the same verb are used (e.g., AT:7:28:f, ἐργασάμενον cf. LXX:E:18b, ἐξεργασάμενοι). Two or three phrases that may have dropped out of the AT in addition E due to haplography have been noted above. The differences in the first twenty verses of addition E between the AT and LXX exhibit no redactional *Tendenz* nor variant *Vorlage* .

One of the differences between addition E in the AT compared to the LXX is that the AT refers to Haman as "Bougaios" (AT:(E)7:25d) where the LXX reads "Macedonian" (LXX:E:10d). This difference reflects a deliberate redaction of the texts. As discussed more fully in chapter 3, this appellation provides a clue to the redactional history of the Greek texts.

There was a Persian general named Bagoas, who assassinated Artaxerxes III in 338 B.C. If "Bougaios" is a variant spelling of this Persian name, Haman is anachronistically being characterized as an assassin in the AT. In fact, addition E does refer to Haman making an attempt on the king's life (AT:(E)7:26). Therefore, the appellation "Bougaios," labelling Haman as an assassin, is quite consistent with the theme of assassination in addition E, and with the amplification of this theme throughout the AT.

The characterization of Haman as a "Bougaios" also goes far in explaining why the LXX text gives the name of the king as Artaxerxes. The translator (or subsequent redactor) who read "Bougaios" as an appellation for Haman knew that Bagoas assassinated Artaxerxes (III), not Xerxes, and accordingly "corrected" the name of the king. This suggests that the AT reading of the king's name, which agrees with the MT, preserves the original reading.

Although addition E is almost identical in both the AT and the LXX,[5] there is almost no correspondence between the AT and LXX in

---

5 My findings contradict those of C.A. Moore, who writes, "there is greater disagreement between [addition E of] the LXX and the AT than in any other Additions" (Moore 1977, 238). His observation is true for chapter 8 as a whole, but not for addition E.

the rest of chapter 8. What little correspondence there is between them is found at the text corresponding to MT:8:15, 16 where the AT and LXX are again almost identical. This is the same pattern observed in chapter 5/D, where a few verses following addition D appear not to be an independent translation of the Hebrew but were copied with the addition from one Greek text to the other.

After E:20 (AT:7:30) the versions show very little agreement, not only through the end of chapter 8, but through the rest of the book up to addition F. Chapter 8 (excluding addition E) has the lowest percent of agreement between the AT and LXX (10% semantic; 7% formal) because there is so little material common to both. An examination of the distribution of the common material shows that it is all located at the end of the chapter, after addition E. There is no material common to the AT and LXX in the first 12 verses of chapter 8 (AT:7:15–21 // LXX:8:1–12). When only the concluding verses of addition E and the end of chapter 8 are examined, there is 39% semantic agreement and 29% formal. The low percentage of agreement between the AT and LXX following addition E does not support the idea that the Greek versions are dependent on one another here. Yet, there is relatively high agreement between the few units they do have in common (see Graphs 6a and b). The average semantic agreement of chapters 8–10 is 89%; the average formal agreement is 64%.

This evidence can be explained if both versions originally translated a similar *Vorlage*, but then these chapters in each version were substantially and independently changed when addition E was introduced to each. A more detailed discussion of this hypothesis explaining how this possibly may have occurred is presented in the conclusion to this work.

Addition C —The Prayers of Mordecai and Esther

The prayers of Mordecai and Esther in addition C introduce into the Esther story the strongest religious element of the Greek additions. The addition of prayers to the story adds an element not found in the MT, that the fast of Mordecai and Esther was accompanied by a direct plea to God for deliverance. The prayers of Mordecai and Esther in addition C express interest in the covenant by alluding to God's previous acts of deliverance and by specifically mentioning Abraham, the temple, the Jews as God's inheritance, the exodus and the sign of the covenant, circumcision. These references make explicit what the MT only perhaps hints, that the Jews in the Persian Diaspora are still God's covenant people. The *Tendenz* of addition C seems to address the question, Are the Jews in the Diaspora still in covenant with God?

Abraham, the patriarch with whom God's covenant was first made, is mentioned in addition C in both the AT and LXX. Only the AT text explicitly mentions Abraham as covenant head. The AT distinctively refers to God as κύριε, ὁ διαθέμενος πρὸς Αβρααμ ("Lord, who made a covenant with Abraham," 4:16e), where the LXX reads simply, ὁ θεὸς Αβρααμ ("the God of Abraham," C:8e). The title ὁ διαθέμενος is unique to the AT and does not occur elsewhere in the Greek versions of the Hebrew Bible.

After the temple in Jerusalem was rebuilt, the covenantal status of Jews who remained outside the land was a point of debate. Concern and reverence for the temple is expressed in addition C, in both the AT and the LXX, when Esther prays that the enemy might not σβέσαι δόξαν οἴκου σου καὶ θυσιαστηρίου σου ("extinguish the glory of your house and your altar," AT:4:22j,k). If the term "Bougaion" is an allusion to the Persian general who assassinated Artaxerxes III and who, according to Josephus, polluted the temple and taxed the daily sacrifice, this concern for the temple and altar may be from the same redactional activity which introduced that term.

In both the AT and LXX addition C shows concern that the Jews not be destroyed because they are God's inheritance, another theme closely related to the covenant. Mordecai tells God that their enemies are about to destroy and remove "the inheritance that has been yours from the beginning. Do not neglect your portion which you redeemed out of the land of Egypt" (AT:4:16). Mordecai's reference to the exodus is present in both the AT and LXX. Addition C echoes the prayer of Moses in the Greek of Deut 9:26, 27 which begins with the unusual invocation found neither in the MT nor elsewhere in the Greek OT, κύριε κύριε βασιλεῦ τῶν θεῶν ("Lord, Lord, king of the gods"). The prayer of Mordecai in the LXX text of addition C (but not in the AT) also begins κύριε κύριε but continues βασιλεῦ πάντων κρατῶν ("king of all powers," LXX:C:2b). In Deut 9:27, Moses asks God to be merciful because of His covenant with Abraham, Isaac and Jacob.

Similarly, Mordecai bases his plea for God's help on the covenant with Abraham (AT:4:16e).

Esther's prayer also echoes the Greek prayer of Moses in Deut 9:26. The peculiar vocative, βασιλεῦ τῶν θεῶν, found in Moses' prayer, occurs in only one other place in the Greek OT, here in addition C where Esther addresses God (in the LXX but not in the AT) as βασιλεῦ τῶν θεῶν ("king of the gods," C:23h).

In the AT, Esther asks God to deliver them ἐν τῇ χειρί σου τῇ κραταιᾷ ("by your mighty hand," AT:4:25k, l), echoing another phrase from the Greek of Deut 9:26. The expression ἐν τῇ χειρί σου τῇ κραταιᾷ and variants of it occur repeatedly in the Greek versions of Exodus (3:19, 6:1, 13:3, 9, 14,16) and Deuteronomy (3:24, 4:34, 5:15, 6:21, 7:8, 19, 9:26, 11:2, 26:8, 34:12). It is a stereotyped phrase used to refer to God's mighty power in history that delivered Israel out of Egypt.

This phrase appears in the post–exilic books in the LXX of 2 Chron 6:32 and in Ezek 20:33, 34. In both books these occurrences are in the context of Jerusalem as the place to which God gathers "by His mighty hand" both gentiles (the 2 Chronicles passage) and the dispersed Jews (the Ezekiel passage). The author of addition C seems to be using Esther's prayer to bring Jerusalem to mind, perhaps to support a call for the dispersed Jews to return to, or at least pray for, the holy city.

The phrase ἐν τῇ χειρί σου τῇ κραταιᾷ is also found in the Theodotionic recension of Daniel's prayer in Dan 9:15 (but not in the OG version), where Daniel's plea is quite similar to that of Esther in addition C.

The deliberate use of the exodus motif by the author of addition C is further evidenced by the phrase describing the situation of the Jews as ἐν πικρασμῷ δουλείας ("in bitter slavery," AT:4:21c). These words in Esther's prayer define a closer parallel between the Jews in 5th century Persia and their ancestors in Pharaoh's Egypt long before, redrawing the line of covenant continuity.

The echoes of Moses' prayer from the LXX Deut 9:26,27 in addition C cast Mordecai and Esther as intercessors for Israel. After the pattern of Moses, they invoke the Abrahamic covenant and the exodus from Egypt as historical precedents justifying their plea for deliverance. The deliverance which follows this prayer implies that the

Jews in the Diaspora were still under God's covenant mercies, a concept only ambiguously implied by the MT.

The sign of the covenant, circumcision, is also a distinctive interest of the AT in addition C. The AT of addition C exhibits this distinctive concern with circumcision by identifying Haman as "uncircumcised." In his prayer Mordecai explains to God that it was in obedience to the first commandment and not from hubris or self–seeking that he refused to bow to the "uncircumcised" Haman (τὸν ἀπερίτμητον Αμαν, 4:15g). (Mordecai's words bring to mind David's indignation with Goliath in 1 Sam 17:26, "Who is this uncircumcised Philistine, that he should taunt the armies of the living God?") Where the AT reads "uncircumcised" the LXX reads "haughty Haman" (τὸν ὑπερήφανον Αμαν). In both the LXX and AT of addition C, Esther reminds God that He knows how she loathes "the bed of the uncircumcised" (βδελύσσομαι κοίτην ἀπεριτμήτου, AT:4:25t), apparently a reference to her marriage to a pagan king. (Compare this sentiment to the relatively contemporaneous text of Ezra 10, which expresses strong opposition to Jews marrying foreigners.)

The concern for circumcision appears first in the Greek Esther in addition C but reappears in chapter 8 after the royal decree (addition E) announces the Jews' deliverance. The AT reads "and many of the Jews were circumcised" (AT:7:41a–c) where the LXX has "many of the gentiles were circumcised" (LXX:8:17h–j). The AT reading appears strange because it is usually assumed that Jews would already have been circumcised. However, if the continuity of the covenant to the Jews in the Diaspora was in question, circumcision, the sign of the covenant, may not have been regularly practiced by the Jews, especially during the Hellenistic period. In addition C, Mordecai and Esther appeal to God for deliverance on the basis of the covenant. Addition E, the royal decree, announces deliverance and was evidence that God was extending covenantal protection to the Jews outside the land. Therefore the practice of circumcision, the sign of the covenant, could be resumed in full faith after God demonstrated that He was restoring covenant blessing and "many Jews were circumcised."

Insofar as MT Esther lacks any reference to God or to the religious symbols of Israel, it leaves the events of the Esther story at the periphery of biblical history and theology. The overall effect of addition C, with its interest in the covenant, the temple and altar, and circumcision and with its literary allusions to the prayer of Moses and the exodus, draws the Esther story from the periphery into the mainstream of the tradition of the Pentateuch. This addition exonerates Mordecai and Esther of the religious and moral ambiguity in which the MT leaves them and shows them worthy of veneration. The question of the continuity of God's covenant with the post–exilic Jews of the Diaspora is answered explicitly and affirmatively by the author of addition C by reference to the symbols of the covenant. This would have been a comfort and encouragement to those Jews who remained outside the land during the Second Temple period.

The Semitic style of the prayers of addition C may have been influenced by the style of the Greek that translated the Pentateuch or it may be evidence of a Semitic *Vorlage*. Although this study finds the results of syntax criticism of addition C inconclusive (see chapter 1), Moore and Martin have found the syntactic evidence sufficient to conclude that these prayers are translations of a Semitic source. Torrey argues more specifically for an Aramaic source for addition C because the AT reading ἐν πειρασμῷ (AT:4:15v) and the parallel LXX reading ἐν ὑπερηφανίᾳ (LXX:C:7l) are both legitimate translations of the two different senses of the Aramaic phrase *b'ithnassa'ah* (Torrey 1944, 8).

In support of a Semitic source, the phrase καὶ νῦν occurs three times in addition C: AT:4:16a (LXX:C:8a), AT:4:22b (LXX:C:17a) and AT:4:29a (LXX omits). This phrase occurs ubiquitously throughout the Greek translation of other Hebrew books, translating, for instance, ועתה (Gen 12:19) and אתם (Ex 19:4). Of particular relevance to the historical period of the original language of Esther, P. Alexander notes that καὶ νῦν translates וכענת, וכען and וכעת, common transition markers in Aramaic (but also in Hebrew) epistolary literature of the Persian period (Alexander 1984, 594). Since the prayers of Mordecai and Esther are not epistolary literature, Alexander's observation may not apply. Furthermore, the expression καὶ νῦν also occurs in additions B:7 and E:23, which are clearly composition Greek (not to mention the phrase occurs twenty–six times in the NT, which is also composition Greek). Although the occurrence of καὶ νῦν in addition C is not clear evidence of a Semitic source, it occurs in the Greek Esther *only* in additions B, C and E. (Recall that additions B and E were without doubt composed in Greek.)

The phrase καὶ νῦν is not the only lexical element that addition C has in common with B and E. Addition C shares other distinctive vocabulary with one or both of these additions exclusively. The vocative title παντοκράτωρ is used to refer to God only in additions C and E, and only in the AT (4:13a, 7:30k). God is referred to as ἀληθινοῦ (the only true God) only in additions C and E, and only in the AT (4:15s, 7:27m). The phrase ἐν καιρῷ θλίψεως ("in the time of affliction") occurs only in additions C and E in both the AT and LXX texts (AT:4:24f, 7:29i). The word ἐξουσία appears only in additions B, C and E at AT:3:15f, 4:13d and 7:23y, respectively, referring to ultimate political authority. This shared vocabulary associates additions C and E, even though they are of different genres and are written in very different styles.

Furthermore, addition E recognizes a shared role of Mordecai and Esther, a concept that is also present in the form and content of addition C. Addition E refers specifically to "Mordecai our perpetual savior and of Esther his blameless partner" (AT:7:26). Although addition C does not refer to Mordecai and Esther as partners, the concept of their partnership is reflected in the form and content of addition C. The author/redactor of addition C did not include only Mordecai's prayer or only Esther's prayer, but presents an intercessory partnership of Mordecai and Esther. Together their two prayers share elements from the one prayer of Moses in the Greek of Deut 9:26,27. Furthermore, the deliverance which gave Mordecai and Esther their place in history occurred through the cooperating circumstances of them both.

The lexical and conceptual features common to additions C and E suggest that the royal decree of addition E announcing the deliverance answers to the prayers for deliverance of Mordecai and Esther in addition C. Whether or not addition C was translated from a Semitic source, it appears as if addition E was composed to echo the Greek text of addition C. This evidence indicates that either *the Greek* of addition C was present in the Greek version(s) prior to the composition of addition E, or that additions C and E, both in Greek, were added to the Greek version of Esther at the same time. This internal evidence suggests that addition C logically preceded addition E, but it does not rule out the possibility that both entered the Greek text at the same time (along with addition B).

Unlike the similarity of syntax, style and vocabulary common to additions B and E, which compels the conclusion of a common author, there is not enough textual similarity between C and E to prove that the same author wrote both. The Semitic tone and simple style of addition C contrasts sharply with the sophisticated Greek vocabulary, syntax and clause structure of additions B and E. If both C and E came from the same author, he deliberately wrote in a style he believed to be appropriate to the genre of each addition.

The logical priority of C over E is consistent with the chronological relationship concluded by other recent studies. Based on a literary analysis of the Greek versions of Esther, C. Dorothy concludes that addition C (and D) preceded addition E. In his redactional history of the text, the addition of C and D were the first stage in the growth of the text, making the Esther story more religious. Because both have religious elements, he believes additions C and D were added at the same time but earlier than additions B and E (Dorothy 1989, 409). Although this study agrees with the priority of C over E, it has found no lexical or syntactic evidence that would associate additions C and D to the same redactional strata.

Dorothy finds motivation for the inclusion of additions B and E in the practice of Hellenistic historiography, which typically added official documents and correspondence to historical narrative (ibid., 409). He explains that the inclusion of additions B and E was intended to give the Esther story historical verisimilitude. The prayer–answer correspondence between C and E suggested by this study does not contradict Dorothy's reconstruction of the redaction of the text. The concerns of Hellenistic historiography may have motivated the genre of addition E, but the prayers of Mordecai and Esther in addition C motivated its content.

K. Wynn, who attempts to identify the socio–historical circumstances of the redaction of the additions, sees in the religious elements of additions C and D "an attempt to resolve the differences between the pious concerns of the Pharisees and the nationalistic concerns of ... the Hasmonean ruler" (Wynn 1990, 217–18). Accordingly, he dates the inclusion of both C and D to the century following the Maccabean revolt. His reconstruction of the history of the text also places the introduction of C and D into the text of Esther prior to additions B and E.

Additions C and D have been associated in the redactional history of the text because they both contain explicit references to God and because they each have parallels to the book of Judith. Moore finds the nature of the parallels and the tenor of additions C and D to be compatible with the socio–historical setting of the 2nd century B.C. (Moore 1977, 166).[6] Although this study has found textual traits shared by additions B and E and by C and E, a similar study of addition D shows it has no distinctive vocabulary or syntax in common with any other addition. Furthermore, the overall agreement of the texts of B, C and E in the AT to the LXX is similar: 68%, 62% and 60% respectively. The agreement between the text of addition D in the AT and LXX is a much higher 76%, which distinguishes it from B, C and E. This extent of agreement is further evidence that the origin and history of addition D is separate from that of B, C and E.

If the similarities between additions C and E are deliberate, as this study suggests, the AT of addition C preserves more of the original readings than does the LXX text of addition C. This shows that the AT preserves the earlier form of addition C, just as it does for additions B and E.

Additions A and F — Mordecai's Dream

Addition A, Mordecai's dream and his discovery of an assassination plot, and addition F, the interpretation of the dream, were introduced at the beginning and end, respectively, of the Greek Esther. By positioning the dream and its interpretation as a frame around the story, the redactor of these additions intends the events in the Persian court to be viewed as a fulfillment of Mordecai's dream. It is difficult to imagine they were not added to the Esther text at the same time. From a literary perspective, C. Dorothy observes that additions A and F make little or no sense without each other and certainly "function together at the final level of the text" (Dorothy 1989, 315).

Given the brevity of the dream and the inanimate nature of its images, it is, in my opinion, unlikely that originally it was a Semitic text that circulated independently of the Esther story, as Moore has suggested (Moore 1977, 249). He suggests this because he sees the

---

[6] See also S. Zeitlin (1972).

dream as not fitting the Esther story very well. For instance, he finds it inappropriate that Mordecai should be symbolized in the dream by a dragon. He also observes differences between the LXX and AT in the way the images of the dream are interpreted in addition F. These observations may have an explanation, as discussed below. In any case, if the dream is as inappropriate as Moore suggests, it is difficult to explain why a redactor would find it a fitting frame for the story.

Additions A and F are not integrated at all into the text of the Esther story. Each stands apart from the intervening chapters. Neither the dream nor its interpretation is referred to within the story. This suggests that A and F may comprise the last redactional strata of the Greek Esther story.

When addition A was added to the AT, chapter 2 was apparently edited somewhat to eliminate material that would otherwise be redundant. The reference to the exile of the Jews by Nebuchadnezzar king of Babylon which is made in chapter 2 of the MT (and LXX) when Mordecai is introduced has been relocated to addition A where Mordecai is first introduced in the AT. The LXX of Esther redundantly preserves the reference at both places. This may indicate that addition A was more carefully redacted into the AT but simply copied into the LXX.

The position of the dream and its interpretation as a frame around the Esther story indicate its function. Consider that the dream could have been inserted within the story, for instance, in chapter 2 where Mordecai is introduced in the MT. In that position, it would have been subordinated to the story line as just another part of the story. The prominent position of the dream as a prologue and its interpretation as an epilogue subordinates the intervening story to a new context defined by the dream.

The positioning of Mordecai's dream and its interpretation as a frame around the story achieves two literary effects. Firstly, additions A and F make Mordecai the unambiguous hero of the story. In the MT, the roles of Mordecai and Esther in the deliverance of the Jews are mutually dependent to the extent that it is difficult to decide which, if either, is to be considered the main character of the story (although the title of the book is notably "Esther" and not "Mordecai").[7] In the MT, Mordecai and Esther are introduced at the same time in 2:5 and 2:7, respectively. In the Greek text, both the king and Haman are introduced with Mordecai in addition A, but there is no mention of Esther. By delaying her entry into the story, her role is diminished and subjugated to Mordecai's.

With the addition of A in the Greek version, Mordecai is not only identified unambiguously as the hero of the story but he also stands in the tradition of Israel's great prophetic dreamers such as Joseph and Daniel. The parallels between Joseph in the court of Pharaoh and Mordecai in the court of Ahasuerus have long been recognized (Rosenthal 1895, 1896, 1897; Ehrlich 1955; Gan 1961; Meinhold 1975, 1976). Both Joseph and Mordecai were faithful to the LORD while living outside of the promised land in high positions in a pagan government. Each received revelatory dreams about future events that would shape the history of their nation. In the MT, Mordecai's spiritual character is ambiguous at best; in the Greek text, he is shown to be the recipient of divine revelation.

The second effect achieved by framing the Esther story with the dream and its interpretation is to show that the events which transpired in the Persian court were not a happenstance of history but were divinely orchestrated and prophetically foretold. The MT is completely silent about God's role in the events of the story. The Greek text specifies the deliverance as God's response to the cries of His people, but addition A presents a premonition of the events before they transpired, reminiscent of a prophetic prediction.

The imagery of Mordecai's dream is apocalyptic. He dreams of thunders, earthquake, darkness and tumult, and dragons, imagery that is distinctively apocalyptic. The dream is comprised of three scenes, each marked by καὶ ἰδού (the AT has only two of the three occurrences of this phrase, AT:A:3d, A:4a):

    (1) noise, thunders and tumult on earth,
    (2) two dragons prepared to fight,

---

[7] An informal poll of a Hebrew language class reading Esther resulted in thirteen students identifying Esther as the main character, six choosing Mordecai and eight undecided.

(3) a day of darkness and affliction, the cry of the people and the little fountain.

These three scenes are comprised of nouns but virtually no verbs of action. That is, the images are stated but remain inanimate. For instance consider, A:4a, καὶ ἰδοὺ δύο δράκοντες ("and behold, two dragons!"). Although the dragons are described as coming out to fight, in the dream they do not actually fight, nor do they devour anything, etc. This inanimate imagery can be compared to Rev 12, where the dragon acts, sweeping away stars and throwing them to earth. In A:7 the fountain is merely described: καὶ ἐγένετο ἐκ πηγῆς μικρᾶς ὕδωρ πολύ, ποταμὸς μέγας ("and it happened from a little fountain much water, a great river").

The inanimate character of the images is a clue to their function. Because they do not act, the images of the dream do not function to extend the action of the story into the heavenly realm. They do not provide clues that become significant as the story unfolds or from which the outcome of the story can be predicted because the story does not allude to dragons, fountains or water. The function of this inanimate imagery appears to be purely associative, invoking connotations which remain unstated. Addition F "interprets" the dream merely by equating characters of the story with the images; the dragons are Haman and Mordecai, the fountain is Esther. But because the images are inanimate, their identification with the characters of the story gives no additional insight into the story, does not assist in character development nor does it enhance the sense of narrative closure. I propose that this inanimate imagery functions not to extend or explain the story, but to associate the political events of the Persian court with some larger context triggered by the imagery.

The images in the dream of Mordecai echo images from earlier biblical texts to draw the Esther story more explicitly into the broader context of the redemptive history of Israel. The way the dream's imagery is simply pronounced, without involving any action, suggests that it was meant only to trigger a context previously defined by that same imagery within which the Esther story should be read. In fact, the imagery of the dream in additions A and F echoes imagery found in the Greek text of Jeremiah, especially the prophecy against Babylon in chapter 28 (MT ch. 51).

Jeremiah was the prophetic voice that heralded God's judgment of His people through the destruction of Jerusalem by Nebuchadnezzar. He was also the prophet who pronounced judgment on Nebuchadnezzar for this same act. Jeremiah lived in the land of Benjamin and it was in Benjamin that he purchased a field as a prophetic sign of the restoration of Israel. His prophecy against Babylon is found in LXX Jer 28 and includes many of the same images found in additions A and F of the Greek Esther.

The MT of Esther introduces Mordecai in 2:5,6 as a Jew of the tribe of Benjamin who had been taken into exile from Jerusalem with Jeconiah king of Judah by Nebuchadnezzar. If Mordecai had personally been taken from Jerusalem by Nebuchadnezzar he would have been over 100 years old as the Esther story opens. Various arguments have been made in the commentaries to explain this difficulty, all assuming that the statement was intended to be biographical.

This reference to Mordecai, Nebuchadnezzar and the exile is relocated in the Greek Esther to addition A where it introduces Mordecai as the recipient of a revelatory dream. In this context, I propose the statement is not intended to describe Mordecai's personal biography but to position him in the prophetic continuum. In this context Nebuchadnezzar and Mordecai are symbols that define a *prophetic* continuity linking the events of the Persian court to the pronouncements of Jeremiah. Nebuchadnezzar symbolizes the complex of historical events set in motion with his destruction of Jerusalem and the exile to Babylon, events that inexorably led to Mordecai's life in Susa. These historical events were interpreted by the prophets to be God's judgment on the sin of His people. Consequently, "Nebu-chadnezzar" is not only the name of a Babylonian king, it is a symbol of divine judgment. In a similar way, Mordecai set in motion a chain of events that led not only to the deliverance of the Persian Jews from annihilation but to their rise to the upper echelon of a political hierarchy that had previously subjugated them. His name symbolizes the Jews' ultimate survival in exile and their eventual restoration to blessing, as was also predicted by Jeremiah.

For his part in the destruction of Jerusalem, Nebuchadnezzar is named in the prophecies of Babylon's downfall but he did not personally suffer the subsequent Persian conquest by Cyrus. Similarly, Mordecai did not personally experience the exile but is a symbol of the subsequent reversal of the Jews fortune predicted by Jeremiah at the time of the exile. The juxtaposition of Nebuchadnezzar and Mordecai as symbols invoking the memory of the judgment–restoration prophecy forms a literary nexus within which the reader is invited to see God's sovereign purposes being worked out in history through, but beyond, the personal lifetimes of these historical figures.

The recollection of Jeremiah's prophecy against Babylon in Mordecai's dream is metaleptic. The dream does not quote Jeremiah nor even overtly allude to it but subtly echoes it. R. Hays explains the function and literary effect of metalepsis, or allusive echo:

> When a literary echo links the text in which it occurs to an earlier text, the figurative effect of the echo can lie in the unstated or suppressed (transumed) points of resonance between the two texts ... Allusive echo functions to suggest to the reader that text B should be understood in light of a broad interplay with text A, encompassing aspects of A beyond those explicitly echoed ... Metalepsis ... places the reader within a field of whispered or unstated correspondences (Hays 1989, 20).

The text of Mordecai's dream and its interpretation whispers echoes of Jeremiah's prophecy and invites the reader to understand the events that unfold in the Persian court within a matrix of unstated correspondences between Jeremiah's predictions and the political circumstances within which the Jews of Persia find themselves.

The echoes of Jeremiah's prophecy are expressed by nine images that are present both in Mordecai's dream and/or its interpretation and that are also present in chapter 28 of LXX Jeremiah: φωνὴ κραυγὴ (28:54), δρακῶν (28:34), σκότος (28:34), πόλεμος (28:20), πηγῆ (28:36) φῶς (28:16), κατέπιον (28:34,44), and κρίμα (28:9,10). (Other elements of additions A and F are found in other places in LXX Jeremiah: ταραχή, σεισμός, κλῆρος, ποταμός, and ὕδωρ.) Mordecai's dream seems to resonate most strongly with the prophecy against Nebuchadnezzar as expressed in verse 36 of LXX Jer 28:

> He [Nebuchadnezzar] has *devoured* me, ... Nebuchadnezzar king of Babylon has *swallowed me up*, like a *dragon* he has filled his stomach with my delicacies ... Therefore thus says the Lord, "Behold, I will

judge your adversary and I will work your vengeance; I will make her
sea desolate and I will dry up her *fountain*."

In Jeremiah's prophecy against Nebuchadnezzar, the dragon is the
Babylonian king. In Mordecai's dream, both Mordecai and Haman are
dragons. In scripture, dragons/serpents are usually the personification
of evil. Nowhere else in scripture is a hero of Israel symbolized as a
δρακών. This peculiar application of the dragon image to a hero of
Israel indicates that the image is not being used generically. The
application to Mordecai is answering to a call found only in the Greek
of Jeremiah for God's people in Babylon to become as dragons
(γένεσθε ὥσπερ δράκοντες, Jer 27:8). This call is absent from the
corresponding Hebrew (MT Jer 50:8) and shows that the author of
additions A and F was using either the Greek scripture (not the MT) or
a Hebrew *Vorlage* of Jeremiah that is no longer extant.

This peculiar application of the dragon image to Mordecai
symbolizes the reversal of fortune predicted by Jeremiah. The dragon
Nebuchadnezzar swallows up God's people in LXX Jer 28, but in the
Greek Esther God's people achieve commensurate power when
Mordecai becomes a dragon and the lowly are exalted and "swallow
up" (same verb as Jer 28) the exalted (AT:A:8).

In LXX Jer 28, the fountain is the symbol of Babylon's power,
that Jeremiah predicts God will dry up. In Mordecai's dream, Esther is
the fountain which gushes forth, symbolizing power given to the Jews
through Esther's reign as queen of Persia. Therefore, the dragon image
and the fountain image, though dissimilar to each other, both refer to
political power.

Although Mordecai's dream echoes the same images found in
Jeremiah's prophecy, the referents of the symbols are different because
the positions of Babylon and the Jews have been reversed between the
time of Jeremiah and Mordecai. This reversal of the referents of the
images is consistent with the major theme and the literary structure of
the book of Esther, which is the reversal of the fortune of the Jews.

The reversal of fortune from judgment to blessing is expressed
throughout scripture as the emergence from darkness to light. The light
of the rising sun in Mordecai's dream (AT:A:8c) is the reversal of the
image of the setting sun found in Jeremiah as the Jews entered the
darkness of exile. Jeremiah describes the disaster looming over

Jerusalem as her sun going "down in the middle of the day" (LXX Jer:15:9). In Mordecai's dream the darkness was fleeing the light of the rising sun (AT:A:8c). By using this imagery the author of additions A and F of the Greek Esther is casting the events of the Esther story as an instance of God reversing the fortunes of the Jews, a sign that the long night of God's judgment was passing as Jeremiah had predicted. This interest in showing that the protection of the Jews in Persia fulfilled Jeremiah's prophecy is consistent with the related interest in the continuity of the covenant found in addition C.

Given that additions A and F employ metalepsis to stir the memory of the Greek Jeremiah, the differences between additions A and F in the AT and the LXX can be examined to see if one or the other better preserves this literary device. The dream in Addition A is almost identical in both the AT and the LXX. As was observed in the canonical portions of the text, the AT often lacks occurrences of the adjective μέγας found in the LXX text (AT:A:4c, A:5:b, A:7e). The presence of this feature in both addition A and the canonical portions of the AT suggests that it was either removed from the AT or added to the LXX throughout the entire book during one redaction after addition A was copied from one Greek text to the other.

There is a striking similarity of the dragon imagery of Mordecai's dream with Rev 12:17, found only in the LXX text of addition A. Compare the imagery of Mordecai's dream in the LXX to Rev 12:17:

> LXX:A:5: δύο δράκοντες ... προῆλθον ἀμφότεροι παλαίειν ... ἡτοιμάσθη πᾶν ἔθνος εἰς πόλεμον ὥστε πολεμῆσαι δικαίων ἔθνος
>
> ("two dragons ... came out ready to fight ... every nation was prepared for war to fight against the righteous nation")

> Rev 12:17: ὁ δράκων ... ἀπῆλθεν ποιῆσαι πόλεμον μετὰ τῶν λοιπῶν τοῦ σπέρματος αὐτῆς τῶν τηρούντων τὰς ἐντολὰς
>
> ("the dragon ... came out to make war with the rest of her seed who keep the commandments")

At this place the AT reads only that "everything was troubled by the sound of this cry [of the dragons]" (AT:A:5f–h). The parallel with Rev 12:12 suggests the possibility that the LXX reading was a later Christian interpolation.

In support of a redaction of addition A during the Christian era, the equivalence between the Macedonian month and Adar–Nisan found at AT:A:1g (but lacking in the LXX) was valid only from A.D. 15/16 – 176. (See a fuller discussion of this in the conclusion to this work.) Although the clause is likely a gloss inserted after the original introduction of addition A into the AT, it does prove that some changes were made to this text in the first century A.D., making a Christian redaction possible.

Even though addition A is often referred to as Mordecai's Apocalypse, it is debatable whether the genre of Mordecai's dream should be identified technically as an apocalypse. If, however, the form of the dream is compared to the four sub–genres of apocalypse identified by J.J. Collins, it seems to be most similar to his Type Ib apocalypses with cosmic and/or poltical eschatology that have neither historical review nor other–worldly journey (Collins 1979). Collins names other texts of this form including the NT book of Revelation, the Apocalypse of Peter, Shepherd of Hermas, and the Gospel of Mary. Of Type Ib apocalypses Collins writes, "No Jewish or Greco–Roman apocalypse conforms to this type" (ibid., 14). Although discussions of Mordecai's dream have always seemed to assume a Jewish origin, the intriguing idea that its extant form may have come from a Christian redaction deserves further thought.

Addition A in both the AT and the LXX contains the assassination plot against the king that Mordecai foiled. However only the AT links the interpretation of Mordecai's dream to this event (AT:A:11). This has led some to construe erroneously the two conspiring eunuchs as the two dragons of the dream in some sort of initial fulfillment of the dream. But Haman is also introduced in addition A as an enemy of Mordecai because he foiled the assassination plot (implying that Haman at least favored the plot). Thus both dragons, Mordecai and Haman are introduced in addition A along with the point of contention between them, which in the Greek Esther is political intrigue not personal conflict. Note that the implication of Haman as favoring the assassination of the king comports with his characterization as a "Bougaion" as mentioned above and discussed in chapter 3. This suggests a redactional association between addition A (at least verses AT:A:16-18) and addition E.

The interpretation of the dream in addition F is quite different in the AT than in the LXX. The dragons in both the AT and LXX are identified as Haman and Mordecai. However, in the AT, Esther is identified as the little fountain and the river as the nations gathered together to destroy the Jews. In the LXX text Esther is the little fountain which becomes a river.

If the author of F intended this dream to echo LXX Jeremiah, the AT is preserving the river imagery as found there, where the nations are symbolized as rivers (e.g., LXX Jer 2:18, 26:7). This suggests that the AT addition F is the earlier form of the interpretation of the dream and that the LXX was changed to conform to other interests after F was copied from one Greek text to the other.

This evidence corroborates the conclusion reached by C. Dorothy that the AT preserves the older form of both additions A and F. He argues on literary grounds that it is harder to imagine the LXX text of the A–F unit being rewritten as the AT version than *vice versa* (Dorothy 1989, 344).

Another significant difference between the AT and LXX in addition F is that the AT of addition F answers specifically to Esther's prayer in addition C. In the AT, but not in the LXX, Esther prays ἐπιφάνηθι ἡμῖν, κύριε, καὶ γνώσθητι ἡμῖν ἐν καιρῷ θλίψεως ἡμᾶς ("Manifest yourself to us, O Lord, and reveal yourself in this time of our affliction," AT:4:24a–f). Addition F in the AT, but not in the LXX, answers this prayer: ἥλιος καὶ φῶς ἣ ἐγένετο τοῖς Ἰουδαίοις ἐπιφανεία τοῦ θεοῦ ("The sun and light which came to the Jews are a manifestation of God," AT:7:54u–w). Given that "sun" and "light" symbolize the restoration of the Jews to God's covenant blessing, the deliverance of the Jews in Persia is being construed as God manifesting Himself once again in their history.

This internal coherence between additions C and F in the AT could be argued as an editor's later work were it not that this imagery of the sun is found also in LXX Jer 15:9 and is part of the complex of prophetic promise invoked by metalepsis. If additions A and F are echoing Jeremiah, as argued, then the light of the rising sun shows that God's judgment on His people is passing, that He is once more hearing their cries and revealing Himself in history on their behalf. This was Esther's plea in addition C, showing a coherence between additions A, C and F. Noting the coherence previously found in the AT addition C with addition E and B, the possibility arises that these texts, so diverse in genre and style, were nevertheless introduced into the Greek Esther at the same time. In any case, there is mounting evidence that the AT preserves the older form of at least five of the six additions (A, B, C, E, F).

SUMMARY

This study has found certain affinities between the additions, not all of which work together consistently. Lexical evidence suggests an association of additions B, C and E. Additions A and F clearly function together and were almost certainly added to the text at the same time and possibly last. There is also an association in content between C and F (the manifestation of God) and between A and E (Haman as would–be assassin). This suggests that A, B, C, E and F either have a common origin (despite their salient difference) or at least were unified by a subsequent redactor. The prominence of Mordecai over Esther achieved by additions A and F does not comport easily with the more shared role of Esther and Mordecai in additions C and E. Addition D was found to have no affinity with any of the other additions.

CONCLUSIONS

• Although the AT and MT sometimes agree against the LXX, the AT and LXX virtually never agree against the MT outside of the additions.
• The AT was not originally produced as a recension of the LXX (or *vice versa*), but is an independent translation of a Semitic *Vorlage* quite similar to that of the LXX where they have text in common.
• There is insufficient agreement between the AT and LXX in chapters 8–10 to support a literary dependence of the two. Both seem to have been redacted extensively and independently when addition E was introduced into each.
• There is evidence that the author of 2 Maccabees alluded to the Esther tradition as it is distinctively preserved in addition D of the AT.
• The AT preserves the older form of additions A, B, C, E and F.

• Addition C shows influence from the LXX of Deut 9:26, Moses' intercessory prayer.

• Addition C shows sufficient common vocabulary with addition E to indicate that addition E was composed to answer to the prayers of Mordecai and Esther.

• The *Greek* addition C logically precedes E and was either already in the text at the time addition E was composed, or was inserted at the same time.

• The characterization of Haman as a "Bougaion" in addition A and E paints him as an assassin and associates A and E to the same redactional strata, sometime after 338 B.C.

• The imagery of additions A and F echo the prophecy against Babylon in LXX Jer 28 and frames the events of the Esther story as a fulfillment of Jeremiah's promise of restored covenant blessing.

• The peculiar use of the dragon image in additions A and F indicates that its author was using either the Greek version of Jeremiah (not the MT) or a Hebrew *Vorlage* of Jeremiah no longer extant.

CHAPTER 5: HOW DOES THIS STUDY COMPARE TO WORK PREVIOUSLY DONE?

The AT of Esther has enjoyed considerable attention since 1965, when C. A. Moore persuasively argued that it was not a Lucianic recension of the LXX but might be an independent translation of a Semitic source.[1] This chapter evaluates work on the AT published by E. Tov (1982), D. J. A. Clines (1984) and M. V. Fox (1991) in light of the findings of this study.

E. TOV: "THE 'LUCIANIC' TEXT OF THE CANONICAL AND THE APOCRYPHAL SECTIONS OF ESTHER: A REWRITTEN BIBLICAL BOOK," 1982

E. Tov challenged the idea that the AT is an independent translation. He argued that it is a revision of the LXX corrected toward a Hebrew midrash of Esther, a Hebrew text different from the MT. His hypothesis is based on the following points:

---

[1] No work approaching the extent of Moore's had previously been done on the AT, although the text has been known at least since the 17th–century. Cardinal Bellarmin (c.1600) first suggested that the major additions in the Greek versions are translations of a lost Hebrew source (Bellarminus, *de verbo Dei* I, c.VII, 10). C. C. Torrey argued that the MT, the two Greek versions and the version of Esther found in Josephus each represented a different Aramaic source (Torrey 1944). E. J. Bickerman rejected the Lucianic origin of the AT but still considered it a recension of the LXX text (Bickerman 1950). –195–

(1) The AT (which Tov refers to as "L") depends upon the LXX text. This is clear from "important common renderings which could not have developed independently" (Tov 1982, 4).

(2) The AT reflects Hebrew readings that are different from the MT. This is evident from the "many (syntactic) Hebraisms in the short additions to MT" (ibid., 7).

(3) The translation of the canonical sections in the AT and the "so–called" additions are one organic unit; that is, the Hebrew (or Aramaic) text toward which the AT was corrected contained the additions and the references to the additions found in the canonical sections (ibid., 11).

(4) The AT was corrected toward a Hebrew (or Aramaic) midrashic rewriting of the Esther story, placing it within a religious setting. The author of this midrashic rewrite a) embellished the story as he saw fit, b) omitted details found in the MT, c) changed and revised whole sections (ibid., 17, 19, 21).

Tov's hypothesis that the production of the AT as it now stands involved both the LXX and a Hebrew text recognizes the puzzling character of the AT, which does have similarities to the LXX text but at the same time seems to reflect a Hebrew *Vorlage* that is both similar to and different from the MT. According to Tov's theory, the AT is similar to the LXX because it was originally produced as a revision of that text; where it reflects a Hebrew *Vorlage* it was corrected toward a midrashic text, which was a rewrite of the MT version.

Tov is undeniably correct that there are readings in the AT that are identical to the LXX and that do indicate a direct literary dependence of one Greek version upon the other at those places. However, these readings do not represent the overall relationship of the AT to the LXX when the texts in their entirety are compared. The readings in the AT that are identical to those in the LXX are greatly outnumbered by readings where such agreement would be expected, but is not found, if the AT were a revision. Specifically, where the LXX disagrees with the MT, one would expect the AT to follow the LXX if the AT were a recension of it. The AT and LXX agree against the MT in only three units. Contra Tov, this study and D. J. A. Clines cite examples where the dependence of the AT on the LXX is contra–indicated (this study, chapter 4; Clines 1984, 87–89). As discussed in chapter 4 of this work, in spite of some identical readings, the AT is overall too unlike the LXX to have been originally a revision of it. Although each reading must be judged on its own merit, this study concludes that such identical agreements between the AT and LXX are secondary impositions of one text upon the other occurring either during textual transmission or when the additions were copied from one Greek version to the other.

Furthermore, as discussed in chapter 1, the syntax of the AT shows it to be a translation of a Semitic source. Tov's hypothesis explains the translation character of the AT syntax as the result of its being corrected toward a Hebrew midrashic text. How would one distinguish translation characteristics inherited from the LXX from the influence of the correction toward a Semitic text? Would the translation character of the LXX's syntax more likely be preserved or attenuated in a subsequent revision? Intuitively it seems more likely that a revision of a translation would move it generally in the direction of composition Greek, obliterating the syntactical evidence of its Semitic *Vorlage*. On the other hand, if the purpose of that revision was to make it more faithful to a Semitic source, the resulting Greek syntax of the revision might be even more strongly Semitic than that of the original translation. It is a difficult question to decide without further study of the revision of texts that are known to be translations. (For a comparison of the syntactic profiles of Old Greek Daniel to Theodotion Daniel see Jobes 1995.)

This study has demonstrated in chapter 3 that there are readings within the AT that could only have arisen from a Hebrew *Vorlage*, not from a Greek parent text. However, those readings can be explained in reference to the extant MT, indicating that the Hebrew *Vorlage* of the AT was in those places virtually identical to the MT. Tov has identified several short pluses in the AT that are not found in the MT but which reflect Hebrew syntax.[2] At least two of these short pluses (in 6:17 and 7:2) reflect the concerns of addition C, and are likely associated with that redaction of the text. Tov's observation of Hebraisms in several of the short pluses may be further evidence that the AT was there translating a Hebrew (or Aramaic) *Vorlage*, however one which in those places differed from the MT. On the other hand, Tov gives

---

[2] These clauses are found in 3:5, 6:4, 6:5, 6:13, 6:17 and 7:2 (Tov 1982, 8–9)

examples, observed also in this study, that at times the AT has an even more literal rendering of the MT than the LXX (Tov 1982, 9). If the *Vorlage* of the AT was not the MT, it apparently had a close, if indirect, relationship to it.

However, it is not certain if the Hebraisms Tov observes actually reflect a Hebrew *Vorlage*. When Tov offered the same explanation for the pluses in the Greek text of 1 Samuel, J. Lust responded,

> The text value of so–called Hebraisms in the pluses of the Greek text should not be overestimated, however tempting this may be. Indeed, it is not always easy to make a sharp distinction between Hebraisms on the one hand and idioms proper to the style and language of the translator on the other. Moreover, when a translator added his own remarks, he often took his inspiration from the context, so that his own Greek could hardly be distinguished from his translation–Greek. (Lust in Barthélemy et al. 1986, 88)

Tov's observations are consistent with the conclusion of this study that, where the AT and MT have corresponding text, the *Vorlage* of the AT was quite like the MT. This, taken together with Tov's observation of Hebraisms in the short pluses, suggests that the AT reflects a Hebrew *Vorlage* quite similar to the MT but in which these short pluses also possibly stood. These pluses either were originally in the Hebrew and dropped out of the MT after the AT was produced, or the AT originally translated a text virtually identical to the MT and was later corrected toward a Hebrew version of Esther that included those pluses.

Tov argues that the major additions, with the exception of B and E, were in the Hebrew or Aramaic midrash toward which the AT was corrected. Based on syntax criticism published by Martin (1975) and Moore (1973), he accepts the hypothesis that additions A, C, D and F are translations of Semitic sources. As chapter 1 of this study has shown, syntax criticism shows unequivocally that additions B and E were originally composed in Greek; however, the syntactical character of additions A, C, D and F does not conclusively indicate a Semitic source. The original language of these additions is likely to remain uncertain unless additional manuscript evidence is unearthed.

If it could be known with greater certainty that additions A, C, D and F are translations of Hebrew or Aramaic, Tov's scenario that all four of these "additions" entered the AT from one source has the appeal of simplicity in its favor. For if these Semitic additions were not in the AT's *Vorlage* (and they are not in the MT, nor the targums), it becomes quite complicated to explain where they came from and when and why they entered the Esther story. Because the additions depend on the rest of the Esther story for their coherence, it seems unlikely that they circulated independently. Furthermore, when concatenated together, the additions do not comprise a coherent source in themselves. Therefore, a hypothesis that posits an independent existence for the additions must explain how each came into the text. Tov's idea that they all (except B and E) once existed in one midrashic Hebrew text of Esther is a simpler scenario that gains much appeal in light of the complexity of the alternatives.

Unfortunately, the arguments Tov gives in support of the additions being "one organic unit" with the canonical sections are not persuasive. He argues that the canonical sections of the AT and the so–called additions form "one organic unit" because the text of the canonical sections contain several references to the additions. He envisions these scattered references being added to the Hebrew text when the major additions (A, C, D and F) were inserted in the Hebrew text. However, it is equally plausible that such references were added within the Greek when the additions were introduced into the Greek text. The existence of such references alone does not strongly support Tov's conclusion.

If the scattered references to the additions consistently reflected Hebrew syntax, Tov's argument would be strengthened. Although Tov does not mention it, as noted above, two of the short Hebraisms he identifies (in 6:17 and 7:2) reflect the interests of addition C. Tov does cite one short addition in 1:1a,b, καὶ ἐγένετο μετὰ τοὺς λόγους τούτους, which forms the narrative transition from addition A to the canonical chapter 1. Tov argues that this short plus reflects Hebrew diction and therefore indicates a Semitic origin for this transition phrase and the preceding addition A. Granted this conclusion, Tov does not note that this phrase is in identical agreement with the LXX text and could have been copied from one Greek version to the other with the addition. Tov construes such identical agreement between the AT and LXX elsewhere as evidence of the literary dependence of the one Greek version on the other.

Tov further argues that a certain redundancy resulted in the LXX when the major additions were inserted into the canonical sections, a redundancy that is not found in the AT. He explains that the author of additions A, C, D and F who introduced them into the Hebrew *Vorlage* avoided this redundancy by carefully omitting sections of the canonical text. The redactor who introduced the same additions into the LXX was not so careful to avoid the resulting redundancies. By Tov's theory, the AT reflects a correction of the LXX toward this Hebrew *Vorlage* by eliminating the redundancies. Here again, this evidence does not compel the conclusion that the additions once existed in a Hebrew *Vorlage*; the same situation could have arisen with equal plausibility within the Greek tradition when a Greek redactor introduced the additions more carefully into the AT than was done in the LXX.

Tov's view that the AT is a revision of the LXX corrected toward a Semitic text that contained additions A, C, D and F has not been adopted by others who have subsequently published on the AT. Clines criticizes Tov's argument for "one organic unit" by pointing out that there are "places where the AT does not harmonize with the Additions" (Clines 1984, 106). Clines' criticism, however, is not to the point, for the fact that a redactor who introduced the additions to the Hebrew text did not consistently harmonize the base text with the additions says nothing about the possible existence of such a Hebrew text. The same judgment on the work of the Greek redactor must be leveled, but it does not therefore disprove the existence of such an imperfectly redacted Greek text.

Clines continues to argue against the organic unity of the additions with the canonical text saying,

> ... the textual character of those additions in the AT (viz. the fact that they exhibit a text–type very much closer to the LXX's than AT usually has) make it more than probable that they are secondary to the original AT, just as they are secondary in the LXX as compared with the MT (ibid., 72).[3]

---

[3] Although he rejects Tov's reconstruction of the AT's origin and redactional history, Clines seems to agree with Tov that some of the additions are translations of a Semitic

The fact that the AT and LXX closely agree to a much greater extent in the additions than they do in the rest of the text indicates only that the additions are secondary to *one* of the Greek versions, having been copied from one to the other. By its nature this argument cannot support the claim that the additions are secondary to *both* Greek versions, for it says nothing about the relationship of the additions to the text in which they *first* appeared. To show that the additions were secondary to the AT requires demonstration that the nature of the text of the additions in the AT is different from the nature of the text in the canonical sections, i.e., that the Greek of each must have come from two different people.

The secondary nature of the additions within the AT was subsequently demonstrated by M. Fox, who has rigorously demonstrated that the AT is composed of at least two redactional levels. Fox persuasively argues that the original text of the AT is a translation of a Hebrew *Vorlage* to which the major additions were subsequently added (Fox 1991,17–30). Fox's work showing that the additions comprise a secondary redactional stratum is discussed in chapter 4 and will not be reviewed here except to say that this study agrees with his conclusion that the additions are secondary to the AT. Anyone who continues to argue that the Greek of additions A, C, D and F was produced by the same translator as the rest of the book must now respond to Fox's analysis.

Fox's work showing the additions to be secondary material in the AT may at first seem to contradict Tov's view that they are "one organic unit" with the canonical text, but the two views are not mutually exclusive. One could argue with Tov that the Greek of the canonical sections of the AT originated with the LXX translator, because the AT is a revision, according to Tov, of those sections. However, the person who produced that revision of the LXX also had before him the Hebrew midrashic text of Esther which Tov argues

---

source. The implication that the additions came from two languages, Greek and Hebrew/Aramaic, and more than one Semitic text at that, greatly complicates the reconstruction of the AT's history. Though rejecting Tov's scenario, Clines admits he cannot reconstruct a textual history which would support his own (Clines 1984, 186n.3).

contained four of the six additions (A, C, D and F). Because the goal of the revision was to correct the LXX to this midrashic text, these additions were translated into Greek and inserted in the base text of the AT, which was a revision of the LXX. Therefore Tov's theory could also account for the differences between the Greek of the additions and the Greek of the canonical sections which Fox correctly observes. The additions were originally one organic unit with the Hebrew midrashic text, but are nevertheless secondary to the AT. (Because Tov has not published on this subject since Fox, I do not know whether Tov would actually argue along these lines.)

However, Clines, Fox and I disagree with Tov's theory that the AT was originally produced as a revision of the LXX on the grounds that the AT is not as similar to the LXX in the canonical sections as Tov's hypothesis requires. The scattered agreement Tov observes between the AT and LXX does not characterize their original relationship but reflects subsequent attempts to correct one Greek version to the other. But by that time, the AT and LXX differed so much that there were few places where the texts corresponded enough to bring them into agreement.

D. J. A. CLINES: "THE ESTHER SCROLL: THE STORY OF THE STORY," 1984

Clines unequivocally rejected Tov's theory: "I do not agree with Tov that AT is based on the LXX and corrects it in the direction of a Hebrew recension variant from MT" (Clines 1984, 94). Clines states his opinion of the relationship of the texts of Esther as follows:

> The AT of Esther, in its essential core (i.e., up to AT 8.17 and excluding the Additions), is a translation of a Semitic original that was different from the MT. The LXX, on the other hand, is a translation of an original that was in all important respects and probably in most details identical with the MT. Any affinity between AT and LXX in the core of the story arises solely from the similarity of their respective *Vorlagen* (ibid., 92).

Clines believes that the MT of Esther originally ended at 8:17 (AT:7:17).[4] Based on an analysis of the story–line, narrative motivation and literary style, he argues that 9:1–19, the etiology of Purim, was added to the Hebrew after the original composition of the story. Furthermore, he sees 9:20–10:3 (the end of the extant text) as an appendix that is also secondary to the original text of the story. Clines finds evidence in the AT that its Semitic *Vorlage* also ended at 8:17 (AT:7:17). He believes the AT to be a translation of this "proto–MT" text, which, at the time the AT was produced, did not include chapters 9 and 10 (and a few scattered verses, e.g., those referring to the irrevocability of the king's decrees).

In this work I do not wish to argue for or against the unity of the MT of Esther. Several others better qualified than I have done so.[5] Fox also presents a persuasive counter–argument for the redactional unity of the MT specifically aimed at Clines' criticism (Fox 1991, 99–115). I do wish to question Clines' claim that the AT is evidence of a "proto–MT" of Esther that ended with chapter 8. Although Clines' major thesis has been adopted and assumed as the starting point for subsequent work (e.g., Dorothy 1989; Wynn 1990; Fox 1991), this study finds textual evidence that is not adequately explained by Clines' theory. Regardless of whether the extant ending of the MT is original or secondary, this study argues that the AT was produced from a *Vorlage* that contained that ending.

Clines applied principles of literary criticism to the AT to reach his conclusion that the AT must have originally ended with 8:17 (AT:7:17), reflecting the ending of its *Vorlage*. He uses this methodology to the exclusion of techniques normally used in Septuagintal studies, techniques that involve a close comparison of the extent of textual agreement of the versions, retroversion of the Greek into Hebrew, etc. His approach is deliberate and he defends it saying:

> And I am, thankfully, not obliged to explain how in every particular
> case the wording of the AT could be prior to the (proto–)Masoretic text,

---

[4] Clines uses the Cambridge versification for the AT. The Göttingen citations used in the parallel texts of this study are given in parentheses for clarity.

[5] See also Anderson (1950), Bardtke (1963), Berg (1979), Gerleman (1966), Jones (1978) and Moore (1971).

since at any particular point AT does not necessarily represent the pre–Masoretic text, and in many individual cases the AT may well be a free or poor translation. *This is the reason why the investigation of the relationship of the texts of Esther can be most profitably conducted on the basis of their various story–lines, rather than by restricting the examination to the wording of individual verses* — as has perhaps too frequently been done in the past (ibid., 114, emphasis mine).

I believe Clines' literary criticism of the versions of Esther is of great value, and there is no scholar more qualified to bring this methodology to bear on the versions of Esther. However, by recognizing that many readings in the AT do not necessarily represent the pre–Masoretic text, Clines is admitting that other factors besides literary concerns complicate the reconstruction of the *Vorlage* of the AT, factors such as translation technique and changes introduced after the original production of the AT. These factors, which within the scope of his work he chooses to set aside, are the concerns more central to Septuagintal studies.

The legitimate literary concerns that Clines presents must be considered in light of the overall characteristics of the text, something Clines does not do. Both a literary analysis and a scrutiny of the fine points of the text are necessary to characterize accurately the AT and to reconstruct its origin and history.

This study agrees with Clines that the AT was not originally produced as a recension of the LXX, but that some of its readings were later corrected by redactors and/or scribes to agree with the LXX (or *vice versa*). Furthermore, this study also agrees that the similarity of the AT to the LXX outside of the additions is due to the similarity of their respective *Vorlagen*. Virtually all agree that the MT is the *Vorlage* from which the LXX was originally produced. The question is, To what extent, if any, was the *Vorlage* of the AT different from the MT? Clines (and Fox, see below) argue that the *Vorlage* of the AT was substantially different from the MT, most especially in its ending. I wish to argue that the AT does *not* strongly attest a *Vorlage* that was quite different from the MT, even in its ending.

Clines uses the previous work of H. J. Cook (1969), who argued that the AT was evidence of a Hebrew text of Esther that ended at MT:8:5. Although Clines disagrees with Cook about the precise location of the original ending, their arguments are sufficiently similar that this critique directed at Clines will also indirectly answer to Cook.

The foundation of Clines' argument is that the text of the AT is different from the MT more in its ending than it is in the preceding seven chapters of the story and that the ending of the AT does not preserve literary coherence. According to Clines, the best explanation is that the AT was translated from an ancestor of the MT before chapters 9 and 10 were added to it. In other words, the ending of the AT developed independently from the ending of the MT, hence the great differences between them.

Clines believes he has proven on literary grounds, independently of the evidence of the AT, that the Hebrew of Esther originally ended at 8:17 (AT:7:17). He approaches the AT looking for evidence to corroborate that conclusion (Clines 1984, 68). He applies literary criticism to the AT to find evidence in its ending that he construes as corroborating his prior conclusion concerning the original ending of the Hebrew. After identifying sixteen places in the AT ending where the narrative logic of the story line disintegrates, he concludes,

> ... the character of the AT does indeed alter quite radically after 8.16 (=MT 8.5). The concluding verses, 8.17–21, 33–52, are a poorly written narrative, almost unintelligible at places, that cannot be attributed to the same author or level of redaction as the principal part of the book, and can only be regarded as secondary to it. Apparently the original form of AT ended at the point in the narrative reached by the time of 8.17 (whether or not 8.17 was itself the original conclusion) (ibid., 84).

Although I disagree with some of his points, I do not wish to argue here with Clines' judgment of the poor character of the AT's ending. Rather, I wish to present evidence that may suggest a different explanation for the qualities Clines observes.

This study also observed that the ending of the AT has a different relationship to the MT from that of the rest of the story. However, referring to Graphs 1a–d in chapter 2 of this work, note that both semantic and formal agreement of the AT with respect to the MT begins to fall off sharply much earlier than the end of chapter 8. If the endings are compared including all of the pluses and minuses, both semantic and formal agreement of the AT with the MT begins to drop with chapter 5, not at the end of chapter 8 (see chapter 2, Graphs 1a, b). (Recall that chapter 5 of the Greek Esther includes addition D, which is the addition most interwoven with the canonical material.)

These pluses and minuses are not solid evidence of the *Vorlage* of the AT since it is equally probable they were a) pluses and minuses in the Semitic *Vorlage vis–à–vis* the MT, or b) expansions and abbreviations by the translator of his *Vorlage*, or c) introduced by a later redactor of the Greek (ibid., 90). Since the extent of agreement including pluses and minuses is difficult to interpret unambiguously, Graphs 1c and d of chapter 2 show the extent of agreement when the pluses and minuses are excluded.

When only those units are considered for which there is Greek text in the AT corresponding to the MT, the agreement between the AT and MT still begins to drop at chapter 5, but not so sharply (see Graphs 1c,d in chapter 2). Of even greater interest, the agreement of the AT with the MT in chapters 8 and 9 approaches the agreement of the LXX with the MT in those chapters. Two inferences follow: (1) If Clines wishes to argue for the location of an original ending on the basis of divergence from the MT, he must look earlier than chapter 8. (2) If Clines believes the MT was the *Vorlage* of the LXX in chapters 8 and 9, a similar extent of agreement suggests it could also have been the *Vorlage* of the AT in those chapters.

Further evidence that the *Vorlage* of the AT could not have ended at 8:17 (AT:7:17) is found in that verse itself. If 8:17 (AT:7:17) was the concluding sentence of the *Vorlage* of the AT, it does not, even in Clines' judgment, provide an adequate resolution of plot tension (ibid., 79). The AT merely says, "And the king put into his [Mordecai's] hand the affairs of the kingdom." As Clines observes, it fails to mention the crucial fact that Haman's decree actually was revoked and the Jews actually were saved from destruction. The sentence as it now stands in the AT does not provide narrative closure for the story. If a concluding sentence originally stood at this place, that sentence was edited beyond recognition to form a transition to the AT's ending when it was added. Therefore, the seam so crucial to Clines' theory, if it ever existed, has been obliterated by subsequent redaction. If, on the other hand, this sentence as it now stands in the AT does faithfully reflect its *Vorlage*, it suggests that more story followed. Hence some ending material must have been present in that *Vorlage*.

Whether the sentence in 8:17 (AT:7:17) is original or not, as it now stands it does not support Clines' claim that the *Vorlage* ended just there. The question is, To what extent does the AT preserve the material in the ending of its *Vorlage?*

The second prong of Clines' argument is that the narrative logic disintegrates in the ending of the AT. This is true. However, when chapters 1–7 of the AT are examined, the same types of narrative dissonance Clines observed in the ending are found throughout the book. For instance:

1. AT:3:13 reads καὶ ἔσπευσε καὶ ἔδωκεν εἰς χεῖρας τρεχόντων ἱππέων. ("And he [Haman] hurried and gave [the letter] to swift horsemen.") In the Greek, the verb ἔδωκεν has no direct object. In translation, it is necessary to supply the direct object implied by the context, "the letter," although no letter has been written in the preceding verses of the AT. Addition B, a copy of the letter, follows AT:3:13, which forms a (poor) transition from the main narrative to a secondary addition.

2. In AT:4:3a Mordecai sends εὐνοῦχον ἕνα ("one/a eunuch") to Esther.[6] When the eunuch returns, Mordecai sends him back to Esther with the instructions οὕτως ἐρεῖτε αὐτῇ ("thus you will say to her," AT:4:4d). The problem is that the verb, ἐρεῖτε, is in the plural number, which makes no sense in the context. The implied plural subject of the verb has no referent in the AT and produces narrative dissonance.

3. In the MT, Esther's first banquet with the king and Haman occurs on the same day that she issues her invitation and Haman eagerly reports his good fortune to his family that same night after attending the banquet. In the AT, the first banquet occurs the day *after* Esther issues the invitation, but oddly Haman does not tell his family about the invitation, though he would have had an entire evening to do so. Rather, in the AT, as in the MT, Haman eagerly reports his invitation to dine with the queen to his wife, his friends and his sons on the night *between* the first and

---

[6] The presence of the explicit numeral ἕνα followed by the noun in this Greek phrase may indicate it is translating a Hebrew phrase that used the numeral אֶחָד as an adjective, which in the Hebrew follows its noun and is sometimes used as an indefinite article.

second banquets (AT:5:21). Since he had learned of his invitation the day before the first banquet, would he not have informed his family of his good fortune sooner? The difference between the AT and MT in the timing of the first banquet with respect to the time of the invitation introduces narrative dissonance.

4. In AT:6:6j, the king asks "Who is outside?" without prior narrative motivation. Unlike the MT, which first reports that Haman had just entered the courtyard (MT:6:4), the king's question in the AT is jarring because it is unmotivated.

Because such narrative dissonance is characteristic of the AT elsewhere, its presence in the ending of the AT does not argue for the independence of the AT from its *Vorlage* after chapter 8. More likely, this dissonance was introduced as the Greek text experienced substantial editing, especially when the additions were introduced.

To summarize my criticism of Clines' argument: (1) The divergence of the AT from the MT that he observes does not coincide with his proposed ending of the proto–MT. (2) The verse he proposes in the AT as the original ending could not have been a concluding statement. More material must have followed it. (3) The (poor) literary quality he observes in the ending of the AT and cites as evidence of textual independence is also found elsewhere in the AT where the question of textual independence is not an issue.

Not only does the AT not support Clines' argument for the ending of the proto–MT at 8:17 (AT:7:17), it presents positive evidence that the original AT ending was in fact much more similar to the extant MT, even in chapters 9 and 10, than Clines recognizes. This evidence, previously discussed in chapter 3, will be only summarized here.

Firstly, the ending of the AT includes at least thirteen of the same major events and points, and in the same sequence, as found in chapters 8–10 of the MT. It is true that the AT abbreviates each one, even to an aesthetically unpleasant extent, but their presence in the text cannot be denied. Furthermore, even the highly abbreviated explanation of Purim in the AT, which Clines judges as "an unintelligent abbreviation" (ibid., 83), contains all of the points found in the MT necessary to explain the origin of the holiday. Moreover, these points are also presented in the AT in the same order as found in the MT.

The AT *does* treat Purim with less interest than the MT, but this may reflect the interests of the target audience and not the text of the *Vorlage*. For instance, as noted in chapter 3, the AT does not explain, nor even mention, the difference between the celebration of Purim by the Jews of Susa on the fifteenth and its celebration on the fourteenth by the rural Jews. As Fox explains,

> AT still has two days of celebration (14–15 Adar: viii 47b), but the redactor has left no historical rationale for the timing, nor has he assigned the days to different locales ... The loss of the Susan/provincial distinction, so important in the MT and the LXX, was very likely occasioned by a lessening of interest. Whereas the MT (and LXX) seems to be sorting out an issue of current contention and offering a compromise between two rival claims as to the correct date of Purim, for R–AT [the redactor of the AT] the matter no longer requires argumentation (ibid., 84–5).

Fox agrees with Clines that the Purim etiology was not present in the *Vorlage* of the AT but was a later addition to the Hebrew when the dates of Purim became an issue. He locates this redactional *Tendenz* in the Hebrew *Vorlage* of the AT. However, an alternative explanation may be that the Greek translator who originally produced the AT did find the Purim material in his *Vorlage*, but considered it irrelevant for his target audience. The explanation of two dates for Purim would have been irrelevant either to Jews in locations where Purim was not (yet?) celebrated (though they possibly knew that Jews elsewhere did celebrate the holiday), or where the date of its celebration was settled. (See the concluding chapter of this work for a discussion of the date and provenance of the AT.)

One's judgment on whether the Purim etiology is original or secondary to the Hebrew text is of course influenced by one's view of when Purim began to be celebrated. If Purim originated in the Persian period in Susa its etiology in the Hebrew text could be original. If one dates the origin of the holiday to the Hellenistic period, then it is more likely to be secondary material subsequently appended to the story.

The agreement between the endings of the AT and MT is not just in content, but as argued in chapter 3, the correspondence between the AT and MT in the ending extends to the level of textual agreement.

Although because of the many pluses and minuses the AT and MT have little corresponding text in the ending, where they do have text in common there is a high degree of both semantic and formal agreement. There are only eighty–four units of text out of 515 common to both the AT and MT in chapters 8–10. But of these eighty–four units, 70% agree semantically and 49% agree formally. Furthermore, the eighty–four units in the ending of the AT that have corresponding Hebrew text are in the same place and sequence as the units in the MT with which they agree.

If the *Vorlage* of the AT did not contain this material, its origin is a complete mystery, for it also could not have been copied from the LXX. The ending of the AT does not show a literary dependence on the LXX in chapters 8–10, except in addition E and a few verses immediately following it. If, as Clines implies, the ending is secondary to the AT and came from the LXX, it should exhibit the same nature as the six major additions. (In fact, if the extant ending is not original to the AT, it should be considered the seventh major addition.) As the following table shows, in the six major additions the AT has a high percentage of material in common with the LXX. If the ending of the AT (i.e., chapters 8–10) had been copied from the LXX, one would expect a similarly high percentage of common material. This is clearly not the case:

Amount of Material Common to the AT and LXX

Chapter	# Units Total	# Units in Common	% in Common
A	156	92	59%
B	119	86	72%
C	237	180	76%
D	115	86	75%
E	200	154	77%
F	81	42	52%
7	148	39	26%
8	222	21	10%
9	237	56	24%
10	34	21	62%

The relationship between the concluding chapters of the AT and the LXX is clearly not the same as in the secondary additions that were copied from one Greek version to the other. The average amount of material common to the AT and LXX in the additions is 68.5%; in chapters 7–10, a much lower 30.5%. A much higher percent of corresponding text would be necessary to demonstrate that the similarity between the AT ending and the MT ending had come from the LXX.

Recall that when the pluses and minuses in the ending are excluded (since they indicate secondary redactional activity in either the Hebrew or the Greek), the agreement of the AT with the MT approaches that of the LXX with the MT. If the MT was the *Vorlage* of the LXX in its ending, the similar extent of agreement suggests the MT could also have been the *Vorlage* of the AT.

As noted in chapter 4, scrutiny of the relatively few units of text the AT ending has in common with the LXX and MT shows evidence that all three versions have a common core. There are fifty–nine units in chapters 8–10 where AT = MT = LXX. All but two of these units exhibit both semantic and formal agreement among all three texts. Because the endings of the AT and LXX are overall so different, the agreement can be best explained in the same way Clines explains affinity between the versions in the rest of the text, that is, arising "solely from the similarity of their respective *Vorlagen*" (ibid., 92). Moreover, their respective *Vorlagen* were identical to the MT at least in these places.

I propose that the agreement of the AT with both the MT and LXX is because both Greek versions are independent translations of the same *Vorlage*. The AT developed independently and substantial changes were made, especially in the ending, probably when addition E was included. After this, only a vestige of its *Vorlage* remained in the ending of the AT. Later, when addition E was present in both Greek versions, an attempt was made to correct the ending of the AT to the LXX. However, because by that time the endings were so different, only a few corresponding units could be made to agree. This scenario is discussed further in the conclusion to this work.

Religious Language

Clines also argues that the ancestor of the MT from which the AT was translated contained the religious language found in the pluses of the AT and was subsequently omitted from the Hebrew text that has come down to us as the MT. Clines identifies nine passages with religious references which he suggests were original to the *Vorlage* of the AT and later omitted from the Hebrew text that was used in the liturgical celebration of Purim (ibid., 107–112). It is often suggested that because Purim was celebrated so raucously all references to God were removed from the Hebrew scroll of Esther read during the celebration so as to not provide opportunity to profane His name. This dubious explanation can at most explain the omission of explicit references to God, but the AT contains much more religious language than just that, including references to Haman's gods.

Although by principles of formal logic one could argue that pluses in the AT actually represent text cut from the Hebrew after the translation was made, it seems to this writer much more natural that religious language was added in the Greek versions to clarify, expand and specify points in the biblical Hebrew text that cry out for theological exposition. It seems counter–intuitive that a text stripped of its religious language would have survived as the canonical version, especially if competing with an older Hebrew text that contained the religious references.

Moreover, as Clines himself discusses, the specific nature of the religious additions to the Greek Esther parallels the references to God found in the Hebrew texts of Ezra, Nehemiah and Daniel. He writes, "... the effect of the Additions was to assimilate the book to the norm established by Ezra, Nehemiah and Daniel" (ibid., 174). In my opinion, such parallels would seem to motivate the addition of religious language to the Greek text as well as to argue strongly against its removal from the Hebrew.

Fox agrees that the religious passages are additions "with easily understandable and well–paralleled motivations" (Fox 1991, 120). In his judgment also "The excision of religious statements would be a far more radical act than simply not writing them into a story to start with" (ibid., 120).

If the Hebrew text once included the religious language of the AT, there are no seams in it to suggest that such material was excised. Redaction criticism depends on just such internal evidence that observably disrupts the literary coherence of a text. Although such evidence is apparent in the AT, there is none in the MT. The literary artistry of the extant Hebrew version in chapters 1–8, which Clines notes (ibid., 31–38), would not likely have survived the cutting and splicing required to eliminate the religious passages. One would expect instead the kind of criticism Clines levels at 9:1–19 and 9:20–10:3, which he claims were the result of secondary redactional activity precisely because he does not see in them the literary quality of the preceding chapters. Since many of the religious pluses in the AT have coherence with the additions (see chapter 4), this study concludes it is much more likely that they were subsequently added to the AT than that they were excised from the Hebrew ancestor of the MT.

To conclude the evaluation of Clines' hypothesis: This study agrees with Clines that the AT is not a recension of the LXX. It also observes the great deviation of the AT from the MT in chapters 8–10 (which in fact begins with chapter 5) but does not agree that this is evidence that the AT's *Vorlage* ended at 8:17 (AT:7:17). Although Clines' hypothesis may explain the differences between the endings of the AT and MT, it fails to recognize, much less explain, the similarity of content and the extent of textual agreement between the AT and MT in the endings. Because there is little material common to the AT and LXX in these chapters, the ending of the AT was not copied from the LXX as Clines implies, therefore, its similarity to the MT did not come via the LXX. The similarity of the ending of the AT to the MT is due to the similarity of the AT's *Vorlage* with the MT. The great differences are due to substantial redactional activity when addition E was introduced and perhaps at other times as well.

MICHAEL V. FOX: "THE REDACTION OF THE BOOKS OF ESTHER," 1991

M. V. Fox has produced the most rigorous evaluation of the relationship of the versions of Esther to date (Fox 1991). In light of Clines' work Fox writes,

The Alpha–Text of Esther

> While I do not consider all of Clines' arguments valid, and while I
> define the scope of AT–end differently, I think that on the whole his
> literary criteria succeed in showing that AT–end belongs to a different
> stage of development than the proto–AT (ibid., 136).

Fox believes that the AT is a translation of a Hebrew text that is
not, as Clines suggests, a direct ancestor of the MT, but is instead a
"collateral relative of the MT" (ibid., 97). This means that the *Vorlage*
of the AT and the ancestors of the MT descended from the same distant
text, but that the *Vorlage* of the AT was not a direct ancestor of the
MT. Fox agrees with Clines that most of the material following 8:17
(AT:7:17) was not in the Hebrew *Vorlage* of the AT. He agrees that the
verse Clines suggests as the original ending, 8:17 (AT:7:17), is not a
suitable concluding statement and there must have been more material
in the conclusion of its *Vorlage*.

To the extent that Fox agrees with Clines concerning the original
ending of the AT, the arguments already presented above also challenge
Fox. The following discussion of Fox's work will focus on those points
which are distinctive to his analysis of the AT.

Fox argues that the extant ending of the AT was not original and
therefore attests a shorter *Vorlage* different from the MT. He proposes
that the original ending of the *Vorlage* is preserved in AT:7:18–21 and
AT:7:33-38 (ibid., 38–9) because this material could not have come
from the LXX or MT, since it is found in neither, and because he sees
no motivation for a redactor to have added it later.

The passage Fox claims is the original conclusion of the AT
(AT:7:38) does form a better ending statement than the one proposed
by Clines. However there may be motivation for the later addition of
AT:7:33–38, in light of the nature of addition E, which intervenes at
AT:7:21, right in the middle of the original ending Fox proposes.

The passage that Fox suggests originally concluded the AT (and
its Hebrew *Vorlage*) is a brief summary of a letter Mordecai sends
revoking Haman's decree and establishing for the Jews a feast of
celebration. It is not found in either the MT or the LXX, so could not
have been copied from those sources. At first glance it seems somewhat
redundant with the longer more detailed decree that immediately
precedes it in the AT. This letter from Mordecai to the Jews is needed
in the AT, however, because addition E is formally from the king

("The Great King, Ahasuerus, to the ...") and in the AT it is introduced by the statement, "and he wrote the following letter," where the nearest antecedent of "he" is also the king, not Mordecai. Furthermore, in the AT, the decree was addressed to the Persian leaders of the empire and did not include the Jews. In contrast, the MT makes it unambiguously clear that the king's decree contained *Mordecai's* orders not only to the leaders of the empire but to the Jews as well (MT:8:9), a statement which is not found in the AT. In the AT it is unclear what, if any, role Mordecai had in the king's decree as recorded in addition E. Therefore the passage that Fox identifies as having no redactional motivation in the AT would have been necessary to establish that not only did a decree go out from the king to the leaders of the empire, but that Mordecai himself wrote to the Jews, establishing the feast of celebration. In other words, a royal decree from a pagan king to his pagan leaders would not carry the authority needed to establish a feast within the Jewish community. Only Mordecai, an esteemed Jew in a high position, had the prerequisite authority to establish tradition for the Jews. In the LXX version, the king's decree seems to issue from Esther's influence. As this study has discussed in chapters 3 and 4, one of the characteristics of the AT is that it amplifies Mordecai's role and minimizes Esther's.

Therefore, the summary of Mordecai's letter in the AT is not at all redundant with the king's decree, but was needed in the AT once addition E was introduced. This provides, contra Fox, some motivation for its inclusion as part of the redactional activity that introduced addition E.

Fox contends that the rest of the material in the ending of the AT was copied from the ending of the LXX. All of the previous arguments aimed at Clines' similar theory argue against Fox as well. However, Fox presents the argument that vocabulary correspondence between the AT and LXX indicates that the AT borrowed its ending from the LXX.

Fox demonstrates the use of the LXX text by the AT by counting the number of words the AT has in common with the LXX in a given passage. He defines a vocabulary match between the AT and LXX as,

> (1) occurrences of the same lexical item, irrespective of grammatical form, (2) close cognates in different parts of speech and (3) prefix-variants of compound verbs and nouns from the same stem... Matches

need not appear in the same position in the sentence in each version,
but they must fill the same syntactical slot (ibid., 20).

After counting the number of vocabulary matches between the AT and LXX, he calculates the percentages of the total number of words in the AT and LXX these matches represent and identifies the median value for each AT passage.[7] Vocabulary correspondence alone cannot adequately demonstrate literary dependence. If a given text was in fact copied from another, a high percentage of vocabulary correspondence (approaching 100%) necessarily results. However, the converse is not true. A high percentage of vocabulary correspondence alone between two texts does not necessarily imply one was copied from the other. Any re–telling of the same story will inevitably use much of the same vocabulary, as would two translations of one source. Evidence that one text was copied from another involves not only vocabulary matches, but also consecutive vocabulary matches in similar, if not identical, word order extending over at least phrases or clauses, if not sentences. This is what is found when the additions (A–F) in the AT are compared to the additions in the LXX. It is not found when the endings of the two versions are compared. (A glance at the parallel texts of the additions compared to chapters 8–10 visually reinforces this difference. See Appendix 1.) Therefore, the vocabulary correspondence Fox observes must be considered in light of the other characteristics of the endings.

The following table is an excerpt of the relevant data Fox published of the percentage of vocabulary matches between the AT and LXX in the six major additions and in the ending of the AT (ibid., 49):

---

[7] The median value indicates half the verses in the passage have a percentage of vocabulary matches greater than the median value, and the other half, a percentage of vocabulary matches less than the median.

AT's Use of the LXX in the Redactional Sections

passage	# word matches	# AT words	% AT matches	# LXX words	% LXX words used by AT	median value
A	189	308	61%	298	63%	0.57
B	210	249	84%	246	85%	0.81
C	447	577	77%	597	75%	0.79
D	206	261	79%	254	81%	0.85
...	...	...	...	...	...	...
E	338	429	79%	472	72%	0.86
AT–end	196	281	70%	718	**27%**	0.76
F	125	171	73%	199	63%	0.97

When this data is compared to the values calculated from the canonical, "proto–AT" sections (ibid., 48), a great difference is found between the number of vocabulary matches in the canonical, "proto–AT" sections and the number in the major additions. This pattern is consistent with the additions having been copied from one Greek version to the other. The question is, does vocabulary correspondence in the AT's ending position it with the canonical sections or the additions (or neither)? Fox's own data displayed above shows clearly that the relationship between the AT and LXX in their endings is drastically different from the relationship between them in the six major additions.

Fox has calculated that in the six major additions, A–F, the percentage of LXX words used by the AT ranges from 63 to 85%. (See sixth column, "% LXX words used by AT".) In the ending, however, the AT uses only 27% of the corresponding LXX vocabulary. Furthermore, for each of the six additions, the number of words in the AT version is comparable to the number of words in the LXX: A, 308/298; B, 249/246; C, 577/597; D, 261/254; E, 429/472; F, 171/199. (Compare columns 2 and 5.) This is expected if one Greek version copied from the other. But, according to Fox's data, the AT ending has only 281 words compared to the 718 of the LXX ending. This indicates a different relationship between the endings of the two versions from that of the additions and raises the question of whether such low vocabulary correspondence could be better explained as resulting from a non–literary relationship. In fact, the low vocabulary correspondence in the AT ending, 27%, is closer to that which Fox calculates for the "proto–AT" sections, which average 21% (ibid., 48). These numbers indicate that the AT ending was not originally copied from the LXX.

On the other hand, this study also observed a high degree of agreement between the AT and LXX in those units they have in common in chapters 9 and 10 (see Graphs 6a and b in chapter 4). This might at first seem to support Fox's claims of a literary dependence; however, a different explanation presents itself. Although there is a high degree of agreement in chapters 9 and 10 where the AT and LXX have corresponding units, there are very few units of text common to the AT and LXX in their endings (98 out of 493). This argues against the AT ending having been originally copied from the LXX. However, those few units which they do have in common do exhibit a fairly high degree of agreement, as reflected in the median value Fox calculates for AT–end (0.76). As Fox suggests, this does indicate a literary dependence, *but only for those few units*.

Both of these characteristics of the AT's ending must be explained and neither at the expense of the other. The evidence suggests, contra Fox, that the AT's ending was not originally copied from the LXX (hence little material in common), but the elements that a redactor/scribe found common to both versions were later corrected to agree with each other (hence the strong agreement of only the material common to both). Except for the relatively few units of common material in the ending, the redactor/scribe found no corresponding text, so the versions could not be corrected to agree in those places. This attempt at reconciling the ending of the two versions would most likely have been made at the time or after addition E was copied from one version to the other.

It would take substantial further study focused on chapters 7–10 and addition E to separate the vestiges of the ending of the original translation from the results of the later and extensive redactional activity in the ending.

THE VORLAGE OF THE AT AND THE MT

This study agrees with both Fox and Clines that the AT was originally produced as a translation of a Hebrew *Vorlage* and was not originally a recension of the LXX. Clines considers the Hebrew *Vorlage* of the AT to have been a direct ancestor of the MT. This ancestor, the "proto–MT," lacked chapters 9 and 10 and perhaps some other material as well (such as the irrevocability of Persian law). For Clines, the AT provides a snapshot of an earlier literary stage of the MT and thus provides direct evidence for the redactional history of the MT.

Fox considers the *Vorlage* of the AT to be "a collateral relative of the MT," not necessarily its direct ancestor (Fox 1991, 97). He proposes a Semitic ancestor common to both the MT and the *Vorlage* of the AT, which he calls "proto–Esther." Fox explains his use of the hypothetical *Vorlage* of the AT for redaction criticism of the MT,

> While the proto–AT is not a *source* of the MT, it does show us a collateral version of the Esther story. This external vantage–point enables us to ascertain, by a sort of triangulation, the main components of the tale underlying the MT version (ibid., 96).

Fox himself admits, "To use the AT in attempting to trace the formation of the MT is undoubtedly a bold, if not precarious, maneuver" (ibid., 96). The redactional history of the MT which Fox then proposes presumes that: (1) the alleged Semitic *Vorlage* of the AT can be reconstructed with confidence from only three (or four) medieval manuscripts of AT itself, (2) "proto–Esther," the hypothetical ancestor common to the MT and AT, can be reconstructed, at least in its salient features, from the hypothetical reconstruction of the AT's *Vorlage*, and (3) an imaginary comparison of these two hypothetical texts, for which there is zero manuscript evidence,[8] with the MT can be

---

[8] In 1992 J. T. Milik published six fragments from cave 4 at Qumran to which he assigned the sigla of 4QprEsth[a], ... 4QprEsth[f] (Milik 1992). He claims these are fragments of an Aramaic source of Esther, a "proto–Esther." It is argued that they are a literary source of the Esther story because the story they tell is set in the Persian court of Xerxes and is a story of a courtier. Such general similarities are not compelling evidence, especially in view of the great differences, such as the name of the

made with confidence to show the development of the Hebrew text which terminated in the extant MT. Fox's use of the AT to propose a redactional history of the MT is speculation, since there is not a fragment of manuscript evidence with which to control or validate the reconstruction of the texts required for redaction criticism. Moreover, Fox's most fundamental premise, that the proto–AT did not derive from the MT (ibid., 97), but from a text that developed independently of it, is challenged by this study.

Although I am quite skeptical of Fox's use of the AT to reconstruct the redactional history of the MT, I also believe that the Hebrew *Vorlage* of the AT reflects the pre–history of the MT. This Greek translation was almost certainly made before the MT as we know it was stabilized in the first century of this era. In that sense, the AT does provide a snapshot of the Hebrew text in an earlier literary stage. This study agrees with Clines, contra Fox, that the *Vorlage* of the AT was a direct ancestor of the MT. It departs from both Clines and Fox in their conclusion that the AT reflects a Hebrew *Vorlage* that was radically different from the extant MT.

While this study agrees that the *Vorlage* of the AT was not identical to the extant MT at every point, it has demonstrated that at many points throughout the text, the *Vorlage* of the AT *was* virtually identical to the extant MT. Furthermore, this study presents evidence that even in the ending, which without dispute differs the most among the three versions, the *Vorlage* of the AT was in its extent and salient points quite similar to the extant MT. The AT originally translated a Hebrew text that was in most respects quite similar to the MT, but which was subsequently edited extensively to produce a Greek version of Esther in which the political dynamics between the Jews and the pagan empire overshadowed the Purim etiology and in which Mordecai's stature overshadowed Esther's. A proposed history of the relationship of the Greek versions of Esther is presented in the concluding chapter of this work.

---

protagonist and his position in the court. Specific details in the fragments that are said to agree with the Esther story are based on conjectural emmendation of the text and are quite debatable.

CONCLUSIONS

• The agreement E. Tov observes between the AT and LXX does not reflect the relationship of the original texts. Rather, it reflects later attempts to correct one Greek version to the other.

• This study challenges the hypothesis advanced by D. J. A. Clines, and later by M. V. Fox, that the ending of the AT is evidence of a Hebrew *Vorlage* shorter than the MT.

• There is a core of material common to the ending of all three versions that indicates the *Vorlagen* of the AT and LXX were quite similar to the MT.

• The AT is a translation of a Hebrew *Vorlage* that was a direct ancestor of the MT and quite similar to it in its content and extent.

CONCLUSION: SO WHAT IS THE ALPHA–TEXT OF ESTHER?

Any explanation of the origin of the AT of Esther involves great uncertainty. Because there are no ancient manuscripts of the AT, any knowledge of its origin and history must be inferred from just four medieval manuscripts. Although the origin of the AT remains shrouded in uncertainty, the inferences resulting from this study of the AT point in some directions and away from others. The conclusions listed at the end of the previous chapters anchor these remarks to the evidence presented by the text itself. Beyond those, some of these concluding remarks are from the more subjective impressions that inevitably formed while spending countless hours with the alpha–text. A few of these concluding remarks are (hopefully) intelligent conjecture, but conjecture nonetheless.

My studied opinion is that the alpha–text of Esther is probably the older of the two extant Greek versions, and probably the first Greek translation made of the Hebrew (or Aramaic) Esther.[1] Its *Vorlage*, while not everywhere identical to the extant MT, was in extent and salient points quite similar to the MT, and in many places throughout the text, it was virtually identical to the MT. After its original production, the AT developed independently of its Hebrew

---

[1] Tov offers evidence that the *Vorlage* of the AT was written in Aramaic (Tov 1982, 25n.). Fox offers equal evidence that it was in Hebrew (Fox 1991, 26, 28). The complexity of the evidence warrants a substantial study which lies outside the scope of this work.

Vorlage, which itself developed into the MT as we know it. When, during the Hasmonean dynasty, Jerusalem again exerted influence over the tradition and practice of the Jews in the Diaspora, the divergence of the Greek AT from the Hebrew text then known in Jerusalem warranted a new translation. This new translation, the LXX version of Esther, made in either 114 or 78 B.C. (see below), supplanted the older Greek AT version within the Jewish tradition. The six major additions, familiar to readers of the AT, were copied into the LXX. Attempts were made to bring the AT into agreement with the LXX, but because the texts were so different, these attempts could produce only scattered identical readings throughout the otherwise dissimilar versions.

This study has revealed at least three indications that the AT is older than the LXX version: (1) the text shows affinity with many of the characteristics of the OG of Daniel (see the excursus at the end of this work); (2) the reference to Bougaios is more likely to have entered the text soon after 338 B.C. than after 114 B.C., the earliest dating of the LXX of Esther (see chapter 3); (3) the AT preserves the older form of most of the six major additions (see chapter 4).

The results of this study also indicate that the *Vorlage* of the AT was in many respects quite similar to the MT and at many places virtually identical with it (see chapter 2). Where the AT has text in common with the MT, it agrees with the MT more than it disagrees (84% semantic agreement, 54% formal). In fact, the extent of agreement between the AT and MT where they have text in common is almost equal to that between the LXX of Esther and the MT (88% semantic, 64% formal). Furthermore, the AT follows the word order of the MT more often than not. Where the text of the AT disagrees with the MT, a substantial percentage (55%) of the differences are unavoidably due to the differences between the syntax of the Hebrew and Greek languages.

Even the ending of the AT, which is where the text deviates most from the MT, shows significant agreement with it in both text and content. What little text the AT's ending has in common with the MT shows a semantic agreement of 70% and a formal agreement of 49%. The AT ending includes at least thirteen of the major points and events found in the MT ending, and in the same sequence (see chapter 3).

It is likely that the AT in its original form did not include the six major additions. If additions A, C, D and F were originally a part of a

Semitic text of the Esther story, as Tov argues, then those additions were translated into Greek and introduced into the AT subsequent to its original production. It is virtually certain that additions B and E, the royal decrees, were composed in Greek and were introduced at the same time as or after addition C, the prayers of Mordecai and Esther. Additions A and F, Mordecai's dream and its interpretation, were both most probably introduced into the AT at the same time, regardless of whether addition A once circulated independently.

As it now stands, the AT is a version of the Esther story that, in comparison to the MT, magnifies Mordecai's role and minimizes Esther's. Instead of highlighting the origin of Purim, it amplifies the political dynamics of the Jews in relationship to a pagan empire powerful enough to threaten their very existence. More than the other two versions, the AT emphasizes that Jews in positions of political power benefit not only the Jewish community, but the king and the empire as well.

Although the date and provenance of the original production of the AT remains unknown, this study offers evidence that sheds light on those questions. If the reference to Bougaios in the AT is an allusion to the assassin of Artaxerxes III in 338 B.C., it was most likely introduced into the Esther story while that event was still a living memory (see chapter 3). This suggests that the reference came into the Esther story late in the Persian period (in that case, probably originally in a Semitic form) or quite early in the Hellenistic period (in a Greek form).

If 2 Macc 2:2 is a deliberate allusion to the Esther story, it demonstrates that addition D as it stands only in the AT version of Esther was known in Jerusalem about 100 B.C. when 2 Maccabees was written to the Jews of Alexandria.

Some redaction of the AT, including addition A, was almost certainly made in the first century of this era. Addition A contains a relative clause that equates two sequential months of the Jewish lunar calendar, Adar–Nisan, with those of the Macedonian calendar, Dystros–Xandikos (AT:A:1). Because of a known intercalating correction to the Macedonian calendar, this particular correspondence between the Jewish Adar–Nisan and the Macedonian Dystros–Xandikos existed only from AD 15/16 until 176. (Samuel 1972, 142–43). Prior to AD 15/16 Adar–Nisan corresponded to Xandikos–Artemisios. This provides firm evidence that the AT was redacted, possibly to its present form, between AD 15 and 176.

Furthermore, the fact that only the AT of Esther gives the corresponding Macedonian month names suggests that the redaction of the AT that introduced this correspondence was intended to produce a version of the Esther story for an audience which was not familiar with the Jewish lunar calendar. The correspondence of the Jewish month names to the Macedonian is also found several times in Josephus, who was writing for Gentile readers apparently more familiar with the Macedonian calendar than the Jewish (*Ant. Jews* i.80; xi.107; xi.148; xi.286; xii.248; xii.319). In comparison, the LXX version of Esther mentions only one Jewish month, Nisan, and does not give its equivalent in the Macedonian calendar, suggesting that the original audience of the LXX text themselves used the Jewish lunar calendar.

I conjecture that the reason the AT mentions two sequential month names, but the LXX only one, is because of the adjustment made between AD 15/16 and 46/47 that introduced an extra intercalating month into the Macedonian lunar calendar. For some time after that adjustment was made, two sequential lunar month names were required to specify unambiguously the equivalence between the Macedonian lunar calendar and any other.

The colophon found in the LXX manuscripts of Esther dates the original production of that translation to either 114 or 78 B.C. (Bickerman 1944; Moore 1971, 112).[2] I suggest that the LXX translation, carrying the imprimatur of Jerusalem, widely supplanted the older AT version within Jewish communities of the Diaspora. Nonetheless, the AT was still in circulation in the first century of this era in a location where its readers used the Macedonian calendar, not the Jewish. Moreover, the fact that the AT is preserved in manuscripts that date to the medieval period implies that some tradition must have valued this version enough to copy it for a thousand years.

If the AT in its final form was not produced within the Jewish community, the possibility of a Christian stage in its history must be considered. Further form critical study of Mordecai's dream as it

---

[2] The identical colophon is found on one manuscript of the AT, ms. 19 (Chigi R.vi.38). It doubtless was copied from an LXX manuscript and is of no value in determining the date of the original production of the AT.

stands in the AT is needed to determine if it is a Christian apocalypse (see chapter 4). The AT, although Jewish in origin, may have been redacted to its final form between AD 15/16 and 176 and subsequently preserved within a Christian tradition. Much further study is needed on the text of Mordecai's dream to identify its genre and compare its form to other texts already classified by J. J. Collins (Collins 1979).

If I were to suggest a provenance of origin for the AT, I would choose Egypt over Jerusalem. If the text had been produced and maintained in Jerusalem, it is difficult to explain the extent of its divergence from the developing Hebrew tradition that terminated in the MT. This opinion disagrees with recent work published that places most of the development of the recensions of Esther in Jerusalem.

In a recent doctoral dissertation, K. Wynn studies the socio-historical settings of the recensions of Esther and proposes seventeen distinct redactional stages (Wynn 1990, 120–24). He writes that at an early stage the Esther text, originally produced in the Babylonian Diaspora, was carried back to Jerusalem with the returning exiles (ibid., 160). He proposes that numerous subsequent redactions were motivated by the Maccabean struggle for independence and the emerging conflicts between the Pharisaic pietists and Hasmonean nationalists. According to Wynn's reconstruction, the final redaction of the text which introduced additions B and E occurred within the Jewish community in Alexandria in the Roman period.

Having carefully compared the three extant versions of Esther, it seems to me that there is not enough textual evidence to differentiate seventeen redactional layers, let alone describe the precise socio-historical motivation of each. I would agree that the Greek Esther story generally spoke to the issues of Hellenization during the politically unstable period following Alexander's conquest. However, Wynn's description of the dozen or so recensions made in Judea within a century or so conjures the image of a textual tug–of–war between parties who each changed the Esther story to support their own position. For instance, he writes,

> The two Esther texts, Esther IIB[4] and Esther IB, were both in use at the time of the attainment of independence in 142 B.C.E. Each text was used by different factions within the Jewish community. The pietistic

community continued to support Esther IB while the nationalistic
movement rallied around Esther IIB[4] (ibid., 206).

According to Wynn, each of the many redactions was penned by
a political faction which adapted the Esther story to its own special
concerns. Purportedly, this intense interest in the Esther story
attempted to resolve a conflict over the celebration of Purim in
Jerusalem. It seems unlikely to me that any text undergoing the intense
redactional activity that Wynn proposes could have carried any
authority or influence for people who watched the text change before
their eyes. Such a situation might be credible only if there was some
independent historical documentation linking the Esther texts to the
political factions as Wynn proposes.

Unfortunately, Wynn does not provide any concrete historical
documentation that directly and specifically associates the Esther story
with the motives of any historically identifiable group. His
reconstruction is based totally on inference from internal evidence,
construing segments of the Esther texts with the presumed sympathies
of opposing political factions, and then identifying those segments as
redactional strata arising from those parties. Moreover, in his proposed
reconstruction, he does not clearly distinguish the origin, development
and relationship of the three distinct versions. While applauding his
effort to reconstruct the socio–historical settings of the recensions of
Esther, I cannot agree that all three versions of Esther developed
concurrently within a relatively short period of time and within the
same geographical location.

The evidence presented by the texts is best explained, in my
opinion, if the AT developed within a community outside of Judea. The
similarity of the AT to the MT indicates a common point in their
history; on the other hand, the extensive differences between them
indicate the AT developed independently of the Hebrew text. This
suggests an origin for the AT in a location where the Hebrew text was
once known but was no longer used. After the Hebrew text of Esther
returned to Jerusalem with the exiles, it had a continuous existence
within that community which terminated in the extant MT version. I
suggest it is therefore more likely that the AT was originally produced
and developed in Egypt where a sizable Jewish population used
Aramaic, and possibly Hebrew, during the Persian age and where

centuries later their descendants adopted the Greek language of the Hellenistic age.

Although there is no manuscript evidence of Esther among the Elephantine papyri, the existence of a large community of Jews at Elephantine during the Persian period provides a historical setting for the Semitic text of Esther to have entered Egypt soon after it was produced (in Persia?). There are no Hebrew documents found among the (Aramaic) papyri from Elephantine, and the use of Hebrew by the Egyptian Jews of this period is debated. Cowley had the impression that the Aramaic of the Elephantine Jews as attested by their papyri showed the influence of Hebrew (Cowley 1923, 118–19). In Porten's opinion, the Jews of Elephantine were quite at home with Aramaic but he doesn't rule out their use of Hebrew also (Porten 1968, 33n.27). In either case, the known presence of a large community of Jews who spoke Aramaic and possibly Hebrew in Egypt during the Persian period provides a reason for the Semitic text of Esther to have entered Egypt soon after its original production.

That same Semitic text was also found in Jerusalem, either because it had originated there or had been brought there by those returning from exile. Although this Semitic text was not everywhere identical to the extant MT, it was quite similar to it in its extent, i.e., it included all the salient points of chapters 9 and 10. (See the discussion of this in chapters 3 and 5.) The AT therefore reflects an early branching in the Semitic textual tradition from which the MT has come.

Unlike the exiles who returned to Jerusalem from Persia, the Jewish community in Egypt had not experienced so close at hand the deliverance that caused the Jews in Persia to rejoice. However, because communication throughout the Persian empire was extensive and rapid, the Jews of Egypt were no doubt aware that the Jews in other places did celebrate the holiday called Purim.

Many years later, in the Ptolemaic period, the story of Esther and Mordecai was valued by the Egyptian Jews more for its example of how Jews should live within a pagan empire than for its explanation of the origin of Purim. When the text was first translated into Greek during this time, the resulting AT reflected less interest in Purim and more in Mordecai as a Jewish political hero.

As the Greek language replaced Aramaic in Egypt, whatever knowledge of Hebrew the Egyptian Jews once had was largely lost, and the Greek AT was free to develop independently of the Hebrew version. The subsequent development of the AT within the Greek-speaking Jewish community in Egypt highlighted the previous history of the Israelites in Egypt. Parallels between the Esther story and Joseph's life in Egypt have long been recognized (Humphreys 1973; Meinhold 1969, 1975; Wills 1990). Gerleman suggested that the Esther story was patterned after the Exodus narrative (Gerleman 1966). These parallels, which are not at all explicit in the Hebrew Esther, were made more prominent in the Greek version. This study has revealed that the prayers of Mordecai and Esther in addition C in the AT echo the prayer of Moses in Deut 9 and also contain explicit references to the Exodus (see chapter 4).

During the Hasmonean dynasty, Jerusalem again became a center for Jewish culture and religion. The ancient Hebrew texts had been maintained in Jerusalem and were the authoritative texts of that community. Letters sent from Jerusalem to the Egyptian Jews (e.g., 2 Maccabees), who were by that time concentrated mostly in Alexandria, exhorted them to observe the same religious feasts as the Jews in Jerusalem, which by that time included both Purim and Hanukkah. The only existing Greek version of Esther, the AT, was by that time not only quite different from the Hebrew text extant in Jerusalem, but reflected only a minimal interest in Purim. To authorize the celebration of Purim and to standardize the Greek version with the Hebrew text, a new translation of Esther was made, known to us as the LXX version.

Bickerman argues that the colophon on the LXX text of Esther was needed to verify the existence of an authoritative Hebrew text of Esther in Jerusalem to Jews who had no direct access to it. Bickerman takes the need for the colophon on the translation as an indication "that the Hebrew Esther was still unknown in Alexandria in 78–77 B.C." (Bickerman 1944, 355). (His point still stands if the LXX was produced in the alternative year of 114 B.C.) The need for the colophon is consistent with the scenario that the Hebrew text of Esther from which the AT was originally produced was no longer circulating among the Greek–speaking Jews of Egypt.

This newer Greek translation supplanted the AT, which then subsequently survived only as a parochial version within a possibly non-Jewish community where the Macedonian calendar was in use. The Macedonian month names found only in the AT version of Esther are also consistent with an Egyptian provenance.

The names of the Macedonian lunar months were in use in Egypt by the middle of the third century B.C. (Samuel 1972, 146). Although the indigenous Egyptian civil calendar was solar, there was also an Egyptian lunar calendar used for religious purposes. By the time of Ptolemy V, the Macedonian calendar was completely assimilated to the Egyptian lunar calendar by simply equating the Egyptian lunar months to the Macedonian. This system persisted in Egypt until the Julian calendar was introduced late in the Roman period.

The Macedonian month names were used not only in Egypt but widely throughout the vast area of Alexander's empire, and were harmonized in different ways with the lunar calendars locally in use. The adjustment that occurred between AD 15/16 and 46/47 making the Nisan–Adar correspondence with Xandikos–Dystros may have originated in the Seleucid court in Syria (Samuel 1972, 142–3). Although the same Macedonian month names were in use in Egypt as in Syria, it is unclear if and when the intercalating correction, which resulted in the correspondence noted in the AT, was adopted in Egypt. Because the use of a given calendar had great political implications, calendars used in a given place changed with the dominant political sympathies. This often meant more than one calendar was concurrently used at a given time.

The complexity of the relationships between the calendars in use in the Hellenistic kingdoms requires special expertise to locate rightly a given date to its provenance and time of origin. A deeper study of the equivalent month names found in the AT would almost certainly shed light on the history of the text. The point remains that the textual evidence presented by the month names in the AT is consistent with an Egyptian provenance for its preservation after it was supplanted by the LXX version.

The presence of two lunar month names in addition A of the AT, compared to just one in the corresponding place in the LXX text, suggests that addition A was already present in the LXX before the intercalating month was introduced sometime between AD 15/16 and 46/47. The change in the AT that specified two month names was necessary only after this shift in the calendar occurred.

The additions, with perhaps the exception of B and E, probably first appeared in the AT and were copied into the LXX text after its original production. The comparative analysis of the additions discussed in this study (chapter 4) shows the form preserved in the AT to be closer to the form of the additions at the point they were copied from one Greek version to the other. Although this says nothing about the text in which they first appeared, this textual evidence corroborates the theory that the additions were copied from the AT to the LXX. The additions as they now stand in the LXX have experienced more editing than they have in the AT. Because the LXX text replaced the AT and circulated more widely than the AT, there was more opportunity for changes to it after the additions were copied.

The proposed direction of the copy of at least additions A, C, D and F from the AT to the LXX makes sense if the LXX supplanted the AT which already contained that material. Consider the scenario where the AT version known to the Egyptian Jews prior to the production of the LXX contained the additions. When the LXX arrived in Egypt, it did not include the additions because the MT text, from which it had been translated, did not contain them. The material familiar to the Egyptian Jews from the AT was then copied into the new LXX version.

At some later time, attempts were made to correct the AT to the authorized Greek version, the LXX, while preserving the distinctive form of the AT. But because the Greek texts were so different, there were relatively few places where they could be corrected to agree. The scattered readings throughout the AT that agree identically with the LXX came from this type of redactional activity.

Although the AT reflects an early stage in the development of the Hebrew Esther story, its value for textual criticism of the MT or for the reconstruction of its own *Vorlage* is quite limited. The AT has obviously experienced a long and complex history of textual transmission over the centuries between the time of its origin in the early Hellenistic period to the date of its oldest surviving medieval manuscript. Since there is no early manuscript of the AT, it is even quite possible that some of its readings originated in the centuries between the 3rd and the 11th. The known popularity of the Esther story in the medieval period may have motivated such readings.[3]

Virtually nothing is known about the circulation of the AT during these many intervening centuries because neither Christian nor Jewish literature mentions or quotes the AT of Esther. The fact that the book of Esther is not quoted at all in the New Testament and is not referred to by the early Church fathers shrouds its place in Christian tradition with silence. Origen apparently did not know of the AT, for none of the readings distinctive to it are found in the Hexapla. (This perhaps argues against an Egyptian provenance, for if the AT survived in Alexandria, it seems probable that Origen would have been aware of it.) The targums and Talmud do not preserve any clear quote of or reference to the AT of Esther.

Unless older manuscripts of the AT are discovered, or fragments of Esther are identified among the Qumran material, theories on the origin of this intriguing text will continue to be punctuated with many questions marks.

---

[3] *Esther in Medieval Garb* (Walfish 1993) documents how popular the Esther story was in the medieval period. To my knowledge, no one has studied the AT within the historical context from which its surviving manuscripts date.

EXCURSUS: THE ALPHA–TEXT COMPARED TO THE OLD GREEK OF DANIEL

Just as there are two versions of Esther in Greek, there are also two Greek versions of Daniel, referred to as the Old Greek (OG) and Theodotion's (θ) recension. These designations given to the Greek versions of Daniel reflect the current consensus about their relationship. The OG text is older than θ, which is a recension of Daniel produced by revising the OG. The majority text of Daniel is θ. Because Theodotion's recension almost universally replaced the OG version, there are few manuscripts extant which preserve the OG of Daniel. One of these is in the Chigi collection of manuscripts in Rome (Vat. Chigi.R.vii.45 = Gött. 88).

The majority text of the Greek Esther is preserved in the 4th–century uncials and is generally referred to as the LXX text. Only four medieval manuscripts preserve the AT of Esther. If the AT is older than the majority text, it, like OG Daniel, was almost universally replaced. However, unlike Daniel, the LXX text of Esther is almost certainly not a recension of the AT, nor *vice versa*.

One of the extant manuscripts that preserves the AT of Esther is also found in the Chigi collection in Rome (Vat. Chigi.R.vi.38 = Gött. 19). Unlike the other three manuscripts, which contain both the LXX and AT versions, the Chigi manuscript has only one text of Esther, and that is the AT. Although it can never be assumed that texts that happen to be gathered together in a given collection of manuscripts have anything further in common, the fact that Chigi happens to preserve both of two relatively rare texts, the OG of Daniel and the AT of Esther, raises the question of whether the OG of Daniel and the AT may in fact have more of substance in common.

Like the two Greek texts of Esther, which both include six major blocks of additional material, the two Greek texts of Daniel also both include substantial additions: the Prayer of Azariah, the Hymn of the Three Young Men, Susanna, and Bel and the Dragon. Like the additions to Esther, there is no extant Hebrew or Aramaic source corresponding to these additions, although the first two, the Prayer of Azariah and the Hymn of the Three Young Men, are thought to be translations of a Semitic source. Syntax criticism of the additions of Esther indicates that some of them (A, C, D, and F) also may be translations of Semitic sources no longer extant (see chapter 1).

The nature and content of these additions to Daniel as they stand in the OG version are quite different from the same additions as they are found in θ. This suggests a complicated textual history for the additions that integrated them into the respective texts, as opposed to this material having just been "tacked on" at some point. A comparison of the additions to the Greek versions of Esther also shows significant differences between the additions preserved in the AT and the same additions in the LXX Esther (see chapter 4). Although it is beyond the scope of this work, it would be interesting to determine if the differences between the OG and θ of Daniel in the additions show similarities to the differences between the AT and LXX of Esther in the additions. If so, this would present evidence that there was a common point in the redactional history of the texts of Daniel and Esther.

As discussed in chapter 2, Tov's criteria are used to indicate the style of a translation. In order to compare the AT to Daniel, this study applied those criteria to chapter 8 of both Greek versions of Daniel. The results can be directly compared to those of the analysis of the Greek texts of Esther. This comparison shows that the style of the text of OG Dan 8 is freer than that of θ and stands closer to the style of the AT than does θ Dan 8:

The Translation Style of Daniel and Esther Compared
(1=same as MT; 5=completely different)

Text	Equiv.	Word order	Corresp.	Linguistic adequacy	Overall Average
θ: Dan 8	1.3	1.2	1.5	1.6	1.4
OG: Dan 8	1.4	1.3	1.9	2.0	1.6
AT Esth 6	1.6	1.6	2.0	1.9	1.8
AT – all	1.8	1.7	2.2	2.0	1.9
AT Esth 8	2.2	1.6	2.2	2.5	2.1

This table shows that of the texts sampled, θ Dan 8 follows the MT most closely overall and AT Esth 8 deviates the most from the MT. Of the two Greek versions of Dan 8, the OG is more similar to the AT of Esther than is θ.

The θ text of Daniel and LXX Esther more closely follow the MT than does the OG Daniel and the AT. In the case of Esther, the LXX is more similar to the MT because it translates much more of the material found in the MT (1236 units out of 1508, or 82%) than does the AT (590 out of 1508, or 39%). Both OG Daniel and the AT have a few chapters which contain so little of the MT material as to raise the question of a *Vorlage* different from the MT. The AT of Esther deviates the most from the MT in chapters 8–10; similarly, chapters 4–6 of the OG of Daniel have only a handful of verses that correspond to the MT. D. O. Wenthe has found that not more than 40% of the material in chapter 4 of OG Daniel corresponds to the MT (Wenthe 1991, 101). This study of the AT has found that, overall, only about 55% of the MT is represented in the AT. The AT and OG Daniel share the general feature that in the chapters where they deviate the most from the MT they both have many pluses and minuses. One might conclude that OG Dan 4–6 and AT 8–10 had absolutely no contact with the MT. However, one intriguing feature questions that conclusion. Even within these most deviant chapters, both the OG Dan and the AT represent the MT so literally in some places that they must, in spite of their differences, have some fairly direct relationship with the MT.

Both OG Daniel and AT Esther deviate from the MT, but they do so in generally similar ways. Could the Greek version of both books have a common point of origin or redaction? Might they (or their

Semitic *Vorlagen*) belong to the same textual family, tradition or recension? A thorough investigation of this question would involve carefully scrutinizing and comparing at least the texts of OG Daniel chapters 4–6 with AT Esther chapters 8–10 to see if any lexical, syntactical or semantic patterns can be discerned. A further fine–scale comparison of the additions to Esther with the additions to Daniel would be necessary to see if the additions to both books could have arisen from the same socio–historical impulse or even by the same translator/redactor. As tempting as it is to pursue this line of research, such investigation falls outside the scope of this study. Accordingly, this chapter attempts only to sketch out how the AT compares to OG Daniel by comparing the distinctive characteristics of the AT discovered in this study (see chapter 3) to the work which others have already published on the OG of Daniel.

How Does the Greek of the AT Compare to the OG of Daniel?

The basis for this comparison is two recent doctoral dissertations which characterize the OG of Daniel. Working under the direction of E. Ulrich at Notre Dame, D. O. Wenthe examined the OG translation of Daniel 1–6 (Wenthe 1991) and S. Pace Jeansonne characterized the OG of Daniel 7–12 (Jeansonne 1988). Many of the characteristics they have identified with the OG of Daniel can be directly compared to characteristics of the AT revealed by this study (chapters 2 and 3).

Both Wenthe and Jeansonne have concluded that OG Daniel preceded θ and that the θ recension was produced by revising the OG (Wenthe, 95; Jeansonne, 21–22). Jeansonne explains that θ revises OG Daniel to be faithful to a contemporaneous Semitic text in the first century of this era, a Semitic text which was significantly different (at least in chapters 4–6) from the *Vorlage* from which OG Daniel was originally translated.

Until the time of C. A. Moore's dissertation (1965), the AT was thought to be a later "Lucianic" recension of LXX Esther. Further study has convinced most scholars that the AT is not a recension of the LXX, but the chronological and textual relationship between LXX Esther and the AT remains uncertain. The redactional history of the

AT in relationship to the other texts of Esther might be illumined if AT Esther and OG Daniel are characteristically similar.

Wenthe summarized two general features of the translation technique of OG Daniel as 1) greater lexical diversity and 2) "its more fluid use of Greek linguistic structures" (Wenthe, 247). How does the AT compare to these general characteristics of OG Daniel?

The lexical consistency of the AT discussed in chapter 2 of this work can be directly compared to Wenthe's study. Of the twenty–four words which Wenthe selected from MT Daniel to examine in translation, nine of them also occur in MT Esther (בוֹא, אָבַד, אָכַל, אָב, יָד, לֵב, יַיִן, רֹאשׁ and אֶרֶץ). (The translation equivalents used in the AT and LXX texts of Esther for these words are listed in the table at the end of chapter 2.) Wenthe found that these nine Hebrew words are represented in the OG of Daniel by nineteen different lexical forms (compared to eleven in θ). These same nine words are represented by twenty–eight different lexical forms in the AT and by thirty–two different forms in the LXX. Both the AT and LXX of Esther are even more lexically diverse than the OG of Daniel. A comparison of the translation equivalents in OG Daniel to those in the Greek versions of Esther shows no apparent pattern in common, with perhaps the exception that the OG of Daniel distinctively uses εἰσπορεύομαι once to translate בוֹא, as does the LXX Esther.

The current theory holds that most subsequent recensions of the Greek biblical texts are less lexically diverse than their predecessors because of a trend toward standardizing the Hebrew–Greek translation equivalents. This translation/revision technique seems to have been in use during the first century of this era. It is uncertain what, if any, relationship this technique had to the emergence of the MT as the standard Hebrew text. If this trend in standardizing translation equivalents is an accurate interpretation of the evidence, the AT exhibits sufficient lexical diversity to qualify it as an OG text. However, the LXX of Esther, which more closely follows the MT, exhibits even greater lexical diversity.

Wenthe uses the frequency with which a given Hebrew word is translated by the same Greek word as an indicator of how closely the translator followed his *Vorlage*. He finds that the relative frequencies of the translation equivalents מַלְכוּת → βασιλεία and מֶלֶך →

βασιλεύς show that the OG of Daniel in chapters 4–6 deviates from the translation pattern found in chapters 1–3 and 7–12 (ibid., 48–9). In chapters 1–3 and 7–12, מַלְכוּת is translated by βασιλεία 78% of the time, but drops to 59% in chapters 4–6. In chapters 1–3 and 7–12, מֶלֶךְ is translated by βασιλεύς 86% of the time, but only 47% of the time in chapters 4–6. Wenthe assumes a given translator would consistently handle these common words producing a uniform pattern throughout the entire book. Assuming that the text was produced by one translator (which is a reasonable assumption), he infers that the translation of chapters 4–6 *has* been handled consistently with the rest of the book, and that the translator was faithful to the words found in his *Vorlage*. What may look like an apparent inconsistency in translation technique when chapters 4–6 are compared to the MT is really evidence that a text different from the MT must have been the *Vorlage* of the Greek text in chapters 4–6. That is to say, the translator did not translate מֶלֶךְ and מַלְכוּת with the same frequency of the expected Greek words in chapters 4–6 because in fact מֶלֶךְ and מַלְכוּת were not in the *Vorlage* of chapters 4–6 to begin with.

The mere ratios of the frequency of occurrence of βασιλεύς/ מֶלֶךְ and βασιλεία/מַלְכוּת, however, are insufficient evidence for this conclusion. The fact that for about 20% of the occurrences in chapters 1–3 and 7–12 the translator chose something other than βασιλεύς and βασιλεία to render מֶלֶךְ and מַלְכוּת indicates that the translator did in fact freely use other lexically adequate expressions.

The inadequacy of frequency of occurrence as evidence of a different *Vorlage* may be illustrated as follows: The phrase יֵין מַלְכוּת could conceivably be translated οἶνος τῆς βασιλείας, using the translation equivalent מַלְכוּת → βασιλείας, or οἶνος βασιλικός, using an adjective, or perhaps even οἶνος τοῦ βασιλέως. From the fact that there are (at least) three different Greek expressions available to the translator, nothing can be inferred about the *Vorlage* by counting the number of times βασιλεύς and βασιλεία occur. Wenthe's argument is further weakened because the two words he is relying on here have such closely related semantic domains that they overlap in some contexts. If the Greek vocabulary of chapters 1–3 and 7–12 that adequately renders מֶלֶךְ and מַלְכוּת without using βασιλεύς and βασιλεία is also found in chapters 4–6, then Wenthe's conclusion is greatly undermined. It is not merely a comparison of frequency ratios, but a comparison of what other choices were used elsewhere, which must be considered.

To make a direct comparison to OG Daniel, the AT was examined to see if it also handles these two Hebrew words, מֶלֶךְ and מַלְכוּת, differently in chapters 8–10 than in the rest of the book. Sure enough, the same break in the pattern found in chapters 4–6 of OG Daniel is found in AT chapters 8–10. In the AT, מֶלֶךְ is translated in chapters 1–7 by βασιλεύς 42% of the time but only 14% of the time in chapters 8–10. (The corresponding values in the LXX are 67% and 54%, respectively.) Forty–one percent of the occurrences of מַלְכוּת in chapters 1–7 are translated by βασιλεία both in the AT and in the LXX (although not always in the same places). The two occurrences of מַלְכוּת in chapters 8–10 are not once translated by βασιλεία in either the AT or the LXX. When the Greek texts of Esther do not represent the given Hebrew word by the expected Greek word, it is due to either a different lexical choice or to the phrase being entirely omitted in the Greek text.

Two observations follow from this data. Firstly, to the extent that the handling of these two Hebrew words is representative of the translator's technique, it should be noted that the AT is in *all* chapters much more diverse with respect to the MT of Esther than are chapters 1–3 and 7–12 of the OG Daniel. In fact, the low frequency with which these two Hebrew words are consistently translated in all chapters of the AT is more similar to chapters 4–6 of OG Daniel (cf. AT chs. 1–7: מֶלֶךְ → βασιλεύς, 42%; מַלְכוּת → βασιλεία, 41% to OG chs. 1–3, 7–12: מֶלֶךְ → βασιλεύς, 47%; מַלְכוּת → βασιλεία, 59%).

Secondly, the fact that a decrease in the ratio of the frequency of occurrence of βασιλεύς/מֶלֶךְ and βασιλεία/מַלְכוּת is also observed in chapters 8–10 of the AT (and to a lesser degree in the LXX) does not support Wenthe's reasoning nor does it necessarily suggest a relationship between the AT and OG Daniel. Although these figures may at first suggest some correspondence between the OG of Daniel in chapters 4–6 and the AT of Esther in chapters 8–10, such a judgment would be premature because the observed pattern may be only a formal coincidence. After all, one must remember that these ratios are really just a numerical way of saying what is already well known: that the text in chapters 4–6 of the OG Daniel and in chapters 8–10 of the AT of Esther deviates greatly from the MT.

It remains to be determined whether or not chapters 4–6 of OG Daniel deviate from the MT *in the same way* as chapters 8–10 of the AT. For instance what must be determined in regard to the Hebrew words מֶלֶךְ and מַלְכוּת is whether their rendering, where different from the expected Greek words βασιλεύς and βασιλεία, is similar in both OG Daniel and the AT. If this could be shown, it would suggest that these Hebrew words really were present in the *Vorlagen* of the texts and that the same translation technique (same translator?) was used both in OG Daniel and in AT Esther. Such a study might explain why these words in chapters 4–6 of OG Daniel and AT chapters 8–10 were handled differently than in the rest of their respective texts, for instance due to the syntax of Hebrew idiom rather than deviant *Vorlagen*. Such a determination would require the kind of careful comparison of the AT to the OG Daniel mentioned above, and lies outside the scope of this work.

Several parallels between OG Dan 1–6 and the AT are worth noting, though none is of itself compelling evidence of a common history:

1. δοχὴν μεγάλην. Chapter 5 of OG Daniel begins with a proem not found in the other versions of Daniel. One of the distinctive features of this proem that Wenthe identifies is that the banquet given by "Baltasar" is referred to as δοχὴν μεγάλην rather than the ἐστιατόριαν μεγάλην of θ (ibid., 161). This same phrase, δοχὴν μεγάλην, is found distinctively in the AT at 1:9d in reference to the banquet Vashti holds for the women of the court. It corresponds to מִשְׁתֶּה (with no adjective) in the Hebrew; the LXX renders it with πότον and no adjective. A two–word phrase of such a nondescript nature cannot be used to show an affinity between any two texts. However, if further study showed that this was a stereotyped phrase in use during a certain period time or within a certain provenance, or that it had some more specific connotation within the context of the Persian court, then its distinctive presence in both OG Dan and AT may be a significant clue.

2. *Handling the "list genre."* The tendency of OG Daniel to shorten or omit the lists found in the MT is also a tendency of the AT, and to a lesser extent, the LXX of Esther (Wenthe, 187, 192, 225). Wenthe cites work by P. Coxon, who explains that the lists in the MT of Daniel (for instance, of officials, musical instruments, metals, etc.) is a rhetorical technique producing "resonant and rhythmic prose by constant repetitions, variations and additions to the staple list" (ibid., 187 quoting Coxon 1986, 106). The artistic impulse to produce rhythmic patterns and sounds pleasing to the ear would explain why a translator might change the length of a list for rhythm and use different proper names in lists where these names had no other significance but for rhythm and euphony.

In Esth 1:3, the list of groups attending the king's banquet is shortened in both the AT and LXX of Esther. The list in 1:10 of the names of the seven eunuchs is replaced by a plural noun in the AT, but is preserved in the LXX. The list of the names of the king's advisors in 1:14 is shortened in the LXX and omitted entirely in the AT. Two lists naming the recipients of royal memos are found in the MT at 3:12 and 8:9; the LXX preserves both intact and the AT omits both verses in their entirety. If Coxon is correct, perhaps the pleasing rhetorical effect produced by the long lists in the Hebrew (or Aramaic) language would have been lost in the translation into Greek. Recognizing this, the translator of the AT (and of OG Daniel) may have chosen either to omit the list entirely or to shorten it, if it was necessary to preserve its semantic referent. The omission or alteration of this kind of a rhetorical structure seems almost certain to occur during translation. For that reason, deviations from the MT which involve a rhetorical structure are, in my opinion, best explained as a translation decision and not as good evidence of a variant *Vorlage*.

3. *Pronouns for Proper Nouns.* The substitution of a proper noun with a general noun or pronoun is the second most frequently occurring type of small substitutions between the AT and MT, occurring sixteen times (see catalog of differences in chapter 3). For instance, in AT:4:9c, "to Esther" in the MT and LXX is replaced with "to her":

LXX	MT	AT
4:13e καὶ εἶπον	לְהָשִׁיב	4:9c καὶ εἶπεν
αὐτῇ Εσθηρ	אֶל־אֶסְתֵּר	αὐτῇ

Wenthe observed a similar tendency in OG Daniel, for instance at 5:13 (Wenthe, 187):

θ	MT	OG
Dan 5:13 εἶπεν τῷ Δανιηλ	וְאָמַר לְדָנִיֵּאל	εἶπεν αὐτῷ

4. "Your friend." A striking parallel is found between the reading of AT:5:14f and OG Dan 6:13. The expression τὸν φίλον σου ("your friend") is a plus shared only by OG Daniel and the AT. In OG Dan 6:13 the phrase refers to Daniel (ibid., 207). This same phrase is a plus at AT: 5:14f where, in addressing the king, Esther refers to Haman, advisor to the king, as ὁ φίλος σου. Although translated into English as "your friend," the common role that both Daniel and Haman had as a close advisor to a Persian king suggests that this phrase may have held a more technical or specific sense. If further study revealed that this was a stereotyped phrase, used almost as a title, for instance, then this parallel between the AT and OG Dan may be evidence of a common point in redactional history.

5. *Passive Voice Verbs.* The AT tends to favor the aorist passive voice for Hebrew verbal forms which could be pointed as either active or passive. In his comment on the OG Dan 6:17 Wenthe mentions in passing that "the OG places the action in the aorist passive (v.18)" (ibid., 230). Jeansonne also noted this trait in OG Dan 8:10 (Jeansonne, 56). The tendency to prefer passive voice when the Hebrew verb form is ambiguous may indicate that OG Daniel and the AT belong to a family, group or textual tradition. It would be interesting to explore whether Greek texts of other books of the Hebrew Bible exhibit this same preference.

In addition to these specific parallels in readings between OG Daniel and the AT, a more general tendency is also noted. In his notes on chapter 5, Wenthe observes that the "ornate and rhetorical addresses which are placed on the lips of Daniel, the king, and the queen–mother" in the MT are not found in the OG. It is my impression that many of the minuses in the AT are also comprised of discourse. Here is another place where a further more detailed comparison of the discourse found in MT Daniel and Esther, but not in OG Dan and the AT, respectively, might reveal a common pattern.

We now compare Jeansonne's work on the character of OG Dan 7–12 with the character of the AT. The AT of Esther shares many of the same characteristics identified by Jeansonne in the OG of Dan 7–12:

1. The translation of כָּל. Jeansonne observed that the Greek adjective πᾶς ("all") was not present in the OG of Dan 8:5 where כָּל is found in the Hebrew (ibid., 52). The Greek adjective πᾶς is also not found in the AT in seven places where כָּל is found in the Hebrew (1:16l, 2:2k, 3:1k, 5:22a, (9)7:42a, (9)7:47f, (9)7:47h). In five of these units, the LXX of Esther also omits the adjective. In her opinion, the Hebrew adjective כָּל was not present in the *Vorlage* of Dan 8, because this adjective is "typically added to Hebrew texts" (Jeansonne, 57).

2. The occurrence of πύλη. Jeansonne cites McCrystall who finds that the OG of Daniel uses, among others, the word πύλη ("gate") to recall Ezekiel, e.g., Dan 8:2 (ibid., 30). However, she disagrees with McCrystall that this distinctive reading is a deliberate allusion. Instead, she explains it as a mechanical error of metathesis in the Hebrew where the translator confused אבול ("gate") for אובל ("river"). The AT twice includes the Greek noun πύλη, but both are in units for which no Hebrew is extant ((E)7:28h, (8)7:37d). (The LXX of Esther also includes this Greek word at 4:2b to translate the Hebrew שַׁעַר.)

3. References to Susa. The OG of Daniel refers to Susa as "the city" (πόλις) where the Hebrew has בִּירָה ("fortress") (ibid., 49). In contrast, θ uses βάρις, which is not a transliteration but a proper Greek equivalent meaning "castle, palace, fortress." Both the AT and the LXX are similar to OG Daniel. Where there is a noun in apposition with the proper name Susa, the AT (and the LXX) also use πόλις consistently to translate בִּירָה (e.g., 1:5l, 2:5b).

4. The Addition of Nouns in Apposition. The OG of Daniel inserts nouns in apposition to proper nouns for clarification (ibid., 62). This is also a distinctive characteristic of the AT where five times a

noun or noun phrase follows a proper noun where there are none in the
MT or the LXX (2:8e, 5:14f [=LXX], 5:17c, 6:5f, 7:8e). For instance,
the MT and LXX at 5:6 read "the king said to Esther ..." where the AT
has "the king said to Esther, the queen, ..." (AT:5:17c).

5. The Addition of Pronouns. Jeansonne found that the OG tends
to add pronouns to clarify the text (ibid., 66). The AT adds pronouns,
where there are none in the Hebrew (or the LXX), four times (1:4g,
1:11f, 1:11k, 1:18c).

6. Passive Voice Verbs. As noted above, the OG of Daniel
construes verbal forms which are ambiguous in the Hebrew as passive
forms (hiphil or niphal); Theodotion uses active forms (ibid., 56). The
AT shares the OG tendency toward passive voice forms in 6:11g and
possibly in 1:12i and 6:2a.

7. The Date Formula. The OG of Dan 8:1 expresses "in the third
year of the reign of Belshazzar" with a genitive of time, ἔτους τρίτου
βασιλεύοντος; θ uses the formula ἐν ἔτει τρίτῳ τῆς βασιλείας
(ibid., 34). In the AT, the date formula (relocated from 1:3 to the first
sentence of addition A) reads ἔτους δευτέρου βασιλεύοντος agreeing
in syntax with the OG formula. The LXX retains the date formula at
1:3, where it agrees with that found in θ, and also at A:1, where it is
identical to that of the AT, agreeing there in syntax with OG Dan 8:1.

8. Tendency to Use Compound Verbs. The OG tendency to use
compound verbs noted by Jeansonne is found also in the AT and the
LXX of Esther (ibid., 58). The AT uses a compound verb at least
eighteen times where the LXX does not; the LXX uses a compound
verb eighteen times where the AT does not.

9. The Omission of רַב. Jeansonne notes that the OG of Dan 7:3
does not represent the adjective רַב present in the Hebrew. She explains
this omission as due to homoioteleuton within the Hebrew (ibid., 79).
Though it may be entirely coincidental, the AT also omits units with
רַב three, and maybe four, times (1:7i, 1:8h, 5:21k and possibly
10:3m). None of these instances could be due to homoioteleuton.

However, all of them except 1:7i involve the omission of more than just that word.

10. *The Omission of* יְקָר. Jeansonne observes that the OG of Dan 7:14 omits יְקָר due to homoiarchton within the Hebrew (ibid., 80). Though probably coincidental, the AT also omits translating this Hebrew word in unit 6:5d, where its omission cannot be similarly explained.

There are also a few characteristics of the AT that make an interesting contrast to the OG of Daniel:

1. *"People of the Land."* Jeansonne cites F.F. Bruce, who argues that the translation of כָּל־עַם הָאָרֶץ ("all the people of the land") as πάντι ἔθνει ἐπὶ τῆς γῆς ("to every nation on earth") in the OG of Dan 9:6 results from interpretation, not from a variant *Vorlage*. Bruce is quoted as arguing that the OG of Dan 9:6 strikes a note of wider universalism, since "the prophets who spoke 'to all the people of the land' … are now said to have spoke [sic] 'to every nation on earth'" (ibid., 29). Bruce sees this as an interpretive translation arising from the political situation of the Greek–speaking Jews in the Diaspora. Jeansonne argues against Bruce on this point, contending that the OG does not exhibit any consistent pattern that would indicate the greater universalism Bruce suggests (ibid., 118).

The phrase in question, מֵעַמֵּי הָאָרֶץ, occurs once in the Hebrew of Esther (8:17). It is translated τῶν ἐθνῶν by the LXX and τῶν Ἰουδαίων by the AT. If Bruce is correct, the AT is not displaying the same tendency toward universalism evidenced by the LXX translation. In fact, the AT reading "the Jews" is even more specific and narrow than the corresponding Hebrew phrase.

2. πρός *for* עַל. Jeansonne notes that πρός is an equivalent reading in the OG for the Hebrew preposition עַל; whereas θ standardizes with ἐπί (ibid., 50). In the Greek versions of Esther עַל is not once translated by πρός, but is most frequently translated in both the LXX and AT by ἐπί.

3. The Translation of חמה/חמת/חמם. The OG of Daniel renders the Hebrew noun חֵמָה ("wrath") with θυμός. Theodotion uses ὁρμή ("rage"), which Jeansonne argues is a standard translation equivalent of חֵמָה. She points out that ὁρμή is also found in θ Ezek 3:14 for חֵמָה and that Aquila and Symmachus both use ὁρμή for חֵמָה in Gen 3:16 (ibid., 52). Where חֵמָה occurs in the Hebrew of Esther and is translated by a Greek noun, the LXX chooses θυμός (2:1, 7:10) in agreement with the OG. The AT in 1:12 and 7:7 chooses, not ὁρμή, but the very similar word ὀργή, which is close in meaning as well as in form (note the difference in breathing and the γ instead of μ). It is uncertain whether an inner–Greek corruption of one form into the other may have occurred, or whether the AT translator simply chose a different word. Nevertheless, the word which renders חֵמָה in the AT is closer in form to θ than to OG in this instance.

4. The Translation of גדל. Jeansonne notes that the verbal form of the root גדל is standardized in θ with the infinitive μεγαλύνειν, where the OG, exhibiting its greater lexical diversity, uses the infinitives ὑψοῦν and κατισχύσειν (ibid., 60). Of the three occurrences of this root in the Hebrew of Esther, the AT translates it only once (3:1c) and that with ἐμεγάλυνεν. The LXX translates it twice, once with ἐδόξασεν (3:1b) and once with περιέθηκεν (5:11g), showing greater lexical diversity. Here the AT shows greater affinity with the θ text of Daniel.

5. ἐν τῇ χειρί σου τῇ κραταιᾷ. This phrase is not discussed by Jeansonne, but its occurrence in both θ Dan 9:15 and addition C of the AT of Esther is worth noting. The expression is strongly associated with the Exodus, occurring repeatedly in that connection in the Greek texts of Exodus and Deuteronomy. (See the further discussion of this in the section on addition C in chapter 4.) This phrase occurs distinctively in the prayer of Daniel in θ, but not in OG Dan. The phrase occurs in addition C in the prayer of Esther (AT:4:25k, l). This evidence suggests an affinity between Esther addition C and θ Dan. Since addition C is clearly secondary to the original production of the AT, it does not weigh against the original AT having affinity with OG Dan.

CONCLUSIONS

This brief comparison of the AT to the OG of Daniel has identified a few general tendencies, such as similar translation style, great lexical diversity, the omission of discourse, and the specific parallels listed above. This limited comparison also shows that the AT shares a few characteristics of θ. Since θ is believed to be a revision of the OG Daniel, it is possible that the AT has affinity with OG Daniel from its original production, but was subsequently revised toward the particularities characteristic of "Theodotion."

On the other hand, perhaps the nature of the parallels identified in this brief study is either too general or too ubiquitous to show any true affinity between OG Daniel and the AT. Substantial further study would be required to demonstrate that the AT has a greater affinity with the OG of Daniel than it does with θ, but this initial comparison points in that direction. It is also not possible to conclude from the evidence presented here that the AT and OG Daniel are contemporaneous texts, or that they originated in the same provenance, or that they stand in the same textual group, recension or tradition. The evidence presented in this brief study does suggest that a comprehensive comparison of the AT to the OG of Daniel is warranted and that such a study would yield valuable information about these two rare texts preserved by the Chigi manuscript.

WORKS CITED

Alexander, P. S.   1984. "Epistolary Literature." *Jewish Writings of the Second Temple Period*. Philadelphia: Fortress Press. 579–96.

Anderson, B. W.   1950. "The Place of the Book of Esther in the Christian Bible." *JR* 30: 32–43.

Bardtke, H.   1963. *Das Buch Esther*. Gütersloh: Gütersloher Verlagshaus Gerd Mohn.

Barthélemy, D., et al.   1986. *The Story of David and Goliath: Textual and Literary Criticism*. Göttingen: Vandenhoeck & Ruprecht.

Berg, S. B.   1979. *The Book of Esther: Motifs, Themes and Structure*. Missoula: Scholars Press.

Bickerman, E. J. 1944. "The Colophon of the Greek Book of Esther." *JBL* 63: 339–62.

——————   1950. "Notes on the Greek Book of Esther." *PAAJR* 20: 101–33.

Brooke, A. E., McLean, N. and Thackeray H. St. John, eds. 1940. "Esther, Judith, Tobit." *The Old Testament in Greek*, III, Pt. I. Cambridge: U. Press.

Cazelles, H.   1961. "Note sur la composition du rouleau d'Esther."*Lex tua veritas: Festschrift for H. Junker.* 17–29.

Clines, D. J. A. 1984. *The Esther Scroll: The Story of the Story.* Sheffield: JSOT Press.

Collins, J. J.   1979. "Apocalypse: The Morphology of a Genre."
                    Semeia 14: 1–20.
Cook, H. J.   1969. "The A–Text of the Greek Versions of the
                    Book of Esther." *Z Altt W* 81: 369–76.
Cowley, A. E.   1923. *Aramaic Papyri of the Fifth Century B. C.*
                    Oxford: Clarendon.
Coxon, P.   1986. "The 'List' Genre and Narrative Style in the
                    Court Tales of Daniel." *J St OT* 35: 95–121.
Cross, F. M.   1961. "The Development of the Jewish Scripts." *The
                    Bible and the Ancient Near East.* Garden City, NY:
                    Doubleday & Co. 133–202.
Day, L. M.   1995. *Three Faces of a Queen: Characterization in
                    the Books of Esther.* JSOTS v. 186. Sheffield:
                    Academic Press.
de Lagarde, P. A. 1883. *Librorum Veteris Testamenti Canonicorum.*
                    Göttingen.
Deissmann, A.   1927. *Light from the Ancient East.* New York:
                    George H. Doran, Co.
Dommershausen, W. 1968. *Die Esterrolle: Stil und Ziel einer_
                    alttestamentlichen Schrift.* Stuttgart: Katholisches
                    Bibelwerk.
Dorothy, C. V. 1989. "The Books of Esther: Structure, Genre, and
                    Textual Integrity." Ph.D. diss. Claremont Graduate
                    School. (JSOTS v. 187, Sheffield: Academic, in press).
Duchesne–Guillemin, J. 1953. "Les Noms des Eunuques d'Assuerus."
                    Studies in the Book of Esther. C. A. Moore, ed.
                    New York: Ktav Publishing House. 273–76.
Ehrlich, E. L.   1955. "Der Traum des Mardochai." *Z Rel G* VII(1):
                    69–74.
Field, F.   1875. *Origenis Hexaplorum.* Hildesheim: Georg
                    Olms Verlagsbuchhandlung.
Fox, M. V.   1991. *The Redaction of the Books of Esther.*
                    Atlanta: Scholars Press.
——————   1992. "The Redaction of the Greek Alpha–Text of
                    Esther." *Sha'arei Talmon.* Winona Lake, IN:
                    Eisenbrauns. 207–20.
Fritzsche, O. F. 1848. *ΕΣΘΗΡ.* Turici: Typis Orellii, Fuesslini
                    et Socc.

Gan, M.   1961. "The Book of Esther in the Light of the Story
                 of Joseph in Egypt" (Hebrew). *Tarbiz* 31: 144–49.

Gardner, A. E.   1984. "The Relationship of the Additions to the Book
                 of Esther to the Maccabean Crisis." *Journal for the
                 Study of Judaism in Persian, Hellenistic and Roman
                 Period* 15: 1–8.

Gehman, H. S.   1924. "Notes on the Persian Words in the Book of
                 Esther." *JBL* 43: 321–28.

Gerleman, G.   1966. "Studien zu Esther: Stoff–Struktur–Stil–Sinn."
                 BS 48: 1–48.

Gordis, R.   1976. "Studies in the Esther Narrative." *JBL* 95:
                 43–58.

Hanhart, R.   1966. "Esther." *Septuaginta. Vetus Testamentum
                 Graecum auctoritate Societatis Gottingensis editum,*
                 ed. J. Ziegler, III. Göttingen: Vanderhoeck &
                 Ruprecht.

Hays, R. B.   1989. *Echoes of Scripture in the Letters of Paul.*
                 New Haven: Yale U. Press.

Hoschander, J.   1923. *The Book of Esther in the Light of History.*
                 Philadelphia: Dropsie College.

Humphreys, W.   1973. "A Life–Style for Diaspora: A Study of the
                 Tales of Esther and Daniel." *JBL* 92: 211–23.

Jeansonne, S. P. 1988. *The Old Greek Translation of Daniel 7–12.*
                 Washington, DC: The Catholic Biblical Association
                 of America.

Jobes, K. H.   1995. "A Comparative Syntactic Analysis of the
                 Greek Versions of Daniel: A Test Case for New
                 Methodology." *BIOSCS* 28, Fall 1995.

Jones, B. W.   1978. "The So–called Appendix to the Book of
                 Esther." *Semitics* 6: 36–43.

Lewy, J.   1939. "The Feast of the 14th Day of Adar." *HUCA*
                 14: 127–51.

Maloney, E. C.   1981. *Semitic Interference in Marcan Syntax.* Chico:
                 Scholars Press.

———————   1989. review of *Syntax Criticism of the Synoptic
                 Gospels,* by R. A Martin. *CBQ* 51: 378–80.

Marquis, G.   1986. "Word Order as a Criterion for the Evaluation of Translation Technique in the LXX and the Evaluation of Word–Order Variants as Exemplified in LXX–Ezekiel." *Textus* 13: 59–84.

Martin, R. A.   1974. *Syntactical Evidence of Semitic Sources in Greek Documents.* Missoula: Scholars Press.

————— 1975. "Syntax Criticism of the LXX Additions to the Book of Esther." *JBL* 94: 65–72.

————— 1987. *Syntax Criticism of the Synoptic Gospels.* Lewiston: Edwin Mellen Press.

————— 1989. *Syntax Criticism of Johannine Literature, the Catholic Epistles, and the Gospel Passion Accounts.* Lewiston, NY: Edwin Mellen Press.

McCrystall, A.   1980. "Studies in the Old Greek Translation of Daniel." D. Phil. diss. Oxford U.

Meinhold, A.   1969. "Die Diasporanovelle — eine alttestamentliche Gattung." Dr. Theol. diss. Ernst–Moritz–Arndt–Universität.

————— 1975. "Die Gattung des Josephsgeschichte und des Estherbuches: Diasporanovelle, I." *Z Altt W* 87: 306–24.

————— 1976. "Die Gattung der Josephsgeschichte und des Estherbuches: Diasporanovelle II." *Z Altt W* 88: 72–93.

Milik, J. T.   1992. "Les Modeles Arameens du Livre D'Esther dans la Grotte 4 de Qumran." *R Qumran* 15: 321–99.

Millard, A. R.   1977. "The Persian Names in Esther and the Reliability of the Hebrew Text." *JBL* 96: 481–88.

Moore, C. A.   1965. "The Greek Text of Esther." Ph.D. diss. Johns Hopkins University.

————— 1967. "A Greek Witness to a Different Hebrew Text of Esther." *Z Altt W* 79(3): 351–58.

————— 1971. *The Anchor Bible: Esther.* New York: Doubleday.

————— 1973. "On the Origins of the LXX Additions to the Book of Esther." *JBL* 92: 382–93.

Moore, C. A.   1977. *Daniel, Esther and Jeremiah: The Additions.*
                    New York: Doubleday.
————————   1982. *Studies in the Book of Esther.* New York:
                    Ktav Publishing House.
Motzo, B.   1934. Il rifacimento Greco di Ester e il III Mac.
                    Saggi de storia e letteratura Guideo–Ellenistica.
                    Florence: 272–90.
Nickelsburg, G.   1984. "The Bible Rewritten and Expanded." *Jewish
                    Writings of the Second Temple Period.* 89–156.
Oppenheim, A.   1965. "On Royal Gardens in Mesopotamia." *J Near
                    East St* 24: 328–33.
Paton, L. B.   1908. "A Text–Critical Apparatus to the Book of
                    Esther." *Old Testament and Semitic Studies in
                    Memory of William Rainey Harper.* Chicago: U. of
                    Chicago Press. 1–52.
————————   1916. *A Critical and Exegetical Commentary on the
                    Book of Esther.* New York: Charles Scribner's Sons.
Porten, B.   1968. *Archives from Elephantine: The Life of an
                    Ancient Jewish Military Colony.* Berkeley: U. Of
                    CA Press.
Roiron, F. X.   1916. "Les parties deuterocanoniques du Livre
                    D'Esther." *Recherches de science religieuse* : 3–16.
Rosenthal, L. A.   1895. "Die Josephsgeschichte mit den Büchern Ester und
                    Daniel verglichen." *Z Altt W* 15: 278–84; 16: 182
                    (1896); 17: 126–28 (1897).
Samuel, A. E.   1972. "Calendars of the Hellenistic Kingdoms."
                    *Greek and Roman Chronology: Calendars and Years
                    in Classical Antiquity.* München: C.H. Beck'sche
                    Verlagsbuchhandlung. 139–51.
Seeligmann, I. L.   1990. "Problems and Perspectives in Modern
                    Septuagint Research." *Textus* 15: 169–232.
Soubigou, L.   1952. Esther traduit et commente. *La Sainte Bible —
                    Bible de Jerusalem.* Paris: Cerf. 2d, ed.
Swete, H. B.   1914. *An Introduction to the Old Testament in
                    Greek.* Peabody, MA: Hendrickson.
Torrey, C. C.   1944. "The Older Book of Esther." *Harv Th R*
                    37(1): 1–40.

Tov, E. 1981. *The Text–Critical Use of the Septuagint.* Jerusalem: Simor, Ltd.

——————— 1982. "The 'Lucianic' Text of the Canonical and the Apocryphal Sections of Esther: A Rewritten Biblical Book." *Textus* 10: 1–25.

——————— 1992. "Interchanges of Consonants between the Masoretic Text and the Vorlage of the Septuagint." *Shaarei Talmon: Studies in the Bible, Qumran, and the Ancient Near East Presented to Shemaryahu Talmon.* Winona Lake, IN: Eisenbrauns. 255–66.

Walfish, B. D. 1993. *Esther in Medieval Garb: Jewish Interpretation of the Book of Esther in the Middle Ages.* Albany: SUNY Press.

Wenthe, D. O. 1991. "The Old Greek Translation of Daniel 1–6." Ph.D. diss. University of Notre Dame.

Wevers, J. W. 1990. *Notes on the Greek Text of Exodus.* Atlanta: Scholars Press.

Wills, L. M. 1990. *The Jew in the Court of the Foreign King: Ancient Jewish Court Legends.* Minneapolis: Fortress Press.

Wynn, K. H. 1990. "The Sociohistorical Contexts of the Recensions of Esther." Ph.D. diss. Southern Baptist Theological Seminary.

Zadok, R. 1986. "Notes on Esther [links of personal names with Persian or chiefly Imperial Aramaic]." *Z Altt W* 98(1): 105–10.

Zeitlin, S. 1972. "The Books of Esther and Judith: A Parallel." *The Book of Judith.* Leiden: E. J. Brill. 1–37.

Appendix 1: The Parallel Texts of Esther

THE TEXTS OF ESTHER — ADDITION A

		LXX (Göttingen o')	MT (BHS 3)		AT (Göttingen L)	
A:1	a	"Ετους δευτέρου βασιλεύοντος	– No Hebrew Text Extant –	A:1	"Ετους δευτέρου βασιλεύοντος	a
	b	'Αρταξέρξου			Ασσυήρου	b
	c	τοῦ μεγάλου			τοῦ μεγάλου	c
	d	τῇ μιᾷ τοῦ			μιᾷ τοῦ	d
	e				μηνὸς Αδαρ	e
	f	Νισα			Νισαν	f
	g				(ὅς ἐστι Δύστρος Ξανθικός)	g
	h	ἐνύπνιον εἶδεν Μαρδοχαῖος			ἐνύπνιον εἶδε Μαρδοχαῖος	h
	i	ὁ τοῦ Ιαίρου τοῦ Σεμεΐου			ὁ τοῦ Ιαείρου τοῦ Σεμεΐου	i
	j	τοῦ Κισαίου			τοῦ Κισαίου	j
	k	ἐκ φυλῆς Βενιαμιν,			τῆς φυλῆς Βενιαμιν,	k
						l
A:2	a	ἄνθρωπος Ἰουδαῖος				m
	b	οἰκῶν ἐν Σούσοις τῇ πόλει,				n
	c	ἄνθρωπος μέγας		(A:2)	ἄνθρωπος μέγας	o
	d	θεραπεύων ἐν τῇ αὐλῇ τοῦ βασιλέως.				p
A:3	a	ἦν δὲ ἐκ				
	b	τῆς αἰχμαλωσίας ἧς		A:2(3)	τῆς αἰχμαλωσίας ἧς	a
	c	ᾐχμαλώτευσεν Ναβουχοδονοσορ			ᾐχμαλώτευσε Ναβουχοδονοσορ	b

Addition A

THE TEXTS OF ESTHER — ADDITION A

LXX (Göttingen o')			MT (BHS 3)	AT (Göttingen L)		
	d	βασιλεὺς Βαβυλῶνος	– No Hebrew Text Extant –		c	ὁ βασιλεὺς Βαβυλῶνος
	e	ἐξ Ιερουσαλημ			d	
	f	μετὰ Ιεχονίου			e	μετὰ Ιεχονίου
	g	τοῦ βασιλέως τῆς Ἰουδαίας.			f	τοῦ βασιλέως τῆς Ἰουδαίας.
A:4	a	καὶ τοῦτο		A:3(4)	a	καὶ τοῦτο
	b				b	ἦν
	c	αὐτοῦ τὸ ἐνύπνιον·			c	αὐτοῦ τὸ ἐνύπνιον·
	d	καὶ ἰδοὺ			d	καὶ ἰδοὺ
A:4	e	φωναὶ καὶ			e	φωνὴ καὶ
	f				f	κραυγή
	g	θόρυβος,			g	θορύβου,
	h	βρονταὶ καὶ σεισμός,			h	βρονταὶ καὶ σεισμὸς
	i				i	καὶ
	j	τάραχος ἐπὶ τῆς γῆς.			j	τάραχος ἐπὶ τῆς γῆς.
A:5	a	καὶ ἰδοὺ		A:4(5)	a	καὶ ἰδοὺ
	b	δύο δράκοντες			b	δύο δράκοντες,
	c	μεγάλοι ἕτοιμοι			c	
	d				d	καὶ

Addition A

THE TEXTS OF ESTHER — ADDITION A

	LXX (Göttingen o')	MT (BHS 3)	AT (Göttingen L)	
e	προσῆλθον	– No Hebrew Text Extant –	προσῆλθον	e
f	ἀμφότεροι παλαίειν,		ἀμφότεροι παλαίειν,	f
g	καὶ ἐγένετο αὐτῶν φωνὴ	A:5 καὶ ἐγένετο αὐτῶν φωνή,	a
h	μεγάλη,			
A:6 a	καὶ τῇ φωνῇ αὐτῶν ἡτοιμάσθη			
b	πᾶν ἔθνος εἰς πόλεμον			
c	ὥστε πολεμῆσαι δικαίων ἔθνος.			
			(A:6) καὶ ἐταράσσετο πάντα	c
			ἀπὸ τῆς φωνῆς	d
			τῆς κραυγῆς ταύτης.	e
				f
				g
				h
			A:6 μαρτυρομένη πᾶσι τοῖς λαοῖς	a
A:7 a	καὶ ἰδοὺ			
b	ἡμέρα σκότους καὶ γνόφου,		(A:7) ἡμέρα σκότους καὶ γνόφου	c
c	θλῖψις καὶ στενοχωρία, κάκωσις			d
d	καὶ τάραχος		(A:8) καὶ ταραχὴ	e
e	μέγας ἐπὶ τῆς γῆς,			f
A:8 a	καὶ ἐταράχθη δίκαιον		πολέμου, καὶ ἡτοιμάσατο	g
b	πᾶν ἔθνος		πᾶν ἔθνος	h

THE TEXTS OF ESTHER — ADDITION A

	LXX (Göttingen o')	MT (BHS 3)		AT (Göttingen L)	
		– No Hebrew Text Extant –			
c	φοβούμενοι τὰ ἑαυτῶν κακά,			πολεμῆσαι,	i
d	καὶ ἡτοιμάσθησαν ἀπολέσθαι,		(A:9)	καὶ ἀνεβοήσαμεν	j
A:9 a	καὶ ἐβόησαν			πρὸς κύριον	k
b	πρὸς τὸν θεόν.			ἀπὸ φωνῆς	l
c	ἀπὸ δὲ τῆς βοῆς			τῆς κραυγῆς	m
d	αὐτῶν			αὐτῶν.	n
e				καὶ	o
f			A:7		a
g	ἐγένετο			ἐγένετο	b
h	ὡσανεὶ ἀπὸ			ἐκ	c
i	μικρᾶς πηγῆς			πηγῆς μικρᾶς	d
j				ὕδωρ πολύ,	e
k	ποταμὸς μέγας,			ποταμὸς μέγας·	f
l	ὕδωρ πολύ.				
A:10 a	φῶς		A:8(10)	φῶς,	a
b	καὶ				b
c	ὁ ἥλιος ἀνέτειλεν,			ἥλιος ἀνέτειλε,	c
d	καὶ οἱ ταπεινοὶ ὑψώθησαν			καὶ οἱ ποταμοὶ ὑψώθησαν	d

Addition A

THE TEXTS OF ESTHER — ADDITION A

	LXX (Göttingen o')	MT (BHS 3)	AT (Göttingen L)	
e	καὶ κατέφαγον τοὺς ἐνδόξους.	– No Hebrew Text Extant –	καὶ κατέπιον τοὺς ἐνδόξους.	e
A:11 a	καὶ διεγερθεὶς Μαρδοχαῖος		A:9(11) καὶ ἀναστὰς Μαρδοχαῖος	a
b	ὁ ἑωρακὼς			b
c			ἐκ τοῦ ὕπνου αὐτοῦ	c
d	τὸ ἐνύπνιον		ἐμερίμνα τί	d
e	τοῦτο		τὸ ἐνύπνιον	e
f	καὶ			f
g	τί ὁ θεὸς		καὶ	g
h	βεβούλευται ποιῆσαι,		τί ὁ δυνατὸς	h
i			ἑτοιμάζει ποιῆσαι.	i
j			A:10 καὶ τὸ ἐνύπνιον αὐτοῦ	a
k			κεκρυμμένον ἦν	b
l	εἶχεν αὐτὸ			c
m	ἐν τῇ καρδίᾳ		ἐν τῇ καρδίᾳ	d
n			αὐτοῦ,	e
o	καὶ ἐν παντὶ λόγῳ		καὶ ἐν παντὶ καιρῷ	f
p	ἤθελεν ἐπιγνῶναι αὐτὸ		ἦν ἀναζητῶν αὐτό.	g
q	ἕως τῆς νυκτός.			h

Addition A

THE TEXTS OF ESTHER — ADDITION A

LXX (Göttingen o')	MT (BHS 3)	AT (Göttingen L)
	– No Hebrew Text Extant –	
	A:11	a ἐπίκρισις αὐτοῦ
		b διασαφήσεται αὐτῷ
		c ἕως τῆς ἡμέρας
A:12 a καὶ ἡσύχασεν	(A:12)	d ἧς ὕπνωσε
b Μαρδοχαῖος		e Μαρδοχαῖος
c ἐν τῇ αὐλῇ		f ἐν τῇ αὐλῇ
d		g τοῦ βασιλέως
e μετὰ Γαβαθα		h μετὰ Αστάου
f καὶ Θαρρα		i καὶ Θεδεύτου
g τῶν δύο εὐνούχων		j τῶν δύο εὐνούχων
h τοῦ βασιλέως		k τοῦ βασιλέως
i τῶν φυλασσόντων τὴν αὐλήν,		
A:13 a ἤκουσέν τε	A:12(13)	a καὶ ἤκουσε
b αὐτῶν τοὺς λογισμοὺς		b τοὺς λόγους αὐτῶν
c καὶ τὰς μερίμνας αὐτῶν		c καὶ τὰς διαβολὰς αὐτῶν,
d ἐξηραύνησεν		d ὡς ἐξηγοῦντο
e καὶ ἔμαθεν		e
f ὅτι ἑτοιμάζουσιν		f

Addition A

THE TEXTS OF ESTHER — ADDITION A

	LXX (Göttingen o')	MT (BHS 3)		AT (Göttingen L)
g	τὰς χεῖρας ἐπιβαλεῖν	– No Hebrew Text Extant –	g	τοῦ ἐπιθέσθαι
h	Ἀρταξέρξη τῷ βασιλεῖ,		h	Ασσυήρῳ τῷ βασιλεῖ
i			i	τοῦ ἀνελεῖν αὐτόν.
j			A:13 a	εὖ δὲ φρονήσας ὁ Μαρδοχαῖος
k	καὶ ὑπέδειξεν		b	ἀπήγγειλε
l	τῷ βασιλεῖ		c	
m	περὶ αὐτῶν.		d	περὶ αὐτῶν.
A:14 a	καὶ ἐξήτασεν ὁ βασιλεὺς		A:14 a	καὶ ἤτασεν ὁ βασιλεὺς
b	τοὺς δύο εὐνούχους,		b	τοὺς δύο εὐνούχους
c			c	καὶ εὗρε τοὺς λόγους
d			d	Μαρδοχαίου,
e	καὶ ὁμολογήσαντες		e	καὶ ὁμολογήσαντες
f			f	οἱ εὐνοῦχοι
g	ἀπήχθησαν.		g	ἀπήχθησαν.
A:15 a	καὶ ἔγραψεν		A:15 a	καὶ ἔγραψεν
b			b	Ασσυῆρος
c	ὁ βασιλεὺς		c	ὁ βασιλεὺς
d	τοὺς λόγους τούτους		d	περὶ τῶν λόγων τούτων,

Addition A

THE TEXTS OF ESTHER — ADDITION A

	LXX (Göttingen o')	MT (BHS 3)	AT (Göttingen L)	
		– No Hebrew Text Extant –		
e	εἰς μνημόσυνον,			e
f	καὶ Μαρδοχαῖος ἔγραψεν		καὶ ἐγράφη Μαρδοχαῖος	f
g	περὶ		ἐν τῷ βιβλίῳ τοῦ βασιλέως	g
h			περὶ	h
i			τοῦ μνημονεύειν	i
j	τῶν λόγων τούτων.		τῶν λόγων τούτων.	j
A:16 a	καὶ ἐπέταξεν ὁ βασιλεὺς		A:16 καὶ ἐνετείλατο ὁ βασιλεὺς	a
b	Μαρδοχαίῳ		περὶ τοῦ Μαρδοχαίου	b
c	θεραπεύειν		θεραπεύειν	c
d			αὐτὸν	d
e	ἐν τῇ αὐλῇ		ἐν τῇ αὐλῇ	e
f			τοῦ βασιλέως	f
g			καὶ πᾶσαν θύραν ἐπιφανῶς	g
h			τηρεῖν	h
i	καὶ ἔδωκεν αὐτῷ		A:17 καὶ ἔδωκεν αὐτῷ	a
j	δόματα			b
k	περὶ τούτων.		περὶ τούτων	c
A:17 a	καὶ ἦν			d

Addition A

THE TEXTS OF ESTHER — ADDITION A

	LXX (Göttingen o')	MT (BHS 3)		AT (Göttingen L)	
b	Αμαν Αμαδάθου	(A:17)	– No Hebrew Text Extant –	Αμαν Αμαδάθου	e
c	Βουγαῖος			Μακεδόνα	f
d	ἔνδοξος				g
e	ἐνώπιον τοῦ βασιλέως,			κατὰ πρόσωπον τοῦ βασιλέως.	h
f	καὶ ἐζήτησεν	A:18		καὶ ἐζήτει	a
g				ὁ Αμαν	b
h	κακοποιῆσαι			κακοποιῆσαι	c
i	τὸν Μαρδοχαῖον			τὸν Μαρδοχαῖον	d
j	καὶ			καὶ	e
k				πάντα	f
l	τὸν λαὸν αὐτοῦ			τὸν λαὸν αὐτοῦ	g
m	ὑπὲρ			ὑπὲρ	h
n				τοῦ λελαληκέναι αὐτὸν	i
o				τῷ βασιλεῖ	j
p				περὶ	k
q	τῶν δύο εὐνούχων			τῶν εὐνούχων,	l
r	τοῦ βασιλέως.				m
				διότι ἀνῃρέθησαν.	n

Addition A

	LXX (Göttingen o')		MT (BHS 3)		AT (Göttingen L)	
1:1	καὶ ἐγένετο	a	וַיְהִי	1:1	καὶ ἐγένετο	a
	μετὰ τοὺς λόγους τούτους	b	בִּימֵי		μετὰ τοὺς λόγους τούτους	b
	ἐν ταῖς ἡμέραις	c	אֲחַשְׁוֵרוֹשׁ הוּא		ἐν ἡμέραις	c
	Ἀρταξέρξου —	d	אֲחַשְׁוֵרֹשׁ הַמֹּלֵךְ		Ασσυήρου	d
	οὗτος ὁ Ἀρταξέρξης	e				e
		f			τοῦ βασιλέως	f
		g	מֵהֹדּוּ		τοῦ μεγάλου,	g
		h	וְעַד־כּוּשׁ		ὑπετάγησαν αὐτῷ	h
	ἀπὸ τῆς Ἰνδικῆς	i			ἀπὸ τῆς Ἰνδικῆς	i
		j			ἕως τῆς Αἰθιοπίας	j
	ἑκατὸν εἴκοσι ἑπτὰ	k	שֶׁבַע וְעֶשְׂרִים וּמֵאָה		ἑκατὸν εἴκοσι ἑπτὰ	k
	χωρῶν	l	מְדִינָה׃		χῶραι.	l
	ἐκράτησεν —	m				m
1:2	ἐν αὐταῖς ταῖς ἡμέραις	a	בַּיָּמִים הָהֵם	1:2		a
	ὅτε ἐθρονίσθη	b	כְּשֶׁבֶת			b
	ὁ βασιλεὺς	c	הַמֶּלֶךְ		ἐν τῷ καθῆσθαι	c
	Ἀρταξέρξης	d	אֲחַשְׁוֵרוֹשׁ עַל כִּסֵּא מַלְכוּתוֹ אֲשֶׁר בְּשׁוּשַׁן הַבִּירָה		Ασσυήρου	d

Chapter 1

THE TEXTS OF ESTHER — CHAPTER 1

	LXX (Göttingen o')	MT (BHS 3)	AT (Göttingen L)	
e			ἐπὶ τοῦ θρόνου	e
f			τῆς βασιλείας αὐτοῦ,	f
g	ἐν Σούσοις τῇ πόλει,			g
1:3 a	ἐν τῷ τρίτῳ ἔτει	1:3		a
b	βασιλεύοντος αὐτοῦ,	בִּשְׁנַת שָׁלוֹשׁ לְמָלְכוֹ		b
c		עָשָׂה	καὶ	c
d	δοχὴν ἐποίησεν	מִשְׁתֶּה	ἐποίησεν	d
e			ὁ βασιλεὺς	e
f	τοῖς φίλοις	לְכָל־שָׂרָיו	πότον	f
g	καὶ τοῖς λοιποῖς ἔθνεσιν	וַעֲבָדָיו	τοῖς ἄρχουσι	g
h		חֵיל		h
i				i
j	καὶ τοῖς		τῆς αὐλῆς	j
k	Περσῶν καὶ Μήδων	פָּרַס וּמָדַי	Περσῶν καὶ Μήδων,	k
l	ἐνδόξοις	הַפַּרְתְּמִים וְשָׂרֵי		l
m	καὶ τοῖς ἄρχουσιν		καὶ οἱ ἄρχοντες	m
n	τῶν σατραπῶν,	הַמְּדִינוֹת לְפָנָיו	τῶν χωρῶν	n

THE TEXTS OF ESTHER — CHAPTER 1

	LXX (Göttingen o')	MT (BHS 3)	AT (Göttingen L)
1:4		1:4	
o			κατὰ πρόσωπον αὐτοῦ,
a	καὶ μετὰ ταῦτα,	בְּהַרְאֹתוֹ	εἰς τὸ ἐπιδειχθῆναι 1:4
b	μετὰ τὸ δεῖξαι αὐτοῖς 1:4	אֶת־עֹשֶׁר	τὸν πλοῦτον
c	τὸν πλοῦτον	כְּבוֹד	τῆς δόξης
d		מַלְכוּתוֹ	τοῦ βασιλέως
e	τῆς βασιλείας αὐτοῦ	וְאֶת־יְקָר	καὶ τὴν τιμὴν
f	καὶ τὴν δόξαν	תִּפְאֶרֶת	τῆς καυχήσεως
g	τῆς εὐφροσύνης	גְּדוּלָּתוֹ	αὐτοῦ
h	τοῦ πλούτου αὐτοῦ	יָמִים רַבִּים	
i		שְׁמוֹנִים וּמְאַת יוֹם׃	
j	ἐπὶ		ἐπὶ
k	ἡμέρας ἑκατὸν ὀγδοήκοντα,		ὀγδοήκοντα καὶ ἑκατὸν ἡμέρας,
1:5 a	ὅτε δὲ 1:5	וּבִמְלוֹאת 1:5	ἕως
b	ἀνεπληρώθησαν	הַיָּמִים הָאֵלֶּה	ἀνεπληρώθησαν
c	αἱ ἡμέραι		αἱ ἡμέραι
d	τοῦ γάμου,		
e			ἃς

Chapter 1

	LXX (Göttingen o')	MT (BHS 3)	AT (Göttingen L)	
f	ἐποίησεν ὁ βασιλεὺς	וַיַּעַשׂ הַמֶּלֶךְ	ἐποίησεν ὁ βασιλεὺς	f
g	πότον	לְכָל-		g
h		הָעָם	πᾶσι	h
i	τοῖς ἔθνεσιν	הַנִּמְצְאִים		i
j	τοῖς εὑρεθεῖσιν	בְּשׁוּשַׁן	τοῖς εὑρεθεῖσιν	j
k	εἰς	הַבִּירָה	ἐν Σούσοις	k
l	τὴν πόλιν	לְמִגָּדוֹל	τῇ πόλει	l
m		וְעַד-קָטָן	ἀπὸ μεγάλου ἕως μικροῦ	m
n		מִשְׁתֶּה שִׁבְעַת	πότον	n
o	ἐπὶ ἡμέρας ἓξ	יָמִים	ἐν ἡμέραις ἑπτὰ	o
p	ἐν αὐλῇ	בַּחֲצַר	ἔνδον ἐν τῇ αὐλῇ	p
q	οἴκου	גִּנַּת בִּיתַן		q
r	τοῦ βασιλέως	הַמֶּלֶךְ׃	τοῦ βασιλέως,	r
s			ἄγων τὰ σωτήρια αὐτοῦ.	s
1:6 a	κεκοσμημένη βυσσίνοις 1:6	1:6 חוּר כַּרְפַּס	ἦν δὲ ἐξεστρωμένα βύσσινα	a
b	καὶ καρπασίνοις τεταμένοις	וּתְכֵלֶת אָחוּז	καὶ καρπάσινα	b
c			καὶ ὑακίνθινα	c

Chapter 1

THE TEXTS OF ESTHER — CHAPTER 1

	LXX (Göttingen o')	_MT (BHS 3)_	_AT (Göttingen L)_
d			καὶ κόκκινα ἐμπεπλεγμένα
e			ἐν ἄνθεσιν,
f			καὶ σκηνὴ τεταμένη
g	ἐπὶ σχοινίοις βυσσίνοις	חוּר כַּרְפַּס וּתְכֵלֶת אָחוּז בְּחַבְלֵי־בוּץ	ἐν σχοινίοις βυσσίνοις
h	καὶ πορφυροῖς	וְאַרְגָּמָן	καὶ πορφυροῖς
i	ἐπὶ κύβοις		ἐπὶ κύβοις
j	χρυσοῖς καὶ	עַל־גְּלִילֵי	
k	ἀργυροῖς,	כֶסֶף	ἀργυροῖς
l	ἐπὶ στύλοις παρίνοις	וְעַמּוּדֵי שֵׁשׁ	καὶ στύλοις παρίνοις
m	καὶ λιθίνοις·		καὶ περιχρύσοις,
n			καὶ
o	κλῖναι χρυσαῖ	מִטּוֹת זָהָב	κλῖναι χρυσαῖ
p	καὶ ἀργυραῖ	וָכֶסֶף	
q	ἐπὶ λιθοστρώτου	עַל רִצְפַת	ἐπὶ λιθόστρωτον
r	σμαραγδίτου		σμαράγδου,
s	λίθου καὶ πιννίνου	בַּהַט וָשֵׁשׁ	
t	καὶ παρίνου λίθου,	וְדַר וְסֹחָרֶת	

THE TEXTS OF ESTHER — CHAPTER 1

	LXX (Göttingen ο')	MT (BHS 3)	AT (Göttingen L)	
u	καὶ στρωμναί	וְהַשְׁקוֹת׃		u
v	διαφανεῖς ποικίλως διηνθισμέναι,			v
w	κύκλῳ ῥόδα		καὶ κύκλῳ ῥόδα,	w
x	πεπασμένα·			x
1:7				
a	ποτήρια χρυσᾶ	וְכֵלִים מִכֵּלִים שׁוֹנִים	καὶ	a
b			ποτήρια χρυσᾶ	b
c	καὶ ἀργυρᾶ,			c
d	καὶ ἀνθράκινον κυλίκιον	וְיֵין מַלְכוּת רָב	ἔξαλλα	d
e	προκείμενον			e
f	ἀπὸ ταλάντων τρισμυρίων·			f
g	οἶνος		καὶ οἶνος	g
h			βασιλικὸς	h
i	πολὺς			i
j	καὶ ἡδὺς			j
k	ὃν αὐτὸς ὁ βασιλεὺς	כְּיַד הַמֶּלֶךְ׃	ὃν ὁ βασιλεὺς	k
l	ἔπινεν.		πίνει,	l
1:8				
a	ὁ δὲ πότος οὗτος	וְהַשְׁתִיָּה	καὶ πότος	a

THE TEXTS OF ESTHER — CHAPTER 1

	LXX (Göttingen o')	MT (BHS 3)	AT (Göttingen L)	
b	οὐ κατὰ προκείμενον νόμον	כְּדָת	κατὰ τὸν νόμον·	b
c	ἐγένετο,	אֵין אֹנֵס		c
d	οὕτως δὲ	כִּי־כֵן	οὕτως γὰρ	d
e	ἠθέλησεν	יִסַּד	ἐπέταξεν	e
f	ὁ βασιλεύς	הַמֶּלֶךְ	ὁ βασιλεύς	f
g	καὶ ἐπέταξεν			g
h	τοῖς οἰκονόμοις	עַל כָּל־רַב בֵּיתוֹ		h
i	ποιῆσαι τὸ θέλημα αὐτοῦ	לַעֲשׂוֹת כִּרְצוֹן	ποιῆσαι τὸ θέλημα	i
j	καὶ τῶν ἀνθρώπων.	אִישׁ־וָאִישׁ׃	τῶν ἀνθρώπων.	j
1:9 a	καὶ Αστιν	1:9 גַּם וַשְׁתִּי	καὶ Ουαστιν	a
b	ἡ βασίλισσα	הַמַּלְכָּה	ἡ βασίλισσα	b
c	ἐποίησεν	עָשְׂתָה	ἐποίησε	c
d	πότον	מִשְׁתֵּה	δοχὴν	d
e			μεγάλην	e
f			πάσαις	f
g	ταῖς γυναιξὶν	נָשִׁים	ταῖς γυναιξὶν	g
h	ἐν τοῖς βασιλείοις	בֵּית הַמַּלְכוּת	ἐν τῇ αὐλῇ τοῦ βασιλέως.	h

Chapter 1

THE TEXTS OF ESTHER — CHAPTER 1

LXX (Göttingen o′)	MT (BHS 3)	AT (Göttingen L)
i ὅπου ὁ βασιλεὺς		
j Ἀρταξέρξης.		
1:10 a ἐν δὲ	**1:10** אֲחַשְׁוֵרֽוֹשׁ׃	**1:10**
b τῇ ἡμέρᾳ τῇ ἑβδόμῃ	בַּיּוֹם הַשְּׁבִיעִ֔י	a ἐγένετο δὲ
c ἡδέως γενόμενος	כְּט֥וֹב לֵב־הַמֶּ֖לֶךְ	b τῇ ἡμέρᾳ τῇ ἑβδόμῃ
d ὁ βασιλεὺς εἶπεν	בַּיָּ֑יִן	c ἐν τῷ εὐφρανθῆναι
e τῷ Αμαν	אָמַ֡ר	d τὸν βασιλέα ἐν τῷ οἴνῳ
f καὶ Βαζαν	לִ֠מְהוּמָן	e εἶπεν ὁ βασιλεὺς
g καὶ Θαρρα	בִּזְּתָ֨א	
h καὶ Βωραζη	חַרְבוֹנָ֜א	
i καὶ Ζαθολθα	בִּגְתָ֤א	
j καὶ Αβαταζα	וַאֲבַגְתָא֙	
k καὶ Θαραβα,	זֵתַ֣ר	
l τοῖς ἑπτὰ εὐνούχοις	וְכַרְכַּ֔ס	
m τοῖς διακόνοις	שִׁבְעַת֙ הַסָּרִיסִ֔ים	
n τοῦ βασιλέως	הַמְשָׁרְתִ֕ים	f τοῖς παισὶν αὐτοῦ
o	אֶת־פְּנֵ֖י הַמֶּ֥לֶךְ	

THE TEXTS OF ESTHER — CHAPTER 1

	LXX (Göttingen o')		MT (BHS 3)		AT (Göttingen L)
	p	Ἀρταξέρξου,			
1:11	a	εἰσαγαγεῖν	1:11 וַיֹּאמֶר׃	1:11 a	ἀγαγεῖν
	b		אֶת־וַשְׁתִּי	b	Ουαστιν
	c	τὴν βασίλισσαν	הַמַּלְכָּה	c	τὴν βασίλισσαν
	d	πρὸς αὐτὸν	לִפְנֵי הַמֶּלֶךְ	d	εἰς τὸ συνεστηκὸς συμπόσιον
	e		בְּכֶתֶר	e	ἐν τῷ διαδήματι
	f		מַלְכוּת	f	τῆς βασιλείας αὐτῆς
	g	βασιλεύειν αὐτὴν			
	h	καὶ περιθεῖναι αὐτῇ τὸ διάδημα	לְהַרְאוֹת הָעַמִּים	h	κατὰ πρόσωπον
	i	καὶ δεῖξαι αὐτὴν	וְהַשָּׂרִים	i	τῆς στρατιᾶς
	j	τοῖς ἄρχουσιν	אֶת־יָפְיָהּ	j	αὐτοῦ.
	k		כִּי־טוֹבַת מַרְאֶה הִיא׃	k	
	l	καὶ τοῖς ἔθνεσιν			
	m	τὸ κάλλος αὐτῆς,			
	n	ὅτι καλὴ ἦν.			
1:12	a	καὶ οὐκ εἰσήκουσεν αὐτοῦ	1:12 וַתְּמָאֵן	1:12 a	καὶ οὐκ ἠθέλησεν

Chapter 1

	LXX (Göttingen o')	MT (BHS 3)	AT (Göttingen L)	
b	Αστιν ἡ βασίλισσα	וַתְּמָאֵן הַמַּלְכָּה	Ουαστιν	b
c	ἐλθεῖν	וַשְׁתִּי לָבוֹא	ποιῆσαι	c
d		בִּדְבַר הַמֶּלֶךְ	τὸ θέλημα τοῦ βασιλέως	d
e	μετὰ τῶν εὐνούχων.	אֲשֶׁר בְּיַד הַסָּרִיסִים	διὰ χειρὸς τῶν εὐνούχων.	e
f			ὡς δὲ ἤκουσεν ὁ βασιλεὺς	f
g			ὅτι ἠκύρωσεν Ουαστιν	g
h			τὴν βουλὴν αὐτοῦ,	h
i	καὶ ἐλυπήθη	וַיִּקְצֹף	ἐλυπήθη	i
j	ὁ βασιλεὺς	הַמֶּלֶךְ		j
k		מְאֹד	σφόδρα,	k
l	καὶ ὠργίσθη	וַחֲמָתוֹ	καὶ ὀργὴ ἐξεκαύθη	l
m		בָּעֲרָה בוֹ	ἐν αὐτῷ.	m
1:13 a	καὶ εἶπεν	וַיֹּאמֶר · 1:13	καὶ εἶπεν	a
b		הַמֶּלֶךְ	ὁ βασιλεὺς	b
c			πᾶσι	c
d	τοῖς φίλοις αὐτοῦ		τοῖς σοφοῖς τοῖς εἰδόσι	d
e	Κατὰ ταῦτα ἐλάλησεν Αστιν, לַחֲכָמִים יֹדְעֵי הָעִתִּים כִּי־כֵן דְּבַר הַמֶּלֶךְ			e

Chapter 1

THE TEXTS OF ESTHER — CHAPTER 1

	LXX (Göttingen o')	MT (BHS 3)	AT (Göttingen L)	
f	ποιήσατε οὖν περὶ τούτου	כָּל־יֹדְעֵי	νόμον καὶ κρίσιν	f
g	νόμον καὶ κρίσιν.	דָּת וָדִין׃	τί ποιῆσαι τῇ βασιλίσσῃ	g
			περὶ τοῦ μὴ τεθεληκέναι αὐτὴ	h
			ποιῆσαι τὸ θέλημα τοῦ βασιλέως.	i
				j
1:14 a	καὶ προσῆλθεν	1:14 וְהַקָּרֹב	καὶ προσῆλθον	a
b	αὐτῷ	אֵלָיו	πρὸς αὐτὸν	b
c	Ἀρκεσαῖος	כַּרְשְׁנָא		
d	καὶ Σαρσαθαῖος	שֵׁתָר		
e	καὶ Μαλησεαρ	אַדְמָתָא		
f		תַרְשִׁישׁ		
g		מֶרֶס		
h		מַרְסְנָא		
i		מְמוּכָן		
j				
k	οἱ ἄρχοντες		οἱ ἄρχοντες	c
l	Περσῶν καὶ Μήδων		Περσῶν καὶ Μήδων	d

	LXX (Göttingen o')		MT (BHS 3)	AT (Göttingen L)	
	m	οἱ ἐγγὺς	אֵלָי	καὶ οἱ ὁρῶντες	e
	n		פָּנָי	τὸ πρόσωπον	f
	o	τοῦ βασιλέως,	הַמֶּלֶךְ	τοῦ βασιλέως	g
	p		וְהַיֹּשְׁבִים	καὶ	h
	q	οἱ πρῶτοι παρακαθήμενοι	רִאשֹׁנָה	οἱ καθήμενοι	i
	r	τῷ βασιλεῖ,	בַּמַּלְכוּת:	ἐν τοῖς βασιλείοις.	j
1:15	a	καὶ ἀπήγγειλαν αὐτῷ			
	b	κατὰ τοὺς νόμους	1:15		
	c	ὡς δεῖ ποιῆσαι			
	d	Αστιν τῇ βασιλίσσῃ,			
	e	ὅτι οὐκ ἐποίησεν			
	f	τὰ ὑπὸ τοῦ βασιλέως			
	g				
	h	προσταχθέντα διὰ τῶν εὐνούχων.			
1:16	a	καὶ εἶπεν	1:16	καὶ παρεκάλεσεν αὐτὸν	a
	b	ὁ Μουχαῖος		Βουγαῖος	b
	c			λέγων	c

Chapter 1

THE TEXTS OF ESTHER — CHAPTER 1

	LXX (Göttingen o')	*MT (BHS 3)*	*AT (Göttingen L)*	
d	πρὸς τὸν βασιλέα	לִפְנֵ֥י הַמֶּ֖לֶךְ		d
e	καὶ τοὺς ἄρχοντας	וְהַשָּׂרִ֑ים		e
f	Οὐ τὸν βασιλέα μόνον	לֹ֤א עַל־הַמֶּ֙לֶךְ֙ לְבַדּ֔וֹ	Οὐ τὸν βασιλέα μόνον	f
g	ἠδίκησεν	עָ֣וְתָ֔ה	ἠδίκηκεν	g
h	Αστιν	וַשְׁתִּ֖י	Ουαστιν	h
i	ἡ βασίλισσα,	הַמַּלְכָּ֑ה	ἡ βασίλισσα,	i
j	ἀλλὰ καὶ	כִּֽי	ἀλλὰ καὶ	j
k	πάντας	עַל־כָּל־		k
l	τοὺς ἄρχοντας	הַשָּׂרִ֗ים	τοὺς ἄρχοντας	l
m	καὶ τοὺς ἡγουμένους	וְעַֽל־כָּל־הָ֣עַמִּ֔ים	Περσῶν καὶ Μήδων·	m
n		אֲשֶׁ֕ר	καὶ εἰς πάντας τοὺς λαοὺς	n
o		בְּכָל־מְדִינ֖וֹת		o
p	τοῦ βασιλέως	הַמֶּ֥לֶךְ		p
q		אֲחַשְׁוֵרֽוֹשׁ׃		q
1:17 a	(καὶ γὰρ διηγήσατο αὐτοῖς	כִּֽי־יֵצֵ֤א דְבַר־הַמַּלְכָּה֙		r
b	τὰ ῥήματα τῆς βασιλίσσης,	עַל־כָּל־הַנָּשִׁ֔ים	ἡ ἀδικία αὐτῆς ἐξῆλθεν,	s
c	καὶ ὡς ἀντεῖπεν	לְהַבְז֥וֹת בַּעְלֵיהֶ֖ן בְּעֵינֵיהֶ֑ן	ὅτι ἠκύρωσε τὸ πρόσταγμα	t

Chapter 1

	LXX (Göttingen o')	MT (BHS 3)	AT (Göttingen L)
d	τῷ βασιλεῖ).	לִרְעוּתָהּ יִתֵּן הַמֶּלֶךְ מַלְכוּתָהּ	τοῦ βασιλέως.
e		אֲחַשְׁוֵרוֹשׁ הַמֶּלֶךְ לִפְנֵי	
f		וַשְׁתִּי תָבוֹא לֹא־אֲשֶׁר	
g		יַעֲבוֹר וְלֹא	
h		פָרַס־וּמָדַי בְּדָתֵי וְיִכָּתֵב	
i		מִלְּפָנָיו דְבַר־מַלְכוּת יֵצֵא	
j		טוֹב הַמֶּלֶךְ אִם־עַל	
k	ὡς οὖν ἀντεῖπεν	וְהַיּוֹם הַזֶּה תֹּאמַרְנָה	
l	τῷ βασιλεῖ Ἀρταξέρξῃ,		
1:18 a	οὕτως σήμερον 1:18	פָּרַס־וּמָדַי שָׂרוֹת	
b		שָׁמְעוּ אֲשֶׁר	
c	αἱ τυραννίδες αἱ λοιπαὶ τῶν ἀρχόντων	הַמַּלְכָּה אֶת־דְּבַר	
d	Περσῶν καὶ Μήδων	הַמֶּלֶךְ שָׂרֵי	
e	ἀκούσασαι	לְכֹל	
f	τὰ τῷ βασιλεῖ λεχθέντα ὑπ᾽ αὐτῆς	בִּזָּיוֹן מֵאַיִן	
g		וָקָצֶף	
h	τολμήσουσιν ὁμοίως ἀτιμάσαι	וּכְדַי	

u

THE TEXTS OF ESTHER — CHAPTER 1

	LXX (Göttingen o')		MT (BHS 3)		AT (Göttingen L)	
1:19	i τοὺς ἄνδρας αὐτῶν.	1:19	אִם־עַל־הַמֶּלֶךְ טוֹב	1:18(19)	εἰ δοκεῖ οὖν	a
	a εἰ οὖν δοκεῖ,		יֵצֵא דְבַר־מַלְכוּת מִלְּפָנָיו אֲשֶׁר			b
	b τῷ βασιλεῖ,				τῷ κυρίῳ	c
	c				ἡμῶν	d
	d				καὶ ἀρεστὸν τῷ φρονήματι	e
	e				αὐτοῦ,	f
	f προσταξάτω βασιλικόν,		אֲשֶׁר לֹא־תָבוֹא וַשְׁתִּי			g
	g καὶ γραφήτω		הַמֶּלֶךְ		γραφήτω	h
					εἰς πάσας τὰς χώρας	i
			וְיִכָּתֵב בְּדָתֵי פָרַס־וּמָדַי		καὶ πρὸς πάντα τὰ ἔθνη,	g
			וְלֹא יַעֲבוֹר		καὶ γνωσθήτω ἠθετηκυῖα	h
			לִפְנֵי וַשְׁתִּי		τὸν λόγον	i
			אֲחַשְׁוֵרוֹשׁ הַמֶּלֶךְ		τοῦ βασιλέως Ουαστιν·	
	h κατὰ τοὺς νόμους					
	i Μήδων καὶ Περσῶν,					
	j καὶ μὴ ἄλλως χρησάσθω,					
	k μηδὲ εἰσελθάτω ἔτι					

	LXX (Göttingen o')		MT (BHS 3)	AT (Göttingen L)	
l	ἡ βασίλισσα		וַשְׁתִּי		
m	πρὸς αὐτόν,		אֲשֶׁר לֹא־בָאָה וַשְׁתִּי הַמַּלְכָּה		
n	καὶ τὴν βασιλείαν		לִפְנֵי הַמֶּלֶךְ אֲחַשְׁוֵרוֹשׁ	ἡ δὲ βασιλεία	j
o	αὐτῆς				
p	δότω		יִתֵּן	δοθήτω	k
q	ὁ βασιλεὺς		הַמֶּלֶךְ		
r	γυναικὶ κρείττονι οὔσῃ αὐτῆς.		לִרְעוּתָהּ הַטּוֹבָה מִמֶּנָּה׃		
1:20	ἄλλῃ, κρείττονι οὔσῃ αὐτῆς,	1:20	וְנִשְׁמַע	καὶ φανέσθω ὑπακούουσα	l
a	καὶ ἀκουσθήτω		פִּתְגָם הַמֶּלֶךְ	τῆς φωνῆς τοῦ βασιλέως	a
b	ὁ νόμος ὁ ὑπὸ τοῦ βασιλέως,		אֲשֶׁר־יַעֲשֶׂה	καὶ	b
c	ὃν ἐὰν ποιῇ		בְּכָל־מַלְכוּתוֹ	ποιήσει ἀγαθὸν	c
d			כִּי רַבָּה הִיא	πάσαις ταῖς βασιλείαις·	d
e	ἐν τῇ βασιλείᾳ				e
f	αὐτοῦ.				f
g					
h	καὶ οὕτως πᾶσαι αἱ γυναῖκες		וְכָל־הַנָּשִׁים	καὶ πᾶσαι αἱ γυναῖκες	h
i	περιθήσουσιν τιμὴν		יִתְּנוּ	δώσουσι τιμὴν	i

Chapter 1

	LXX (Göttingen o')	MT (BHS 3)	AT (Göttingen L)	
j			καὶ δόξαν	j
k	τοῖς ἀνδράσιν	בְכָל־נָשֶׁיהָ?	τοῖς ἀνδράσιν	k
l	ἑαυτῶν		αὐτῶν	l
m	ἀπὸ πτωχοῦ ἕως πλουσίου.	:וּמִגָּדוֹל וְעַד־קָטָן	ἀπὸ πτωχῶν ἕως πλουσίων.	m
1:21 a	καὶ ἤρεσεν	וַיִּיטַב	1:21 καὶ ἀγαθὸς	a
b	ὁ λόγος	הַדָּבָר	ὁ λόγος	b
c	τῷ βασιλεῖ	בְּעֵינֵי הַמֶּלֶךְ	ἐν καρδίᾳ τοῦ βασιλέως,	c
d	καὶ τοῖς ἄρχουσι	וְהַשָּׂרִים		d
e	καὶ ἐποίησεν	וַיַּעַשׂ	καὶ ἐποίησεν	e
f		הַמֶּלֶךְ	ἕτοιμος	f
g	ὁ βασιλεὺς	כִּדְבַר		g
h	καθὰ ἐλάλησεν	מְמוּכָן:	κατὰ τὸν λόγον τοῦτον.	h
i	ὁ Μουχαῖος·	וַיִּשְׁלַח		
1:22 a	καὶ ἀπέστειλεν	סְפָרִים		
b		אֶל־כָּל־מְדִינוֹת הַמֶּלֶךְ		
c	εἰς πᾶσαν τὴν βασιλείαν	הַמֶּלֶךְ		
d				

Chapter 1

The Texts of Esther — Chapter 1

LXX (Göttingen o')	MT (BHS 3)	AT (Göttingen L)

e   κατὰ χώραν   אֶל־עַמּ֔וֹ כִּלְשׁוֹן֣וֹ וּכְמָדִינָ֣ה וּמְדִינָ֤ה

f   κατὰ τὴν λέξιν αὐτῶν   כִּכְתָבָ֗הּ

g   אִישׁ־שֹׂרֵ֣ר כָּל־לִהְי֨וֹת

h   בְּבֵית֔וֹ

i   ὥστε εἶναι φόβον αὐτοῖς

j   ἐν ταῖς οἰκίαις αὐτῶν.   וּמְדַבֵּ֖ר כִּלְשׁ֥וֹן עַמּֽוֹ׃

k

	LXX (Göttingen o')		MT (BHS 3)		AT (Göttingen L)	
2:1	a	καὶ μετὰ τοὺς λόγους τούτους	2:1	אַחַר הַדְּבָרִים הָאֵלֶּה כְּשֹׁךְ חֲמַת הַמֶּלֶךְ אֲחַשְׁוֵרוֹשׁ	Καὶ οὕτως ἔστη	a
	b	ἐκόπασεν ὁ βασιλεὺς τοῦ θυμοῦ			τοῦ μνημονεύειν τῆς Ουαστιν	b
	c				καὶ ὧν ἐποίησεν	c
	d	καὶ οὐκέτι ἐμνήσθη		זָכַר אֶת־וַשְׁתִּי	Ασσυήρῳ τῷ βασιλεῖ.	d
	e	τῆς Αστιν μνημονεύων		וְאֵת אֲשֶׁר־עָשָׂתָה		e
	f	οἷα ἐλάλησεν		וְאֵת אֲשֶׁר־נִגְזַר עָלֶיהָ׃		
	g					
	h	καὶ ὡς κατέκρινεν αὐτήν				
2:2	a	καὶ εἶπαν	2:2	וַיֹּאמְרוּ	καὶ εἶπον	a
	b	οἱ διάκονοι τοῦ βασιλέως		נַעֲרֵי־הַמֶּלֶךְ מְשָׁרְתָיו	οἱ λειτουργοὶ τοῦ βασιλέως	b
	c	Ζητηθήτω		יְבַקְשׁוּ	Ζητήσωμεν	c
	d	τῷ βασιλεῖ		לַמֶּלֶךְ		d
	e	κοράσια ἄφθορα		נְעָרוֹת בְּתוּלוֹת		e
	f	καλὰ τῷ εἴδει		טוֹבוֹת מַרְאֶה׃		f
2:3	a	καὶ καταστήσει ὁ βασιλεὺς	2:3	וְיַפְקֵד הַמֶּלֶךְ		g
	b	κωμάρχας ἐν πάσαις ταῖς χώραις		פְּקִידִים בְּכָל־מְדִינוֹת		h
	c	τῆς βασιλείας αὐτοῦ,		מַלְכוּתוֹ		i

THE TEXTS OF ESTHER — CHAPTER 2

	LXX (Göttingen o')	MT (BHS 3)		AT (Göttingen L)	
d	καὶ ἐπιλεξάτωσαν	וְיַפְקֵד׃			j
e	κοράσια παρθενικὰ	וְיִקְבְּצוּ אֶת־כָּל־נַעֲרָה־		παρθένους	k
f	καλὰ τῷ εἴδει	טוֹבַת מַרְאֶה אֶל־שׁוּ		καλὰς τῷ εἴδει,	l
g	εἰς Σουσαν τὴν πόλιν	אֶל־בֵּית הַנָּשִׁים אֶל־יַד הֵ			m
h	εἰς τὸν γυναικῶνα,	סְרִיס הַמֶּלֶךְ שֹׁמֵר הַנָּשִׁים			n
i	καὶ παραδοθήτωσαν		(2:3)	καὶ δοθήτωσαν	o
j				προστατεῖσθαι	p
k		אֶל־יַד		ὑπὸ χεῖρα	q
l		הֵגֶא		Γωγαίου	r
m	τῷ εὐνούχῳ	סְרִיס		τοῦ εὐνούχου	s
n	τοῦ βασιλέως	הַמֶּלֶךְ			t
o	τῷ φύλακι τῶν γυναικῶν,	שֹׁמֵר הַנָּשִׁים		τοῦ φύλακος τῶν γυναικῶν·	u
p	καὶ δοθήτω σμῆγμα	וְנָתוֹן תַּמְרוּקֵיהֶן׃			v
q	καὶ ἡ λοιπὴ ἐπιμέλεια.	וְהַנַּעֲרָה			w
2:4 a	καὶ ἡ γυνή,	אֲשֶׁר תִּיטַב 2:4	2:4	καὶ ἡ παῖς,	a
b	ἣ ἂν ἀρέσῃ	בְּעֵינֵי הַמֶּלֶךְ		ἣ ἐὰν ἀρέσῃ	b
c	τῷ βασιλεῖ,	תִּמְלֹךְ		τῷ βασιλεῖ,	c

Chapter 2

THE TEXTS OF ESTHER — CHAPTER 2

LXX (Göttingen o')	MT (BHS 3)	AT (Göttingen L)
d βασιλεύσει ἀντὶ Αστιν.	יְמַלְךְ תַּחַת וַשְׁתִּי	d κατασταθήσεται ἀντὶ Ουαστιν.
e καὶ ἤρεσεν τῷ βασιλεῖ	וַיִּיטַב הַדָּבָר בְּעֵינֵי הַמֶּלֶךְ	e
f τὸ πρᾶγμα,		f
g καὶ ἐποίησεν οὕτως.	וַיַּעַשׂ כֵּן׃	g καὶ ἐποίησαν ἑτοίμως κατὰ ταῦτα.
g		
2:5 a καὶ ἄνθρωπος ἦν Ἰουδαῖος	2:5 אִישׁ יְהוּדִי הָיָה	2:5 a καὶ ἦν ἀνὴρ Ἰουδαῖος
b ἐν Σούσοις τῇ πόλει,	בְּשׁוּשַׁן הַבִּירָה	b ἐν Σούσοις τῇ πόλει,
c καὶ ὄνομα αὐτῷ Μαρδοχαῖος	וּשְׁמוֹ מָרְדֳּכַי	c ᾧ ὄνομα Μαρδοχαῖος
d ὁ τοῦ Ιαΐρου	בֶּן יָאִיר	d υἱὸς Ιαείρου
e τοῦ Σεμεΐου	בֶּן שִׁמְעִי	e τοῦ Σεμεΐου
f τοῦ Κισαίου	בֶּן קִישׁ	f τοῦ Κισαίου
g ἐκ φυλῆς Βενιαμιν,	אִישׁ יְמִינִי׃	g τῆς φυλῆς Βενιαμιν.
2:6 a ὃς ἦν αἰχμάλωτος	2:6 אֲשֶׁר הָגְלָה מִירוּשָׁלִַם	
b ἐξ Ιερουσαλημ,	עִם הַגֹּלָה אֲשֶׁר הָגְלְתָה	
c	עִם יְכָנְיָה מֶלֶךְ יְהוּדָה	
d	אֲשֶׁר הֶגְלָה נְבוּכַדְנֶאצַּר	
e	מֶלֶךְ בָּבֶל׃	

THE TEXTS OF ESTHER — CHAPTER 2

	LXX (Göttingen o')		MT (BHS 3)		AT (Göttingen L)	
	f	ἦν ᾐχμαλώτευσεν		׃הַבִּירָה אֲשֶׁר		
	g	Ναβουχοδονοσορ		וַיִּגְלָה נְבוּ‍		
	h	βασιλεὺς Βαβυλῶνος.		כַדְרֶאצַּר מֶלֶךְ		
				׃בָּבֶל		
2:7	a	καὶ ἦν τούτῳ	2:7	אֹמֵן וַיְהִי	2:7	καὶ ἦν ἐκτρέφων πιστῶς	a
	b	παῖς θρεπτή,		הִיא אֶסְתֵּר אֶת־הֲדַסָּה		τὴν Εσθηρ	b
	c	θυγάτηρ		בַּת־		θυγατέρα	c
	d	Αμιναδαβ		דֹּדוֹ			d
	e	ἀδελφοῦ πατρὸς αὐτοῦ				ἀδελφοῦ τοῦ πατρὸς αὐτοῦ·	e
	f	καὶ ὄνομα αὐτῇ Εσθηρ·		וְאֵם אָב לָהּ אֵין כִּי			f
	g	ἐν δὲ τῷ μεταλλάξαι αὐτῆς					g
	h	τοὺς γονεῖς					h
	i	ἐπαίδευσεν αὐτὴν					i
	j	ἑαυτῷ εἰς γυναῖκα·					j
	k	καὶ ἦν τὸ κοράσιον		וְהַנַּעֲרָה		καὶ ἦν ἡ παῖς	k
	l	καλὸν τῷ εἴδει.		יְפַת־תֹּאַר		καλὴ τῷ εἴδει	l
	m					σφόδρα	m
	n			מַרְאֶה וְטֹובַת		καὶ ὡραία τῇ ὄψει.	n

THE TEXTS OF ESTHER — CHAPTER 2

	LXX (Göttingen o')	MT (BHS 3)	AT (Göttingen L)	
o		וַיְהִי בְּהִשָּׁמַע דְּבַר־הַמֶּלֶךְ וְדָתוֹ		o
p		וּבְהִקָּבֵץ		p
2:8 a	καὶ ὅτε ἠκούσθη	נְעָרוֹת רַבּוֹת		q
b	τὸ τοῦ βασιλέως πρόσταγμα,	אֶל־שׁוּשַׁן הַבִּירָה		r
c		אֶל־יַד הֵגָי		s
d	συνήχθησαν κοράσια πολλὰ			t
e	εἰς Σουσαν τὴν πόλιν			u
f	ὑπὸ χεῖρα Γαι,			v
g	καὶ ἤχθη	**2:8** וַתִּלָּקַח אֶסְתֵּר	**2:8** καὶ ἐλήφθη	a
h	Εσθηρ	אֶל־בֵּית הַמֶּלֶךְ	τὸ κοράσιον	b
i		אֶל־יַד הֵגַי	εἰς τὸν οἶκον τοῦ βασιλέως·	c
j	πρὸς Γαι	שֹׁמֵר הַנָּשִׁים׃	καὶ εἶδε Βουγαῖος	d
k			ὁ εὐνοῦχος	e
l	τὸν φύλακα τῶν γυναικῶν.		ὁ φυλάσσων τὸ κοράσιον,	f
2:9 a	καὶ ἤρεσεν αὐτῷ	**(2:9)** וַתִּיטַב הַנַּעֲרָה בְעֵינָיו	**(2:9)** καὶ ἤρεσεν αὐτῷ	g
b		וַתִּשָּׂא חֶסֶד לְפָנָיו	ὑπὲρ πάσας τὰς γυναῖκας.	h
c	τὸ κοράσιον			i

	LXX (Göttingen o')		MT (BHS 3)	AT (Göttingen L)	
		2:9	חֶסֶד וַתִּשָּׂא	καὶ εὗρεν Εσθηρ χάριν	a
d	καὶ εὗρεν χάριν			καὶ ἔλεον	b
e			לְפָנָיו	κατὰ πρόσωπον αὐτοῦ,	c
f	ἐνώπιον αὐτοῦ,		וַיְבַהֵל	καὶ ἔσπευσε	d
g	καὶ ἔσπευσεν			προστατῆσαι αὐτῆς	e
h			אֶת־תַּמְרוּקֶיהָ וְאֶת־		f
i			מָנוֹתֶהָ לָתֶת לָהּ		g
j				καὶ ἐπέδωκεν	h
k	αὐτῇ δοῦναι				i
l	τὸ σμῆγμα				j
m	καὶ τὴν μερίδα		אֵת שֶׁבַע הַנְּעָרוֹת הָרְאֻיוֹת	ὑπὲρ τὰ ἑπτὰ κοράσια,	k
n	καὶ τὰ ἑπτὰ κοράσια		לָתֶת־לָהּ		l
o	τὰ ἀποδεδειγμένα αὐτῇ		מִבֵּית הַמֶּלֶךְ		m
p	ἐκ βασιλικοῦ		וַיְשַׁנֶּהָ וְאֶת־נַעֲרוֹתֶיהָ		n
q	καὶ ἐχρήσατο αὐτῇ καλῶς		לְטוֹב בֵּית הַנָּשִׁים׃	τὰς ἅβρας αὐτῆς.	o
r	καὶ ταῖς ἅβραις αὐτῆς				p
s	ἐν τῷ γυναικῶνι.				
2:10 a	καὶ οὐχ ὑπέδειξεν Εσθηρ	2:10	לֹא־הִגִּידָה אֶסְתֵּר		

THE TEXTS OF ESTHER — CHAPTER 2

LXX (Göttingen o')		MT (BHS 3)	AT (Göttingen L)
b	τὸ γένος αὐτῆς	אֶת־עַמָּהּ	
c	οὐδὲ τὴν πατρίδα·	וְאֶת־מוֹלַדְתָּהּ	
d	ὁ γὰρ Μαρδοχαῖος	כִּי	
e	ἐνετείλατο αὐτῇ	מָרְדֳּכַי	
f	μὴ ἀπαγγεῖλαι.	צִוָּה עָלֶיהָ	
2:11 a	καθ' ἑκάστην δὲ ἡμέραν 2:11	אֲשֶׁר לֹא־תַגִּיד׃	
b	ὁ Μαρδοχαῖος περιεπάτει	וּבְכָל־יוֹם וָיוֹם	
c	κατὰ τὴν αὐλὴν τὴν γυναικείαν	מָרְדֳּכַי מִתְהַלֵּךְ	
d	ἐπισκοπῶν τί Εσθηρ	לִפְנֵי חֲצַר בֵּית־הַנָּשִׁים	
e	συμβήσεται.	לָדַעַת אֶת־שְׁלוֹם אֶסְתֵּר	
		וּמַה־יֵּעָשֶׂה בָּהּ׃	
2:12 a	οὗτος δὲ ἦν καιρὸς 2:12	וּבְהַגִּיעַ	
b	κορασίου εἰσελθεῖν	תֹּר נַעֲרָה וְנַעֲרָה	
c	πρὸς τὸν βασιλέα,	לָבוֹא	
d		אֶל־הַמֶּלֶךְ	
e	ὅταν ἀναπληρώσῃ		
f			
g	μῆνας δέκαδύο·		

LXX (Göttingen o')

h οὕτως γὰρ ἀναπληροῦνται
i αἱ ἡμέραι τῆς θεραπείας,
j μῆνας ἓξ ἀλειφόμεναι
k ἐν σμυρίνῳ ἐλαίῳ
l καὶ μῆνας ἓξ
m ἐν τοῖς ἀρώμασιν
n καὶ ἐν τοῖς σμήγμασιν
o τῶν γυναικῶν,

2:13 a καὶ τότε εἰσπορεύεται
b πρὸς τὸν βασιλέα·
c καὶ ᾧ ἐὰν εἴπῃ,
d παραδώσει αὐτὴν
e συνεισέρχεσθαι αὐτῷ
f ἀπὸ τοῦ γυναικῶνος
g ἕως τῶν βασιλείων.

2:14a δείλης εἰσπορεύεται,
b καὶ πρὸς ἡμέραν ἀποτρέχει

MT (BHS 3)

כִּי כֵן יִמְלְאוּ יְמֵי
מְרוּקֵיהֶן שִׁשָּׁה חֳדָשִׁים
בְּשֶׁמֶן הַמֹּר
וְשִׁשָּׁה חֳדָשִׁים בַּבְּשָׂמִים
וּבְתַמְרוּקֵי הַנָּשִׁים׃

2:13 וּבָזֶה הַנַּעֲרָה בָאָה
אֶל־הַמֶּלֶךְ
אֵת כָּל־אֲשֶׁר תֹּאמַר
יִנָּתֵן לָהּ
לָבוֹא עִמָּהּ
מִבֵּית הַנָּשִׁים
עַד־בֵּית הַמֶּלֶךְ׃

2:14 בָּעֶרֶב הִיא בָאָה
וּבַבֹּקֶר הִיא שָׁבָה

AT (Göttingen L)

LXX (Göttingen o')	MT (BHS 3)	AT (Göttingen L)
c εἰς τὸν γυναικῶνα τὸν δεύτερον,	שֵׁנִי אֶל־בֵּית הַנָּשִׁים שֵׁנִי	
d οὗ	אֶל־יַד	
e Γαι	הֵגֶא	
f ὁ εὐνοῦχος	סְרִיס	
g τοῦ βασιλέως	הַמֶּלֶךְ	
h ὁ φύλαξ τῶν γυναικῶν,	שֹׁמֵר הַנָּשִׁים	
i καὶ οὐκέτι εἰσπορεύεται	לֹא־תָבוֹא עוֹד	
j πρὸς τὸν βασιλέα,	אֶל־הַמֶּלֶךְ	
k ἐὰν μὴ	כִּי	
l	אִם־חָפֵץ בָּהּ הַמֶּלֶךְ	
m κληθῇ ὀνόματι.	:וְנִקְרְאָה בְשֵׁם	
2:15 a ἐν δὲ τῷ ἀναπληροῦσθαι 2:15	וּבְהַגִּיעַ תֹּר־אֶסְתֵּר	
b τὸν χρόνον Εσθηρ	בַּת־אֲבִיחַיִל	
c τῆς θυγατρὸς Αμιναδαβ	דֹּד מָרְדֳּכַי	
d ἀδελφοῦ πατρὸς Μαρδοχαίου	אֲשֶׁר לָקַח־לוֹ לְבַת	
e	לָבֹא אֶל־הַמֶּלֶךְ	
f εἰσελθεῖν πρὸς τὸν βασιλέα,	אֶל־הַמֶּלֶךְ	

THE TEXTS OF ESTHER — CHAPTER 2

LXX (Göttingen o')	MT (BHS 3)	AT (Göttingen L)	
g οὐδὲν ἠθέτησεν	לֹא עָשְׂתָה אֶת־דְּבַר הַמֶּלֶךְ		q
h ὧν ἐνετείλατο	כִּי אִם אֶת־אֲשֶׁר יֹאמַר		r
i	לָהּ		s
j ὁ εὐνοῦχος	הֵגַי סְרִיס־הַמֶּלֶךְ		t
k ὁ φύλαξ τῶν γυναικῶν·	שֹׁמֵר הַנָּשִׁים		u
l ἦν γὰρ Εσθηρ εὑρίσκουσα	וַתְּהִי אֶסְתֵּר נֹשֵׂאת		v
m χάριν	חֵן		w
n παρὰ	בְּעֵינֵי		x
o πάντων τῶν βλεπόντων αὐτήν.	כָּל־רֹאֶיהָ׃		
2:16 a καὶ εἰσῆλθεν	2:9 וַתֵּיטַב	ὡς δὲ εἰσήχθη	
b Εσθηρ	הַנַּעֲרָה	Εσθηρ	
c πρὸς ᾽Αρταξέρξην τὸν βασιλέα	2:16 וַתִּלָּקַח אֶסְתֵּר אֶל־הַמֶּלֶךְ אֲחַשְׁוֵרוֹשׁ אֶל־בֵּית מַלְכוּתוֹ	πρὸς τὸν βασιλέα,	
d	בַּחֹדֶשׁ הָעֲשִׂירִי		
e τῷ δωδεκάτῳ μηνί,	הוּא־חֹדֶשׁ טֵבֵת		
f ὅς ἐστιν Αδαρ,	בִּשְׁנַת־שֶׁבַע		
g τῷ ἑβδόμῳ ἔτει	לְמַלְכוּתוֹ׃		
h τῆς βασιλείας αὐτοῦ.			

LXX (Göttingen o')			MT (BHS 3)		AT (Göttingen L)	
2:17	a	καὶ ἠράσθη	2:17	וַיֶּאֱהַב	ἤρεσεν	y
	b	ὁ βασιλεὺς		הַמֶּלֶךְ	αὐτῷ	z
	c				σφόδρα.	aa
	d	Εσθηρ,				bb
	e		2:14	אֶת־אֶסְתֵּר	καὶ ὅταν ἐγένετο ἑσπέρα,	a
	f				εἰσήγετο, καὶ τὸ πρωὶ ἀπελύετο.	b
	g				ὡς δὲ κατεμάνθανεν ὁ βασιλεὺς	c
	h		2:17	מִכָּל־הַנָּשִׁים	πάσας τὰς παρθένους,	a
	i				ἐφάνη ἐπιφανεστάτη Εσθηρ,	b
	j	καὶ εὗρεν χάριν		וַתִּשָּׂא־חֵן	καὶ εὗρε	c
	k			וָחֶסֶד לְפָנָיו	χάριν καὶ ἔλεον	d
	l				κατὰ πρόσωπον αὐτοῦ,	e
	m	παρὰ πάσας τὰς παρθένους,		מִכָּל־הַבְּתוּלֹת		f
	n	καὶ ἐπέθηκεν		וַיָּשֶׂם	καὶ ἐπέθηκε	g
	o	αὐτῇ				h
	p	τὸ διάδημα		כֶּתֶר־מַלְכוּת	τὸ διάδημα	i
	q	τὸ γυναικεῖον.		בְּרֹאשָׁהּ וַיַּמְלִיכֶהָ	τῆς βασιλείας	j

Chapter 2

LXX (Göttingen o')		MT (BHS 3)	AT (Göttingen L)	
r		תֵּעָשֶׂה	ἐπὶ τὴν κεφαλὴν αὐτῆς.	k
s		עַל־רֹאשָׁהּ וְנֵעֶרְ:		l
2:18 a καὶ ἐποίησεν ὁ βασιλεὺς	2:18	וַיַּעַשׂ הַמֶּלֶךְ	2:18 καὶ ἤγαγεν ὁ βασιλεὺς	a
b πότον		מִשְׁתֶּה גָדוֹל		b
c πᾶσιν τοῖς φίλοις αὐτοῦ		לְכָל־שָׂרָיו		c
d καὶ ταῖς δυνάμεσιν		וַעֲבָדָיו		d
e ἐπὶ ἡμέρας ἑπτὰ		אֵת מִשְׁתֵּה		e
f καὶ ὕψωσεν τοὺς γάμους Εσθηρ		אֶסְתֵּר	τὸν γάμον τῆς Εσθηρ ἐπιφανῶς	f
g καὶ ἄφεσιν		וַהֲנָחָה	καὶ ἐποίησεν ἀφέσεις	g
h		לַמְּדִינוֹת	πάσαις ταῖς χώραις.	h
i ἐποίησεν		עָשָׂה		i
j τοῖς ὑπὸ τὴν βασιλείαν αὐτοῦ.		וַיִּתֵּן		
k		מַשְׂאֵת		k
		כְּיַד הַמֶּלֶךְ:		
2:19 a ὁ δὲ Μαρδοχαῖος ἐθεράπευεν	2:19	וּבְהִקָּבֵץ בְּתוּלוֹת שֵׁנִית		
b ἐν τῇ αὐλῇ.		וּמָרְדֳּכַי יֹשֵׁב בְּשַׁעַר־הַמֶּלֶךְ:		

THE TEXTS OF ESTHER — CHAPTER 2

LXX (Göttingen o')	*MT (BHS 3)*	*AT (Göttingen L)*

2:20 a ἡ δὲ Εσθηρ οὐχ ὑπέδειξεν 2:20 אֵ֣ין אֶסְתֵּ֗ר מַגֶּ֤דֶת

b τὴν πατρίδα αὐτῆς· מֽוֹלַדְתָּהּ֙

c וְאֶת־עַמָּ֔הּ

d οὕτως γὰρ כַּאֲשֶׁ֛ר

e ἐνετείλατο αὐτῇ Μαρδοχαῖος, צִוָּ֥ה עָלֶ֖יהָ מָרְדֳּכָ֑י

f φοβεῖσθαι τὸν θεὸν

g καὶ ποιεῖν τὰ προστάγματα αὐτοῦ, וְאֶת־מַאֲמַ֤ר מָרְדֳּכַי֙

h אֶסְתֵּ֣ר עֹשָׂ֔ה

i καθὼς ἦν μετ' αὐτοῦ· כַּאֲשֶׁ֛ר הָיְתָ֥ה בְאׇמְנָ֖ה אִתּֽוֹ׃

j καὶ Εσθηρ οὐ μετήλλαξεν

k τὴν ἀγωγὴν αὐτῆς.

2:21 בַּיָּמִ֣ים הָהֵ֔ם

2:21 a καὶ ἐλυπήθησαν וּמׇרְדֳּכַ֖י יֹשֵׁ֣ב בְּשַֽׁעַר־הַמֶּ֑לֶךְ

b קָצַ֣ף בִּגְתָ֣ן וָתֶ֡רֶשׁ

c οἱ δύο εὐνοῦχοι τοῦ βασιλέως שְׁנֵֽי־סָרִיסֵ֨י הַמֶּ֜לֶךְ

d οἱ ἀρχισωματοφύλακες מִשֹּׁמְרֵ֣י הַסַּ֗ף

THE TEXTS OF ESTHER — CHAPTER 2

LXX (Göttingen o')	MT (BHS 3)	AT (Göttingen L)

	LXX (Göttingen o')	MT (BHS 3)
e	ὅτι προῆχθη Μαρδοχαῖος,	כִּי הִגִּיד לָהֶם אֲשֶׁר־
f	καὶ ἐζήτουν ἀποκτεῖναι	וְכָל־הַיְהוּדִים אֲשֶׁר בְּכָל־
g	Ἀρταξέρξην τὸν βασιλέα.	הַמֶּלֶךְ הוּא וּמָרְדֳּכָי:
2:22 a	καὶ ἐδηλώθη Μαρδοχαίῳ	וַיִּוָּדַע הַדָּבָר
b	ὁ λόγος,	לְמָרְדֳּכַי
c	καὶ ἐσήμανεν Εσθηρ,	וַיַּגֵּד לְאֶסְתֵּר הַמַּלְכָּה
d		
e	καὶ αὐτὴ ἐνεφάνισεν	וַתֹּאמֶר אֶסְתֵּר
f	τῷ βασιλεῖ	לַמֶּלֶךְ
g	τὰ τῆς ἐπιβουλῆς.	בְּשֵׁם מָרְדֳּכָי:
2:23 a	ὁ δὲ βασιλεὺς ἤτασεν	2:23 וַיְבֻקַּשׁ הַדָּבָר וַיִּמָּצֵא
b	τοὺς δύο εὐνούχους	
c	καὶ ἐκρέμασεν αὐτούς.	וַיִּתָּלוּ שְׁנֵיהֶם עַל־עֵץ
d	καὶ προσέταξεν ὁ βασιλεὺς	
e	καταχωρίσαι εἰς μνημόσυνον	וַיִּכָּתֵב בְּסֵפֶר
f	ἐν τῇ βασιλικῇ βιβλιοθήκῃ	דִּבְרֵי הַיָּמִים
g		לִפְנֵי הַמֶּלֶךְ:

THE TEXTS OF ESTHER — CHAPTER 2

LXX (Göttingen o′)	_MT (BHS 3)_	_AT (Göttingen L)_
h ὑπὲρ τῆς εὐνοίας		
i Μαρδοχαίου ἐν ἐγκωμίῳ.		

	LXX (Göttingen o')		MT (BHS 3)		AT (Göttingen L)	
3:1	a	Μετὰ δὲ ταῦτα	3:1	אַחַר ׀ הַדְּבָרִים הָאֵלֶּה	3:1	Καὶ ἐγένετο
	b	ἐδόξασεν ὁ Βασιλεὺς		גִּדַּל		μετὰ τοὺς λόγους τούτους,
	c	ὁ Βασιλεὺς		הַמֶּלֶךְ		ἐμεγάλυνεν
	d	Ἀταξέρξης		אֲחַשְׁוֵרוֹשׁ		ὁ βασιλεὺς
	e	Αμαν Αμαδάθου		אֶת־הָמָן		Ασσυῆρος
	f	Βουγαῖον		בֶּן־הַמְּדָתָא		Αμαν Αμαδάθου
	g	καὶ ὕψωσεν αὐτὸν		הָאֲגָגִי		Βουγαῖον
	h	καὶ ἐπρωτοβάθρει		וַיְנַשְּׂאֵהוּ		καὶ ἐπῆρεν αὐτὸν
	i			וַיָּשֶׂם אֶת־כִּסְאוֹ		καὶ ἔθηκε τὸν θρόνον αὐτοῦ
	j	πάντων		מֵעַל		ὑπεράνω
	k	τῶν φίλων αὐτοῦ,		כָּל־		
				הַשָּׂרִים אֲשֶׁר אִתּוֹ׃	l	τῶν φίλων αὐτοῦ
					m	ὥστε κάμπτεσθαι
					n	καὶ προσκυνεῖν αὐτῷ
					o	ἐπὶ τὴν γῆν πάντας.
3:2	a	καὶ πάντες	3:2	וְכָל־	3:2	πάντων οὖν
	b			עַבְדֵי הַמֶּלֶךְ		

Chapter 3

	LXX (Göttingen o´)	MT (BHS 3)	AT (Göttingen L)	
c	οἱ ἐν τῇ αὐλῇ	הַמֶּלֶךְ אֲשֶׁר־בְּשַׁעַר	προσκυνούντων	c
d	προσεκύνουν	כֹּרְעִים וּמִשְׁתַּחֲוִים	αὐτῷ	d
e	αὐτῷ.	לְהָמָן	κατὰ	e
f	οὕτως γὰρ	כִּי־כֵן	τὸ πρόσταγμα τοῦ βασιλέως	f
g	προσέταξεν ὁ Βασιλεὺς	צִוָּה־לוֹ הַמֶּלֶךְ		g
h	ποιῆσαι.			h
i	ὁ δὲ Μαρδοχαῖος	וּמָרְדֳּכַי	Μαρδοχαῖος	i
j	οὐ προσεκύνει	לֹא יִכְרַע	οὐ προσεκύνει	j
k	αὐτῷ.	וְלֹא יִשְׁתַּחֲוֶה׃	αὐτῷ.	k
3:3				3:3
			καὶ εἶδον	a
			οἱ παῖδες τοῦ βασιλέως	b
			ὅτι ὁ Μαρδοχαῖος	c
			οὐ προσκυνεῖ τὸν Αμαν,	d
			καὶ εἶπον	e
			οἱ παῖδες τοῦ βασιλέως	f
				g
			πρὸς τὸν Μαρδοχαῖον	h
3:3 a	καὶ ἐλάλησαν	3:3		
b		עַבְדֵי הַמֶּלֶךְ		
c	οἱ ἐν τῇ αὐλῇ τοῦ βασιλέως	אֲשֶׁר־בְּשַׁעַר הַמֶּלֶךְ		
d	τῷ Μαρδοχαίῳ	לְמָרְדֳּכָי		

THE TEXTS OF ESTHER — CHAPTER 3

	LXX (Göttingen o')		MT (BHS 3)		AT (Göttingen L)	
e	Μαρδοχαῖε,		מַדּוּעַ אַתָּה עוֹבֵר		Τί σὺ παρακούεις	i
f	τί παρακούεις		אֵת מִצְוַת הַמֶּלֶךְ׃		τοῦ βασιλέως	j
g	τὰ ὑπὸ τοῦ βασιλέως λεγόμενα;				καὶ οὐ προσκυνεῖς τὸν Αμαν;	k
						l
3:4 a	καθ' ἑκάστην ἡμέραν	3:4	וַיְהִי כְּאָמְרָם אֵלָיו יוֹם			
b	ἐλάλουν αὐτῷ,		וָיוֹם			
c	καὶ οὐχ ὑπήκουεν αὐτῶν.		וְלֹא שָׁמַע אֲלֵיהֶם			
d	καὶ ὑπέδειξαν τῷ Αμαν		וַיַּגִּידוּ לְהָמָן לִרְאוֹת הֲיַעַמְדוּ			
e	Μαρδοχαῖον		דִּבְרֵי מָרְדֳּכַי כִּי־הִגִּיד לָהֶם אֲשֶׁר־הוּא יְהוּדִי׃			
f	τοῖς τοῦ βασιλέως λόγοις					
g	ἀντιτασσόμενον,					
h	καὶ ὑπέδειξεν αὐτοῖς	3:4	מָרְדֳּכַי־לוֹ		καὶ ἀπήγγειλεν αὐτοῖς	a
i	ὁ Μαρδοχαῖος					b
j	ὅτι Ἰουδαῖός ἐστιν.		אֲשֶׁר־הוּא יְהוּדִי׃		ὅτι Ἰουδαῖός ἐστιν.	c
					καὶ ἀπήγγειλαν	d
					περὶ αὐτοῦ τῷ Αμαν.	e
3:5 a	καὶ ἐπιγνοὺς Αμαν	3:5	וַיַּרְא הָמָן		ὡς δὲ ἤκουσεν Αμαν,	a

Chapter 3

	LXX (Göttingen o')		MT (BHS 3)	AT (Göttingen L)	
	b ὅτι οὐ προσκυνεῖ		כִּי־אֵין מָרְדֳּכַי		b
	c		וּמִשְׁתַּחֲוֶה		c
	d αὐτῷ		לוֹ		d
	e Μαρδοχαῖος,				e
	f ἐθυμώθη σφόδρα		וַיִּמָּלֵא הָמָן חֵמָה׃	f ἐθυμώθη τῷ Μαρδοχαίῳ,	f
				g καὶ ὀργὴ ἐξεκαύθη ἐν αὐτῷ,	g
3:6		a	וַיִּבֶז בְּעֵינָיו לִשְׁלֹחַ		h
		b	יָד בְּמָרְדֳּכַי לְבַדּוֹ		i
		c	כִּי־הִגִּידוּ לוֹ		j
		d	אֶת־עַם מָרְדֳּכָי		k
3:6	a καὶ ἐβουλεύσατο ἀφανίσαι		וַיְבַקֵּשׁ הָמָן לְהַשְׁמִיד	l καὶ ἐζήτει ἀνελεῖν	l
	b πάντας τοὺς	f	אֶת־כָּל־הַיְּהוּדִים	m τὸν Μαρδοχαῖον	m
	c	g	אֲשֶׁר בְּכָל־מַלְכוּת	n καὶ πάντα τὸν λαὸν αὐτοῦ	n
	n				
	d ὑπὸ τὴν	h	אֲחַשְׁוֵרוֹשׁ		
	e	i	עַם מָרְדֳּכָי		
	f Ἀρταξέρξου βασιλείαν	j		o ἐν ἡμέρᾳ μιᾷ. (see MT 3:13)	o

THE TEXTS OF ESTHER — CHAPTER 3

LXX (Göttingen o')	MT (BHS 3)	AT (Göttingen L)
g 'Ιουδαίους.	k	
	l עַם מָרְדֳּכָי:	
		3:6 a καὶ παραζηλώσας ὁ Αμαν
		b καὶ κινηθεὶς
		c ἐν παντὶ τῷ θυμῷ αὐτοῦ
		d ἐρυθρὸς ἐγένετο
		e ἐκτρέπων αὐτὸν
		f ἐξ ὀφθαλμῶν αὐτοῦ
3:7 a καὶ ἐποίησεν ψήφισμα	a וַיְבַקֵּשׁ הָמָן וַיֹּאמֶר	
b 3:7	b וַיֹּ֫אמֶר לֹ֫אׁ	
c	c בְּחֹ֫דֶשׁ הָרִאשׁוֹן	
d ἐν ἔτει δωδεκάτῳ	d הוּא חֹ֫דֶשׁ נִיסָ֫ן	
e τῆς βασιλείας Ἀρταξέρξου	e בְּיַ֫ד פּוּר	
f καὶ ἔβαλεν κλήρους	f וְגוֹרָל לִפְנֵי הָמָן	
g	g מִיּוֹם לְיוֹם	
h ἡμέραν ἐξ ἡμερας	h וּמֵחֹ֫דֶשׁ	
i καὶ μῆνα ἐκ μηνὸς		

	LXX (Göttingen o')		MT (BHS 3)		AT (Göttingen L)
	j ὥστε ἀπολέσαι	i			
	k ἐν μιᾷ ἡμέρᾳ	j			
	l τὸ γένος Μαρδοχαίου,	k			
	m καὶ ἔπεσεν ὁ κλῆρος	l			
	n εἰς τὴν τεσσαρεσκαιδεκάτην	m			
	o τοῦ μηνός,	n			
	p	o			
	q ὅς ἐστιν Αδαρ.	p	וַיַּפֵּל פּוּר הוּא הַגּוֹרָל ... הוּא־חֹדֶשׁ אֲדָר׃	g	καὶ καρδία φαύλη
				h	ἐλάλει
				i	τῷ βασιλεῖ
				j	
				k	κακὰ περὶ Ισραηλ
3:8	a καὶ ἐλάλησεν	3:8	וַיֹּאמֶר הָמָן	3:8 a	λέγων
	b πρὸς τὸν βασιλέα		אֲחַשְׁוֵרוֹשׁ לַמֶּלֶךְ	b	Ἔστι λαὸς
	c Ἀρταξέρξην		יֶשְׁנוֹ עַם־אֶחָד	c	διεσπαρμένος
	d λέγων		מְפֻזָּר וּמְפֹרָד	d	
	e				
	f Ὑπάρχει ἔθνος				
	g διεσπαρμένον				
	h				

THE TEXTS OF ESTHER — CHAPTER 3

LXX (Göttingen o')	MT (BHS 3)	AT (Göttingen L)	
i ἐν τοῖς ἔθνεσιν	בֵּ֥ין הָֽעַמִּ֗ים	ἐν πάσαις ταῖς βασιλείαις,	e
j ἐν πάσῃ τῇ βασιλείᾳ σου,	בְּכֹל֙ מְדִינֹ֣ות מַלְכוּתֶ֔ךָ	λαὸς πολέμου καὶ ἀπειθής,	f
k	וְדָתֵיהֶ֞ם שֹׁנֹ֣ות מִכָּל־עָ֗ם	ἔξαλλα νόμιμα ἔχων,	g
l οἱ δὲ νόμοι αὐτῶν ἔξαλλοι	וְאֶת־דָּתֵ֤י הַמֶּ֙לֶךְ֙		h
m παρὰ πάντα τὰ ἔθνη,	אֵינָ֣ם עֹשִׂ֔ים	τοῖς δὲ νομίμοις	i
n τῶν δὲ νόμων	לְ֠מֶלֶךְ	σοῦ, βασιλεῦ,	j
o τοῦ βασιλέως	אֵֽין־שֹׁוֶ֖ה	οὐ προσέχουσι	k
p παρακούουσιν,	לְהַנִּיחָֽם׃	γνωριζόμενοι	l
q		ἐν πᾶσι τοῖς ἔθνεσι	m
r		πονηροὶ ὄντες	n
s		καὶ τὰ προστάγματά σου ἀθετοῦσι	o
t		πρὸς καθαίρεσιν τῆς δόξης σου.	p
u			q
v καὶ οὐ συμφέρει τῷ βασιλεῖ			r
w ἐᾶσαι αὐτούς.			s
3:9 a εἰ δοκεῖ τῷ βασιλεῖ,	3:9 אִם־עַל־הַמֶּ֣לֶךְ טֹ֔וב יִכָּתֵ֖ב	3:9 εἰ δοκεῖ οὖν τῷ βασιλεῖ,	a
b	לְאַבְּדָ֑ם׃	καὶ ἀγαθὴ ἡ κρίσις	b

Chapter 3

LXX (Göttingen o')	MT (BHS 3)	AT (Göttingen L)
c		c ἐν καρδίᾳ αὐτοῦ,
d δογματισάτω		d δοθήτω μοι τὸ ἔθνος
e ἀπολέσαι αὐτούς,	b לְאַבֵּד	e εἰς ἀπώλειαν,
e καγὼ διαγράψω		f καὶ διαγράψω
f εἰς τὸ γαζοφυλάκιον		g εἰς τὸ γαζοφυλάκιον
g τοῦ βασιλέως		h
h ἀργυρίου τάλαντα μύρια.	c בְּכָל־מְלֶאכֶת	i ἀργυρίου τάλαντα μύρια.
	d	j
	e	k
	f	l
3:10 a καὶ περιελόμενος ὁ βασιλεὺς 3:10		(see 3:10 below)
b τὸν δακτύλιον		
c ἔδωκεν εἰς χεῖρα τῷ Αμαν		
d		
e		
f σφραγίσαι		
g κατὰ τῶν γεγραμμένων		

THE TEXTS OF ESTHER — CHAPTER 3

		LXX (Göttingen o')	MT (BHS 3)		AT (Göttingen L)	
3:11	h	κατὰ τῶν Ἰουδαίων.		3:11	καὶ εἶπεν αὐτῷ ὁ βασιλεύς	a
	a	καὶ εἶπεν ὁ βασιλεὺς	הַכֶּסֶף נָתוּן לָךְ			b
	b	τῷ Αμαν	וְהָעָם			
	c	Τὸ μὲν			Τὸ μὲν	c
	d	ἀργύριον ἔχε,	לַעֲשׂוֹת בּוֹ כַּטּוֹב		ἀργύριον ἔχε,	d
	e	τῷ δὲ ἔθνει χρῶ	בְּעֵינֶיךָ׃		τῷ δὲ ἔθνει χρῶ	e
	f	ὡς βούλει.			ὡς ἂν σοι ἀρεστὸν ᾖ.	f
				3:10	καὶ περιείλετο ὁ βασιλεὺς	a
					τὸ δακτύλιον	b
					ἀπὸ τῆς χειρὸς αὐτοῦ	c
					καὶ ἔδωκε τῷ Αμαν λέγων	d
					Γράφε εἰς πάσας τὰς χώρας	e
					καὶ σφραγίζου	f
					τῷ δακτυλίῳ τοῦ βασιλέως·	g
					οὗ γὰρ ἔστιν ὃς ἀποστρέψει	h
					τὴν σφραγῖδα.	i
				3:7	καὶ ἐπορεύθη Αμαν	a

THE TEXTS OF ESTHER — CHAPTER 3

LXX (Göttingen o')	MT (BHS 3)	AT (Göttingen L)
3:12 a καὶ ἐκλήθησαν		
b οἱ γραμματεῖς τοῦ βασιλέως		b πρὸς τοὺς θεοὺς αὐτοῦ
c μηνὶ πρώτῳ		c τοῦ ἐπιγνῶναι
d τῇ τρισκαιδεκάτῃ		d ἡμέραν θανάτου αὐτῶν,
e καὶ ἔγραψαν		e καὶ βάλλει κλήρους
f ὡς ἐπέταξεν Αμαν		f εἰς τὴν τρισκαιδεκάτην
g τοῖς στρατηγοῖς		g τοῦ μηνὸς Αδαρ Νισαν
		h φονεύειν πάντας
		i τοὺς Ἰουδαίους
		j ἀπὸ ἀρσενικοῦ ἕως θηλυκοῦ
		k καὶ διαρπάζειν τὰ νήπια.

MT (BHS 3) 3:12:

וַיִּקָּרְאוּ
סֹפְרֵי הַמֶּלֶךְ בַּחֹדֶשׁ
הָרִאשׁוֹן בִּשְׁלוֹשָׁה
עָשָׂר יוֹם בּוֹ וַיִּכָּתֵב
כְּכָל־אֲשֶׁר־צִוָּה הָמָן
אֶל אֲחַשְׁדַּרְפְּנֵי־הַמֶּלֶךְ

THE TEXTS OF ESTHER — CHAPTER 3

LXX (Göttingen o')	MT (BHS 3)	AT (Göttingen L)
h καὶ τοῖς ἄρχουσιν	הַמֶּלֶךְ־אֶל	
i κατὰ πᾶσαν χώραν	וַיִּכָּתֵב בְּכָל־מְדִינָה וּמְדִינָה	
j ἀπὸ Ἰνδικῆς		
k ἕως τῆς Αἰθιοπίας,		
l ταῖς ἑκατὸν εἴκοσι ἑπτὰ χώραις,		
m τοῖς τε ἄρχουσιν τῶν ἐθνῶν	עַם וָעָם מְדִינָה	
n κατὰ τὴν αὐτῶν λέξιν	כִּכְתָבָהּ מְדִינָה וּמְדִינָה	
o	וַעֲבָדִים כִּכְתָבָם	
p διὰ	וְעַם	
q Ἀρταξέρξου τοῦ βασιλέως.	בְּשֵׁם הַמֶּלֶךְ אֲחַשְׁוֵרֹשׁ נִכְתָּב	
r	וְנֶחְתֹּם בְּטַבַּעַת הַמֶּלֶךְ׃	
		3:13 καὶ ἔσπευσε
		b καὶ ἔδωκεν
3:13 a καὶ ἀπεστάλη	3:13 וְנִשְׁלוֹחַ	
b	סְפָרִים	
c διὰ βιβλιαφόρων	בְּיַד הָרָצִים	c
d εἰς τὴν Ἀρταξέρξου βασιλείαν	אֶל־כָּל־מְדִינוֹת הַמֶּלֶךְ	d εἰς χεῖρας τρεχόντων ἱππέων.
e ἀφανίσαι	לְהַשְׁמִיד לַהֲרֹג	

Chapter 3

LXX (Göttingen o')	MT (BHS 3)	AT (Göttingen L)
	לֶאֱבֹד	
	לַהֲרֹג	
	לְהַשְׁמִיד	
f		
g		
h τὸ γένος τῶν Ἰουδαίων	אֵת כָּל־הַיְּהוּדִים	
i	מִנַּעַר וְעַד־זָקֵן	
j ἐν ἡμέρᾳ μιᾷ	טַף וְנָשִׁים בְּיוֹם אֶחָד	
k	בִּשְׁלוֹשָׁה עָשָׂר	
l μηνὸς δωδεκάτου,	לְחֹדֶשׁ שְׁנֵים־עָשָׂר	
m ὅς ἐστιν Αδαρ,	הוּא־חֹדֶשׁ אֲדָר	
n καὶ διαρπάσαι τὰ ὑπάρχοντα αὐτῶν.	וּשְׁלָלָם לָבוֹז׃	
B:1		**3:14 (B:1)**
a Τῆς δὲ ἐπιστολῆς ἐστιν		Καὶ ὑπέγραψε a
b τὸ ἀντίγραφον τόδε		τὴν ὑποτεταγμένην ἐπιστολήν b
c Βασιλεὺς μέγας		Βασιλεὺς μέγας c
d Ἀρταξέρξης		Ασσυῆρος d
e τοῖς ἀπὸ τῆς Ἰνδικῆς		τοῖς ἀπὸ τῆς Ἰνδικῆς e
f ἕως τῆς Αἰθιοπίας		ἕως τῆς Αἰθιοπίας f
g ἑκατὸν εἴκοσι ἑπτὰ		ἑκατὸν καὶ εἴκοσι καὶ ἑπτὰ g

Chapter 3

THE TEXTS OF ESTHER — ADDITION B

	LXX (Göttingen o')	MT (BHS 3)	AT (Göttingen L)	
		– No Hebrew Text Extant –		
h	χωρῶν		χωρῶν	h
i	ἄρχουσιν καὶ τοπάρχαις		ἄρχουσι καὶ σατράπαις	i
j	ὑποτεταγμένοις			j
k	τάδε γράφει		τάδε γράφει	k
B:2 a	Πολλῶν ἐπάρξας ἐθνῶν		3:15 (B:2) Πολλῶν ἐπάρξας ἐθνῶν	a
b	καὶ πάσης ἐπικρατήσας		καὶ πάσης ἐπικρατήσας	b
c	οἰκουμένης		τῆς οἰκουμένης	c
c	ἐβουλήθην —		ἐβουλήθην —	d
e	μὴ τῷ θράσει		μὴ τῷ θράσει	e
f	τῆς ἐξουσίας ἐπαιρόμενος,		τῆς ἐξουσίας ἐπαιρόμενος,	f
g	ἐπιεικέστερον		ἐπιεικέστερον	g
h	δὲ καὶ		δὲ καὶ	h
i	μετὰ ἠπιότητος		μετὰ ἠπιότητος	i
j	ἀεὶ διεξάγων —		ἀεὶ διεξάγων —	j
k	τοὺς τῶν ὑποτεταγμένων		τοὺς τῶν ὑποτεταγμένων	k
l	ἀκυμάτους		ἀταράχους	l
m	διὰ παντὸς καταστῆσαι βίους,		διὰ παντὸς καταστῆσαι βίους,	m
n	τήν τε βασιλείαν		τὴν δὲ βασιλείαν	n

Addition B

THE TEXTS OF ESTHER — ADDITION B

	LXX (Göttingen o')	MT (BHS 3)	AT (Göttingen L)	
		– No Hebrew Text Extant –		
o	ἥμερον καὶ πορευτὴν		ἥμερον καὶ πορευτὴν	o
p	μέχρι		ἄχρι	p
q	περάτων παρεξόμενος		περάτων παρεχόμενος	q
r	ἀνανεώσασθαι		ἀνανεώσασθαι	r
s	τε τὴν ποθουμένην τοῖς πᾶσιν ἀνθρώποις		τὴν πᾶσιν ἀνθρώποις ποθουμένη	s
t	εἰρήνην.		εἰρήνην.	t
B:3 a	πυθομένου δέ μου		3:16 (B:3) πυνθανομένου δέ μου	a
b	τῶν συμβούλων		τῶν συμβούλων	b
c	πῶς ἂν ἀχθείη τοῦτο		πῶς ἂν ἀχθείη τοῦτο	c
d	ἐπὶ πέρας		ἐπὶ πέρας	d
e	ὁ σωφροσύνη		ὁ σωφροσύνη	e
f	παρ' ἡμῖν διενέγκας		παρ' ἡμῖν διενηνοχὼς,	f
g	καὶ ἐν τῇ εὐνοίᾳ		εὐνοίᾳ	g
h	ἀπαραλλάκτως		ἀπαραλλάκτῳ	h
i	καὶ βεβαίᾳ πίστει		καὶ βεβαίᾳ πίστει	i
j	ἀποδεδειγμένος			j
k	καὶ δεύτερον		τὸ δεύτερον	k
l	τῶν βασιλειῶν γέρας		τῶν βασιλειῶν γέρας	l

Addition B

THE TEXTS OF ESTHER — ADDITION B

	LXX (Göttingen o')	MT (BHS 3)		AT (Göttingen L)
		– No Hebrew Text Extant –		
m	ἀπενηνεγμένος Αμαν		m	ἀπενεγκάμενος Αμαν
B:4 a	ἐπέδειξεν ἡμῖν	(B:4)	n	ὑπέδειξεν ἡμῖν
b			o	πάροικον
c	ἐν πάσαις ταῖς		p	ἐν πάσαις ταῖς
d	κατὰ τὴν οἰκουμένην φυλαῖς		q	κατὰ τὴν οἰκουμένην φυλαῖς
e	ἀναμεμῖχθαι δυσμενῆ		r	ἀναμεμῖχθαι δυσμενῆ
f	λαόν τινα		s	τινὰ λαόν,
g	τοῖς νόμοις		t	τοῖς μὲν νόμοις
h	ἀντίθετον		u	ἀντιδικοῦντα
i	πρὸς πᾶν ἔθνος		v	πρὸς πᾶν ἔθνος,
j	τά τε τῶν βασιλέων		w	τὰ δὲ τῶν βασιλέων
k	παραπέμποντας διηνεκῶς		x	παραπέμποντα διηνεκῶς
l	διατάγματα		y	προστάγματα
m	πρὸς τὸ μὴ κατατίθεσθαι		z	πρὸς τὸ μηδέποτε
n	τὴν ὑφ' ἡμῶν κατευθυνομένην		aa	τὴν βασιλείαν
o	ἀμέμπτως συναρχίαν.		bb	εὐσταθείας τυγχάνειν.
B:5 a	διειληφότες οὖν τόδε		3:17 (B:5)	διειληφότες οὖν
b	τὸ ἔθνος μονώτατον			μονώτατον τὸ ἔθνος

Addition B

THE TEXTS OF ESTHER — ADDITION B

		LXX (Göttingen o')	MT (BHS 3)	AT (Göttingen L)	
			– No Hebrew Text Extant –		
c		ἐν ἀντιπαραγωγῇ		ἐναντία παραγωγῇ	c
d		παντὶ			d
e		διὰ παντὸς ἀνθρώπῳ κείμενον		παντὸς κείμενον τῶν ἀνθρώπων	e
f		διαγωγὴν νόμων		διὰ τῶν νόμων	f
g		ξενίζουσαν		ξενίζουσαν	g
h		παραλλάσσον		παραγωγὴν	h
i		καὶ δυσνοοῦν		καὶ δυσνοοῦν	i
j		τοῖς ἡμετέροις πράγμασιν		τοῖς ἡμετέροις προστάγμασιν	j
k				ἀεὶ	k
l		τὰ χείριστα		τὰ χείριστα	l
m		συντελοῦν κακὰ		συντελεῖν κακὰ	m
n		καὶ			n
o		πρὸς τὸ		πρὸς τὸ	o
p		μὴ τὴν βασιλείαν		μηδέποτε κατατίθεσθαι	p
q		εὐσταθείας τυγχάνειν,		τῇ ὑφ' ἡμῶν κατευθυνομένη	q
				μοναρχίᾳ,	r
B:6	a	προστετάχαμεν οὖν		3:18 (B:6) προστετάχαμεν οὖν	a
	b			ὑμῖν	b

Addition B

THE TEXTS OF ESTHER — ADDITION B

	LXX (Göttingen o')	MT (BHS 3)	AT (Göttingen L)	
c	τοὺς σημαινομένους ὑμῖν	– No Hebrew Text Extant –	τοὺς σημαινομένους ὑμῖν	c
d	ἐν τοῖς γεγραμμένοις		ἐν τοῖς γεγραμμένοις	d
e	ὑπὸ Αμαν		ὑπὸ Αμαν	e
f	τοῦ τεταγμένου		τοῦ τεταγμένου	f
g	ἐπὶ τῶν πραγμάτων		ἐπὶ τῶν πραγμάτων	g
h	καὶ δευτέρου πατρὸς ἡμῶν		καὶ δευτέρου πατρὸς ἡμῶν	h
i	πάντας		ὁλορίζους ἀπολέσαι	i
j	σὺν γυναιξὶν		σὺν γυναιξὶ	j
k	καὶ τέκνοις		καὶ τέκνοις	k
l	ἀπολέσαι ὁλορίζει			l
m	ταῖς τῶν ἐχθρῶν		ταῖς τῶν ἐχθρῶν	m
n	μαχαίραις ἄνευ παντὸς		μαχαίραις ἄνευ παντὸς	n
o	οἴκτου καὶ φειδοῦς		οἴκτου καὶ φειδοῦς	o
p	τῇ τεσσαρεσκαιδεκάτῃ		τῇ τεσσαρεσκαιδεκάτῃ	p
q	τοῦ δωδεκάτου μηνὸς		τοῦ μηνὸς τοῦ δωδεκάτου	q
r	Αδαρ		(οὗτος ὁ μὴν Αδαρ,	r
s			ὅς ἐστι Δύστρος),	s
t	τοῦ ἐνεστῶτος ἔτους,			t

Addition B

THE TEXTS OF ESTHER — ADDITION B

		LXX (Göttingen o')	MT (BHS 3)	AT (Göttingen L)	

MT (BHS 3) — No Hebrew Text Extant –

LXX (Göttingen o')

B:7	a	ὅπως οἱ πάλαι
	b	καὶ νῦν δυσμενεῖς
	c	ἐν ἡμέρᾳ μιᾷ
	d	βιαίως
	e	εἰς τὸν ᾅδην
	f	κατελθόντες
	g	εἰς τὸν μετέπειτα
	h	χρόνον
	i	εὐσταθῇ καὶ
	j	ἀτάραχα
	k	παρέχωσιν ἡμῖν
	l	διὰ τέλους τὰ πράγματα.
3:14	a	Τὰ δὲ ἀντίγραφα
	b	τῶν ἐπιστολῶν
	c	ἐξετίθετο

AT (Göttingen L)

u	φονεύειν
v	πάντας τοὺς Ἰουδαίους
w	καὶ ἁρπάζειν τὰ νήπια,
x	(B:7) ἵνα οἱ πάλαι
y	δυσμενεῖς καὶ νῦν
z	ἐν ἡμέρᾳ μιᾷ
aa	συνελθόντες
bb	εἰς τὸν ᾅδην
cc	
dd	εἰς τὰ μετέπειτα
ee	
ff	εὐσταθήσωσιν καὶ
gg	μὴ διὰ τέλους
hh	παρέχωσιν ἡμῖν
ii	πράγματα.

פַּתְשֶׁ֣גֶן הַכְּתָ֗ב
דָּ֣ת לְהִנָּתֵ֤ן בְּכָל

THE TEXTS OF ESTHER — CHAPTER 3

LXX (Göttingen o')	MT (BHS 3)	AT (Göttingen L)
d κατὰ χώραν,	פַּתְשֶׁ֣גֶן הַכְּתָ֗ב לְהִנָּ֤תֵֽן	
e καὶ προσετάγη	דָּת֙	
f πᾶσιν τοῖς ἔθνεσιν	בְּכָל־מְדִינָ֣ה וּמְדִינָ֔ה	
g ἑτοίμους εἶναι	גָּל֖וּי לְכָל־הָעַמִּ֑ים	
h εἰς τὴν ἡμέραν ταύτην.	לִהְי֥וֹת עֲתִדִ֖ים	
	לַיּ֥וֹם הַזֶּֽה׃	
	3:15 הָרָצִ֞ים יָצְא֤וּ a	
	דְחוּפִים֙ b	
3:15 a ἐσπεύδετο δὲ τὸ πρᾶγμας·	בִּדְבַ֣ר הַמֶּ֔לֶךְ	
b καὶ εἰς Σουσαν·	וְהַדָּ֥ת נִתְּנָ֖ה d	
c ὁ δὲ βασιλεὺς καὶ Αμανε	בְּשׁוּשַׁ֣ן הַבִּירָ֑ה	
d ἐκωθωνίζουτο,	וְהַמֶּ֤לֶךְ וְהָמָן֙ f	
e ἐταράσσετο δὲ ἡ πόλις.	יָשְׁב֣וּ לִשְׁתּ֔וֹת	3:19 (15) Καὶ ἐν Σούσοις a
	וְהָעִ֥יר שׁוּשָׁ֖ן נָבֽוֹכָה׃ g	ἐξετέθη τὸ πρόσταγμα τοῦτο. b

	LXX (Göttingen o')		MT (BHS 3)		AT (Göttingen L)	
4:1	a Ὁ δὲ Μαρδοχαῖος	4:1	וּמָרְדֳּכַי	4:1	Ὁ δὲ Μαρδοχαῖος	a
	b ἐπιγνοὺς		יָדַע		ἐπέγνω	b
	c τὸ συντελούμενον		אֶת־כָּל־אֲשֶׁר נַעֲשָׂה		πάντα τὰ γεγονότα,	c
	d				καὶ ἡ πόλις Σοῦσα ἐταράσσετο	d
	e				ἐπὶ τοῖς γεγενημένοις,	e
	f				καὶ πᾶσι τοῖς Ἰουδαίοις ἦν	f
	g				πένθος μέγα καὶ πικρὸν	g
	h				ἐν πάσῃ πόλει.	h
	i			4:2	ὁ δὲ Μαρδοχαῖος ἐλθὼν	a
	j διέρρηξεν		וַיִּקְרַע מָרְדֳּכַי		εἰς τὸν οἶκον αὐτοῦ	b
	k		אֶת־בְּגָדָיו		περιείλετο	c
	l τὰ ἱμάτια ἑαυτοῦ		וַיִּלְבַּשׁ שַׂק		τὰ ἱμάτια αὐτοῦ	d
	m καὶ ἐνεδύσατο σάκκον		וָאֵפֶר		καὶ περιεβάλετο σάκκον	e
	n καὶ κατεπάσατο σποδὸν		וַיֵּצֵא		καὶ σποδωθείς	f
	o καὶ ἐκπηδήσας		בְּתוֹךְ הָעִיר			g
	p διὰ τῆς πλατείας					h
	q τῆς πόλεως					i

Chapter 4

LXX (Göttingen o')		MT (BHS 3)	AT (Göttingen L)	
r	ἔβόα φωνῇ μεγάλῃ	בְּתוֹךְ הָעִיר וַיִּזְעַק זְעָקָה		j
s	Αἴρεται ἔθνος			k
t	μηδὲν ἠδικηκός.			l
4:2 a	καὶ ἦλθεν	וַיָּבוֹא	ἐξῆλθεν	m
b	ἕως τῆς πόλης τοῦ βασιλέως	עַד לִפְנֵי שַׁעַר־הַמֶּלֶךְ	ὡς ἐπὶ τὴν αὐλὴν τὴν ἔξω	n
c	καὶ ἔστη·	כִּי אֵין	καὶ ἔστη·	o
d	οὐ γὰρ ἦν ἐξὸν αὐτῷ	לָבוֹא	οὐ γὰρ ἠδύνατο	p
e	εἰσελθεῖν	אֶל־שַׁעַר הַמֶּלֶךְ	εἰσελθεῖν	q
f	εἰς τὴν αὐλὴν	בִּלְבוּשׁ שָׂק׃	εἰς τὰ βασιλεια	r
g	σάκκον ἔχοντι		ἐν σάκκῳ.	s
h	καὶ σποδόν.	וּבְכָל־מְדִינָה וּמְדִינָה		
4:3 a	καὶ ἐν πάσῃ χώρᾳ,	מְקוֹם אֲשֶׁר דְּבַר־הַמֶּלֶךְ		
b	οὗ	וְדָתוֹ מַגִּיעַ אֵבֶל גָּדוֹל		
c	ἐξετίθετο τὰ γράμματα,	לַיְּהוּדִים		
d	κραυγὴ	וְצוֹם וּבְכִי		
e		וּמִסְפֵּד שַׂק		
f	καὶ κοπετὸς	וָאֵפֶר יֻצַּע לָרַבִּים׃		

THE TEXTS OF ESTHER — CHAPTER 4

LXX (Göttingen o')		MT (BHS 3)	AT (Göttingen L)	
g	καὶ πένθος μέγα	וְאֵבֶל		
h		גָּדוֹל		
i	τοῖς Ἰουδαίοις,	לַיְּהוּדִים		
j	σάκκον καὶ σποδὸν	שַׂק וָאֵפֶר		
k	ἔστρωσαν ἑαυτοῖς.	יֻצַּע לָרַבִּים׃		
4:4 a	καὶ εἰσῆλθον	4:4 וַתְּבוֹאֶינָה	4:3(4) καὶ ἐκάλεσεν εὐνοῦχον ἕνα	a
b	αἱ ἅβραι καὶ οἱ εὐνοῦχοι	נַעֲרוֹת אֶסְתֵּר וְסָרִיסֶיהָ וַיַּגִּידוּ	καὶ ἀπέστειλε πρὸς Εσθηρ,	b
c	τῆς βασιλίσσης			c
d	καὶ ἀνήγγειλαν αὐτῇ,	לָהּ וַתִּתְחַלְחַל		d
e	καὶ ἐταράχθη	הַמַּלְכָּה		e
f		מְאֹד		f
g	ἀκούσασα τὸ γεγονός	וַתִּשְׁלַח בְּגָדִים		g
h	καὶ ἀπέστειλεν	לְהַלְבִּישׁ אֶת־מָרְדֳּכַי		h
i	στολίσαι			i
j	τὸν Μαρδοχαῖον			j
				k
				l

LXX (Göttingen o')

k καὶ ἀφελέσθαι
l αὐτοῦ τὸν σάκκον,
m
n
o ὁ δὲ οὐκ ἐπείσθη.
4:5 a ἡ δὲ Εσθηρ προσεκαλέσατο
b Αχραθαῖον
c τὸν εὐνοῦχον αὐτῆς,
d ὃς παρειστήκει αὐτῇ,
e καὶ ἀπέστειλεν
f
g μαθεῖν
h αὐτῇ
i παρὰ τοῦ Μαρδοχαίου
j τὸ ἀκριβές.

MT (BHS 3)

וְסָרִיסֶ֙יהָ֙
וַיַּגִּ֣ידוּ לָ֔הּ

4:4
וַתִּתְחַלְחַ֥ל
הַמַּלְכָּ֖ה מְאֹ֑ד
וַתִּשְׁלַ֨ח
בְּגָדִ֜ים לְהַלְבִּ֣ישׁ
אֶֽת־מָרְדֳּכַ֗י
וּלְהָסִ֥יר
שַׂקּ֛וֹ מֵעָלָ֖יו
וְלֹ֥א קִבֵּֽל׃

4:6 a וַיֵּצֵ֥א הֲתָ֖ךְ אֶֽל־מָרְדֳּכָ֑י
b אֶל־רְח֣וֹב הָעִ֔יר
אֲשֶׁ֖ר לִפְנֵ֥י שַֽׁעַר־הַמֶּֽלֶךְ׃

AT (Göttingen L)

m καὶ εἶπεν ἡ βασίλισσα
n Περίελεσθε
o τὸν σάκκον
p καὶ εἰσαγάγετε αὐτόν·
a ὃς δὲ οὐκ ἤθελεν.

	LXX (Göttingen o')	MT (BHS 3)	AT (Göttingen L)
4:7		c	
		d	
4:7 a	ὁ δὲ Μαρδοχαῖος	וַיַּגֶּד־לוֹ מָרְדֳּכַי	
b	ὑπέδειξεν αὐτῷ	אֵת כָּל־אֲשֶׁר קָרָהוּ	
c	τὸ γεγονὸς	וְאֵת פָּרָשַׁת הַכֶּסֶף אֲשֶׁר	
d	καὶ τὴν ἐπαγγελίαν,	אָמַר הָמָן לִשְׁקוֹל	
e	ἣν ἐπηγγείλατο Αμαν	עַל־גִּנְזֵי הַמֶּלֶךְ	
f	τῷ βασιλεῖ	בַּיְּהוּדִים לְאַבְּדָם׃	
g	εἰς τὴν γάζαν		
h	ταλάντων μυρίων,		
i	ἵνα ἀπολέσῃ τοὺς Ἰουδαίους.		
4:8 a	καὶ τὸ ἀντίγραφον 4:8	וְאֶת־פַּתְשֶׁגֶן	
b	τὸ ἐν Σούσοις ἐκτεθὲν	כְּתָב־הַדָּת אֲשֶׁר־נִתַּן	
c	ὑπὲρ τοῦ ἀπολέσθαι αὐτοὺς	בְּשׁוּשָׁן לְהַשְׁמִידָם	
d	ἔδωκεν αὐτῷ	נָתַן לוֹ לְהַרְאוֹת	
e	δεῖξαι τῇ Εσθηρ	אֶת־אֶסְתֵּר וּלְהַגִּיד לָהּ	(4:8) ἀλλ' εἶπεν b
f	καὶ εἶπεν	וּלְצַוּוֹת עָלֶיהָ	

THE TEXTS OF ESTHER — CHAPTER 4

	LXX (Göttingen o')	MT (BHS 3)	AT (Göttingen L)	
g	αὐτῷ		Οὕτως ἐρεῖτε αὐτῇ	c
h	ἐντελλασθαι αὐτῇ	הִיא	Μὴ ἀποστρέψῃς	d
i		עָלֶיהָ הַתֹּאמַרְן	τοῦ εἰσελθεῖν	e
j	εἰσελθούσῃ	אַל־תָּבֹא	πρὸς τὸν βασιλέα	f
k		לְהִמָּלֵט בֵּית־הַמֶּלֶךְ		g
l	παραιτήσασθαι	מִכָּל־		h
m	τὸν βασιλέα	כִּי אִם־	καὶ κολακεῦσαι	i
n	καὶ ἀξίωσαι	הַחֲרֵשׁ		j
o	αὐτὸν		τὸ πρόσωπον αὐτοῦ	k
p	περὶ		ὑπὲρ	l
q			ἐμοῦ καὶ	m
r	τοῦ λαοῦ	׃נַפְשֵׁהּ	τοῦ λαοῦ	n
s	μνησθεῖσα ἡμερῶν		μνησθεῖσα ἡμερῶν	o
t	ταπεινώσεώς σου		ταπεινώσεώς σου	p
u	ὡς ἐτράφης		ὧν ἐτράφης	q
v	ἐν χειρί μου,		ἐν τῇ χειρί μου,	r
w	διότι Αμαν		ὅτι Αμαν	s

	LXX (Göttingen o')	MT (BHS 3)	AT (Göttingen L)	
x	ὁ δευτερεύων		ὁ δευτερεύων	t
y	τῷ βασιλεῖ ἐλάλησεν		λελάληκε τῷ βασιλεῖ	u
z	καθ' ἡμῶν εἰς θάνατον·		καθ' ἡμῶν εἰς θάνατον.	v
aa	ἐπικάλεσαι	4:5	ἐπικαλεσαμένη οὖν	a
bb	τὸν κύριον,		τὸν θεὸν	b
cc	καὶ λάλησον		λάλησον	c
dd	τῷ βασιλεῖ περὶ ἡμῶν		περὶ ἡμῶν τῷ βασιλεῖ,	d
ee	καὶ ῥῦσαι ἡμᾶς ἐκ θανάτου.		καὶ ῥῦσαι ἡμᾶς ἐκ θανάτου.	e
4:9 a	εἰσελθὼν δὲ ὁ Αχραθαῖος	וַיָּבֹא הֲתָךְ	καὶ ἀπήγγειλεν	4:6(9) a
b	ἐλάλησεν	וַיַּגֵּד	αὐτῇ	b
c	αὐτῇ	לְאֶסְתֵּר	τὴν ὀδύνην τοῦ Ισραηλ.	c
d	πάντας τοὺς λόγους τούτους.	אֵת דִּבְרֵי מָרְדֳּכָי׃		
4:10 a	εἶπεν δὲ Εσθηρ	וַתֹּאמֶר אֶסְתֵּר	καὶ ἀπέστειλεν	4:7(10) a
b	πρὸς Αχραθαῖον	לַהֲתָךְ	αὐτῷ	b
c	Πορεύθητι		κατὰ τάδε λέγουσα	c
d	πρὸς Μαρδοχαῖον	אֶל־מָרְדֳּכָי		
e	καὶ εἶπον			

THE TEXTS OF ESTHER — CHAPTER 4

	LXX (Göttingen o')		MT (BHS 3)	AT (Göttingen L)	
	4:11			(4:11)	
a	ὅτι Τὰ ἔθνη πάντα		כׇּל־עַבְדֵי	Σὺ	d
b	τῆς βασιλείας		הַמֶּלֶךְ		e
c			וְעַם־מְדִינוֹת הַמֶּלֶךְ		f
d	γινώσκει		יֹֽדְעִים	γινώσκεις	g
e			אֲשֶׁר	παρὰ πάντας	h
f	ὅτι		כׇּל־	ὅτι	i
g	πᾶς ἄνθρωπος ἡ γυνή,		אִישׁ וְאִשָּׁה אֲשֶׁר		j
h	ὅς		יָבוֹא־	ὃς ἂν	k
i	εἰσελεύσεται		אֶל־	εἰσέλθη	l
j	πρὸς τὸν βασιλέα		הַמֶּלֶךְ אֶל־הֶחָצֵר	πρὸς τὸν βασιλέα	m
k	εἰς τὴν αὐλὴν τὴν ἐσωτέραν		הַפְּנִימִית אֲשֶׁר לֹֽא־יִקָּרֵא		n
l	ἄκλητος,		אַחַת דָּתוֹ לְהָמִית	ἄκλητος,	o
m					p
n	οὐκ ἔστιν αὐτῷ σωτηρία·				
o	πλὴν ᾧ ἐκτείνει		לְבַד מֵאֲשֶׁר יֽוֹשִׁיט־לוֹ	ᾧ οὐκ ἐκτενεῖ	r
p	ὁ βασιλεὺς		הַמֶּלֶךְ		s

Chapter 4

	LXX (Göttingen o')		MT (BHS 3)		AT (Göttingen L)	
q	τὴν χρυσῆν ῥάβδον,		אֲשֶׁר־יוֹשִׁיט־לוֹ הַמֶּלֶךְ		τὴν ῥάβδον αὐτοῦ τὴν χρυσῆν,	t
r	οὗτος σωθήσεται.		וְחָיָה		θανάτου ἔνοχος ἔσται.	u
s	κἀγὼ οὐ κέκλημαι	4:8	וַאֲנִי לֹא נִקְרֵאתִי			v
t	εἰσελθεῖν		לָבוֹא		καὶ ἐγὼ οὐ κέκλημαι	a
u			אֶל־הַמֶּלֶךְ			b
v	πρὸς τὸν βασιλέα,		זֶה שְׁלוֹשִׁים		πρὸς αὐτόν,	c
w	εἰσιν αὗται ἡμέραι τριάκοντα.		יוֹם:		ἡμέραι εἰσὶ τριάκοντα·	d
					καὶ πῶς εἰσελεύσομαι νῦν	e
					ἄκλητος οὖσα;	f
4:12 a	καὶ ἀπήγγειλεν	4:12	וַיַּגִּידוּ			
b	Αχραθαῖος					
c	Μαρδοχαίῳ		לְמָרְדֳּכָי			
d	πάντας τοὺς λόγους Εσθηρ.		אֵת דִּבְרֵי אֶסְתֵּר:			
4:13 a	καὶ εἶπεν Μαρδοχαῖος	4:13	וַיֹּאמֶר מָרְדֳּכַי	4:9(13)	καὶ ἀπέστειλε	a
b	πρὸς Αχραθαῖον		לְהָשִׁיב אֶל־אֶסְתֵּר		πρὸς αὐτὴν Μαρδοχαῖος	b
c	Πορεύθητι					
d						

Chapter 4

THE TEXTS OF ESTHER — CHAPTER 4

	LXX (Göttingen o')	MT (BHS 3)	AT (Göttingen L)	
e	καὶ εἶπον αὐτῇ Εσθηρ,	אֶל־אֶסְתֵּר הָשִׁיב	καὶ εἶπεν αὐτῇ	c
f	μὴ εἴπῃς σεαυτῇ	אַל־תְּדַמִּי בְנַפְשֵׁךְ		d
g	ὅτι σωθήσῃ μόνη	לְהִמָּלֵט בֵּית־הַמֶּלֶךְ		e
h	ἐν τῇ βασιλείᾳ	מִכָּל־הַיְּהוּדִים׃		f
i	παρὰ πάντας τοὺς Ἰουδαίους·			g
4:14 a	ὡς ὅτι ἐὰν παρακούσῃς	(4:14) כִּי אִם־הַחֲרֵשׁ תַּחֲרִישִׁי	(4:14) Ἐὰν ὑπερίδῃς τὸ ἔθνος σου	h
b			τοῦ μὴ βοηθῆσαι αὐτοῖς,	i
c	ἐν τούτῳ τῷ καιρῷ,	בָּעֵת הַזֹּאת		j
d	ἄλλοθεν		ἀλλ' ὁ θεὸς ἔσται αὐτοῖς	k
e	βοήθεια		βοηθὸς	l
f	καὶ σκέπη		καὶ σωτηρία,	m
g	ἔσται τοῖς Ἰουδαίοις,	רֶוַח וְהַצָּלָה יַעֲמוֹד לַיְּהוּדִים מִמָּקוֹם אַחֵר		n
h				o
i	σὺ δὲ καὶ ὁ οἶκος	וְאַתְּ וּבֵית־אָבִיךְ	σὺ δὲ καὶ ὁ οἶκος	p
j	τοῦ πατρός σου	תֹּאבֵדוּ וּמִי	τοῦ πατρός σου	q
	ἀπολεῖσθε·		ἀπολεῖσθε·	
k	καὶ τίς οἶδεν	4:10 וַתֹּאמֶר אֶסְתֵּר	4:10 καὶ τίς οἶδεν	a

Chapter 4

LXX (Göttingen o')	MT (BHS 3)	AT (Göttingen L)
l εἰ εἰς τὸν καιρὸν τοῦτον	וַתֹּאמֶר אֶסְתֵּר	b εἰ εἰς τὸν καιρὸν τοῦτον
m ἐβασίλευσας;	לְהָשִׁיב אֶל־מָרְדֳּכָי׃	c ἐβασίλευσας;
4:15 a καὶ ἐξαπέστειλεν 4:15		a 4:11(15) καὶ ἀπέστειλεν
b Εσθηρ	לֵךְ כְּנוֹס	b ἡ βασίλισσα
c τὸν ἥκοντα	אֶת־כָּל־הַיְּהוּדִים הַנִּמְצְאִים	c
d πρὸς αὐτὴν	בְּשׁוּשָׁן וְצוּמוּ עָלַי	d
e πρὸς Μαρδοχαῖον	וְאַל־תֹּאכְלוּ וְאַל־תִּשְׁתּוּ	e
f λέγουσα	שְׁלֹשֶׁת יָמִים לַיְלָה וָיוֹם	f λέγουσα
4:16 a Βαδίσας ἐκκλησίασον 4:16	גַּם־אֲנִי וְנַעֲרֹתַי	g (4:16) Παραγγείλατε θεραπείαν
b τοὺς Ἰουδαίους		h
c τοὺς ἐν Σούσοις		i
d καὶ νηστεύσατε ἐπ᾽ ἐμοὶ		j καὶ δεήθητε τοῦ θεοῦ ἐκτενῶς·
e καὶ μὴ φάγητε		k
f μηδὲ πίητε		l
g ἐπὶ ἡμέρας τρεῖς		m
h νύκτα καὶ ἡμέραν·		n
i κἀγὼ δὲ καὶ αἱ ἅβραι μου		o κἀγὼ δὲ καὶ τὰ κοράσιά μου

THE TEXTS OF ESTHER — CHAPTER 4

LXX (Göttingen o')	MT (BHS 3)	AT (Göttingen L)
j ἀσιτήσομεν,	אֹבֵד֙ מִ֤ן	ποιήσομεν οὕτως, p
k καὶ τότε εἰσελεύσομαι	וּבְכֵ֞ן אָב֤וֹא	καὶ εἰσελεύσομαι q
l πρὸς τὸν βασιλέα	אֶל־הַמֶּ֙לֶךְ֙	πρὸς τὸν βασιλέα r
m παρὰ τὸν νόμον,	אֲשֶׁ֣ר לֹֽא־כַדָּ֔ת	ἄκλητος, s
n ἐὰν καὶ ἀπολέσθαι με ᾖ.	וְכַאֲשֶׁ֥ר אָבַ֖דְתִּי אָבָֽדְתִּי׃	εἰ δέοι καὶ ἀποθανεῖν με. t
4:17 a καὶ βαδίσας Μαρδοχαῖος	4:17 וַֽיַּעֲבֹ֖ר	4:12(17) καὶ ἐποίησεν a
b ἐποίησεν	מָרְדֳּכָ֑י	οὕτως Μαρδοχαῖος. b
c		
d ὅσα ἐνετείλατο	וַיַּ֕עַשׂ כְּכֹ֛ל אֲשֶׁר־צִוְּתָ֥ה	
e αὐτῷ Εσθηρ.	עָלָ֖יו אֶסְתֵּֽר׃	

Chapter 4

TEXTS OF ESTHER — CHAPTER C

		LXX (Göttingen o')	MT (BHS 3)	AT (Göttingen L)	
			– No Hebrew Text Extant –		
C:1	a	Καὶ ἐδεήθη		4:12(C:1) Καὶ ἐδεήθη	c
	b	κυρίου		τοῦ κυρίου	d
	c	μνημονεύων		μνημονεύων	e
	d	πάντα		αὐτοῦ	f
	e	τὰ ἔργα		τὰ ἔργα	g
	f	κυρίου			h
C:2	a	καὶ εἶπεν		(C:2) καὶ εἶπεν	i
	b	Κύριε, κύριε,		4:13 Δέσποτα παντοκράτορ,	a
	c	βασιλεῦ πάντων κρατῶν,			b
	d	ὅτι		οὗ	c
	e	ἐν τῇ ἐξουσίᾳ		ἐν τῇ ἐξουσίᾳ	d
	f	σου			e
	g	τὸ πᾶν ἐστιν,		ἐστὶ τὰ πάντα,	f
	h	καὶ οὐκ ἔστιν		καὶ οὐκ ἔστιν	g
	i	ὁ ἀντιδοξῶν σοι		ὃς ἀντιτάξεταί σοι	h
	j	ἐν τῷ θέλειν σε		ἐν τῷ θέλειν σε	i
	k	σῶσαι τὸν Ισραηλ·		σῶσαι τὸν οἶκον Ισραηλ·	j
C:3	a	ὅτι σὺ ἐποίησας		(C:3) ὅτι σὺ ἐποίησας	k

Addition C

TEXTS OF ESTHER — CHAPTER C

	LXX (Göttingen o')	MT (BHS 3)	AT (Göttingen L)	
		– No Hebrew Text Extant –		
b	τὸν οὐρανὸν καὶ τὴν γῆν		τὸν οὐρανὸν καὶ τὴν γῆν	l
c	καὶ πᾶν θαυμαζόμενον		καὶ πᾶν τὸ θαυμαζόμενον	m
d	ἐν τῇ ὑπ' οὐρανὸν		ἐν τῇ ὑπ' οὐρανόν,	n
C4 a	καὶ κύριος εἶ πάντων,	(C:4)	καὶ σὺ κυριεύεις πάντων.	o
b	καὶ οὐκ ἔστιν			
c	ὃς ἀντιτάξεταί σοι			
d	τῷ κυρίῳ.			
C:5 a	σὺ πάντα γινώσκεις·	4:14	σὺ γὰρ πάντα γινώσκεις,	a
b	σὺ οἶδας,	(C:5)	καὶ τὸ γένος Ισραηλ	b
c	κύριε,		σὺ οἶδας·	c
d				
e	ὅτι οὐκ ἐν ὕβρει	4:15	καὶ οὐχ ὅτι ἐν ὕβρει	a
f	οὐδὲ ἐν ὑπερηφανίᾳ			b
g	οὐδὲ ἐν φιλοδοξίᾳ		οὐδὲ ἐν φιλοδοξίᾳ	c
h	ἐποίησα		ἐποίησα	d
i	τοῦτο,			e
j	τὸ μὴ προσκυνεῖν		τοῦ μὴ προσκυνεῖν	f
k	τὸν ὑπερήφανον Αμαν,		τὸν ἀπερίτμητον Αμαν,	g

Addition C

TEXTS OF ESTHER — CHAPTER C

	LXX (Göttingen o')		MT (BHS 3)	AT (Göttingen L)	
C:6	a	ὅτι ηὐδόκουν φιλεῖν	– No Hebrew Text Extant –	(C:6) ἐπεὶ εὐδόκουν φιλῆσαι	h
	b	πέλματα ποδῶν αὐτοῦ		τὰ πέλματα τῶν ποδῶν αὐτοῦ	i
	c	πρὸς σωτηρίαν Ισραηλ·		ἕνεκεν τοῦ Ισραηλ·	j
C:7	a	ἀλλὰ ἐποίησα		(C:7) ἀλλ' ἐποίησα	k
	b	τοῦτο			l
	c	ἵνα μὴ θῶ		ἵνα μηδένα προτάξω	m
	d	δόξαν ἀνθρώπου		τῆς δόξης σοῦ,	n
	e			δέσποτα,	o
	f	ὑπεράνω δόξης θεοῦ,			p
	g	καὶ οὐ προσκυνήσω οὐδένα		καὶ μηδένα προσκυνήσω	q
	h	πλὴν σοῦ		πλὴν σοῦ	r
	i	τοῦ κυρίου μου		τοῦ ἀληθινοῦ	s
	j	καὶ οὐ ποιήσα		καὶ οὐ ποιήσω	t
	k	αὐτὰ		αὐτὸ	u
	l	ἐν ὑπερηφανίᾳ.		ἐν πειρασμῷ.	v
C:8	a	καὶ νῦν,	4:16	καὶ νῦν,	a
	b	κύριε		κύριε,	b
	c	ὁ θεός,			c

Addition C

TEXTS OF ESTHER — CHAPTER C

LXX (Göttingen o')	MT (BHS 3)	AT (Göttingen L)
	– No Hebrew Text Extant –	
d ὁ βασιλεύς,		d ὁ διαθέμενος πρὸς Αβρααμ,
e ὁ θεὸς Αβρααμ,		e φεῖσαι τοῦ λαοῦ σου,
f φεῖσαι τοῦ λαοῦ σου,		f ὅτι ἐπιτέθεινται ἡμῖν
g ὅτι ἐπιβλέπουσιν ἡμῖν		g εἰς καταφθορὰν
h εἰς καταφθορὰν		h καὶ ἐπιθυμοῦσιν ἀφανίσαι
i καὶ ἐπεθύμησαν ἀπολέσαι		i καὶ ἐξᾶραι
j		j τὴν ἐξ ἀρχῆς κληρονομίαν σου·
k τὴν ἐξ ἀρχῆς κληρονομίαν σου·		k (C:9) μὴ ὑπερίδῃς τὴν μερίδα σου,
C:9 a μὴ ὑπερίδῃς τὴν μερίδα σου,		l ἦν
b ἦν		m
c σεαυτῷ		n
d ἐλυτρώσω ἐκ γῆς Αἰγύπτου·		o ἐλυτρώσω ἐκ γῆς Αἰγύπτου·
C:10 a ἐπάκουσον τῆς δεήσεώς		a 4:17 (C:10) ἐπάκουσον τῆς δεήσεως
b μου		b ἡμῶν
c καὶ ἱλάσθητι		c καὶ ἱλάσθητι
d τῷ κλήρῳ σου		d τῆς κληρονομίας σου
e καὶ στρέψον τὸ πένθος ἡμῶν		e καὶ στρέψον τὸ πένθος ἡμῶν
f εἰς εὐωχίαν,		f εἰς εὐφροσύνην,

Addition C

TEXTS OF ESTHER — CHAPTER C

LXX (Göttingen o')	MT (BHS 3)	AT (Göttingen L)
g ἵνα ζῶντες ὑμνῶμέν	– No Hebrew Text Extant –	g ἵνα ζῶντες ὑμνήσωμέν
h σου τὸ ὄνομα, κύριε,		h σε,
i καὶ μὴ ἀφανίσῃς στόμα		i καὶ μὴ ἀφανίσῃς στόμα
j αἰνούντων σοι.		j ὑμνούντων σε.
C:11 a καὶ πᾶς Ισραηλ		
b ἐκέκραξαν		
c ἐξ ἰσχύος αὐτῶν,		
d ὅτι θάνατος αὐτῶν		
e ἐν ὀφθαλμοῖς αὐτῶν.		
C:12 a Καὶ Εσθηρ ἡ βασίλισσα κατέφυγεν		4:18 (C:12) a Καὶ Εσθηρ ἡ βασίλισσα κατέφυγεν
b ἐπὶ τὸν κύριον		b ἐπὶ τὸν κύριον
c ἐν ἀγῶνι θανάτου κατειλημμένη,		c ἐν ἀγῶνι θανάτου κατειλημμένη
C:13 a καὶ ἀφελομένη		(C:13) d καὶ ἀφείλατο
b τὰ ἱμάτια τῆς δόξης		e τὰ ἱμάτια τῆς δόξης
c αὐτῆς		f ἀφ' ἑαυτῆς
d		g καὶ πᾶν σημεῖον ἐπιφανείας αὐτῆς

Addition C

TEXTS OF ESTHER — CHAPTER C

	LXX (Göttingen o')	MT (BHS 3)	AT (Göttingen L)	
		– No Hebrew Text Extant –		
e	ἐνεδύσατο		καὶ ἐνεδύσατο	h
f	ἱμάτια			i
g	στενοχωρίας		στενοχωρίαν	j
h	καὶ πένθους		καὶ πένθος	k
i	καὶ ἀντὶ		καὶ ἀντὶ	l
j	τῶν ὑπερηφάνων ἡδυσμάτων σποδοῦ		ὑπερηφάνων ἡδυσμάτων σποδοῦ	m
k	καὶ κοπριῶν ἔπλησεν		καὶ κόπρου ἔπλησε	n
l	τὴν κεφαλὴν αὐτῆς		τὴν κεφαλὴν αὐτῆς	o
m	καὶ τὸ σῶμα αὐτῆς		καὶ τὸ σῶμα αὐτῆς	p
n	ἐταπείνωσεν σφόδρα		ἐταπείνωσε σφόδρα	q
o	καὶ πάντα τόπον κόσμου		καὶ πᾶν σημεῖον κόσμου	r
p			αὐτῆς	s
q	ἀγαλλιάματος		καὶ ἀγαλλιάματος	t
r	αὐτῆς			u
s	ἔπλησεν στρεπτῶν τριχῶν		τερπνῶν τριχῶν ἔπλησε	v
t	αὐτῆς		ταπεινώσεως	w
C:14 a	καὶ ἐδέετο		4:19 (C:14) καὶ ἐδεήθη	a
b	κυρίου		τοῦ κυρίου	b

Addition C

TEXTS OF ESTHER — CHAPTER C

	LXX (Göttingen o')	MT (BHS 3)	AT (Göttingen L)	
		– No Hebrew Text Extant –		
c	θεοῦ Ισραηλ		καὶ εἶπεν	c
d	καὶ εἶπεν		Κύριε	d
e	Κύριέ μου		βασιλεῦ,	e
f	ὁ βασιλεὺς ἡμῶν,		σὺ εἶ μόνος	f
g	σὺ εἶ μόνος·		βοηθός·	g
h			βοήθησόν μοι	h
i	βοήθησόν μοι		τῇ ταπεινῇ	i
j	τῇ μόνῃ		καὶ οὐκ ἐχούσῃ βοηθὸν	j
k	καὶ μὴ ἐχούσῃ βοηθὸν		πλὴν σοῦ,	k
l	εἰ μὴ σέ,			l
C:15 a	ὅτι κίνδυνός μου		(C:15) ὅτι κίνδυνός μου	m
b	ἐν χειρί μου.		ἐν τῇ χειρί μου.	n
C:16 a	ἐγὼ ἤκουον		4:20 (C:16) ἐγὼ δὲ ἤκουσα	a
b	ἐκ γενετῆς μου		πατρικῆς μου βίβλου	b
c	ἐν φυλῇ πατριᾶς μου			c
d	ὅτι		ὅτι	d
e	σύ, κύριε,			e
f	ἔλαβες τὸν Ισραηλ		ἐλυτρώσω τὸν Ισραηλ	f

Addition C

TEXTS OF ESTHER — CHAPTER C

	LXX (Göttingen o')	MT (BHS 3)	AT (Göttingen L)	
		– No Hebrew Text Extant –		
g	ἐκ πάντων τῶν ἐθνῶν		ἐκ πάντων τῶν ἐθνῶν	g
h	καὶ τοὺς πατέρας		καὶ τοὺς πατέρας	h
i	ἡμῶν		αὐτῶν	i
j	ἐκ		ἐκ	j
k	πάντων			k
l	τῶν προγόνων αὐτῶν		τῶν προγόνων αὐτῶν	l
m			ἐπιθέμενος αὐτοῖς Ισραηλ	m
n	εἰς κληρονομίαν αἰώνιον		κληρονομίαν αἰώνιον	n
o	καὶ ἐποίησας αὐτοῖς		καὶ ἐποίησας αὐτοῖς	o
p	ὅσα ἐλάλησας.		ἃ ἐλάλησας	p
q			αὐτοῖς	q
r			καὶ παρέσχου ὅσα ᾔτησαν.	r
C:17 a	καὶ νῦν			
b	ἡμάρτομεν ἐνώπιόν σου,		4:21 (C:17) ἡμάρτομεν ἐναντίον σου,	a
c	καὶ παρέδωκας ἡμᾶς		καὶ παρέδωκας ἡμᾶς	b
d	εἰς χεῖρας τῶν ἐχθρῶν ἡμῶν,		εἰς χεῖρας τῶν ἐχθρῶν ἡμῶν,	c
C:18 a	ἀνθ᾽ ὧν		(C:18) εἰ	d
b	ἐδοξάσαμεν τοὺς θεοὺς αὐτῶν·		ἐδοξάσαμεν τοὺς θεοὺς αὐτῶν·	e

Addition C

		LXX (Göttingen o')	*MT (BHS 3)*	*AT (Göttingen L)*	
	c	δίκαιος εἶ, κύριε.	– No Hebrew Text Extant –	4:22 δίκαιος εἶ, κύριε.	a
C:19	a	καὶ νῦν οὐχ ἱκανώθησαν		(C:19) καὶ νῦν οὐχ ἱκανώθησαν	b
	b	ἐν πικρασμῷ δουλείας ἡμῶν,		ἐν πικρασμῷ δουλείας ἡμῶν,	c
	c	ἀλλὰ ἔθηκαν		ἀλλ᾽ ἐπέθηκαν	d
	d	τὰς χεῖρας αὐτῶν		τὰς χεῖρας αὐτῶν	e
	e	ἐπὶ τὰς χεῖρας τῶν εἰδώλων αὐτῶν		ἐπὶ τὰς χεῖρας τῶν εἰδώλων αὐτῶν	f
C:20	a	ἐξᾶραι ὁρισμὸν στόματός σου		(C:20) ἐξᾶραι ὁρισμὸν στόματός σου,	g
	b	καὶ ἀφανίσαι κληρονομίαν σου		ἀφανίσαι κληρονομίαν σου	h
	c	καὶ ἐμφράξαι στόμα αἰνούντων σοι		καὶ ἐμφάξαι στόμα αἰνούντων σε	i
	d	καὶ σβέσαι δόξαν οἴκου σου		καὶ σβέσαι δόξαν οἴκου σου	j
	e	καὶ θυσιαστήριόν σου		καὶ θυσιαστηρίου σου	k
C:21	a	καὶ ἀνοῖξαι στόμα		(C:21) καὶ ἀνοῖξαι στόματα	l
	b	ἐθνῶν		ἐχθρῶν	m
	c	εἰς ἀρετὰς ματαίων		εἰς ἀρετὰς ματαίων	n
	d	καὶ θαυμασθῆναι βασιλέα σάρκινον		καὶ θαυμασθῆναι βασιλέα σάρκινον	o
	e	εἰς αἰῶνα.		εἰς τὸν αἰῶνα.	p
C:22	a	μὴ παραδῷς, κύριε,		4:23 (C:22) μὴ δὴ παραδῷς, κύριε,	a
	b	τὸ σκῆπτρόν σου		τὸ σκῆπτρόν σου	b

Addition C

TEXTS OF ESTHER — CHAPTER C

	LXX (Göttingen o')	MT (BHS 3)	AT (Göttingen L)	
		– No Hebrew Text Extant –		
c	τοῖς μὴ οὖσιν,		τοῖς μισοῦσί σε ἐχθροῖς,	c
d	καὶ μὴ καταγελασάτωσαν		καὶ μὴ χαρείησαν	d
e	ἐν τῇ πτώσει ἡμῶν,		ἐπὶ τῇ πτώσει ἡμῶν·	e
f	ἀλλὰ στρέψον		στρέψον	f
g	τὴν βουλὴν αὐτῶν		τὰς βουλὰς αὐτῶν	g
h	ἐπ᾽ αὐτούς,		ἐπ᾽ αὐτούς,	h
i	τὸν δὲ ἀρξάμενον		τὸν δὲ ἀρξάμενον	i
j	ἐφ᾽ ἡμᾶς		ἐφ᾽ ἡμᾶς	j
k			εἰς κακὰ	k
l	παραδειγμάτισον.		παραδειγμάτισον.	l
C:23 a	μνήσθητι,		4:24 (C:23) ἐπιφάνηθι	a
b			ἡμῖν,	b
c	κύριε,		κύριε,	c
d	γνώσθητι		καὶ γνώσθητι	d
e			ἡμῖν	e
f	ἐν καιρῷ θλίψεως ἡμῶν		ἐν καιρῷ θλίψεως ἡμῶν	f
g	καὶ ἐμὲ θάρσυνον,		καὶ μὴ θραύσῃς ἡμᾶς.	g
h	βασιλεῦ τῶν θεῶν			

Addition C

LXX (Göttingen o')

i	καὶ πάσης ἀρχῆς ἐπικρατῶν.
C:24 a	δὸς λόγον εὔρυθμον
b	εἰς τὸ στόμα μου
c	
d	ἐνώπιον τοῦ λέοντος
e	καὶ μετάθες
f	τὴν καρδίαν αὐτοῦ
g	εἰς μῖσος τοῦ πολεμοῦντος ἡμᾶς
h	εἰς συντέλειαν αὐτοῦ
i	καὶ τῶν ὁμονοούντων αὐτῷ·
C:25 a	ἡμᾶς δὲ ῥῦσαι
b	ἐν χειρί σου
c	
d	καὶ βοήθησόν μοι
e	τῇ μόνῃ
f	καὶ μὴ ἐχούσῃ
g	εἰ μὴ σέ, κύριε.
h	

MT (BHS 3)

– No Hebrew Text Extant –

AT (Göttingen L)

4:25 (C:24) δὸς λόγον εὔρυθμον	a
εἰς τὸ στόμα μου	b
καὶ χαρίτωσον τὰ ῥήματά μου	c
ἐνώπιον τοῦ βασιλέως	d
καὶ μετάστρεψον	e
τὴν καρδίαν αὐτοῦ	f
εἰς μῖσος τοῦ πολεμοῦντος ἡμᾶς	g
εἰς συντέλειαν αὐτοῦ	h
καὶ τῶν ὁμονοούντων αὐτῷ·	i
(C:25) ἡμᾶς δὲ ῥῦσαι	j
ἐν τῇ χειρί σου	k
τῇ κραταιᾷ	l
καὶ βοήθησόν μοι,	m
	n
	o
	p
ὅτι σύ	q

Addition C

TEXTS OF ESTHER — CHAPTER C

	LXX (Göttingen o')	MT (BHS 3)	AT (Göttingen L)	
		– No Hebrew Text Extant –		
i	πάντων γνῶσιν ἔχεις		πάντων γνῶσιν ἔχεις	r
C:26 a	καὶ οἶδας ὅτι		καὶ οἶδας ὅτι	s
b		(C:26)	βδελύσσομαι κοίτην ἀπεριτμήτου	t
c	ἐμίσησα δόξαν ἀνόμων		καὶ ἐμίσησα δόξαν ἀνόμου	u
d	καὶ βδελύσσομαι κοίτην ἀπεριτμήτων			v
e	καὶ παντὸς ἀλλοτρίου.		καὶ παντὸς ἀλλογενοῦς.	w
C:27 a	σὺ		4:26 (C:27) σὺ	a
b			κύριε,	b
c	οἶδας τὴν ἀνάγκην μου,		οἶδας τὴν ἀνάγκην μου,	c
d	ὅτι βδελύσσομαι		ὅτι βδελύσσομαι	d
e	τὸ σημεῖον τῆς ὑπερηφανίας		τὸ σημεῖον τῆς ὑπερηφανίας,	e
f	μου,			f
g	ὅ ἐστιν ἐπὶ τῆς κεφαλῆς μου		ὅ ἐστιν ἐπὶ τῆς κεφαλῆς μου,	g
h			καὶ οὐ φορῶ αὐτὸ εἰ μὴ	h
i	ἐν ἡμέραις ὀπτασίας μου·		ἐν ἡμέρᾳ ὀπτασίας μου	i
j	βδελύσσομαι αὐτὸ		καὶ βδελύσσομαι αὐτὸ	j
k	ὡς ῥάκος καταμηνίων		ὡς ῥάκος ἀποκαθημένης·	k
l	καὶ οὐ φορῶ αὐτὸ			

Addition C

TEXTS OF ESTHER — CHAPTER C

	LXX (Göttingen o')	MT (BHS 3)	AT (Göttingen L)	
C:28 m	ἐν ἡμέραις ἡσυχίας μου.	– No Hebrew Text Extant –		
a	καὶ οὐκ ἔφαγεν		4:27 (C:28) καὶ οὐκ ἔφαγεν	a
b	ἡ δούλη σου		ἡ δούλη σου	b
c	τράπεζαν Αμαν,		ἐπὶ τῶν τραπεζῶν αὐτῶν ἅμα,	c
d	καὶ οὐκ ἐδόξασα		4:28 καὶ οὐκ ἐδόξασα	a
e	συμπόσιον βασιλέως		βασιλέως συμπόσια	b
f	οὐδὲ ἔπιον οἶνον σπονδῶν·		καὶ οὐκ ἔπιον σπουδῆς οἶνον.	c
C:29 a	καὶ οὐκ ηὐφράνθη		(C:29) καὶ οὐκ εὐφράνθη	d
b	ἡ δούλη σου		ἡ δούλη σου	e
c	ἀφ' ἡμέρας μεταβολῆς μου		ἐφ' ἡμέρας μεταβολῆς μου	f
d	μέχρι νῦν			g
e	πλὴν ἐπὶ σοί,		εἰ μὴ ἐπὶ σοί,	h
f	κύριε ὁ θεὸς Αβρααμ.		δέσποτα.	i
C:30 a	ὁ θεὸς ὁ ἰσχύων		4:29 (C:30) καὶ νῦν,	a
b	ἐπὶ πάντας,		δυνατὸς	b
c	εἰσάκουσον φωνὴν		ὢν ἐπὶ πάντας,	c
d	ἀπηλπισμένων καὶ ῥῦσαι ἡμᾶς		εἰσάκουσον φωνῆς	d
			ἀπηλπισμένων καὶ ῥῦσαι ἡμᾶς	e

Addition C

LXX (Göttingen o')	MT (BHS 3)	AT (Göttingen L)
	– No Hebrew Text Extant –	
e ἐκ χειρὸς τῶν πονηρευομένων		f ἐκ χειρὸς τῶν πονηρευομένων
f		g ἐφ᾽ ἡμᾶς
g καὶ ῥῦσαί με		h καὶ ἐξελοῦ με,
h		i κύριε,
i ἐκ τοῦ φόβου μου.		j ἐκ χειρὸς τοῦ φόβου μου.

The Texts of Esther — Chapter 5/D

	LXX (Göttingen o')		MT (BHS 3)		AT (Göttingen L)	
D:1	a	Καὶ ἐγενήθη	5:1 a	וַיְהִי	5(D):1 a	Καὶ ἐγενήθη
	b	ἐν τῇ ἡμέρᾳ τῇ τρίτῃ,	b	בַּיּוֹם הַשְּׁלִישִׁי	b	ἐν τῇ ἡμέρᾳ τῇ τρίτῃ,
	c	ὡς ἐπαύσατο			c	ὡς ἐπαύσατο
	d				d	Εσθηρ
	e	προσευχομένη,			e	προσευχομένη,
	f	ἐξεδύσατο			f	ἐξεδύσατο
	g	τὰ ἱμάτια τῆς θεραπείας	c	וַתִּלְבַּשׁ	g	τὰ ἱμάτια τῆς θεραπείας
	h	καὶ περιεβάλετο	d	אֶסְתֵּר	h	καὶ περιεβάλετο
	i		e	מַלְכוּת	i	
	j	τὴν δόξαν			j	τὰ ἱμάτια
	k	αὐτῆς			k	τῆς δόξης
D:2	a	καὶ γενηθεῖσα			5(D):2 a	καὶ γενομένη
	b	ἐπιφανὴς			b	ἐπιφανὴς
	c	ἐπικαλεσαμένη			c	καὶ ἐπικαλεσαμένη
	d	τὸν πάντων			d	τὸν πάντων
	e	ἐπόπτην			e	γνώστην
	f	θεὸν καὶ σωτῆρα			f	καὶ σωτῆρα θεὸν

Chapter 5/Addition D

THE TEXTS OF ESTHER — CHAPTER 5/D

	LXX (Göttingen o')	MT (BHS 3)		AT (Göttingen L)	
g	παρέλαβεν			παρέλαβε	g
h				μεθ᾽ ἑαυτῆς	h
i	τὰς δύο ἄβρας			δύο ἄβρας	i
D:3 a	καὶ τῇ μὲν μιᾷ ἐπηρείδετο		(D:3)	καὶ τῇ μὲν μιᾷ ἐπηρείδετο	j
b	ὡς τρυφερευομένη,			ὡς τρυφερευομένη,	k
D:4 a	ἡ δὲ ἑτέρα		(D:4)	ἡ δὲ ἑτέρα	l
b	ἐπηκολούθει κουφίζουσα			ἐπηκολούθει ἐπικουφίζουσα	m
c	τὴν ἔνδυσιν αὐτῆς,			τὸ ἔνδυμα αὐτῆς,	n
D:5 a	καὶ αὐτὴ ἐρυθριῶσα		5:3 (D:5)	καὶ αὐτὴ ἐρυθριῶσα	a
b	ἀκμῇ κάλλους αὐτῆς,			ἐν ἀκμῇ κάλλους αὐτῆς,	b
c	καὶ τὸ πρόσωπον αὐτῆς			καὶ τὸ πρόσωπον αὐτῆς	c
d	ἱλαρὸν				d
e	ὡς προσφιλές,			ὡς προσφιλές,	e
f	ἡ δὲ καρδία αὐτῆς			ἡ δὲ καρδία αὐτῆς	f
g	ἀπεστενωμένη			ἀπεστενωμένη.	g
h	ἀπὸ τοῦ φόβου.				h
D:6 a	καὶ εἰσελθοῦσα		5:4 (D:6)	καὶ εἰσελθοῦσα	a
b	πάσας τὰς θύρας			τὰς θύρας	b

Chapter 5/Addition D

	LXX (Göttingen o')		MT (BHS 3)		AT (Göttingen L)
c	κατέστη	f	וַתַּעֲמֹד	c	ἔστη
d		g	בַּחֲצַר בֵּית־הַמֶּלֶךְ	d	
e		h	הַפְּנִימִית נֹכַח בֵּית הַמֶּלֶךְ	e	
f	ἐνώπιον τοῦ βασιλέως,	i	וְהַמֶּלֶךְ	f	ἐνώπιον τοῦ βασιλέως,
g	καὶ αὐτὸς	j	יוֹשֵׁב עַל־כִּסֵּא	g	καὶ ὁ βασιλεὺς
h	ἐκάθητο ἐπὶ τοῦ θρόνου	k	מַלְכוּתוֹ	h	ἐκάθητο ἐπὶ τοῦ θρόνου
i	τῆς βασιλείας αὐτοῦ	l	בְּבֵית הַמַּלְכוּת	i	τῆς βασιλείας αὐτοῦ
		m	נֹכַח פֶּתַח הַבָּיִת׃		
		5:2 a	וַיְהִי כִרְאוֹת הַמֶּלֶךְ		
		b	אֶת־אֶסְתֵּר הַמַּלְכָּה		
		c	עֹמֶדֶת בֶּחָצֵר		
		d	נָשְׂאָה חֵן בְּעֵינָיו		
j	καὶ πᾶσαν στολὴν			j	καὶ πᾶσαν στολὴν
k	τῆς ἐπιφανείας			k	ἐπιφανείας
l	αὐτοῦ			l	
m	ἐνδεδύκει,			m	ἐνδεδύκει,

Chapter 5/Addition D

THE TEXTS OF ESTHER — CHAPTER 5/D

	LXX (Göttingen o')	MT (BHS 3)	AT (Göttingen L)	
n	ὅλος διὰ χρυσοῦ		ὅλος διάχρυσος,	n
o	καὶ λίθων πολυτελῶν,		καὶ λίθοι πολυτελεῖς	o
p			ἐπ᾽ αὐτῷ,	p
q	καὶ ἦν φοβερὸς σφόδρα.		καὶ φοβερὸς σφόδρα.	q
D:7 a	καὶ ἄρας τὸ πρόσωπον αὐτοῦ		5:5 (D:7) καὶ ἄρας τὸ πρόσωπον αὐτοῦ	a
b	πεπυρωμένον		πεπυρωμένον	b
c	δόξῃ		ἐν δόξῃ	c
d			ἐνέβλεψεν αὐτῇ ὡς ταῦρος	d
e	ἐν ἀκμῇ θυμοῦ		ἐν ἀκμῇ θυμοῦ	e
f			αὐτοῦ,	f
g	ἔβλεψεν,			
h	καὶ ἔπεσεν ἡ βασίλισσα		5:6 καὶ ἐφοβήθη ἡ βασίλισσα	a
i	καὶ μετέβαλεν		καὶ μετέβαλε	b
j	τὸ χρῶμα αὐτῆς		τὸ πρόσωπον αὐτῆς	c
k	ἐν ἐκλύσει		ἐν ἐκλύσει	d
l	καὶ κατεπέκυψεν		καὶ ἐπέκυψεν	e
m	ἐπὶ τὴν κεφαλὴν		ἐπὶ τὴν κεφαλὴν	f
n	τῆς ἅβρας τῆς προπορευομένης.		τῆς ἅβρας τῆς προπορευομένης.	g

	LXX (Göttingen o')	MT (BHS 3)	AT (Göttingen L)	
D:8 a	καὶ μετέβαλεν ὁ θεὸς		5:7 (D:8) καὶ μετέβαλεν ὁ θεὸς	a
b	τὸ πνεῦμα τοῦ βασιλέως		τὸ πνεῦμα τοῦ βασιλέως	b
c	εἰς πραΰτητα,		καὶ μετέθηκε τὸν θυμὸν αὐτοῦ	c
d			εἰς πραΰτητα,	d
e	καὶ ἀγωνιάσας		5:8 καὶ ἀγωνιάσας	a
f			ὁ βασιλεὺς	b
g	ἀνεπήδησεν		κατεπήδησεν	c
h	ἀπὸ τοῦ θρόνου αὐτοῦ		ἀπὸ τοῦ θρόνου αὐτοῦ	d
i	καὶ ἀνέλαβεν αὐτὴν		καὶ ἀνέλαβεν αὐτὴν	e
j	ἐπὶ τὰς ἀγκάλας αὐτοῦ,		ἐπὶ τὰς ἀγκάλας αὐτοῦ	f
k	μέχρις οὗ κατέστη,			g
l	καὶ παρεκάλει αὐτὴν		καὶ παρεκάλεσεν αὐτὴν	h
m	λόγοις εἰρηνικοῖς			i
D:9 a	καὶ εἶπεν		(D:9) καὶ εἶπεν	j
b	αὐτῇ			k
c	Τί ἐστιν, Εσθηρ;		Τί ἐστιν, Εσθηρ;	l
d	ἐγὼ ὁ ἀδελφός σου,		ἐγὼ εἰμι ἀδελφός σου,	m
e	θάρσει,		5:9 θάρσει,	a

Chapter 5/Addition D

	LXX (Göttingen o')	MT (BHS 3)		AT (Göttingen L)	
D:10			D:10	b οὐ μὴ ἀποθάνῃς,	
a	οὐ μὴ ἀποθάνῃς,			c ὅτι κοινόν	
b	ὅτι κοινὸν			d ἐστι τὸ πρᾶγμα ἡμῶν,	
c	τὸ πρόσταγμα ἡμῶν ἐστιν·			e καὶ οὐ πρὸς σὲ ἡ ἀπειλή·	
				f ἰδοὺ τὸ σκῆπτρον	
				ἐν τῇ χειρί σου.	
D:11 a	πρόσελθε.		5:10 (D:12)	καὶ ἄρας	a
D:12 a	καὶ ἄρας	וַיּוֹשֶׁט	e		b
		הַמֶּלֶךְ לְאֶסְתֵּר	f	τὸ σκῆπτρον	c
c	τὴν χρυσῆν ῥάβδον	אֵת שַׁרְבִט הַזָּהָב	g		d
		אֲשֶׁר בְּיָדוֹ	h		e
		וַתִּקְרַב אֶסְתֵּר	i		
f	ἐπέθηκεν	וַתִּגַּע בְּרֹאשׁ הַשַּׁרְבִיט׃	j	ἐπέθηκεν	f
g	ἐπὶ τὸν τράχηλον αὐτῆς			ἐπὶ τὸν τράχηλον αὐτῆς	g
h	καὶ ἡσπάσατο αὐτὴν			καὶ ἡσπάσατο αὐτὴν	h
i	καὶ εἶπεν			καὶ εἶπεν	i
j	Λάλησόν μοι.			Λάλησόν μοι.	j

	LXX (Göttingen o')	MT (BHS 3)	AT (Göttingen L)	
D:13 a	καὶ εἶπεν αὐτῷ		5:11 (D:13) καὶ εἶπεν αὐτῷ	a
b	Εἶδόν σε,		Εἶδόν σε	b
c	κύριε,			c
d	ὡς ἄγγελον θεοῦ,		ὡς ἄγγελον θεοῦ,	d
e	καὶ ἐταράχθη		καὶ ἐτάκη	e
f	ἡ καρδία μου		ἡ καρδία μου	f
g	ἀπὸ φόβου τῆς δόξης σου·		ἀπὸ τῆς δόξης τοῦ θυμοῦ σου,	g
h			κύριε.	h
D:14 a	ὅτι θαυμαστὸς εἶ, κύριε,		5:12 (D:14) καὶ ἐπὶ τὸ πρόσωπον αὐτῆς	a
b	καὶ τὸ πρόσωπόν σου		μέτρον ἱδρῶτος·	b
c	χαρίτων μεστόν.			
D:15 a	ἐν δὲ τῷ διαλέγεσθαι αὐτὴν			
b	ἔπεσεν ἀπὸ ἐκλύσεως·			
D:16 a	καὶ ὁ βασιλεὺς ἐταράσσετο,		(D:16) καὶ ἐταράσσετο ὁ βασιλεὺς	c
b	καὶ πᾶσα ἡ θεραπεία αὐτοῦ		καὶ πᾶσα ἡ θεραπεία αὐτοῦ,	d
c	παρεκάλει αὐτήν.		καὶ παρεκάλουν αὐτήν.	e
5:3 a	καὶ εἶπεν	5:3 וַיֹּאמֶר	5:13 (5:3) καὶ εἶπεν	a
b		לָהּ		b

Chapter 5/Addition D

	LXX (Göttingen o')	MT (BHS 3)	AT (Göttingen L)	
c	ὁ βασιλεύς	הַמֶּלֶךְ	ὁ βασιλεύς	c
d	Τί θέλεις, Εσθηρ,	מַה־לָּךְ אֶסְתֵּר	Τί ἐστιν, Εσθηρ;	d
e		הַמַּלְכָּה		e
f	καὶ τί σού ἐστιν τὸ ἀξίωμα;	וּמַה־בַּקָּשָׁתֵךְ	ἀνάγγειλόν μοι, καὶ ποιήσω σοι·	f
g	ἕως τοῦ ἡμίσους	עַד־חֲצִי	ἕως ἡμίσους	g
h	τῆς βασιλείας μου,	הַמַּלְכוּת	τῆς βασιλείας μου.	h
i	καὶ ἔσται σοι.	וְיִנָּתֵן לָךְ׃		i
5:4 a	εἶπεν δὲ Εσθηρ	5:4 וַתֹּאמֶר אֶסְתֵּר	5:14 (5:4) καὶ εἶπεν Εσθηρ	a
b	Ἡμέρα μου ἐπίσημος		Ἡμέρα ἐπίσημός μοι	b
c	σήμερόν ἐστιν·	הַיּוֹם	αὔριον·	c
d	εἰ οὖν δοκεῖ τῷ βασιλεῖ,	אִם־עַל־הַמֶּלֶךְ טוֹב	εἰ δοκεῖ οὖν τῷ βασιλεῖ,	d
e	ἐλθάτω καὶ αὐτὸς καὶ Αμαν	יָבוֹא הַמֶּלֶךְ וְהָמָן	εἰσελθέ σὺ καὶ Αμαν	e
f		הַיּוֹם	ὁ φίλος σου	f
g		אֶל־הַמִּשְׁתֶּה		g
h	εἰς τὴν δοχήν,	אֲשֶׁר־עָשִׂיתִי לוֹ׃	εἰς τὸν πότον,	h
i	ἣν ποιήσω		ὃν ποιήσω	i
j	σήμερον.		αὔριον.	j

	LXX (Göttingen oʹ)	MT (BHS 3)	AT (Göttingen L)	
5:5			**5:15 (5:5)**	
a	καὶ εἶπεν ὁ βασιλεύς	וַיֹּאמֶר הַמֶּלֶךְ	καὶ εἶπεν ὁ βασιλεύς	a
b	Κατασπεύσατε Αμαν,	מַהֲרוּ אֶת־הָמָן	Κατασπεύσατε τὸν Αμαν,	b
c	ὅπως ποιήσωμεν	לַעֲשׂוֹת	ὅπως ποιήσωμεν	c
d	τὸν λόγον Εσθηρ.	אֶת־דְּבַר אֶסְתֵּר	τὸν λόγον Εσθηρ.	d
e	καὶ παραγίνονται	וַיָּבֹא	**5:16** καὶ παραγίνονται	a
f	ἀμφότεροι	הַמֶּלֶךְ וְהָמָן	ἀμφότεροι	b
g	εἰς τὴν δοχήν,	אֶל־הַמִּשְׁתֶּה	εἰς τὴν δοχήν,	c
h	ἣν εἶπεν Εσθηρ.	אֲשֶׁר־עָשְׂתָה אֶסְתֵּר׃	ἣν ἐποίησεν Εσθηρ,	d
i			δεῖπνον πολυτελές.	e
5:6			**5:17 (5:6)**	
a	ἐν δὲ τῷ πότῳ		καὶ εἶπεν ὁ βασιλεύς	a
b	εἶπεν ὁ βασιλεύς	וַיֹּאמֶר הַמֶּלֶךְ	πρὸς Εσθηρ	b
c	πρὸς Εσθηρ	לְאֶסְתֵּר	Ἡ βασίλισσα,	c
d		בְּמִשְׁתֵּה הַיַּיִן		d
e			τί τὸ θέλημά σου;	e
f	Τί ἐστιν,			f
g	Βασίλισσα Εσθηρ;		αἴτησαι ἕως ἡμίσους	g
h				

Chapter 5

LXX (Göttingen o')	MT (BHS 3)	AT (Göttingen L)
i		h τῆς βασιλείας μου,
j καὶ ἔσται ὅσα ἀξιοῖς.		i καὶ ἔσται σοι ὅσα ἀξιοῖς.
k	f וַתַּעַן אֶסְתֵּר וַתֹּאמַר [שְׁאֵלָתִי]	j
5:7 a καὶ εἶπεν	g וּבַקָּשָׁתִי׃	5:18 (5:7) a καὶ εἶπεν
b	אִם־מָצָאתִי	b Εσθηρ
c	חֵן	c
d Τὸ αἴτημά μου	בְּעֵינֵי הַמֶּלֶךְ	d Τὸ αἴτημά μου
e καὶ τὸ ἀξίωμα·	וְאִם־עַל־הַמֶּלֶךְ	e καὶ τὸ ἀξίωμά μου·
5:8 a εἰ εὗρον χάριν	5:8 טוֹב	(5:8) f εἰ εὗρον χάριν
b ἐνώπιον τοῦ βασιλέως,	לָתֵת אֶת־שְׁאֵלָתִי	g ἐναντίον σου, βασιλεῦ,
c	וְלַעֲשׂוֹת	h καὶ εἰ ἐπὶ τὸν βασιλέα ἀγαθὸν
d	אֶת־בַּקָּשָׁתִי	i δοῦναι τὸ αἴτημά μου
e	יָבוֹא הַמֶּלֶךְ וְהָמָן	j καὶ ποιῆσαι τὸ ἀξίωμά μου,
f ἐλθέτω ὁ βασιλεὺς καὶ Αμαν	אֶל־הַמִּשְׁתֶּה	k ἐλθέτω ὁ βασιλεὺς καὶ Αμαν
g ἔτι τὴν αὔριον	אֲשֶׁר אֶעֱשֶׂה לָהֶם	l
h εἰς τὴν δοχήν,	וּמָחָר אֶעֱשֶׂה	m εἰς τὴν δοχήν,
i ἣν ποιήσω αὐτοῖς·	כִּדְבַר הַמֶּלֶךְ׃	n ἣν ποιήσω αὐτοῖς

	LXX (Göttingen o')		MT (BHS 3)		AT (Göttingen L)	
	j	καὶ αὔριον			καὶ τῇ αὔριον·	o
	k	ποιήσω	וּמָחָר		καὶ αὔριον γὰρ	p
	l		אֶעֱשֶׂה		ποιήσω	q
	m	τὰ αὐτά.	כִּדְבַר הַמֶּלֶךְ׃		κατὰ τὰ αὐτά.	r
				5:19	καὶ εἶπεν ὁ βασιλεύς	a
					Ποίησον κατὰ το θέλημά σου.	b
				5:20 (5:9)	καὶ ἀπήγγελη	a
					τῷ Αμαν κατὰ τὰ αὐτά,	
					καὶ ἐθαύμασεν,	b
					καὶ ὁ βασιλεὺς ἀναλύσας	c
					ἡσύχασεν.	d
5:9	a	καὶ ἐξῆλθεν ὁ Αμαν	5:9	וַיֵּצֵא		
	b			הָמָן בַּיּוֹם הַהוּא		
	c	ἀπὸ τοῦ βασιλέως				
	d	ὑπερχαρής,	שָׂמֵחַ			
	e	εὐφρανόμενος·	וְטוֹב לֵב			
	f	ἐν δὲ τῷ ἰδεῖν Αμαν	וְכִרְאוֹת הָמָן			

Chapter 5

LXX (Göttingen o')		MT (BHS 3)		AT (Göttingen L)	
g	Μαρδοχαῖον		אֶת־מָרְדֳּכַי		
h	τὸν Ἰουδαῖον		הַיְּהוּדִי		
i	ἐν τῇ αὐλῇ		בְּשַׁעַר הַמֶּלֶךְ		
j			וְלֹא־קָם וְלֹא־זָע מִמֶּנּוּ		
k	ἐθυμώθη σφόδρα.		וַיִּמָּלֵא הָמָן		
l		5:10 a	עַל־מָרְדֳּכַי חֵמָה׃	5:21 (5:10)	ὁ δὲ Αμαν εἰσῆλθεν a
5:10 a		b	וַיִּתְאַפַּק הָמָן		εἰς τὸν οἶκον αὐτοῦ b
b	καὶ εἰσελθὼν	c	וַיָּבוֹא אֶל־בֵּיתוֹ		καὶ συνήγαγε c
c	εἰς τὰ ἴδια	d	וַיִּשְׁלַח וַיָּבֵא		τοὺς φίλους αὐτοῦ d
d	ἐκάλεσεν	e	אֶת־אֹהֲבָיו		καὶ τοὺς υἱοὺς αὐτοῦ e
e	τοὺς φίλους		וְאֶת־זֶרֶשׁ		καὶ Ζωσάραν f
f		f	אִשְׁתּוֹ׃		τὴν γυναῖκα αὐτοῦ g
g	καὶ Ζωσάραν	g	הָמָן		h
	τὴν γυναῖκα αὐτοῦ		אֶת־		i
5:11 a	καὶ ὑπέδειξεν αὐτοῖς	5:11	וַיְסַפֵּר לָהֶם		j
b			כְּבוֹד		
c	τὸν πλοῦτον αὐτοῦ		עָשְׁרוֹ הָמָן אֶת־		

	LXX (Göttingen o')	MT (BHS 3)	AT (Göttingen L)	
d		וְכֹל בְּנָיו		k
e	καὶ τὴν δόξαν,	וְאֵת כָּל־אֲשֶׁר		l
f	ἦν	גִּדְּלוֹ הַמֶּלֶךְ		m
g	ὁ βασιλεὺς αὐτῷ περιέθηκεν,	וַאֲשֶׁר נִשְּׂאוֹ		n
h	καὶ ὡς ἐποίησεν αὐτὸν	עַל־הַשָּׂרִים וְעַבְדֵי		o
i	πρωτεύειν καὶ ἡγεῖσθαι	הַמֶּלֶךְ׃		p
j	τῆς βασιλείας.			q
5:12 a	καὶ εἶπεν Αμαν	וַיֹּאמֶר הָמָן (5:12)	καὶ ἐκαυχᾶτο λέγων	r
b	Οὐ κέκληκεν	אַף לֹא־הֵבִיאָה אֶת	ὡς οὐδένα κέκληκεν	s
c		אֶסְתֵּר		t
d	ἡ βασίλισσα	הַמַּלְכָּה	ἡ βασίλισσα	u
e		עִם־הַמֶּלֶךְ	ἐν ἐπισήμῳ ἡμέρᾳ αὐτῆς	v
f	μετὰ τοῦ βασιλέως οὐδένα	אֶל־הַמִּשְׁתֶּה אֲשֶׁר־	εἰ μὴ τὸν βασιλέα	w
g	εἰς τὴν δοχὴν	עָשָׂתָה		x
h		כִּי אִם־אוֹתִי		y
i	ἀλλ' ἢ ἐμέ·	וְגַם־לְמָחָר	καὶ ἐμὲ μόνον·	z
j	καὶ εἰς τὴν αὔριον		καὶ αὔριον	aa

Chapter 5

	LXX (Göttingen o')		MT (BHS 3)		AT (Göttingen L)
k	κέκλημαι.			bb	κέκλημαι·
l					
5:13 a	καὶ ταῦτά μοι οὐκ ἀρέσκει,	5:13	וְכָל־זֶה אֵינֶנּוּ שֹׁוֶה לִי	5:22 (5:13) a	τοῦτο δὲ λυπεῖ με μόνον,
b	ὅταν ἴδω		בְּכָל־עֵת אֲשֶׁר אֲנִי רֹאֶה אֶת־מָרְדֳּכַי הַיְּהוּדִי	b	ὅταν ἴδω
c	Μαρδοχαῖον		יֹושֵׁב בְּשַׁעַר הַמֶּלֶךְ:	c	τὸν Μαρδοχαῖον
d	τὸν Ἰουδαῖον			d	τὸν Ἰουδαῖον
e				e	
f	ἐν τῇ αὐλῇ.			f	ἐν τῇ αὐλῇ
g				g	τοῦ βασιλέως,
h				h	καὶ μὴ προσκυνεῖ με.
5:14 a	καὶ εἶπεν	5:14 a	וַתֹּאמֶר	5:23 (5:14) a	καὶ εἶπεν
b	πρὸς αὐτὸν	b	לֹו	b	αὐτῷ
c	Ζωσάρα ἡ γυνὴ αὐτοῦ	c	זֶרֶשׁ אִשְׁתֹּו	c	Ζωσάρα ἡ γυνὴ αὐτοῦ
d	καὶ οἱ φίλοι	d	וְכָל־אֹהֲבָיו	d	
e				e	Ἐκ γένους Ἰουδαίων ἐστίν·
f				f	ἐπεὶ συγκεχώρηκέ σε ὁ βασιλεὺς
g				g	ἀφανίσαι τοὺς Ἰουδαίους,

THE TEXTS OF ESTHER — CHAPTER 5

	LXX (Göttingen o')		MT (BHS 3)		AT (Göttingen L)
h				h	καὶ ἔδωκάν σοι οἱ θεοὶ
i				i	εἰς ἐκδίκησιν αὐτῶν
j				j	ἡμέραν ὀλέθριον,
k	Κοπήτω σοι ξύλον	e	יַעֲשׂוּ־עֵץ	k	κοπήτω σοι ξύλον
l	πηχῶν πεντήκοντα,	f	גָּבֹהַּ חֲמִשִּׁים אַמָּה	l	πηχῶν πεντήκοντα,
m				m	καὶ κείσθω,
n				n	καὶ κρέμασον αὐτὸν
o				o	ἐπὶ τοῦ ξύλου,
p	ὄρθρου δὲ	g	וּבַבֹּקֶר	p	ὀρθρίσας δὲ
q		h	אֱמֹר לַמֶּלֶךְ	q	πρὸς τὸν βασιλέα
r	εἶπον τῷ βασιλεῖ,	i	וְיִתְלוּ	r	λαλήσεις αὐτῷ·
s	καὶ κρεμασθήτω	j	אֶת־מׇרְדֳּכַי		
t	Μαρδοχαῖος	k	עָלָיו		
u	ἐπὶ τοῦ ξύλου·	l	וּבֹא־עִם־הַמֶּלֶךְ		
v	σὺ δὲ εἴσελθε	m	אֶל־הַמִּשְׁתֶּה שָׂמֵחַ	v	καὶ νῦν εἰσελθὼν
w	εἰς τὴν δοχὴν				
x	σὺν τῷ βασιλεῖ				

	LXX (Göttingen o')		MT (BHS 3)		AT (Göttingen L)	
y	καὶ εὐφραίνου.	n	שָׂמֵחַ		εὐφραίνου	y
z		o	5:24 וַיִּיטַב		πρὸς τὸν βασιλέα.	z
aa	καὶ ἤρεσεν	p	הַדָּבָר		καὶ ἤρεσε	a
bb	τὸ ῥῆμα	q	לִפְנֵי הָמָן			b
cc	τῷ Αμαν,	r	וַיַּעַשׂ הָעֵץ׃		τῷ Αμαν,	c
dd	καὶ ἡτοιμάσθη τὸ ξύλον.				καὶ ἐποίησεν οὕτως.	d

THE TEXTS OF ESTHER – CHAPTER 6

	LXX (Göttingen o')		MT (BHS 3)		AT (Göttingen)
6:1		6:1		6:1	
a	Ὁ δὲ κύριος ἀπέστησεν			a	Ὁ δὲ δυνατὸς ἀπέστησε
b	τὸν ὕπνον			b	τὸν ὕπνον
c	ἀπὸ τοῦ βασιλέως			c	τοῦ βασιλέως
d	τὴν νύκτα ἐκείνην,	a	בַּלַּיְלָה הַהוּא	d	τὴν νύκτα ἐκείνην,
e		b	נָדְדָה	e	καὶ ἦν ἀγρυπνῶν.
f	καὶ εἶπεν	c	שְׁנַת הַמֶּלֶךְ	6:2	
g	τῷ διδασκάλῳ αὐτοῦ	d	וַיֹּאמֶר	a	καὶ ἐκλήθησαν
h	εἰσφέρειν	e	לְהָבִיא	b	οἱ ἀναγνῶσται,
i	γράμματα	f	אֶת־סֵפֶר	c	καὶ τὸ βιβλίον
j	μνημόσυνα τῶν ἡμερῶν	g	הַזִּכְרֹנוֹת דִּבְרֵי הַיָּמִים	d	τῶν μνημοσυνῶν
k	ἀναγινώσκειν	h	וַיִּהְיוּ נִקְרָאִים	e	ἀνεγινώσκετο
l	αὐτῷ.	i	לִפְנֵי הַמֶּלֶךְ׃	f	αὐτῷ.
				6:3(2)	
				a	καὶ ἦν ὑπόθεσις τῶν εὐνούχων
				b	καὶ ὃ ἐποίησε Μαρδοχαῖος
				c	εὐεργέτημα τῷ βασιλεῖ.
				6:4	
				a	καὶ ἐπέστησεν ὁ βασιλεὺς

THE TEXTS OF ESTHER – CHAPTER 6

LXX (Göttingen o')	MT (BHS 3)	AT (Göttingen)
		b τὸν νοῦν σφόδρα λέγων
		c Πιστὸς ἀνὴρ Μαρδοχαῖος
		d εἰς παραφυλακὴν τῆς ψυχῆς μου,
		e διότι αὐτὸς ἐποίησέ με ζῆν
		f ἄχρι τοῦ νῦν,
		g καὶ κάθημαι σήμερον
		h ἐπὶ τοῦ θρόνου μου
		i καὶ οὐκ ἐποίησα αὐτῷ οὐθέν·
		j οὐκ ὀρθῶς ἐποίησα.
6:2 a εὗρεν δὲ	6:2 וַיִּמָּצֵא כָתוּב אֲשֶׁר	
b τὰ γράμματα τὰ γραφέντα	אֶת-	
c περὶ Μαρδοχαίου,	מָרְדֳּכַי	
d ὡς ἀπήγγειλεν	אֲשֶׁר הִגִּיד	
e	בִּגְתָנָא	
f τῷ βασιλεῖ	נִמְצָא	
g περὶ		
h		

	LXX (Göttingen o')		MT (BHS 3)		AT (Göttingen)
i	τῶν δύο εὐνούχων τοῦ βασιλέως		לְמָרְדֳּכַי עַל־	a	καὶ εἶπεν ὁ βασιλεύς
j	ἐν τῷ φυλάσσειν αὐτοὺς		זֶה וַיֹּאמְרוּ	b	τοῖς παισὶν αὐτοῦ
k	καὶ ζητῆσαι ἐπιβαλεῖν		נַעֲרֵי הַמֶּלֶךְ	c	Τί ποιήσωμεν
l	τὰς χεῖρας		מְשָׁרְתָיו	d	
m				e	τῷ Μαρδοχαίῳ
n	᾿Αρταξέρξῃ.	6:5(3)	וַיֹּאמֶר הַמֶּלֶךְ	f	τῷ σωτῆρι τῶν λόγων τούτων;
6:3 a	εἶπεν δὲ ὁ βασιλεύς	6:3		g	
b				h	
c	Τίνα δόξαν ἢ χάριν		מַה־נַּעֲשָׂה יְקָר	i	
d	ἐποιήσαμεν		וּגְדוּלָּה	j	
e	τῷ Μαρδοχαίῳ;			k	
f					
g					
h	καὶ εἶπαν		לֹא־נַעֲשָׂה		
i	οἱ διάκονοι τοῦ βασιλέως		עִמּוֹ דָּבָר׃		
j					
k	Οὐκ ἐποίησας αὐτῷ οὐδέν.				

Chapter 6

LXX (Göttingen o')	MT (BHS 3)	AT (Göttingen)	
		καὶ νοήσαντες	l
		οἱ νεανίσκοι διεφθόνουν αὐτῷ.	m
		ἐνέκειτο γὰρ φόβος Αμαν	n
		ἐν τοῖς σπλάγχνοις αὐτῶν.	o
6:4 a ἐν δὲ τῷ πυνθάνεσθαι	6:6	καὶ ἐνόησεν ὁ βασιλεύς.	a
b τὸν βασιλέα		καὶ ἐγένετο ὄρθρος.	b
c περὶ τῆς εὐνοίας			c
d Μαρδοχαίου			d
e ἰδοὺ Αμαν			e
f ἐν τῇ αὐλῇ·			f
g εἶπεν δὲ ὁ βασιλεύς 6:4 a	(6:4) מִי בֶחָצֵר וַיֹּאמֶר לַמֶּלֶךְ	καὶ ἠρώτησεν ὁ βασιλεύς	g
h Τίς ἐν τῇ αὐλῇ; b		Τίς ἐστιν ἔξω;	h
i		καὶ ἦν Αμαν.	i
j ὁ δὲ Αμαν εἰσῆλθεν c	6:7 וַיֹּאמֶר הָמָן אֶל־הַמֶּלֶךְ	Αμαν δὲ ὤρθρικει	j
k d	לְאִישׁ אֲשֶׁר הַמֶּלֶךְ חָפֵץ בִּיקָרוֹ		k
			a
			b

Chapter 6

THE TEXTS OF ESTHER – CHAPTER 6

LXX (Göttingen o')		MT (BHS 3)		AT (Göttingen)	
l	εἰπεῖν τῷ βασιλεῖ		לְדַבֵּר לַמֶּלֶךְ	c	λαλῆσαι τῷ βασιλεῖ,
m	κρεμάσαι		לִתְלֹתוֹ	d	ἵνα κρεμάσῃ
n	τὸν Μαρδοχαῖον		אֶת־מָרְדֳּכַי	e	τὸν Μαρδοχαῖον.
o	ἐπὶ τῷ ξύλῳ,		עַל־הָעֵץ		
p	ᾧ ἡτοίμασεν.		אֲשֶׁר־הֵכִין לוֹ		
6:5		**6:5**			
a	καὶ εἶπαν οἱ διάκονοι		וַיֹּאמְרוּ נַעֲרֵי		
b	τοῦ βασιλέως		הַמֶּלֶךְ אֵלָיו		
c			הִנֵּה הָמָן		
d	Ἰδοὺ Αμαν		עֹמֵד בֶּחָצֵר		
e	ἔστηκεν ἐν τῇ αὐλῇ.		וַיֹּאמֶר הַמֶּלֶךְ		
f	καὶ εἶπεν ὁ βασιλεὺς		יָבוֹא׃	**6:8(5)** a	καὶ εἶπεν ὁ βασιλεὺς
g	Καλέσατε αὐτόν.			b	εἰσαγαγεῖν αὐτόν.
6:6		**6:6**		**6:9(6)**	
a	εἶπεν δὲ ὁ βασιλεὺς τῷ Αμαν	a	וַיָּבוֹא הָמָן וַיֹּאמֶר לוֹ הַמֶּלֶךְ	a	ὡς δὲ εἰσῆλθεν,
b	Τί ποιήσω τῷ ἀνθρώπῳ,	b	מַה־לַעֲשׂוֹת בָּאִישׁ	b	εἶπεν αὐτῷ ὁ βασιλεὺς
c		c	אֲשֶׁר הַמֶּלֶךְ חָפֵץ בִּיקָרוֹ	c	Τί ποιήσων τῷ ἀνδρὶ
d	ὃν ἐγὼ θέλω	d	אֲשֶׁר הַמֶּלֶךְ חָפֵץ בִּיקָרוֹ	d	τῷ τὸν βασιλέα τιμῶντι,
				e	ὃν ὁ βασιλεὺς βούλεται

Chapter 6

THE TEXTS OF ESTHER – CHAPTER 6

	LXX (Göttingen o')		MT (BHS 3)		AT (Göttingen)	
e	δοξάσαι;	e	יְקָר֑	f	δοξάσαι;	f
f	εἶπεν δὲ ἐν ἑαυτῷ	f	וַיֹּ֤אמֶר	6:10	καὶ ἐλογίσατο	a
g	ὁ Αμαν	g	הָמָן֙ בְּלִבּ֔וֹ		ὁ Αμαν	b
h		h	לְמִ֞י יַחְפֹּ֥ץ הַמֶּ֛לֶךְ		λέγων ὅτι	c
i	Τίνα θέλει ὁ βασιλεύς	i	לַעֲשׂ֥וֹת יְקָ֖ר		Τίνα βούλεται ὁ βασιλεύς	d
j	δοξάσαι	j	יוֹתֵ֣ר מִמֶּ֑נִּי		δοξάσαι	e
k	εἰ μὴ ἐμέ;				εἰ μὴ ἐμέ;	f
6:7 a	εἶπεν δὲ	6:7	וַיֹּ֥אמֶר	6:11(7)	καὶ εἶπεν	a
b			הָמָ֖ן		ὁ Αμαν	b
c	πρὸς τὸν βασιλέα		אֶל־הַמֶּ֑לֶךְ			c
d	"Ανθρωπον,		אִ֕ישׁ		"Ανθρωπος,	d
e	ὃν ὁ βασιλεύς		אֲשֶׁ֥ר הַמֶּ֖לֶךְ		ὃν ὁ βασιλεύς	e
f	θέλει δοξάσαι,		חָפֵ֥ץ בִּיקָרֽוֹ׃		βούλεται δοξάσαι,	f
6:8 a	ἐνεγκάτωσαν οἱ παῖδες	6:8	יָבִ֙יאוּ֙	(6:8)	ληφθήτω	g
b	τοῦ βασιλέως		לְב֣וּשׁ מַלְכ֔וּת			h
c	στολὴν βυσσίνην,		אֲשֶׁ֥ר לָֽבַשׁ־בּ֖וֹ הַמֶּ֑לֶךְ		στολὴ	i
d			וְס֗וּס		βασιλική	j

	LXX (Göttingen o')		MT (BHS 3)	AT (Göttingen)	
e	ἦν ὁ βασιλεὺς περιβάλλεται,		יָבִיא לְבוּשׁ מַלְכוּת אֲשֶׁר לָבַשׁ־בּוֹ הַמֶּלֶךְ	καὶ ἵππος βασιλικός	k
f	καὶ ἵππον,		וְסוּס	ἐφ' ὃν	l
g	ἐφ' ὃν		אֲשֶׁר	ὁ βασιλεὺς ἐπιβαίνει,	m
h	ὁ βασιλεὺς ἐπιβαίνει,		רָכַב עָלָיו הַמֶּלֶךְ		n
i			וַאֲשֶׁר נִתַּן		o
j			כֶּתֶר מַלְכוּת בְּרֹאשׁוֹ׃		p
6:9 a	καὶ δότω	6:9	וְנָתוֹן הַלְּבוּשׁ וְהַסּוּס		q
b			עַל־יַד־אִישׁ		r
c	ἑνὶ	(6:9)	מִשָּׂרֵי הַמֶּלֶךְ הַפַּרְתְּמִים	καὶ εἷς τῶν ἐνδόξων,	s
d	τῶν φίλων τοῦ βασιλέως		וְהִלְבִּישׁוּ אֶת־הָאִישׁ	τῶν φίλων τοῦ βασιλέως,	t
e	τῶν ἐνδόξων		אֲשֶׁר הַמֶּלֶךְ חָפֵץ בִּיקָרוֹ		u
f	καὶ στολισάτω τὸν ἄνθρωπον,		וְהִרְכִּיבֻהוּ עַל־הַסּוּס	λαβέτω ταῦτα	v
g	ὃν ὁ βασιλεὺς ἀγαπᾷ,		בִּרְחוֹב הָעִיר	καὶ ἐνδυσάτω αὐτὸν	w
h	καὶ ἀναβιβασάτω αὐτὸν		וְקָרְאוּ לְפָנָיו		x
i				καὶ ἀναβιβασάτω αὐτὸν	y
j	ἐπὶ τὸν ἵππον			ἐπὶ τὸν ἵππον	z
k				καὶ περιελθέτω τὴν πόλιν	aa

THE TEXTS OF ESTHER – CHAPTER 6

	LXX (Göttingen o')		MT (BHS 3)	AT (Göttingen)	
l				ἔμπροσθεν αὐτοῦ	bb
m	καὶ κηρυσσέτω		אֹתֹ֑ו	κηρύσσων	cc
n			וְקָרְא֣וּ		dd
o	διὰ τῆς πλατείας τῆς πόλεως				ee
p	λέγων				ff
q	Οὕτως ἔσται		כָּ֚כָה יֵעָשֶׂ֣ה	Κατὰ τάδε ποιηθήσεται	gg
r	παντὶ ἀνθρώπῳ,		לָאִ֔ישׁ	τῷ τὸν βασιλέα τιμῶντι,	hh
s	ὃν ὁ βασιλεὺς		אֲשֶׁ֥ר הַמֶּ֖לֶךְ	ὃν ὁ βασιλεὺς	ii
t			חָפֵ֣ץ	βούλεται	jj
u	δοξάζει.		בִּיקָרֹֽו׃	δοξάσαι.	kk
6:10 a	εἶπεν δὲ ὁ βασιλεὺς	6:10	וַיֹּ֨אמֶר הַמֶּ֜לֶךְ	6:12(10) καὶ εἶπεν ὁ βασιλεὺς	a
b	τῷ Αμαν		לְהָמָ֗ן	τῷ Αμαν	b
c			מַהֵ֞ר	Ταχὺ	c
d			קַ֣ח	δράμε	d
e				καὶ λάβε	e
f			אֶת־הַלְּב֤וּשׁ וְאֶת־הַסּוּס֙	τὸν ἵππον καὶ στολὴν	f
g	Καλῶς ἐλάλησας·		כַּאֲשֶׁ֣ר דִּבַּ֔רְתָּ	ὡς εἴρηκας	g

	LXX (Göttingen o')	MT (BHS 3)	AT (Göttingen)	
h	οὕτως ποίησον	כֵּן עֲשֵׂה	καὶ ποίησον	h
i	τῷ Μαρδοχαίῳ τῷ Ἰουδαίῳ,	לְמָרְדֳּכַי הַיְּהוּדִי	Μαρδοχαίῳ τῷ Ἰουδαίῳ	i
j	τῷ θεραπεύοντι	הַיּוֹשֵׁב	τῷ καθημένῳ	j
k	ἐν τῇ αὐλῇ,	בְּשַׁעַר הַמֶּלֶךְ	ἐν τῷ πυλῶνι,	k
l	καὶ μὴ παραπεσάτω σου	אַל־תַּפֵּל דָּבָר	καὶ μὴ παραπεσάτω	l
m	λόγος ὧν ἐλάλησας.	מִכֹּל אֲשֶׁר דִּבַּרְתָּ׃	ὁ λόγος σου.	m
6:13			ὡς δὲ ἔγνω Αμαν	a
			ὅτι οὐκ ἦν αὐτὸς ὁ δοξαζόμενος,	b
			ἀλλ᾽ ὅτι Μαρδοχαῖος,	c
			συνετρίβη ἡ καρδία αὐτοῦ σφόδρα,	d
			καὶ μετέβαλε τὸ πνεῦμα αὐτοῦ	e
			ἐν ἐκλύσει.	f
6:11 a	ἔλαβεν δὲ Αμαν	6:11 וַיִּקַּח הָמָן	6:14(11) καὶ ἔλαβεν Αμαν	a
b	τὴν στολὴν καὶ τὸν ἵππον	אֶת־הַלְּבוּשׁ וְאֶת־הַסּוּס	τὴν στολὴν καὶ τὸν ἵππον	b
			ἐντρεπόμενος τὸν Μαρδοχαῖον,	c
			καθότι ἐκείνῃ τῇ ἡμέρᾳ ἐκέκρικει	d
			ἀνασκολοπίσαι αὐτόν,	e

LXX (Göttingen o')	MT (BHS 3)	AT (Göttingen)		
		6:15	καὶ εἶπε τῷ Μαρδοχαίῳ	a
			Περιελοῦ τὸν σάκκον.	b
		6:16	καὶ ἐταράχθη Μαρδοχαῖος	a
			ὡς ἀποθνῄσκων	b
			καὶ ἀπεδύσατο	c
			μετ᾽ ὀδύνης τὸν σάκκον	d
			καὶ ἐνεδύσατο ἱμάτια δόξης.	e
		6:17	καὶ ἐδόκει Μαρδοχαῖος	a
			τέρας θεωρεῖν,	b
			καὶ ἡ καρδία αὐτοῦ	c
			πρὸς τὸν κύριον,	d
			καὶ ἐξίστατο ἐν ἀφασίᾳ.	e
				f
		6:18	καὶ ἔσπευσεν Αμαν	a
			ἀναλαβεῖν αὐτὸν ἔφιππον.	b
		6:19	καὶ ἐξήγαγεν	a
			Αμαν τὸν ἵππον ἔξω	b
			καὶ προσήγαγεν αὐτὸν	c

LXX (Göttingen o')	MT (BHS 3)		
c καὶ ἐστόλισεν τὸν Μαρδοχαῖον	וַיַּלְבֵּשׁ אֶת־מָרְדֳּכָי		
d καὶ ἀνεβίβασεν αὐτὸν ἐπὶ τὸν ἵππον	וַיַּרְכִּיבֵהוּ		
e			
f			
g			
h καὶ διῆλθεν			

THE TEXTS OF ESTHER – CHAPTER 6

	LXX (Göttingen o')	MT (BHS 3)	AT (Göttingen)	
i	διὰ τῆς πλατείας τῆς πόλεως	בִּרְחוֹב הָעִיר		d
j	καὶ ἐκήρυσσεν	וַיִּקְרָא לְפָנָיו	κηρύσσων	e
k	λέγων			f
l	Οὕτως ἔσται παντὶ ἀνθρώπῳ,	אִישׁ כָּכָה יֵעָשֶׂה לָ	Κατὰ τάδε ποιηθήσεται τῷ ἀνδρὶ	g
m			τῷ τὸν βασιλέα τιμῶντι,	h
n	ὃν ὁ βασιλεὺς θέλει δοξάσαι.	אֲשֶׁר הַמֶּלֶךְ חָפֵץ בִּיקָרוֹ׃	ὃν ὁ βασιλεὺς βούλεται δοξάσαι.	i
6:12 a	ἐπέστρεψεν δὲ	6:12 וַיָּשָׁב	6:20(12) καὶ ὁ μὲν Αμαν ἀπῆλθε	a
b	ὁ Μαρδοχαῖος	מָרְדֳּכַי אֶל־שַׁעַר הַמֶּלֶךְ	πρὸς ἑαυτὸν	b
c	εἰς τὴν αὐλήν,	וְהָמָן נִדְחַף אֶל־בֵּיתוֹ	ἐσκυθρωπωμένος,	c
d	Αμαν δὲ ὑπέστρεψεν	אָבֵל		d
e	εἰς τὰ ἴδια	וַחֲפוּי	ὁ δὲ Μαρδοχαῖος ἀπῆλθεν	e
f	λυπούμενος	רֹאשׁ׃	εἰς τὸν οἶκον αὐτοῦ.	f
g	κατὰ κεφαλῆς.			
6:13 a	καὶ διηγήσατο Αμαν	6:13 וַיְסַפֵּר הָמָן	6:21(13) καὶ διηγήσατο Αμαν	a
b	τὰ συμβεβηκότα αὐτῷ			b

Chapter 6

THE TEXTS OF ESTHER – CHAPTER 6

	LXX (Göttingen o')	MT (BHS 3)		AT (Göttingen)	
c	Ζωσάρᾳ τῇ γυναικὶ αὐτοῦ	לְאֹהֲבָיו		τῇ γυναικὶ αὐτοῦ	c
d	καὶ τοῖς φίλοις,	וּלְזֶרֶשׁ אִשְׁתּוֹ			d
e	καὶ εἶπαν	וַיְסַפֵּר אֵת כָּל־אֲשֶׁר קָרָהוּ		πάντα τὰ γενόμενα αὐτῷ,	e
f	πρὸς αὐτὸν	לוֹ	6:22	καὶ εἶπεν	a
g	οἱ φίλοι	וַיֹּאמְרוּ			b
h		חֲכָמָיו			c
i		וְזֶרֶשׁ			d
j	καὶ ἡ γυνή	אִשְׁתּוֹ		ἡ γυνὴ αὐτοῦ	e
k				καὶ οἱ σοφοὶ αὐτοῦ	f
l				Ἀφ᾽ ὅτε λαλεῖς	g
m				περὶ αὐτοῦ κακά,	h
n				προσπορεύεταί σοι τὰ κακά·	i
o	Εἰ ἐκ γένους Ἰουδαίων	אִם מִזֶּרַע הַיְּהוּדִים מָרְדֳּכַי		ἡσύχαζε,	j
p	Μαρδοχαῖος,	אֲשֶׁר			k
q	ἦρξαι ταπεινοῦσθαι	הַחִלּוֹתָ לִנְפֹּל לְפָנָיו			l
r					m
s	ἐνώπιον αὐτοῦ,	לֹא			n

Chapter 6

THE TEXTS OF ESTHER – CHAPTER 6

	LXX (Göttingen o')	MT (BHS 3)	AT (Göttingen)	
t	πεσὼν πεσῇ·			o
u	οὐ μὴ δύνῃ αὐτὸν ἀμύνασθαι,	לוֹ לֹ֣א־תוּכַ֣ל		p
v		כִּֽי־נָפ֥וֹל תִּפּ֖וֹל לְפָנָֽיו׃		q
w	ὅτι θεὸς ζῶν μετ' αὐτοῦ.		ὅτι ὁ θεὸς ἐν αὐτοῖς.	r
6:14 a	ἔτι αὐτῶν λαλούντων	עוֹדָ֣ם מְדַבְּרִ֣ים עִמּ֔וֹ	6:23(14) καὶ αὐτῶν λαλούντων	a
b	παραγίνονται οἱ εὐνοῦχοι	וְסָרִיסֵ֤י הַמֶּ֙לֶךְ֙ הִגִּ֔יעוּ	παρῆν τις	b
c	ἐπισπεύδοντες		ἐπὶ τὸν πότον	c
d	τὸν Αμαν	וַיַּבְהִ֙לוּ֙ לְהָבִ֣יא אֶת־הָמָ֔ן	σπουδάζων	d
e	ἐπὶ τὸν πότον,	אֶל־הַמִּשְׁתֶּ֖ה אֲשֶׁר־עָשְׂתָ֥ה	αὐτόν·	e
f	ὃν ἡτοίμασεν Εσθηρ.	אֶסְתֵּֽר:		f
g				g
				h
			(7:1) καὶ οὕτως ἱλαρώθη	i
			καὶ πορευθεὶς ἀνέπεσε	j
			μετ' αὐτῶν ἐν ὥρᾳ.	

THE TEXTS OF ESTHER — CHAPTER 7

	LXX (Göttingen o')		MT (BHS 3)		AT (Göttingen L)	
7:1	a	Εἰσῆλθεν δὲ	7:1	וַיָּבֹא		
	b	ὁ βασιλεὺς καὶ Αμαν		הַמֶּלֶךְ וְהָמָן		
	c	συμπιεῖν		לִשְׁתּוֹת		
	d			עִם־אֶסְתֵּר		
	e	τῇ βασιλίσσῃ.		הַמַּלְכָּה׃		
7:2	a	εἶπεν δὲ ὁ βασιλεὺς	7:2	וַיֹּאמֶר הַמֶּלֶךְ	7:1(2)	ὡς δὲ προῆγεν ἡ πρόποσις, a
	b	Εσθηρ		לְאֶסְתֵּר		εἶπεν ὁ βασιλεὺς b
	c	τῇ δευτέρᾳ ἡμέρᾳ		גַּם בַּיּוֹם		τῇ Εσθηρ c
	d	ἐν τῷ πότῳ		הַשֵּׁנִי		d
	e	Τί ἐστιν,		בְּמִשְׁתֵּה		e
	f			הַיַּיִן		Τί ἐστιν f
	g	Εσθηρ βασίλισσα,		מַה־שְּׁאֵלָתֵךְ אֶסְתֵּר		ὁ κίνδυνος g
	h			הַמַּלְכָּה וְתִנָּתֵן		h
	i	καὶ τί τὸ αἴτημά σου		לָךְ		i
	j	καὶ τί τὸ ἀξίωμά σου;		וּמַה־בַּקָּשָׁתֵךְ		καὶ τί τὸ αἴτημά σου; j
	k	καὶ ἔστω σοι		עַד־חֲצִי הַמַּלְכוּת		k
				וְתֵעָשׂ׃		l

Chapter 7

THE TEXTS OF ESTHER — CHAPTER 7

	LXX (Göttingen o')		MT (BHS 3)		AT (Göttingen L)
				m	ἕως τοῦ ἡμίσους
l	ἕως τοῦ ἡμίσους		עַד־חֲצִי	n	τῆς βασιλείας μου.
m	τῆς βασιλείας μου.		הַמַּלְכוּת	o	
n			וְתֵעָשׂ׃		
				7:2 a	καὶ ἠγωνίασεν Εσθηρ
				b	ἐν τῷ ἀπαγγέλλειν,
				c	ὅτι ὁ ἀντίδικος
				d	ἐν ὀφθαλμοῖς αὐτῆς,
				e	καὶ ὁ θεὸς ἔδωκεν αὐτῇ θάρσος
				f	ἐν τῷ αὐτὴν ἐπικαλεῖσθαι αὐτόν.
7:3 a	καὶ ἀποκριθεῖσα	7:3	וַתַּעַן אֶסְתֵּר	7:3 a	καὶ εἶπεν
b	εἶπεν		הַמַּלְכָּה וַתֹּאמַר	b	Εσθηρ
c			אִם־מָצָאתִי חֵן	c	
d	Εἰ εὗρον χάριν		בְּעֵינֶיךָ הַמֶּלֶךְ	d	
e	ἐνώπιον τοῦ βασιλέως,		וְאִם־עַל־הַמֶּלֶךְ טוֹב	e	
f				f	Εἰ δοκεῖ τῷ βασιλεῖ,
g				g	καὶ ἀγαθὴ ἡ κρίσις ἐν καρδίᾳ αὐτοῦ,

Chapter 7

The Texts of Esther — Chapter 7

	LXX (Göttingen o')	MT (BHS 3)	AT (Göttingen L)	
h	δοθήτω ἡ ψυχὴ	תִּנָּתֶן־לִי נַפְשִׁי	δοθήτω ὁ λαός μου	h
i	τῷ αἰτήματί μου	בִּשְׁאֵלָתִי	τῷ αἰτήματί μου	i
j	καὶ ὁ λαός μου	וְעַמִּי	καὶ τὸ ἔθνος	j
k		בְּבַקָּשָׁתִי:	τῆς ψυχῆς μου.	k
l	τῷ ἀξιώματί μου.			l
7:4 a	ἐπράθημεν γὰρ	7:4 כִּי נִמְכַּרְנוּ	ἐπράθημεν γὰρ	a
b	ἐγώ τε καὶ ὁ λαός μου	אֲנִי וְעַמִּי	ἐγὼ καὶ ὁ λαός μου	b
c	εἰς ἀπώλειαν	לְהַשְׁמִיד		c
d	καὶ διαρπαγὴν	לַהֲרוֹג		d
e	καὶ δουλείαν,	וּלְאַבֵּד		e
f	ἡμεῖς καὶ τὰ τέκνα ἡμῶν			f
g	εἰς παῖδας καὶ παιδίσκας,	וְאִלּוּ לַעֲבָדִים וְלִשְׁפָחוֹת נִמְכַּרְנוּ	εἰς δούλωσιν,	g
h		הֶחֱרַשְׁתִּי	καὶ τὰ νήπια αὐτῶν	h
i			εἰς διαρπαγήν,	i
j				j
k	καὶ παρήκουσα·	כִּי אֵין הַצָּר שֹׁוֶה בְּנֵזֶק הַמֶּלֶךְ:	καὶ οὐκ ἤθελον ἀπαγγεῖλαι,	k
l			ἵνα μὴ λυπήσω τὸν κύριόν μου·	l

		LXX (Göttingen o')	_MT (BHS 3)_	_AT (Göttingen L)_		
	m	οὐ γὰρ ἄξιος ὁ διάβολος		ἐγένετο γὰρ μεταπεσεῖν	m	
	n	τῆς αὐλῆς τοῦ βασιλέως.		τὸν ἄνθρωπον	n	
				τὸν κακοποιήσαντα ἡμᾶς.	o	
				καὶ ἐθυμώθη ὁ βασιλεὺς	a	
				καὶ εἶπεν	b	
7:5	a	εἶπεν δὲ ὁ βασιλεύς	7:5		c	
	b		וַיֹּאמֶר הַמֶּלֶךְ		d	
	c		אֲחַשְׁוֵרוֹשׁ	Τίς ἐστιν οὗτος,	e	
	d	Τίς οὗτος,	וַיֹּאמֶר לְאֶסְתֵּר		f	
	e		הַמַּלְכָּה	ὃς ἐτόλμησε	g	
	f	ὅστις ἐτόλμησεν	מִי הוּא זֶה	ταπεινῶσαι	h	
	g	ποιῆσαι τὸ πρᾶγμα τοῦτο;	וְאֵי־זֶה הוּא	τὸ σημεῖον τῆς βασιλείας μου	i	
			אֲשֶׁר־מְלָאוֹ לִבּוֹ	ὥστε παρελθεῖν τὸν φόβον σου;	j	
			לַעֲשׂוֹת כֵּן׃	ὡς δὲ εἶδεν ἡ βασίλισσα	a	7:6
				ὅτι δεινὸν ἐφάνη τῷ βασιλεῖ,	b	
				καὶ μισοπονηρεῖ,	c	
				εἶπεν Μὴ ὀργίζου, κύριε·	d	

LXX (Göttingen o')	MT (BHS 3)	AT (Göttingen L)
		e ἱκανὸν γὰρ ὅτι ἔτυχον
		f τοῦ ἱλασμοῦ σου·
		g εὐωχοῦ, βασιλεῦ.
		h αὔριον δὲ ποιήσω
		i κατὰ τὸ ῥημά σου.
	7:7	7:7 a καὶ ὤμοσεν ὁ βασιλεὺς
		b τοῦ ἀπαγγεῖλαι αὐτὴν αὐτῷ
		c τὸν ὑπερηφανευσάμενον
		d τοῦ ποιῆσαι τοῦτο
		e καὶ μετὰ ὅρκου
		f ὑπέσχετο ποιῆσαι αὐτῇ
		g ὃ ἂν βούληται.
	7:8(6)	7:8(6) a καὶ θαρσήσασα
		b ἡ Εσθηρ εἶπεν
		c Αμαν
		d ὁ φίλος σου ὁ ψευδὴς οὗτοσί,
		e ὁ πονηρὸς ἄνθρωπος οὗτος.
7:6 a εἶπεν δὲ Εσθηρ	7:6	
b ῎Ανθρωπος ἐχθρός·	אִישׁ־צַר וְאוֹיֵב	
c Αμαν	הָמָן	
d	הָרָע הַזֶּה	
e ὁ πονηρὸς οὗτος.	וְהָמָן נִבְעַת	

Chapter 7

THE TEXTS OF ESTHER — CHAPTER 7

	LXX (Göttingen o')		MT (BHS 3)		AT (Göttingen L)	
		7:7	וְהַמֶּ֜לֶךְ קָ֤ם			
f	Αμαν δὲ ἐταράχθη		בַּחֲמָתוֹ֙ מִמִּשְׁתֵּ֣ה			
g	ἀπὸ τοῦ βασιλέως		הַיַּ֔יִן			
h	καὶ τῆς βασιλίσσης.		אֶל־גִּנַּ֖ת הַבִּיתָ֑ן			
7:7 a	ὁ δὲ βασιλεὺς ἐξανέστη	7:9(7)		ἔκθυμος δὲ γενόμενος ὁ βασιλεὺς	a
b				καὶ πλησθεὶς ὀργῆς	b
c				ἀνεπήδησε	c
d				καὶ ἦν περιπατῶν.	d
e	ἐκ τοῦ συμποσίου		וְהָמָן֙ נֹעֲמַ֔ד			
f	εἰς τὸν κῆπον.		לְבַקֵּ֤שׁ עַל־נַפְשׁוֹ֙			
g	ὁ δὲ Αμαν		מֵאֶסְתֵּ֣ר	7:10	καὶ ὁ Αμαν	a
h				ἐταράχθη	b
i	παρῃτεῖτο		הַמַּלְכָּ֔ה כִּ֣י רָאָ֔ה		καὶ προσέπεσεν ἐπὶ τοὺς πόδας	c
j				Εσθηρ	d
k	τὴν βασίλισσαν·		כִּֽי־כָלְתָ֥ה		τῆς βασιλίσσης	e
l				ἐπὶ τὴν κοίτην ἔτι ἀνακειμένης.	f
m	ἑώρα γὰρ ἑαυτὸν		אֵלָ֛יו הָרָעָ֖ה			g
n	ἐν κακοῖς ὄντα.		מֵאֵ֥ת הַמֶּֽלֶךְ׃			h

Chapter 7

	LXX (Göttingen o')	MT (BHS 3)	AT (Göttingen L)	
7:8			7:11(8)	
a	ἐπέστρεψεν δὲ ὁ βασιλεὺς 7:8	וְהַמֶּלֶךְ	καὶ ὁ βασιλεὺς ἐπέστρεψεν	a
b	ἐκ τοῦ κήπου.	שָׁב מִגִּנַּת הַבִּיתָן		b
c		אֶל־בֵּית מִשְׁתֵּה הַיַּיִן	ἐπὶ τὸ συμπόσιον	c
d	Αμαν δὲ ἐπιπεπτώκει	וְהָמָן נֹפֵל עַל־הַמִּטָּה		d
e	ἐπὶ τὴν κλίνην,	אֲשֶׁר אֶסְתֵּר עָלֶיהָ		e
f		וַיֹּאמֶר הַמֶּלֶךְ הֲגַם		f
g	ἀξιῶν τὴν βασίλισσαν.	לִכְבּוֹשׁ אֶת־הַמַּלְכָּה עִמִּי בַּבָּיִת		g
h			καὶ ἰδὼν	h
i	εἶπεν δὲ	הַדָּבָר	εἶπεν	i
j	ὁ βασιλεύς	יָצָא מִפִּי הַמֶּלֶךְ		j
k			Οὐχ ἱκανόν σοι	k
l			ἡ ἁμαρτία τῆς βασιλείας,	l
m	Ὥστε καὶ τὴν γυναῖκα	וּפְנֵי הָמָן חָפוּ	ἀλλὰ καὶ τὴν γυναῖκά μου	m
n	βιάζῃ		ἐκβιάζῃ	n
o	ἐν τῇ οἰκίᾳ μου;	עָמַד לִפְנֵי הַמֶּלֶךְ	ἐνώπιόν μου;	o
p			ἀπαχθήτω Αμαν καὶ μὴ ζήτω.	p

THE TEXTS OF ESTHER — CHAPTER 7

	LXX (Göttingen o')		MT (BHS 3)		AT (Göttingen L)	
q	Αμαν δὲ ἀκούσας		וְהָמָן נִבְעַת מִלִּפְנֵי		καὶ οὕτως ἀπήγετο.	q
r	διετράπη τῷ προσώπῳ.		הַמֶּלֶךְ וְהַמַּלְכָּה׃		καὶ εἶπεν	r
7:9				7:12	Αγαθας	a
a	εἶπεν δὲ	7:9	וַיֹּאמֶר	(7:9)	εἰς τῶν παίδων	b
b	Βουγαθαν		חַרְבוֹנָה		αὐτοῦ	c
c	εἰς τῶν εὐνούχων		אֶחָד מִן־הַסָּרִיסִים		Ἰδοὺ ξύλον	d
d	πρὸς τὸν βασιλέα		לִפְנֵי הַמֶּלֶךְ גַּם		ἐν τῇ αὐλῇ αὐτοῦ	e
e	Ἰδοὺ καὶ ξύλον		הִנֵּה־הָעֵץ		πηχῶν πεντήκοντα,	f
f			אֲשֶׁר־עָשָׂה הָמָן לְמָרְדֳּכַי		ὃ ἔκοψεν Αμαν	g
g					ἵνα κρεμάσῃ	h
h	ἡτοίμασεν Αμαν		אֲשֶׁר דִּבֶּר־טוֹב עַל־הַמֶּלֶךְ		Μαρδοχαῖον τὸν λαλήσαντα	i
i					ἀγαθὰ	j
j	Μαρδοχαίῳ τῷ λαλήσαντι		עֹמֵד בְּבֵית הָמָן גָּבֹהַּ		περὶ τοῦ βασιλέως·	k
k	περὶ τοῦ βασιλέως,					l
l	καὶ ὤρθωται ἐν τοῖς Αμαν		חֲמִשִּׁים אַמָּה			m
m	ξύλον πηχῶν πεντήκοντα.					n

	LXX (Göttingen o')		MT (BHS 3)		AT (Göttingen L)	
		n				o
	εἶπεν δὲ ὁ βασιλεὺς	o			κέλευσον οὖν, κύριε,	p
	Σταυρωθήτω ἐπ' αὐτοῦ.	p			ἐπ' αὐτῷ αὐτὸν κρεμασθῆναι.	a
		q	7:13	𐤄𐤓𐤏𐤄 𐤀𐤌𐤓	καὶ εἶπεν ὁ βασιλεὺς	b
				𐤏𐤋 𐤓𐤀𐤔𐤅	Κρεμασθήτω ἐπ' αὐτῷ.	c
					καὶ ἀφεῖλεν ὁ βασιλεὺς	d
					τὸ δακτύλιον	e
					ἀπὸ τῆς χειρὸς αὐτοῦ,	f
					καὶ ἐσφραγίσθη ἐν αὐτῷ	g
					ὁ βίος αὐτοῦ.	
7:10	καὶ ἐκρεμάσθη Αμαν	a	7:10			
	ἐπὶ τοῦ ξύλου	b				
	ὃ ἡτοιμάσθη Μαρδοχαίῳ.	c				
	καὶ τότε ὁ βασιλεὺς	d				
	ἐκόπασεν τοῦ θυμοῦ.	e				
			7:14		καὶ εἶπεν ὁ βασιλεὺς τῇ Εσθηρ	a
					Καὶ Μαρδοχαῖον ἐβουλεύσατο	b
					κρεμάσαι τὸν σώσαντά με	c

THE TEXTS OF ESTHER — CHAPTER 7

LXX (Göttingen o')	MT (BHS 3)	AT (Göttingen L)	
		ἐκ χειρὸς τῶν εὐνούχων;	d
		οὐκ ᾔδει ὅτι πατρῷον αὐτοῦ	e
		γένος ἐστὶν ἡ Εσθηρ;	f

	LXX (Göttingen o')		MT (BHS 3)		AT (Göttingen L)	
8:1	a	Καὶ ἐν αὐτῇ τῇ ἡμέρᾳ	8:1	בַּיּוֹם הַהוּא		a
	b			נָתַן		b
	c		7:15		καὶ ἐκάλεσεν	c
	d	ὁ βασιλεὺς		הַמֶּלֶךְ	ὁ βασιλεὺς	d
	e	Ἀρταξέρξης		אֲחַשְׁוֵרֹשׁ		e
	f				τὸν Μαρδοχαῖον	f
	g	ἐδωρήσατο		לְאֶסְתֵּר	καὶ ἐχαρίσατο	g
	h	Εσθηρ		הַמַּלְכָּה	αὐτῷ	h
	i					i
	j	ὅσα ὑπῆρχεν Αμαν		אֶת־בֵּית הָמָן	πάντα τὰ τοῦ Αμαν.	j
	k	τῷ διαβόλῳ,		צֹרֵר הַיְּהוּדִּים		
	l	καὶ Μαρδοχαῖος		וּמָרְדֳּכַי בָּא		
	m	προσεκλήθη		לִפְנֵי הַמֶּלֶךְ		
	n	ὑπὸ τοῦ βασιλέως·		כִּי־הִגִּידָה		
	o	ὑπέδειξεν γὰρ Εσθηρ		אֶסְתֵּר מַה הוּא־לָהּ		
	p	ὅτι ἐνοικείωται αὐτῇ.		וְאֵיךָ הוּא לָהּ׃		

LXX (Göttingen o')	MT (BHS 3)	AT (Göttingen L)

AT (Göttingen L)

7:16
a καὶ εἶπεν αὐτῷ Τί θέλεις;
b καὶ ποιήσω σοι.
c καὶ εἶπε Μαρδοχαῖος
d "Ὅπως ἀνέλῃς τὴν ἐπιστολὴν
e τοῦ Αμαν.
7:17
a καὶ ἐνεχείρισεν αὐτῷ
b ὁ βασιλεὺς
c τὰ κατὰ τὴν βασιλείαν.

MT (BHS 3)

8:2
וַיָּסַר הַמֶּלֶךְ אֶת־טַבַּעְתּוֹ
אֲשֶׁר הֶעֱבִיר מֵהָמָן
וַיִּתְּנָהּ לְמָרְדֳּכָי
וַתָּשֶׂם אֶסְתֵּר אֶת־מָרְדֳּכַי
עַל־בֵּית הָמָן׃

8:3
וַתּוֹסֶף אֶסְתֵּר

LXX (Göttingen o')

8:2
a ἔλαβεν δὲ ὁ βασιλεὺς
b τὸν δακτύλιον,
c ὃν ἀφείλατο Αμαν,
d καὶ ἔδωκεν αὐτὸν Μαρδοχαίῳ,
e καὶ κατέστησεν Εσθηρ
f Μαρδοχαῖον
g ἐπὶ πάντων τῶν Αμαν.
8:3
a καὶ προσθεῖσα

	LXX (Göttingen o')	MT (BHS 3)	AT (Göttingen L)
b		ותוסף	
c	ἐλάλησεν	ותדבר	
d	πρὸς τὸν βασιλέα	לפני המלך	
e	καὶ προσέπεσεν	ותפל	
f	πρὸς τοὺς πόδας αὐτοῦ	לפני רגליו	
g		ותבך	
h	καὶ ἠξίου ἀφελεῖν	ותתחנן לו להעביר את־רעת	
i	τὴν Αμαν κακίαν	המן האגגי	
j		ואת מחשבתו	
k	καὶ ὅσα ἐποίησεν	אשר חשב	
l		על־היהודים:	
m	τοῖς Ἰουδαίοις.		
8:4 a	ἐξέτεινεν δὲ ὁ βασιλεὺς 8:4	ויושט המלך	
b	Εσθηρ	לאסתר	
c	τὴν ῥάβδον τὴν χρυσῆν·	את שרבט הזהב	
d	ἐξηγέρθη δὲ Εσθηρ	ותקם אסתר	

THE TEXTS OF ESTHER — CHAPTER 8

LXX (Göttingen o')	MT (BHS 3)	AT (Göttingen L)
e παρεστηκέναι τῷ βασιλεῖ.		
8:5 a καὶ εἶπεν	8:5	a καὶ εἶπεν
b Εσθηρ		b Εσθηρ
c		c τῷ βασιλεῖ
d		d τῇ ἐξῆς Δός μοι
e		e κολάσαι τοὺς ἐχθρούς μου φόνῳ.
f Εἰ δοκεῖ σοι,		
g καὶ εὗρον χάριν,		
h		
i		
j		
k πεμφθήτω		
l ἀποστραφῆναι		
m τὰ γράμματα τὰ ἀπεσταλμένα		
n ὑπὸ Αμαν		
o		

MT (BHS 3) column:

וַתַּעֲמֹד לִפְנֵי הַמֶּלֶךְ׃

7:18   וַתֹּאמֶר

LXX (Göttingen o')

p	τὰ γραφέντα
q	ἀπολέσθαι
r	τοὺς Ἰουδαίους,
s	οἵ εἰσιν
t	ἐν τῇ βασιλείᾳ σου.
8:6 a	πῶς γὰρ δυνήσομαι
b	ἰδεῖν τὴν κάκωσιν
c	τοῦ λαοῦ μου,
d	καὶ πῶς δυνήσομαι
e	σωθῆναι
f	ἐν τῇ ἀπωλείᾳ
g	τῆς πατρίδος μου;

MT (BHS 3)

8:6

כִּי אֵיכָכָה אוּכַל
וְרָאִיתִי
בָּרָעָה אֲשֶׁר־יִמְצָא אֶת־עַמִּי
וְאֵיכָכָה אוּכַל
וְרָאִיתִי בְּאָבְדַן מוֹלַדְתִּי׃

AT (Göttingen L)

7:19		
ἐνέτυχε δὲ ἡ βασίλισσα Εσθηρ	a
καὶ κατὰ τῶν τέκνων Αμαν	b
τῷ βασιλεῖ, ὅπως ἀποθάνωσι	c
καὶ αὐτοὶ μετὰ τοῦ πατρὸς αὐτῶν.	d

Chapter 8

THE TEXTS OF ESTHER — CHAPTER 8

LXX (Göttingen o')	MT (BHS 3)	AT (Göttingen L)	
		καὶ εἶπεν ὁ βασιλεύς Γινέσθω.	e
	7:20	καὶ ἐπάταξε τοὺς ἐχθροὺς εἰς πλῆθος.	a
	7:21	ἐν δὲ Σούσοις	b
		ἀνθωμολογήσατο ὁ βασιλεὺς	c
		τῇ βασιλίσσῃ ἀποκτανθῆναι ἄνδρας	d
		καὶ εἶπεν Ἰδοὺ δίδωμί σοι	e
		τοῦ κρεμάσαι.	f
		καὶ ἐγένετο οὕτως.	g

		MT (BHS 3) 8:7
8:7	a	καὶ εἶπεν ὁ βασιλεύς
	b	וַיֹּאמֶר
	c	πρὸς Εσθηρ הַמֶּלֶךְ אֲחַשְׁוֵרֹשׁ לְאֶסְתֵּר
	d	וּלְמָרְדֳּכַי
	e	הַיְּהוּדִי
	f	הִנֵּה־בֵית
	g	Εἰ πάντα הָמָן נָתַתִּי לְאֶסְתֵּר

THE TEXTS OF ESTHER — CHAPTER 8

	LXX (Göttingen o')	MT (BHS 3)	AT (Göttingen L)
h	τὰ ὑπάρχοντα Αμαν	וּבֵית־הָמָן	
i	ἔδωκα	נָתַתִּי	
j		לְאֶסְתֵּר	
k	καὶ ἐχαρισάμην σοι	וְאֹתוֹ תָּלוּ עַל־הָעֵץ	
l	καὶ αὐτὸν ἐκρέμασα ἐπὶ ξύλου,	עַל אֲשֶׁר־שָׁלַח יָדוֹ בַּיְּהוּדִים	
m	ὅτι τὰς χεῖρας ἐπήνεγκεν		
n	τοῖς Ἰουδαίοις,		
o	τί ἔτι ἐπιζητεῖς;		
8:8			
a	γράψατε καὶ ὑμεῖς　8:8	וְאַתֶּם כִּתְבוּ עַל־הַיְּהוּדִים	
b		כַּטּוֹב בְּעֵינֵיכֶם	
c		בְּשֵׁם הַמֶּלֶךְ	
d	ἐκ τοῦ ὀνόματός μου	וְחִתְמוּ בְּטַבַּעַת הַמֶּלֶךְ	
e	ὡς δοκεῖ ὑμῖν	כִּי־כְתָב אֲשֶׁר־נִכְתָּב בְּשֵׁם־הַמֶּלֶךְ	
f	καὶ σφραγίσατε τῷ δακτυλίῳ μου·	וְנַחְתּוֹם בְּטַבַּעַת הַמֶּלֶךְ	
g	ὅσα γὰρ γράφεται	אֵין לְהָשִׁיב	
h	τοῦ βασιλέως ἐπιτάξαντος		

THE TEXTS OF ESTHER — CHAPTER 8

LXX (Göttingen o')	MT (BHS 3)	AT (Göttingen L)
i καὶ σφραγισθῇ	וְנַחְתּוֹם	
j τῷ δακτυλίῳ μου,	בְּטַבַּעַת הַמֶּלֶךְ	
k οὐκ ἔστιν αὐτοῖς ἀντειπεῖν.	אֵין לְהָשִׁיב׃	
8:9 a ἐκλήθησαν δὲ οἱ γραμματεῖς 8:9	וַיִּקָּרְאוּ סֹפְרֵי־הַמֶּלֶךְ	
b	בָּעֵת־הַהִיא בַּחֹדֶשׁ הַשְּׁלִישִׁי	
c ἐν τῷ πρώτῳ μηνί,	הוּא־חֹדֶשׁ	
d ὅς ἐστιν Νισα,	סִיוָן בִּשְׁלוֹשָׁה	
e τρίτῃ καὶ εἰκάδι	וְעֶשְׂרִים בּוֹ	
f τοῦ αὐτοῦ ἔτους,	וַיִּכָּתֵב כְּכָל־אֲשֶׁר־צִוָּה מָרְדֳּכַי	
g καὶ ἐγράφη	אֶל־הַיְּהוּדִים	
h		
i τοῖς Ἰουδαίοις		
j ὅσα ἐνετείλατο		
k τοῖς οἰκονόμοις		
l καὶ τοῖς ἄρχουσιν τῶν σατραπῶν	וְאֶל הָאֲחַשְׁדַּרְפְּנִים־וְהַפַּחוֹת וְשָׂרֵי הַמְּדִינוֹת	
m ἀπὸ τῆς Ἰνδικῆς	אֲשֶׁר מֵהֹדּוּ	

THE TEXTS OF ESTHER — CHAPTER 8

LXX (Göttingen o')	MT (BHS 3)	AT (Göttingen L)

LXX (Göttingen o')

n   ἕως τῆς Αἰθιοπίας,

o   ἑκατὸν εἴκοσι ἑπτὰ

p   σατραπείαις

q   κατὰ χώραν καὶ χώραν,

r   κατὰ τὴν ἑαυτῶν λέξιν.

s

t

u

8:10 a   ἐγράφη δὲ διὰ τοῦ βασιλέως

b

c   καὶ ἐσφραγίσθη

d   τῷ δακτυλίῳ αὐτοῦ,

e   καὶ ἐξαπέστειλαν τὰ γράμματα

f   διὰ βιβλιαφόρων,

g

h

THE TEXTS OF ESTHER — CHAPTER 8

LXX (Göttingen o')	MT (BHS 3)	AT (Göttingen L)
8:11	8:11	

8:11
a ὡς ἐπέταξεν
b
c αὐτοῖς
d
e χρῆσθαι τοῖς νόμοις αὐτῶν
f
g
h
i
j
k
l
m ἐν πάσῃ πόλει
n βοηθῆσαί τε αὐτοῖς
o καὶ χρῆσθαι τοῖς ἀντιδίκοις αὐτῶν
p καὶ τοῖς ἀντικειμένοις αὐτῶν

MT (BHS 3):

וַיִּתֵּן לַמֶּלֶךְ׃
אֲשֶׁר נָתַן הַמֶּלֶךְ
אֵת כָּל־חֵיל עַם־
וָמְדִינָה הַצָּרִים אֹתָם
טַף וְנָשִׁים
וּשְׁלָלָם
לָבוֹז׃

	LXX (Göttingen o')		_MT (BHS 3)_	_AT (Göttingen L)_	

	LXX (Göttingen o')		_MT (BHS 3)_	_AT (Göttingen L)_	
8:12	q ὡς βούλονται,	8:12			
	a ἐν ἡμέρᾳ μιᾷ		בְּי֣וֹם אֶחָ֔ד		
	b ἐν πάσῃ τῇ βασιλείᾳ		בְּכָל־מְדִינ֖וֹת		
	c Ἀρταξέρξου,		הַמֶּ֣לֶךְ אֲחַשְׁוֵר֑וֹשׁ		
	d τῇ τρισκαιδεκάτῃ		בִּשְׁלוֹשָׁ֥ה עָשָׂ֖ר		
	e τοῦ δωδεκάτου μηνός,		לְחֹ֥דֶשׁ שְׁנֵים־עָשָׂ֛ר		
	f ὅς ἐστιν Αδαρ.		ה֥וּא־חֹ֖דֶשׁ אֲדָֽר׃		
E:1	a ῍Ων ἐστιν ἀντίγραφον	7:22 (E:1)		Καὶ ἔγραψε	a
	b τῆς ἐπιστολῆς τὰ ὑπογεγραμμένα			τὴν ὑποτεταγμένην ἐπιστολὴν	b
	c Βασιλεὺς μέγας			Βασιλεὺς μέγας	c
	d Ἀρταξέρξης			Ασσυῆρος	d
	e τοῖς ἀπὸ τῆς Ἰνδικῆς			τοῖς ἀπὸ τῆς Ἰνδικῆς	e
	f ἕως τῆς Αἰθιοπίας			ἕως τῆς Αἰθιοπίας	f
	g ἑκατὸν εἴκοσι ἑπτὰ			ἑκατὸν καὶ εἴκοσι καὶ ἑπτὰ	g
	h σατραπείαις χωρῶν ἄρχουσιν			χωρῶν ἄρχουσι καὶ σατράπαις	h
	i καὶ τοῖς τὰ ἡμέτερα φρονοῦσιν			τοῖς τὰ ἡμέτερα φρονοῦσι	i

Chapter 8

THE TEXTS OF ESTHER — ADDITION E

	LXX (Göttingen o')	MT (BHS 3)		AT (Göttingen L)	
		– No Hebrew Text Extant –			
	j χαίρειν.			χαίρειν.	j
E:2	a πολλοὶ τῇ πλείστῃ		7:23 (E:2)	πολλοὶ τῇ πλείστῃ	a
	b τῶν εὐεργετούντων χρηστότητι			τῶν εὐεργετούντων χρηστότητι	b
	c πυκνότερον τιμώμενοι			πυκνότερον τιμώμενοι	c
	d μεῖζον ἐφρόνησαν			μεῖζον φρονήσαντες	d
E:3	a καὶ οὐ μόνον		(E:3)	οὐ μόνον	e
	b τοὺς ὑποτεταγμένους ἡμῖν			τοὺς ὑποτεταγμένους ἡμῖν	f
	c ζητοῦσιν κακοποιεῖν,			ζητοῦσι κακοποιεῖν,	g
	d τόν τε κόρον			τὸν δὲ κόρον	h
	e οὐ δυνάμενοι φέρειν			οὐ δυνάμενοι φέρειν	i
	f καὶ τοῖς ἑαυτῶν εὐεργέταις			καὶ τοῖς ἑαυτῶν εὐεργέταις	j
	g ἐπιχειροῦσιν μηχανᾶσθαι·			ἐπιχειροῦσι μηχανᾶσθαι κακά·	k
E:4	a καὶ τὴν εὐχαριστίαν		(E:4)	καὶ τὴν εὐχαριστίαν	l
	b οὐ μόνον			οὐ μόνον	m
	c ἐκ τῶν ἀνθρώπων			ἐκ τῶν ἀνθρώπων	n
	d ἀνταναιροῦντες,			ἀναιροῦντες,	o
	e ἀλλὰ καὶ τοῖς τῶν ἀπειραγάθων			ἀλλὰ καὶ τοῖς τῶν ἀπειραγάθων	p

Addition E

THE TEXTS OF ESTHER — ADDITION E

	LXX (Göttingen o')	MT (BHS 3)	AT (Göttingen L)	
		– No Hebrew Text Extant –		
f	κόμποις ἐπαρθέντες		κόμποις παρελθόντες	q
g	τοῦ τὰ πάντα		τὸ τοῦ πάντα	r
h	κατοπτεύοντος ἀεὶ θεοῦ		δυναστεύοντος δικαιοκρίτου	s
i	μισοπόνηρον		μισοπόνηρον	t
j	ὑπολαμβάνουσιν ἐκφεύξεσθαι		ἐκφυγεῖν διειληφότες,	u
k	δίκην.		τὴν δίκην,	v
E:5 a	πολλάκις δὲ	(E:5)	πολλάκις	w
b	καὶ πολλοὺς			x
c	τῶν ἐπ' ἐξουσίαις		ἐπ' ἐξουσιῶν	y
d	τεταγμένων		τεταγμένοι	z
e	τῶν πιστευθέντων		τὰ τῶν ἐμπιστευομένων	aa
f	χειρίζειν		φίλων πράγματα	bb
g	φίλων τὰ πράγματα		χειρίζειν	cc
h	παραμυθία			dd
i	μετόχους		αἰτίους ἀθῴων	ee
j	αἱμάτων ἀθῴων καταστήσασα		αἱμάτων καταστήσαντες	ff
k	περιέβαλεν συμφοραῖς ἀνηκέστοις		περιέβαλον συμφοραῖς ἀνηκέστοις	gg

Addition E

THE TEXTS OF ESTHER — ADDITION E

		LXX (Göttingen o')	MT (BHS 3)	AT (Göttingen L)	
E:6	a	τῷ τῆς κακοηθείας ψευδεῖ	(E:6)	τῷ τῆς κακοποιίας ψεύδει	hh
	b	παραλογισμῷ			ii
	c	παραλογισαμένων		παραλογισάμενοι	jj
	d	τὴν τῶν ἐπικρατούντων		τὴν τῶν ἐπικρατούντων	kk
	e	ἀκέραιον εὐγνωμοσύνην.		ἀκέραιον εὐγνωμοσύνην.	ll
E:7	a	σκοπεῖν δὲ ἔξεστιν,	7:24 (E:7)	σκοπεῖν δὲ ἔστιν	a
	b	οὐ τοσοῦτον			b
	c	ἐκ τῶν		ἐκ τῶν	c
	d	παλαιοτέρων ὡς			d
	e	παρεδώκαμεν		παραδεδομένων	e
	f			ἡμῖν	f
	g	ἱστοριῶν,		ἱστοριῶν	g
	h	ὅσα ἐστὶν		καὶ ὅσον	h
	i	παρὰ πόδας ὑμᾶς		τὰ παρὰ πόδας	i
	j	ἐκζητοῦντας ἀνοσίως			j
	k	συντετελεσμένα			k
	l			θεωροῦντες ἀξίως	l

LXX (Göttingen o') _MT (BHS 3)_ — No Hebrew Text Extant — _AT (Göttingen L)_

Addition E

THE TEXTS OF ESTHER — ADDITION E

	LXX (Göttingen o')	MT (BHS 3)	AT (Göttingen L)	
		– No Hebrew Text Extant –		
m	τῇ τῶν ἀνάξια δυναστευόντων		τῇ τῶν δυναστευόντων	m
n	λοιμότητι,		ὠμότητι	n
E:8 a	καὶ προσέχειν	(E:8)	προσέχειν	o
b	εἰς τὰ μετὰ ταῦτα		εἰς τὰ μετέπειτα	p
c	εἰς τὸ τὴν βασιλείαν ἀτάραχον		καὶ τὴν βασιλείαν ἀτάραχον	q
d			παρέχειν	r
e	τοῖς πᾶσιν ἀνθρώποις		πᾶσι τοῖς ἔθνεσι	s
f	μετ' εἰρήνης		μετ' εἰρήνης	t
g	παρεξόμεθα			u
E:9 a	χρώμενοι	(E:9)	οὐ χρώμενοι	v
b	ταῖς μεταβολαῖς,		ταῖς διαβολαῖς,	w
c	τὰ δὲ ὑπὸ τὴν ὄψιν ἐρχόμενα		τὰ δὲ ὑπὸ τὴν ὄψιν ἐρχόμενα	x
d	διακρίνοντες ἀεὶ			y
e	μετ' ἐπιεικεστέρας		μετ' ἐπιεικείας	z
f	ἀπαντήσεως.		διεξάγοντες.	aa
E:10 a	ὡς γὰρ	7:25 (E:10)	ἐπιξενωθεὶς γὰρ	a
b			ἡμῖν	b

Addition E

THE TEXTS OF ESTHER — ADDITION E

	LXX (Göttingen o')	MT (BHS 3)	AT (Göttingen L)	
		– No Hebrew Text Extant –		
c			Αμαν Αμαδάθου	c
d			ὁ Βουγαῖος	d
e			ταῖς ἀληθείαις ἀλλότριος	e
f			τοῦ τῶν Περσῶν	f
g			φρονήματος	g
h			καὶ πολὺ διεστὼς	h
i			τῆς ἡμετέρας χρηστότητος	i
c	Αμαν Αμαδάθου			j
d	Μακεδὼν			k
e	ταῖς ἀληθείαις ἀλλότριος			l
f	τοῦ τῶν Περσῶν			m
g	αἵματος			n
h	καὶ πολὺ διεστηκὼς			o
i	τῆς ἡμετέρας χρηστότητος,			p
j	ἐπιξενωθεὶς ἡμῖν			q
E:11 a	ἔτυχεν	(E:11)	ἔτυχε	r
b	ἧς ἔχομεν		τῆς ἐξ ἡμῶν	s
c	πρὸς πᾶν ἔθνος φιλανθρωπίας		πρὸς πᾶν ἔθνος φιλανθρωπίας	
d	ἐπὶ τοσοῦτον		ἐπὶ τοσοῦτον	
e	ὥστε ἀναγορεύεσθαι		ὥστε ἀναγορευθῆναι	
f	ἡμῶν πατέρα		πατέρα ἡμῶν	
g	καὶ προσκυνούμενον		καὶ προσκυνεῖσθαι	
h	ὑπὸ πάντων		ὑπὸ πάντων	
i	τὸ δεύτερον τοῦ βασιλικοῦ θρόνου		τὸ δεύτερον τῶν βασιλικῶν θρόνων	

Addition E

THE TEXTS OF ESTHER — ADDITION E

	LXX (Göttingen o')	MT (BHS 3)	AT (Göttingen L)	
		– No Hebrew Text Extant –		
j	πρόσωπον		διατελεῖν.	t
k	διατελεῖν,		οὐκ ἐνέγκων δὲ	u
E:12 a	οὐκ ἐνέγκας δέ.	7:26 (E:12)	τὴν ὑπερηφανίαν ἐπετήδευσεν	a
b	τὴν ὑπερηφανίαν ἐπετήδευσεν		ἡμᾶς τῆς ἀρχῆς	b
c	τῆς ἀρχῆς στερῆσαι ἡμᾶς		καὶ τοῦ πνεύματος	c
d	καὶ τοῦ πνεύματος,		μεταστῆσαι,	d
e				e
E:13 a	τόν τε ἡμέτερον σωτῆρα	(E:13)	τὸν δὲ ἡμέτερον σωτῆρα	f
b	καὶ διὰ παντὸς		διὰ παντὸς	g
c	εὐεργέτην			h
d	Μαρδοχαῖον		Μαρδοχαῖον	i
e	καὶ τὴν ἄμεμπτον		καὶ τὴν ἄμεμπτον	j
f	τῆς βασιλείας		τούτου	k
g	κοινωνὸν Εσθηρ		κοινωνὸν Εσθηρ	l
h	σὺν παντὶ τῷ τούτων ἔθνει		σὺν τῷ παντὶ τούτων ἔθνει	m
i	πολυπλόκοις μεθόδων		πολυπλόκοις μεθόδοις	n
j	παραλογισμοῖς αἰτησάμενος		διαπλασάμενος	o

Addition E

THE TEXTS OF ESTHER — ADDITION E

		LXX (Göttingen o')	MT (BHS 3)	AT (Göttingen L)	
			– No Hebrew Text Extant –		
E:14	k	εἰς ἀπώλειαν.		εἰς ἀπώλειαν·	p
	a	διὰ γὰρ	(E:14)	διὰ γὰρ	q
	b	τῶν τρόπων τούτων ᾦήθη		τούτων τῶν τρόπων ᾦήθη	r
	c	λαβὼν ἡμᾶς ἐρήμους		λαβὼν ἡμᾶς ἐρήμους	s
	d			ἐξαλλοτρίωσιν	t
	e	τὴν τῶν Περσῶν ἐπικράτησιν		τῆς τῶν Περσῶν ἐπικρατείας	u
	f	εἰς τοὺς Μακεδόνας		ἕως εἰς τοὺς Μακεδόνας	v
	g	μετάξαι.		ἀγαγεῖν.	w
E:15	a	ἡμεῖς δὲ τοὺς	7:27 (E:15)	τοὺς οὖν	a
	b	ὑπὸ τοῦ τρισαλιτηρίου		ὑπὸ τοῦ τρισαλιτηρίου	b
	c	παραδεδομένους		παραδεδομένους	c
	d			ὑμῖν	d
	e	εἰς ἀφανισμὸν			e
	f	Ἰουδαίους εὑρίσκομεν		Ἰουδαίους εὑρίσκομεν	f
	g	οὐ κακούργους ὄντας,		μὴ ὄντας κακούργους,	g
	h	δικαιοτάτοις δὲ		δικαιοτάτοις δὲ	h
	i	πολιτευομένους νόμοις,		πολιτευομένους νόμοις,	i

Addition E

THE TEXTS OF ESTHER — ADDITION E

	LXX (Göttingen o')	MT (BHS 3)	AT (Göttingen L)	
		– No Hebrew Text Extant –		
E:16 a	ὄντας δὲ υἱοὺς	(E:16)	ὄντας δὲ καὶ υἱοὺς	j
b	τοῦ ὑψίστου μεγίστου ζῶντος		τοῦ μόνου	k
c	θεοῦ,		θεοῦ	l
d			καὶ ἀληθινοῦ,	m
e	τοῦ κατευθύνοντος ἡμῖν τε		τοῦ κατευθύναντος ἡμῖν	n
f	καὶ τοῖς προγόνοις ἡμῶν			o
g	τὴν βασιλείαν		τὴν βασιλείαν	p
h			μέχρι τοῦ νῦν	q
i	ἐν τῇ καλλίστῃ διαθέσει.		ἐν τῇ καλλίστῃ διαθέσει.	r
E:17 a	καλῶς οὖν ποιήσετε	7:28 (E:17)	καλῶς οὖν ποιήσατε	a
b	μὴ προσχρησάμενοι		μὴ προσέχοντες	b
c	τοῖς ὑπὸ Αμαν Αμαδάθου		τοῖς προαπεσταλμένοις ὑμῖν	c
d	ἀποσταλεῖσιν γράμμασιν		ὑπὸ Αμαν γράμμασιν	d
E:18 a	διὰ τὸ αὐτὸν	(E:18)	διὰ τὸ καὶ αὐτὸν	e
b	τὸν ταῦτα ἐξεργασάμενον		τὸν τὰ τοιαῦτα ἐργασάμενον	f
c	πρὸς ταῖς Σούσων		πρὸς ταῖς Σούσων	g
d	πύλαις ἐσταυρῶσθαι		πύλαις ἐσταυρῶσθαι,	h

Addition E

THE TEXTS OF ESTHER — ADDITION E

	LXX (Göttingen o')	MT (BHS 3)	AT (Göttingen L)	
		– No Hebrew Text Extant –		
e	σὺν τῇ πανοικίᾳ,		ἀποδεδωκότος αὐτῷ	i
f	τὴν καταξίαν		τὴν καταξίαν	j
g			δίκην	k
h				l
i	τοῦ τὰ πάντα		τοῦ τὰ πάντα	m
j	ἐπικρατοῦντος θεοῦ		κατοπτεύοντος ἀεὶ κριτοῦ.	n
k	διὰ τάχους ἀποδόντος αὐτῷ κρίσιν,			
E:19 a	τὸ δὲ ἀντίγραφον	7:29 (E:19)	ἐκτεθήτω δὲ τὸ ἀντίγραφον	a
b	τῆς ἐπιστολῆς ταύτης ἐκθέντες		τῆς ἐπιστολῆς	b
c	ἐν παντὶ τόπῳ		ἐν παντὶ τόπῳ	c
d	μετὰ παρρησίας			d
e	ἐᾶν τοὺς Ἰουδαίους		χρῆσθαι	e
f	χρῆσθαι		τε τοὺς Ἰουδαίους	f
g	τοῖς ἑαυτῶν νομίμοις		τοῖς ἑαυτῶν νόμοις	g
E:20 a	καὶ συνεπισχύειν αὐτοῖς,	(E:20)	καὶ ἐπισχύειν αὐτοῖς,	h
b	ὅπως τοὺς ἐν καιρῷ θλίψεως		ὅπως τοὺς ἐν καιρῷ θλίψεως	i
c	ἐπιθεμένους		ἐπιθεμένους	j

Addition E

THE TEXTS OF ESTHER — ADDITION E

	LXX (Göttingen o')		MT (BHS 3)		AT (Göttingen L)	
			– No Hebrew Text Extant –			
d	αὐτοῖς			k	ἀμύνωνται.	
e	ἀμύνωνται			l	ἐκρίθη δὲ	
f			7:30	a	ὑπὸ τῶν κατὰ τὴν βασιλείαν	
g				b	Ἰουδαίων	
h				c	ἄγειν	
i				d	τὴν τεσσαρεσκαιδεκάτην	
j	τῇ τρισκαιδεκάτῃ			e	τοῦ μηνός,	
k	τοῦ δωδεκάτου μηνὸς			f	ὅς ἐστιν Αδαρ,	
l	Αδαρ			g		
m	τῇ αὐτῇ ἡμέρᾳ·			h		
E:21 a	ταύτην γὰρ	(E:21)		i	καὶ τῇ πεντεκαιδεκάτῃ ἑορτάσαι,	
b	ὁ τὰ πάντα δυναστεύων θεὸς			j	ὅτι ἐν αὐταῖς	
c	ἀντ' ὀλεθρίας			k	ὁ παντοκράτωρ	
d	τοῦ ἐκλεκτοῦ γένους			l		
e	ἐποίησεν αὐτοῖς			m		
f				n	ἐποίησεν αὐτοῖς	
				o	σωτηρίαν καὶ	

Addition E

THE TEXTS OF ESTHER — ADDITION E

	LXX (Göttingen o')	MT (BHS 3)	AT (Göttingen L)	
		– No Hebrew Text Extant –		
			εὐφροσύνην.	p
E:22 g	εὐφροσύνην.			
a	καὶ ὑμεῖς οὖν			
b	ἐν ταῖς ἐπωνύμοις ὑμῶν			
c	ἑορταῖς ἐπίσημον ἡμέραν			
d	μετὰ πάσης εὐωχίας ἄγετε,			
E:23 a	ὅπως καὶ νῦν καὶ μετὰ ταῦτα		7:31 (E:23) καὶ νῦν μετὰ ταῦτα	a
b	σωτηρία		σωτηρίαν	b
c	ᾖ ἡμῖν καὶ τοῖς εὐνοοῦσιν Πέρσαις,		μὲν εὖ ποιοῦσι τοῖς Πέρσαις,	c
d	τοῖς δὲ ἡμῖν ἐπιβουλεύουσιν		τῶν δὲ ἐπιβουλευσάντων	d
e	μνημόσυνον τῆς ἀπωλείας.		μνημόσυνον τῆς ἀπωλείας.	e
E:24 a	πᾶσα δὲ πόλις ἢ χώρα		7:32 (E:24) ἡ δὲ πόλις καὶ ἡ χώρα,	a
b	τὸ σύνολον,			b
c	ἥτις κατὰ ταῦτα		ἥτις κατὰ ταῦτα	c
d	μὴ ποιήσῃ,		μὴ ποιῆσαι,	d
e	δόρατι καὶ πυρὶ καταναλωθήσεται		δόρατι καὶ πυρὶ καταναλωθήσεται	e
f	μετ᾽ ὀργῆς·		μετ᾽ ὀργῆς	f
g	οὐ μόνον ἀνθρώποις ἄβατος,		καὶ οὐ μόνον ἀνθρώποις ἄβατος,	g

Addition E

THE TEXTS OF ESTHER — ADDITION E

LXX (Göttingen o')	_MT (BHS 3)_	_AT (Göttingen L)_
	– No Hebrew Text Extant –	

AT (Göttingen L):

ἀλλὰ καὶ θηρίοις καὶ πετεινοῖς ἐκταθήσεται. h i

LXX (Göttingen o'):

- h ἀλλὰ καὶ θηρίοις καὶ πετεινοῖς
- i
- j εἰς τὸν ἅπαντα χρόνον
- k ἔχθιστος καταστατθήσεται.
- **8:13** a τὰ δὲ ἀντίγραφα 8:13
- b ἐκτιθέσθωσαν
- c ὀφθαλμοφανῶς
- d ἐν πάσῃ τῇ βασιλείᾳ,
- e
- f ἑτοίμους τε εἶναι
- g πάντας τοὺς Ἰουδαίους
- h εἰς ταύτην τὴν ἡμέραν
- i πολεμῆσαι αὐτῶν τοὺς ὑπεναντίους.
- **8:14** a Οἱ μὲν οὖν ἱππεῖς 8:14
- b
- c ἐξῆλθον

MT (BHS 3) — Hebrew text (opposite 8:13–8:14):

פַּתְשֶׁגֶן הַכְּתָב
חֹק נִתָּן

בְּכָל־מְדִינָה וּמְדִינָה
גָּלוּי לְכָל־הָעַמִּים
וְלִהְיוֹת היהודיים [הַיְּהוּדִים]
עתודים [עֲתִידִים] לַיּוֹם הַזֶּה
לְהִנָּקֵם מֵאֹיְבֵיהֶם׃
הָרָצִים רֹכְבֵי הָרֶכֶשׁ
הָאֲחַשְׁתְּרָנִים
יָצְאוּ מְבֹהָלִים
וּדְחוּפִים בִּדְבַר הַמֶּלֶךְ

THE TEXTS OF ESTHER — CHAPTER 8

LXX (Göttingen o')	MT (BHS 3)	AT (Göttingen L)	
	מְבֹהָלִים וּדְחוּפִים בִּדְבַר הַמֶּלֶךְ		
	וְהַדָּת נִתְּנָה		
d σπεύδοντες			
e τὰ ὑπὸ τοῦ βασιλέως λεγόμενα			
f ἐπιτελεῖν.	בְּשׁוּשַׁן הַבִּירָה	7:33 (8:14) Ἐξετέθη δὲ	
g ἐξετέθη δὲ			
h τὸ πρόσταγμα		καὶ ἐν Σούσοις	a
i καὶ ἐν Σούσοις.		ἔκθεμα περιέχον τάδε,	b
		καὶ ὁ βασιλεὺς ἐνεχείρισε	c
		τῷ Μαρδοχαίῳ	d
		γράφειν ὅσα βούλεται.	e
			f
			g
		7:34 ἀπέστειλε δὲ Μαρδοχαῖος	a
		διὰ γραμμάτων καὶ ἐσφραγίσατο	b
		τῷ τοῦ βασιλέως δακτυλίῳ	c
		μένειν τὸ ἔθνος αὐτοῦ	d
		κατὰ χώρας ἕκαστον αὐτῶν	e
		καὶ ἑορτάζειν τῷ θεῷ.	f

Chapter 8

LXX (Göttingen o')	MT (BHS 3)	AT (Göttingen L)	
		7:35	
		ἡ δὲ ἐπιστολή,	a
		ἣν ἀπέστειλεν ὁ Μαρδοχαῖος,	b
		ἦν ἔχουσα ταῦτα	c
		7:36	
		Αμαν ἀπέστειλεν ὑμῖν	a
		γράμματα ἔχοντα οὕτως	b
		Ἔθνος Ἰουδαίων ἀπειθὲς	c
		σπουδάσατε ταχέως ἀναπέμψαι μοι	d
		εἰς ἀπώλειαν.	e
		7:37	
		ἐγὼ δὲ ὁ Μαρδοχαῖος	a
		μηνύω ὑμῖν τὸν ταῦτα	b
		ἐργασάμενον πρὸς	c
		ταῖς Σούσων πύλαις	d
		κεκρεμάσθαι καὶ	e
		τὸν οἶκον αὐτοῦ διακεχειρίσθαι·	f
		7:38	
		οὗτος γὰρ ἐβούλετο	a
		ἀποκτεῖναι ἡμᾶς	b

LXX (Göttingen o')		MT (BHS 3)	AT (Göttingen L)	

8:15 a	ὁ δὲ Μαρδοχαῖος ἐξῆλθεν 8:15	אֵצֵי וּמָרְדֳּכַי	7:39 (8:15) καὶ ὁ Μαρδοχαῖος ἐξῆλθεν	c
b		מִלִּפְנֵי הַמֶּלֶךְ	τῇ τρίτῃ καὶ δεκάτῃ τοῦ μηνός, ὅς ἐστιν Αδαρ.	d
				a
c	ἐστολισμένος	בִּלְבוּשׁ	ἐστολισμένος	b
d	τὴν βασιλικὴν στολὴν	מַלְכוּת	τὴν βασιλικὴν ἐσθῆτα	c
		תְּכֵלֶת וָחוּר		d
e		וַעֲטֶרֶת זָהָב גְּדוֹלָה		e
f	καὶ στέφανον ἔχων χρυσοῦν	וְתַכְרִיךְ בּוּץ וְאַרְגָּמָן		f
g	καὶ διάδημα	וְהָעִיר שׁוּשָׁן	καὶ διάδημα	g
h	βύσσινον πορφυροῦν·	צָהֲלָה וְשָׂמֵחָה׃	βύσσινον περιπόρφυρον·	h
i	ἰδόντες δὲ		7:40 ἰδόντες δὲ	a
j	οἱ ἐν Σούσοις		οἱ ἐν Σούσοις	b
k				c
l	ἐχάρησαν.	לַיְּהוּדִים	ἐχάρησαν.	d
8:16 a	τοῖς δὲ Ἰουδαίοις 8:16	הָיְתָה אוֹרָה	(8:16) καὶ τοῖς Ἰουδαίοις	e
b	ἐγένετο φῶς	וְשִׂמְחָה	ἐγένετο φῶς,	f

Chapter 8

		LXX (Göttingen o')	MT (BHS 3)	AT (Göttingen L)
	c	καὶ εὐφροσύνη·		
8:17	a	κατὰ πόλιν 8:17	לַיְּהוּדִים הָיְתָה	g πότος, κώθων.
	b	καὶ χώραν,	אוֹרָה וְשִׂמְחָה	
	c	οὗ ἂν ἐξετέθη τὸ πρόσταγμα,	וְשָׂשֹׂן וִיקָר	
	d	οὗ ἂν ἐξετέθη τὸ ἔκθεμα,	וּבְכָל־מְדִינָה וּמְדִינָה	
	e	χαρὰ καὶ εὐφροσύνη	וּבְכָל־עִיר וָעִיר	
	f	τοῖς Ἰουδαίοις,	מְקוֹם אֲשֶׁר	
	g	κώθων καὶ εὐφροσύνη.	דְּבַר־הַמֶּלֶךְ וְדָתוֹ	
	h	καὶ πολλοὶ	מַגִּיעַ	a 7:41 (8:17) καὶ πολλοὶ
	i	τῶν ἐθνῶν	שִׂמְחָה וְשָׂשׂוֹן	b τῶν Ἰουδαίων
	j	περιετέμοντο,	לַיְּהוּדִים	c περιετέμνοντο,
	k		מִשְׁתֶּה וְיוֹם טוֹב	d καὶ οὐδεὶς ἐπανέστη αὐτοῖς·
	l	καὶ ἰουδάιζον	וְרַבִּים מֵעַמֵּי הָאָרֶץ	e
	m	διὰ τὸν φόβον τῶν Ἰουδαίων.	מִתְיַהֲדִים	f ἐφοβοῦντο γὰρ αὐτούς.
	n		כִּי־נָפַל פַּחַד־הַיְּהוּדִים עֲלֵיהֶם	

THE TEXTS OF ESTHER — CHAPTER 9

LXX (Göttingen o')	MT (BHS 3)	AT (Göttingen L)

9:1 a Ἐν γὰρ τῷ δωδεκάτῳ μηνὶ   9:1 וּבִשְׁנֵים עָשָׂר חֹדֶשׁ

    b   הוּא־חֹדֶשׁ אֲדָר

    c τρισκαιδεκάτῃ τοῦ μηνός, בִּשְׁלוֹשָׁה עָשָׂר יוֹם בּוֹ

    d ὅς ἐστιν Αδαρ, אֲשֶׁר הִגִּיעַ דְּבַר־הַמֶּלֶךְ

    e παρῆν וְדָתוֹ לְהֵעָשׂוֹת

    f τὰ γράμματα τὰ γραφέντα בַּיּוֹם אֲשֶׁר שִׂבְּרוּ

    g ὑπὸ τοῦ βασιλέως. אֹיְבֵי הַיְּהוּדִים לִשְׁלוֹט בָּהֶם

    h   וְנַהֲפוֹךְ הוּא

    i

    j   אֲשֶׁר יִשְׁלְטוּ הַיְּהוּדִים

    k   הֵמָּה בְּשֹׂנְאֵיהֶם

    l

    m

9:2 a נִקְהֲלוּ הַיְּהוּדִים בְּעָרֵיהֶם

    b בְּכָל־מְדִינוֹת הַמֶּלֶךְ אֲחַשְׁוֵרוֹשׁ

    c לִשְׁלֹחַ יָד בִּמְבַקְשֵׁי רָעָתָם

    d וְאִישׁ לֹא־עָמַד לִפְנֵיהֶם

THE TEXTS OF ESTHER — CHAPTER 9

LXX (Göttingen o')

9:2
a ἐν αὐτῇ τῇ ἡμέρᾳ
b ἀπώλοντο οἱ ἀντικείμενοι
c τοῖς Ἰουδαίοις·
d οὐδεὶς γὰρ ἀντέστη,
e φοβούμενος αὐτούς.

9:3
a οἱ γὰρ ἄρχοντες
b τῶν σατραπῶν
c καὶ οἱ τύραννοι
d καὶ οἱ βασιλικοὶ γραμματεῖς
e ἔτιμων τοὺς Ἰουδαίους·
f ὁ γὰρ φόβος Μαρδοχαίου
g ἐνέκειτο αὐτοῖς.

MT (BHS 3)

9:2
e נִקְהֲלוּ הַיְּהוּדִים בְּעָרֵיהֶם בְּכָל־מְדִינוֹת הַמֶּלֶךְ אֲחַשְׁוֵרוֹשׁ
f לִשְׁלֹחַ יָד בִּמְבַקְשֵׁי רָעָתָם וְאִישׁ לֹא־
g עָמַד לִפְנֵיהֶם
h כִּי־נָפַל פַּחְדָּם עַל־כָּל־הָעַמִּים׃

9:3
וְכָל־שָׂרֵי הַמְּדִינוֹת וְהָאֲחַשְׁדַּרְפְּנִים וְהַפַּחוֹת וְעֹשֵׂי הַמְּלָאכָה אֲשֶׁר לַמֶּלֶךְ מְנַשְּׂאִים אֶת־הַיְּהוּדִים כִּי־נָפַל פַּחַד־מָרְדֳּכַי עֲלֵיהֶם׃

9:4
a כִּי־גָדוֹל מָרְדֳּכַי בְּבֵית הַמֶּלֶךְ
b וְשָׁמְעוֹ הוֹלֵךְ בְּכָל־הַמְּדִינוֹת

AT (Göttingen L)

7:42 (9:3)
a Οἱ δὲ ἄρχοντες
b
c καὶ οἱ τύραννοι
d καὶ οἱ σατράπαι
e καὶ οἱ βασιλικοὶ γραμματεῖς
f ἔτιμων τοὺς Ἰουδαίους·
g ὁ γὰρ φόβος Μαρδοχαίου
h ἐπέπεσεν ἐπ' αὐτούς.

THE TEXTS OF ESTHER — CHAPTER 9

		LXX (Göttingen o')			MT (BHS 3)	AT (Göttingen L)	
9:4	a	προσέπεσεν γὰρ	9:4	c	כִּֽי־גָד֤וֹל מָרְדֳּכַי֙	7:43 (9:4) καὶ προσέπεσεν	a
	b					ἐν Σούσοις	b
	c	τὸ πρόσταγμα τοῦ βασιλέως				ὀνομασθῆναι	c
	d	ὀνομασθῆναι		d	בְּבֵ֣ית הַמֶּ֔לֶךְ	Αμαν καὶ τοὺς ἀντικειμένους	d
	e			e	וְשָׁמְע֖וֹ הוֹלֵ֣ךְ	ἐν πάσῃ βασιλείᾳ.	e
	f	ἐν πάσῃ τῇ βασιλείᾳ.		f	בְּכָל־הַמְּדִינ֑וֹת		f
					כִּֽי־הָאִ֣ישׁ מָרְדֳּכַ֔י		
					הוֹלֵ֥ךְ וְגָדֽוֹל׃		
			9:5	a	וַיַּכּ֤וּ הַיְּהוּדִים֙ בְּכָל־אֹ֣יְבֵיהֶ֔ם		
				b	מַכַּת־חֶ֥רֶב וְהֶ֖רֶג וְאַבְדָ֑ן		
				c	וַיַּֽעֲשׂ֥וּ בְשֹׂנְאֵיהֶ֖ם		
				d	כִּרְצוֹנָֽם׃		
9:6	a	καὶ ἐν Σούσοις τῇ πόλει	9:6		וּבְשׁוּשַׁ֣ן הַבִּירָ֗ה	7:44 (9:6) καὶ ἀπέκτεινον	a
	b	ἀπέκτειναν			הָרְג֤וּ הַיְּהוּדִים֙	ἐν Σούσοις	b
	c	οἱ Ἰουδαῖοι			וְאַבֵּ֔ד		c
	d					οἱ Ἰουδαῖοι	d
							e

THE TEXTS OF ESTHER — CHAPTER 9

	LXX (Göttingen o')	MT (BHS 3)	AT (Göttingen L)	
e	ἄνδρας πεντακοσίους,	אֲנָשִׁים מֵאֹות חֲמֵשׁ :	ἄνδρας ἑπτακοσίους	f
9:7 a	τόν τε Φαρσαννεσταιν	9:7 אֵת פַּרְשַׁנְדָּתָא וְאֵת	καὶ τὸν Φαρσαν	g
b	καὶ Δελφων	דַּלְפֹון וְאֵת	καὶ τὸν ἀδελφὸν αὐτοῦ	h
c	καὶ Φασγα	אַסְפָּתָא וְאֵת :	καὶ τὸν Φαρνα	i
9:8 a	καὶ Φαρδαθα	9:8 פֹּורָתָא וְאֵת	καὶ τὸν Γαγαφαρδαθα	j
b	καὶ Βαρεα	אֲדַלְיָא וְאֵת		k
c	καὶ Σαρβαχα	אֲרִידָתָא וְאֵת :		l
9:9 a	καὶ Μαρμασιμ	9:9 פַּרְמַשְׁתָּא וְאֵת	καὶ τὸν Μαρμασαιμα	m
b	καὶ Αρουφαιον	אֲרִיסַי וְאֵת		n
c	καὶ Αρσαιον	אֲרִדַי וְאֵת		o
d	καὶ Ζαβουθαιον,	וַיְזָתָא אֵת :	καὶ τὸν Ιζαθουθ	p
9:10 a	τοὺς δέκα υἱοὺς Αμαν	9:10 בְּנֵי עֲשֶׂרֶת	καὶ τοὺς δέκα υἱοὺς Αμαν	q
b	Αμαδάθου	הֲמָן הַמְּדָתָא	Αμαδάθου	r
c	Βουγαίου	צֹרֵר הַיְּהוּדִים	τοῦ Βουγαίου	s
d	τοῦ ἐχθροῦ τῶν Ἰουδαίων,	הָרָגוּ	τοῦ ἐχθροῦ τῶν Ἰουδαίων,	t
e		וּבַבִּזָּה אֶת־יָדָם שָׁלְחוּ לֹא :		u
f	καὶ διήρπασαν		καὶ διήρπασαν	v

THE TEXTS OF ESTHER — CHAPTER 9

LXX (Göttingen o')	MT (BHS 3)	AT (Göttingen L)	
		πάντα τὰ αὐτῶν.	w
9:11a ἐν αὐτῇ τῇ ἡμέρᾳ·	**9:11** בַּיּוֹם הַהוּא		
b ἐπεδόθη τε	בָּא		
c ὁ ἀριθμὸς	מִסְפַּר		
d τῷ βασιλεῖ	הַהֲרוּגִים		
e τῶν ἀπολωλότων	בְּשׁוּשַׁן הַבִּירָה		
f ἐν Σούσοις.			
g			
9:12 a εἶπεν δὲ ὁ βασιλεὺς	**9:12**	7:45 (9:12) καὶ εἶπεν ὁ βασιλεὺς	a
b πρὸς Εσθηρ	וַיֹּאמֶר	τῇ Εσθηρ	b
c	הַמֶּלֶךְ לְאֶסְתֵּר		c
d	הַמַּלְכָּה		d
e Ἀπώλεσαν οἱ Ἰουδαῖοι	בְּשׁוּשַׁן		e
f	הַבִּירָה הָרְגוּ		f
g ἐν Σούσοις τῇ πόλει	הַיְּהוּדִים וְאַבֵּד		g
h ἄνδρας πεντακοσίους·	חֲמֵשׁ מֵאוֹת אִישׁ		h
i	וְאֵת עֲשֶׂרֶת בְּנֵי־הָמָן		i
	בִּשְׁאָר מְדִינוֹת הַמֶּלֶךְ מֶה עָשׂוּ		

THE TEXTS OF ESTHER — CHAPTER 9

	LXX (Göttingen o')	MT (BHS 3)	AT (Göttingen L)	
j		הַמֶּ֗לֶךְ מַה־שְּׁאֵלָתֵ֖ךְ	Πῶς σοι οἱ ἐνταῦθα	j
k	ἐν δὲ τῇ περιχώρῳ	וְיִנָּ֣תֶן לָ֑ךְ	καὶ οἱ ἐν τῇ περιχώρῳ	k
l	πῶς οἴει ἐχρήσαντο;	וּמַה־בַּקָּשָׁתֵ֛ךְ ע֖וֹד	κέχρηνται;	l
m	τί οὖν ἀξιοῖς ἔτι;	וְתֵעָֽשׂ׃		m
n	καὶ ἔσται σοι.			n
o				o
9:13 a	καὶ εἶπεν Εσθηρ	9:13 וַתֹּ֣אמֶר אֶסְתֵּ֗ר	7:46 (9:13) καὶ εἶπεν Εσθηρ	a
b	τῷ βασιλεῖ	אִם־עַל־הַמֶּ֣לֶךְ ט֔וֹב		b
c				c
d	Δοθήτω	יִנָּתֵן֙	Δοθήτω	d
e		גַּם־מָחָ֔ר		e
f	τοῖς Ἰουδαίοις	לַיְּהוּדִים֙	τοῖς Ἰουδαίοις	f
g		אֲשֶׁ֣ר בְּשׁוּשָׁ֔ן		g
h	χρῆσθαι	לַעֲשׂ֖וֹת		h
i		כְּדָ֣ת הַיּ֑וֹם	οὓς ἐὰν θέλωσιν	i
j			ἀνελεῖν καὶ διαρπάζειν.	j
k	ὡσαύτως τὴν αὔριον,		καὶ συνεχώρησεν.	

THE TEXTS OF ESTHER — CHAPTER 9

LXX (Göttingen o')		MT (BHS 3)	AT (Göttingen L)

| | | LXX (Göttingen o') | | MT (BHS 3) | AT (Göttingen L) |

1 ὥστε τοὺς δέκα υἱοὺς   וַיֹּאמֶר הַמֶּלֶךְ לַעֲשׂוֹת כֵּן

m κρεμάσαι Αμαν.   וַתִּנָּתֵן דָּת בְּשׁוּשָׁן

9:14   9:14   וְאֵת עֲשֶׂרֶת בְּנֵי־הָמָן תָּלוּ׃

a καὶ ἐπέτρεψεν   וְאֵת עֲשֶׂרֶת בְּנֵי הָמָן

b οὕτως γενέσθαι,   בֶּן־הַמְּדָתָא צֹרֵר הַיְּהוּדִים

c

d καὶ ἐξέθηκεν   וַיִּקָּהֲלוּ הַיְּהוּדִיִים אֲשֶׁר־

e τοῖς Ἰουδαίοις τῆς πόλεως

f τὰ σώματα τῶν υἱῶν   בְּשׁוּשָׁן גַּם בְּיוֹם אַרְבָּעָה עָשָׂר לְחֹדֶשׁ אֲדָר׃

g Αμαν κρεμάσαι.

9:15 a καὶ συνήχθησαν οἱ Ἰουδαῖοι   9:15   וַיַּהַרְגוּ בְשׁוּשָׁן שְׁלֹשׁ

b ἐν Σούσοις   מֵאוֹת אִישׁ

c τῇ τεσσαρεσκαιδεκάτη   וּבַבִּזָּה לֹא

d τοῦ Αδαρ   שָׁלְחוּ אֶת־יָדָם׃

e καὶ ἀπέκτειναν

f

g ἄνδρας τριακοσίους

h καὶ οὐδὲν διήρπασαν.

THE TEXTS OF ESTHER — CHAPTER 9

LXX (Göttingen o′)	MT (BHS 3)	AT (Göttingen L)
9:16 a οἱ δὲ λοιποὶ τῶν Ἰουδαίων	**9:16** וּשְׁאָר הַיְּהוּדִים	
b οἱ ἐν τῇ βασιλείᾳ	אֲשֶׁר בִּמְדִינוֹת הַמֶּלֶךְ	
c συνήχθησαν	נִקְהֲלוּ	
d καὶ ἑαυτοῖς ἐβοήθουν	וְעָמֹד עַל־נַפְשָׁם	
e καὶ ἀνεπαύσαντο	וְנוֹחַ מֵאֹיְבֵיהֶם	
f ἀπὸ τῶν πολεμίων·	וְהָרֹג בְּשֹׂנְאֵיהֶם	
g ἀπώλεσαν γὰρ αὐτῶν	חֲמִשָּׁה וְשִׁבְעִים אָלֶף	
h μυρίους πεντακισχιλίους		**7:46(9:16)** καὶ ἀπώλεσαν k
		μυριάδας ἑπτὰ καὶ ἑκατὸν l
i τῇ τρισκαιδεκάτῃ τοῦ Αδαρ,		ἄνδρας.
j καὶ οὐδὲν διήρπασαν.	וּבַבִּזָּה לֹא שָׁלְחוּ אֶת־יָדָם׃	
	9:17 a בְּיוֹם־שְׁלֹשָׁה עָשָׂר	
	b לְחֹדֶשׁ אֲדָר	
9:17 a καὶ ἀνεπαύσαντο	c וְנוֹחַ	
b τῇ τεσσαρεσκαιδεκάτῃ	d בְּאַרְבָּעָה עָשָׂר בּוֹ	
c τοῦ αὐτοῦ μηνὸς	e וְעָשֹׂה	
d καὶ ἦγον αὐτὴν ἡμέραν	f אֹתוֹ יוֹם	

	LXX (Göttingen o')	MT (BHS 3)	AT (Göttingen L)
e	ἀναπαύσεως		
f	μετὰ χαρᾶς καὶ εὐφροσύνης.	וְהַיְּהוּדִיִּים	
9:18 a	οἱ δὲ Ἰουδαῖοι 9:18	אֲשֶׁר־בְּשׁוּשָׁן	
b	οἱ ἐν Σούσοις	נִקְהֲלוּ	
c	τῇ πόλει	בִּשְׁלֹשָׁה עָשָׂר בּוֹ	
d	συνήχθησαν	וּבְאַרְבָּעָה עָשָׂר בּוֹ	
e		וְנוֹחַ	
f	καὶ τῇ τεσσαρεσκαιδεκάτῃ	בַּחֲמִשָּׁה עָשָׂר בּוֹ	
g	καὶ οὐκ ἀνεπαύσαντο·	וְעָשֹׂה אֹתוֹ	
h	ἦγον δὲ καὶ τὴν πεντεκαιδεκάτην	יוֹם מִשְׁתֶּה	
i	μετὰ χαρᾶς καὶ εὐφροσύνης.	וְשִׂמְחָה׃	
j		עַל־כֵּן הַיְּהוּדִים	
9:19 a	διὰ τοῦτο οὖν 9:19	הַפְּרָזִים	
b	οἱ Ἰουδαῖοι οἱ διεσπαρμένοι	הַיֹּשְׁבִים בְּעָרֵי הַפְּרָזוֹת	
c	ἐν πάσῃ χώρᾳ τῇ ἔξω	עֹשִׂים אֵת	
d	ἄγουσιν	יוֹם אַרְבָּעָה עָשָׂר	
e	τὴν τεσσαρεσκαιδεκάτην	לַחֹדֶשׁ אֲדָר	

LXX (Göttingen o')	MT (BHS 3)	AT (Göttingen L)	
f τοῦ Αδαρ	אֶת יוֹם		
g ἡμέραν ἀγαθὴν	אַרְבָּעָה עָשָׂר		
h μετ᾽ εὐφροσύνης	לְחֹדֶשׁ אֲדָר		
i ἀποστέλλοντες μερίδας	אֹתוֹ יוֹם		
j ἕκαστος τῷ πλησίον·	מִשְׁתֶּה וְשִׂמְחָה		
k οἱ δὲ κατοικοῦντες	וּמִשְׁלוֹחַ		
l ἐν ταῖς μητροπόλεσιν	מָנוֹת אִישׁ לְרֵעֵהוּ׃		
m καὶ τὴν πεντεκαιδεκάτην τοῦ Αδαρ			
n ἡμέραν εὐφροσύνην ἀγαθὴν			
o ἄγουσιν ἐξαποστέλλοντες			
p μερίδας τοῖς πλησίον.			
9:20 a Ἔγραψεν δὲ Μαρδοχαῖος	9:20 וַיִּכְתֹּב מָרְדֳּכַי	7:47 (9:20) Ἔγραψε δὲ Μαρδοχαῖος	a
b τοὺς λόγους τούτους	אֶת הַדְּבָרִים הָאֵלֶּה	τοὺς λόγους τούτους	b
c εἰς βιβλίον	בַּסֵּפֶר	εἰς βιβλίον	c
d καὶ ἐξαπέστειλεν	וַיִּשְׁלַח סְפָרִים	καὶ ἐξαπέστειλε	d
e	אֶל כָּל הַיְּהוּדִים		e
f τοῖς Ἰουδαίοις,		τοῖς Ἰουδαίοις,	f

Chapter 9

THE TEXTS OF ESTHER — CHAPTER 9

	LXX (Göttingen o')	MT (BHS 3)	AT (Göttingen L)	
g	ὅσοι ἦσαν	אֲשֶׁר	οἳ ἦσαν	g
h	ἐν τῇ	בְּכָל־מְדִינוֹת	ἐν τῇ	h
i	Ἀρταξέρξου βασιλεια,	הַמֶּלֶךְ אֲחַשְׁוֵרוֹשׁ	Ασσυήρου βασιλείᾳ,	i
j	τοῖς ἐγγὺς καὶ τοῖς μακράν,	הַקְּרוֹבִים וְהָרְחוֹקִים	τοῖς μακρὰν καὶ τοῖς ἐγγύς,	j
9:21 a	στῆσαι	לְקַיֵּם עֲלֵיהֶם (9:21)	στῆσαι	k
b	τὰς ἡμέρας ταύτας	לִהְיוֹת עֹשִׂים	τὰς ἡμέρας ταύτας	l
c	ἀγαθὰς	אֵת יוֹם אַרְבָּעָה	εἰς ὕμνους καὶ εὐφροσύνας	m
d		עָשָׂר וְאֵת	ἀντὶ ὀδυνῶν καὶ πένθους,	n
e	ἄγειν τε	יוֹם־		o
f	τὴν τεσσαρεσκαιδεκάτην	חֲמִשָּׁה עָשָׂר	τὴν τεσσαρεσκαιδεκάτην	p
g		בּוֹ בְּכָל־שָׁנָה		q
h	καὶ τὴν πεντεκαιδεκάτην	וְשָׁנָה׃	καὶ τὴν πεντεκαιδεκάτην.	r
i	τοῦ Αδαρ —			s
j		כַּיָּמִים אֲשֶׁר־נָחוּ		t
9:22 a	ἐν γὰρ ταύταις ταῖς ἡμέραις 9:22	בָהֶם הַיְּהוּדִים		u
b	ἀνεπαύσαντο οἱ Ἰουδαῖοι	מֵאֹיְבֵיהֶם		
c	ἀπὸ τῶν ἐχθρῶν αὐτῶν —			

Chapter 9

LXX (Göttingen o')	_MT (BHS 3)_	_AT (Göttingen L)_	
d καὶ τὸν μῆνα,	לַחֹדֶשׁ		
e ἐν ᾧ ἐστράφη αὐτοῖς,	אֲשֶׁר נֶהְפַּךְ לָהֶם		
f ὃς ἦν Αδαρ	מִיָּגוֹן לְשִׂמְחָה		
g ἀπὸ πένθους εἰς χαρὰν	וּמֵאֵבֶל לְיוֹם טוֹב		
h καὶ ἀπὸ ὀδύνης	לַעֲשׂוֹת אוֹתָם		
i εἰς ἀγαθὴν ἡμέραν,	יְמֵי מִשְׁתֶּה		
j ἄγειν ὅλον ἀγαθὰς ἡμέρας	וְשִׂמְחָה		
k γάμων καὶ εὐφροσύνης	וּמִשְׁלֹחַ מָנוֹת		
l ἐξαποστέλλοντας μερίδας	אִישׁ לְרֵעֵהוּ	7:48 (9:22) καὶ ἀπέστειλε μερίδας	a
m τοῖς φίλοις			b
n			c
o καὶ τοῖς πτωχοῖς.	וּמַתָּנוֹת לָאֶבְיֹנִים׃	τοῖς πένησιν,	d
9:23 a καὶ προσεδέξαντο	9:23 וְקִבֵּל הַיְּהוּדִים	καὶ προσεδέξαντο.	e
b οἱ Ἰουδαῖοι,	אֵת אֲשֶׁר־הֵחֵלּוּ לַעֲשׂוֹת		
b			
c καθὼς ἔγραψεν	וְאֵת אֲשֶׁר־כָּתַב		
d αὐτοῖς ὁ Μαρδοχαῖος,	מָרְדֳּכַי אֲלֵיהֶם		

THE TEXTS OF ESTHER — CHAPTER 9

LXX (Göttingen o')		_MT (BHS 3)_	_AT (Göttingen L)_
9:24	a	πῶς Αμαν	9:24	כִּי הָמָן
	b	Αμαδάθου		בֶּן־הַמְּדָ֫תָא
	c	ὁ Μακεδὼν		הָאֲגָגִי
	d			צֹרֵר
	e	ἐπολέμει αὐτούς,		כָּל־הַיְּהוּדִים
	f			חָשַׁב עַל־הַיְּהוּדִים
	g	καθὼς ἔθετο ψήφισμα		לְאַבְּדָם
	h	καὶ κλῆρον ἀφανίσαι αὐτούς,		וְהִפִּיל פּוּר הוּא הַגּוֹרָל
	i			לְהֻמָּם וּֽלְאַבְּדָֽם:
	j			וּבְבֹאָהּ לִפְנֵי הַמֶּ֫לֶךְ
9:25	a	καὶ ὡς εἰσῆλθεν	9:25	אָמַר
	b	πρὸς τὸν βασιλέα		עִם־הַסֵּ֫פֶר
	c	λέγων		יָשׁוּב
	d			מַחֲשַׁבְתּוֹ הָרָעָה
	e			אֲשֶׁר־חָשַׁב עַל־הַיְּהוּדִים
	f			עַל־רֹאשׁוֹ
	g	κρεμάσαι τὸν Μαρδοχαῖον·		וְתָלוּ אֹתוֹ וְאֶת־בָּנָיו עַל־הָעֵֽץ׃

THE TEXTS OF ESTHER — CHAPTER 9

	LXX (Göttingen o')	MT (BHS 3)	AT (Göttingen L)	
			7:49 (9:26)	
h	ὅσα δὲ ἐπεχείρησεν ἐπάξαι		διὰ τοῦτο ἐκλήθησαν	a
i	ἐπὶ τοὺς Ἰουδαίους κακά,		αἱ ἡμέραι αὗται	b
j	ἐπ' αὐτὸν ἐγένοντο,		Φουραια	c
k	καὶ ἐκρεμάσθη αὐτὸς		διὰ τοὺς κλήρους	d
l	καὶ τὰ τέκνα αὐτοῦ.		τοὺς πεσόντας	e
m				
9:26 a	διὰ τοῦτο ἐπεκλήθησαν	9:26		
b	αἱ ἡμέραι αὗται			
c	Φρουραι			
d	διὰ τοὺς κλήρους,			
e				
f				
g	ὅτι τῇ διαλέκτῳ αὐτῶν			
h	καλοῦνται Φρουραι,			
i	διὰ τοὺς λόγους			
j	τῆς ἐπιστολῆς ταύτης			
k	καὶ ὅσα πεπόνθασιν			

MT (BHS 3):

עַל־הַיְּהוּדִים
עַל־רֹאשׁוֹ
וְתָלוּ אֹתוֹ
וְאֶת־בָּנָיו
עַל־הָעֵץ׃

עַל־כֵּן קָרְאוּ
לַיָּמִים הָאֵלֶּה
פוּרִים עַל־שֵׁם הַפּוּר
עַל־כֵּן

עַל־כָּל־דִּבְרֵי הָאִגֶּרֶת הַזֹּאת
וּמָה־רָאוּ עַל־כָּכָה

	LXX (Göttingen o')	MT (BHS 3)	AT (Göttingen L)
l	διὰ ταῦτα	עַל־כָּכָה	
m	καὶ ὅσα αὐτοῖς ἐγένετο·	:וְעַל מָה הִגִּיעַ אֲלֵיהֶם	
9:27 a	καὶ ἔστησεν, 9:27	קִיְּמ֣וּ	
b	καὶ προσεδέχοντο	וְקִבְּל֣וּ	
c	οἱ Ἰουδαῖοι ἐφ' ἑαυτοῖς	הַיְּהוּדִים ׀ עֲלֵיהֶ֣ם	
d	καὶ ἐπὶ τῷ σπέρματι αὐτῶν	וְעַל־זַרְעָ֗ם	
e	καὶ ἐπὶ τοῖς προστεθειμένοις	וְעַ֤ל כָּל־הַנִּלְוִ֣ים	
f	ἐπ' αὐτῶν,	עֲלֵיהֶ֔ם	εἰς τὰς ἡμέρας ταύτας
g	οὐδὲ μὴν ἄλλως χρήσονται.	וְלֹ֣א יַעֲב֔וֹר	εἰς μνημόσυνον.
h		לִהְי֣וֹת עֹשִׂ֗ים אֵ֣ת שְׁנֵ֤י	
i		הַיָּמִ֣ים הָאֵ֔לֶּה	
j		כִּכְתָבָ֖ם וְכִזְמַנָּ֑ם	
k	αἱ δὲ ἡμέραι αὗται 9:28	בְּכָל־שָׁנָ֖ה וְשָׁנָֽה׃ a	
l	μνημόσυνον ἐπιτελούμενον	וְהַיָּמִ֣ים הָ֠אֵלֶּה b	
m	κατὰ γενεὰν καὶ γενεὰν	נִזְכָּרִ֨ים וְנַעֲשִׂ֜ים c	
n		בְּכָל־דּ֣וֹר וָד֗וֹר d	
o		מִשְׁפָּחָה֙ וּמִשְׁפָּחָ֔ה e	
		מְדִינָ֥ה וּמְדִינָ֖ה	
		וְעִ֣יר וָעִ֑יר	
		וִימֵ֞י הַפּוּרִ֣ים הָאֵ֗לֶּה	
		לֹ֤א יַֽעַבְרוּ֙ מִתּ֣וֹךְ	
		הַיְּהוּדִ֔ים וְזִכְרָ֖ם	
		:לֹא־יָס֥וּף מִזַּרְעָֽם	

	LXX (Göttingen o')		MT (BHS 3)	AT (Göttingen L)
p	καὶ πόλιν	f	וְעִיר וָעִיר	
q	καὶ πατριὰν καὶ χώραν.			
9:28 a	αἱ δὲ ἡμέραι αὗται τῶν Φρουραι		וְהַיָּמִים הָאֵלֶּה נִזְכָּרִים	
b	ἀχθήσονται	h	אֲשֶׁר אֵ נַעֲשִׂים	
c		i	בְּכָל־דּוֹר וָדוֹר	
d	εἰς τὸν ἅπαντα χρόνον,			
e	καὶ τὸ μνημόσυνον αὐτῶν	j	מִשְׁפָּחָה	
f	οὐ μὴ ἐκλίπῃ	k	וּמְדִינָה	
g	ἐκ τῶν γενεῶν.	l	וְעִיר וָעִיר:	
			וִימֵי	
			הַפּוּרִים	
9:29 a	καὶ ἔγραψεν	9:29	הָאֵלֶּה	
b	Εσθηρ ἡ βασίλισσα		לֹא יַעַבְרוּ מִתּוֹךְ	
c	θυγάτηρ Αμιναδαβ		הַיְּהוּדִים,	
d	καὶ Μαρδοχαῖος ὁ Ἰουδαῖος		וְזִכְרָם לֹא	
e			יָסוּף מִזַּרְעָם:	
f	ὅσα ἐποίησαν		וַתִּכְתֹּב	
g	τό τε στερέωμα			
h	τῆς ἐπιστολῆς τῶν Φρουραι.		אֶת אֶסְתֵּר הַמַּלְכָּה	

LXX (Göttingen o')	MT (BHS 3)	AT (Göttingen L)

MT (BHS 3)

9:30
a וַיִּשְׁלַח סְפָרִים אֶל־כָּל־הַיְּהוּדִים
b אֶל־שֶׁבַע וְעֶשְׂרִים וּמֵאָה מְדִינָה
c מַלְכוּת אֲחַשְׁוֵרוֹשׁ
d דִּבְרֵי שָׁלוֹם
e וֶאֱמֶת׃

9:31
a לְקַיֵּם אֶת־יְמֵי הַפֻּרִים הָאֵלֶּה
b בִּזְמַנֵּיהֶם
c כַּאֲשֶׁר קִיַּם עֲלֵיהֶם מָרְדֳּכַי הַיְּהוּדִי
d וְאֶסְתֵּר הַמַּלְכָּה
e וְכַאֲשֶׁר קִיְּמוּ עַל־נַפְשָׁם
f וְעַל־זַרְעָם
g דִּבְרֵי הַצֹּמוֹת
h וְזַעֲקָתָם׃
i

LXX (Göttingen o')

9:30
a καὶ Μαρδοχαῖος
b καὶ Εσθηρ ἡ βασίλισσα
c ἔστησαν ἑαυτοῖς
d
e
f καθ' ἑαυτῶν
g καὶ τότε στήσαντες

THE TEXTS OF ESTHER — CHAPTER 9

LXX (Göttingen o')	_MT (BHS 3)_	_AT (Göttingen L)_

h κατὰ τῆς ὑγιείας ἑαυτῶν

i καὶ τὴν βουλὴν αὐτῶν·

9:31 a καὶ Εσθηρ λόγῳ   9:32   דְּבַ֣ר אֶסְתֵּ֔ר

b ἔστησεν   קִיַּ֕ם

c   חֲמֻֽלֵּ֖ל הָאֵ֑לֶּה וְנִכְתָּ֖ב

d εἰς τὸν αἰῶνα,   בַּסֵּֽפֶר׃

e καὶ ἐγράφη   וְנִכְתָּ֖ב

f εἰς μνημόσυνον.   בַּסֵּֽפֶר׃

THE TEXTS OF ESTHER — CHAPTER 10

	LXX (Göttingen o')	MT (BHS 3)	AT (Göttingen L)	
10:1 a	"Ἔγραψεν δὲ ὁ βασιλεὺς	7:50 (10:1) וַיָּ֩שֶׂם֩	7:50 (10:1) Καὶ ἔγραψεν ὁ βασιλεὺς	a
b		הַמֶּ֨לֶךְ אֲחַשְׁרֹ֧שׁ ׀		b
c		מַ֛ס		c
d	ἐπὶ	עַל־		d
e	τὴν βασιλείαν	הָאָ֖רֶץ	τὰ τέλη	e
f	τῆς τε γῆς	וְאִיֵּ֥י הַיָּֽם׃	τῆς γῆς	f
g	καὶ τῆς θαλάσσης		καὶ θαλάσσης	g
				h
10:2 a	καὶ τὴν ἰσχὺν αὐτοῦ	(10:2) וְכָל־מַעֲשֵׂ֤ה	(10:2) καὶ τὴν ἰσχὺν αὐτοῦ,	i
b		תָקְפּוֹ֙ וּגְב֣וּרָת֔וֹ		j
c		וּפָרָשַׁת֙ גְּדֻלַּ֣ת		k
d	καὶ ἀνδραγαθίαν,	מָרְדֳּכַ֔י אֲשֶׁ֥ר גִּדְּל֖וֹ		l
e	πλοῦτόν τε	הַמֶּ֑לֶךְ הֲלוֹא־הֵ֣ם	πλοῦτόν τε	m
f	καὶ δόξαν τῆς βασιλείας αὐτοῦ·	כְּתוּבִ֗ים עַל־סֵ֙פֶר֙ דִּבְרֵ֣י הַיָּמִ֔ים	καὶ δόξαν τῆς βασιλείας αὐτοῦ.	n
g		7:51	καὶ ἐδόξασε Μαρδοχαῖος καὶ	a
h	ἰδοὺ			b
i	γέγραπται	מָדַ֥י וּפָרָֽס׃ לְמַלְכֵ֣י	ἔγραψεν	c

Chapter 10

THE TEXTS OF ESTHER — CHAPTER 10

	LXX (Göttingen o')		MT (BHS 3)	AT (Göttingen L)	
j	ἐν βιβλίῳ	f	עַל־סֵ֫פֶר	ἐν τοῖς βιβλίοις	d
k	βασιλέων	g	לְמַלְכֵי		e
l	Περσῶν καὶ Μήδων	h	פָּרַ֫ס וּמָדָֽי׃	Περσῶν καὶ Μήδων	f
m	εἰς μνημόσυνον.			εἰς μνημόσυνον.	g
10:3 a	ὁ δὲ Μαρδοχαῖος	10:3	כִּֽי מָרְדֳּכַ֫י	7:52 (10:3) ὁ δὲ Μαρδοχαῖος	a
b			הַיְּהוּדִ֞י		b
c	διεδέχετο		מִשְׁנֶה֙	διεδέχετο	c
d	τὸν βασιλέα		לַמֶּ֣לֶךְ	τὸν βασιλέα	d
e	Ἀρταξέρξην		אֲחַשְׁוֵר֔וֹשׁ	Ἀσσυῆρον	e
f	καὶ μέγας		וְגָדוֹל֙	καὶ μέγας	f
g	ἦν ἐν τῇ βασιλείᾳ		לַיְּהוּדִ֔ים	ἦν ἐν τῇ βασιλείᾳ	g
h	καὶ δεδοξασμένος		וְרָצ֖וּי	καὶ φιλούμενος	h
i	ὑπὸ τῶν Ἰουδαίων·		לְרֹ֣ב אֶחָ֑יו	ὑπὸ πάντων τῶν Ἰουδαίων	i
j	καὶ φιλούμενος				j
k	διηγεῖτο τὴν ἀγωγὴν			καὶ ἡγεῖτο αὐτῶν	k
l			דֹּרֵ֥שׁ טוֹב֙ לְעַמּ֔וֹ	καὶ δόξαν	l
m	παντὶ τῷ ἔθνει αὐτοῦ.		וְדֹבֵ֥ר שָׁל֖וֹם לְכָל־זַרְעֽוֹ׃	παντὶ τῷ ἔθνει αὐτοῦ	m

LXX (Göttingen o')	MT (BHS 3)	AT (Göttingen L)
	וַיָּשֶׂם הַמֶּלֶךְ אֲחַשְׁרֹשׁ ׀ מַס עַל־הָאָרֶץ וְאִיֵּי הַיָּם׃	περιετίθει.

n
o
p

THE TEXTS OF ESTHER — ADDITION F

		LXX (Göttingen o')	MT (BHS 3)	AT (Göttingen L)	
			– No Extant Hebrew Text –		
F:1	a	Καὶ εἶπεν Μαρδοχαῖος	7:53 (F:1)	Καὶ εἶπε Μαρδοχαῖος	a
	b	Παρὰ τοῦ θεοῦ ἐγένετο ταῦτα·		Παρὰ τοῦ θεοῦ ἐγένετο ταῦτα·	b
F:2	a	ἐμνήσθην γὰρ περὶ τοῦ ἐνυπνίου,	7:54 (F:2)	ἐμνήσθη γὰρ τοῦ ἐνυπνίου,	a
	b	οὗ εἶδον		οὗ εἶδεν.	b
	c	περὶ τῶν λόγων τούτων·			c
	d	οὐδὲ γὰρ παρῆλθεν ἀπ᾽ αὐτῶν λόγος.		καὶ ἀπετελέσθη	d
				καὶ εἶπεν	e
F:3	a	ἡ μικρὰ πηγή,	(F:3)	Ἡ μικρὰ πηγὴ	f
	b	ἣ ἐγένετο ποταμὸς			g
	c	καὶ ἦν φῶς			h
	d	καὶ ἥλιος			i
	e	καὶ ὕδωρ πολύ·			j
	f	Εσθηρ ἐστιν		Εσθηρ ἐστίν,	k
	g	ὁ ποταμός,			l
	h	ἣν ἐγάμησεν ὁ βασιλεὺς			m
	i	καὶ ἐποίησεν βασίλισσαν.			n
F:4	a	οἱ δὲ δύο δράκοντες	(F:4)	καὶ οἱ δύο δράκοντες	o

Addition F

THE TEXTS OF ESTHER — ADDITION F

	LXX (Göttingen o')	MT (BHS 3)	AT (Göttingen L)	
		– No Extant Hebrew Text –		
b	ἐγώ εἰμι καὶ Αμαν.		ἐγώ εἰμι καὶ Αμαν·	p
c		(F:5)	ποταμὸς	q
F:5 a	τὰ δὲ ἔθνη τὰ ἐπισυναχθέντα		τὰ ἔθνη τὰ συναχθέντα	r
b	ἀπολέσαι		ἀπολέσαι	s
c	τὸ ὄνομα τῶν Ἰουδαίων.		τοὺς Ἰουδαίους·	t
			ἥλιος καὶ φῶς	u
			ἢ ἐγένετο τοῖς Ἰουδαίοις	v
			ἐπιφανεία τοῦ θεοῦ,	w
			τοῦτο τὸ κρίμα.	x
F:6 a	τὸ δὲ ἔθνος τὸ ἐμὸν			
b	οὗτός ἐστιν Ισραηλ,			
c	οἱ βοήσαντες πρὸς τὸν θεον			
d	καὶ σωθέντες·			
e	καὶ ἔσωσεν κύριος τὸν λαὸν αὐτοῦ,			
f	καὶ ἐρρύσατο κύριος ἡμᾶς			
g	ἐκ πάντων τῶν κακῶν τούτων,			
h	καὶ ἐποίησεν ὁ θεὸς		7:55 (F:6) καὶ ἐποίησεν ὁ θεὸς	a

Addition F

THE TEXTS OF ESTHER — ADDITION F

	LXX (Göttingen o')	MT (BHS 3)		AT (Göttingen L)
		– No Extant Hebrew Text –		
i	τὰ σημεῖα		b	τὰ σημεῖα
j	καὶ τὰ τέρατα τὰ μεγάλα,		c	καὶ τὰ τέρατα ταῦτα,
k	ἃ οὐ γέγονεν ἐν τοῖς ἔθνεσιν.		d	ἃ οὐ γέγονεν ἐν τοῖς ἔθνεσιν.
F:7			e	
a	διὰ τοῦτο	(F:7)		
b	ἐποίησεν κλήρους δύο,		f	καὶ ἐποίησε κλήρους δύο,
c	ἕνα τῷ λαῷ τοῦ θεοῦ		g	ἕνα τῷ λαῷ τοῦ θεοῦ
d	καὶ ἕνα πᾶσιν τοῖς ἔθνεσιν·		h	καὶ ἕνα τοῖς ἔθνεσιν·
F:8		7:56 (F:8)	a	καὶ προσῆλθον
a	καὶ ἦλθον		b	οἱ δύο κλῆροι οὗτοι
b	οἱ δύο κλῆροι οὗτοι		c	εἰς ὥρας
c	εἰς ὥραν		d	κατὰ καιρὸν
d	καὶ καιρὸν		e	καὶ ἡμέρας
e	καὶ εἰς ἡμέραν		f	κυριεύσεως τοῦ αἰωνίου
f	κρίσεως ἐνώπιον τοῦ θεοῦ		g	ἐν πᾶσι τοῖς ἔθνεσιν.
g	καὶ πᾶσιν τοῖς ἔθνεσιν.			
F:9		7:57 (F:9)	a	καὶ ἐμνήσθη
a	καὶ ἐμνήσθη		b	ὁ θεὸς τοῦ λαοῦ αὐτοῦ ·
b	ὁ θεὸς τοῦ λαοῦ αὐτου		c	καὶ ἐδικαίωσε
c	καὶ ἐδικαίωσεν			

Addition F

THE TEXTS OF ESTHER — ADDITION F

	LXX (*Göttingen o'*)	MT (*BHS 3*)	AT (*Göttingen L*)
d	τὴν κληρονομίαν ἑαυτοῦ.		τὴν κληρονομίαν αὐτοῦ.
a		7:58	καὶ πᾶς ὁ λαὸς
b			ἀνεβόησε φωνῇ μεγάλῃ
c			καὶ εἶπεν Εὐλογητὸς εἶ, κύριε,
d			ὁ μνησθεὶς τῶν διαθηκῶν
e			τῶν πρὸς τοὺς πατέρας ἡμῶν·
f			ἀμήν.
F:10 a	καὶ ἔσονται αὐτοῖς	7:59 (F:10)	καὶ ἔσονται αὐτοῖς
b	αἱ ἡμέραι αὗται		αἱ ἡμέραι αὗται
c	ἐν μηνὶ Αδαρ		ἐν μηνὶ Αδαρ
d	τῇ τεσσαρεσκαιδεκάτῃ		ἐν τῇ τεσσαρεσκαιδεκάτῃ
e	καὶ τῇ πεντεκαιδεκάτῃ		καὶ τῇ πεντεκαιδεκάτῃ
f	τοῦ αὐτοῦ μηνὸς		τοῦ αὐτοῦ μηνὸς
g	μετὰ συναγωγῆς		μετὰ συναγωγῆς
h	καὶ χαρᾶς		καὶ χαρᾶς
i	καὶ εὐφροσύνης		καὶ εὐφροσύνης

– No Extant Hebrew Text –

Addition F

THE TEXTS OF ESTHER — ADDITION F

LXX (Göttingen o')	*MT (BHS 3)*	*AT (Göttingen L)*
	– No Extant Hebrew Text –	

	LXX (Göttingen o')		*AT (Göttingen L)*	
j	ἐνώπιον τοῦ θεοῦ		ἐνώπιον τοῦ θεοῦ	j
k	κατὰ γενεὰς εἰς τὸν αἰῶνα		κατὰ γενεὰς εἰς τὸν αἰῶνα	k
l	ἐν τῷ λαῷ αὐτοῦ Ισραηλ.		ἐν τῷ λαῷ αὐτοῦ Ισραηλ.	l
F:11 a	Ἔτους τετάρτου βασιλεύοντος			
b	Πτολεμαίου καὶ Κλεοπάτρας			
c	εἰσήνεγκεν Δοσίθεος,			
d	ὃς ἔφη εἶναι ἱερεὺς καὶ Λευίτης,			
e	καὶ Πτολεμαῖος ὁ υἱὸς αὐτοῦ			
f	τὴν προκειμένην ἐπιστολὴν			
g	τῶν Φρουραι			
h	ἣν ἔφασαν εἶναι,			
i	καὶ ἑρμηνευκέναι			
j	Λυσίμαχον Πτολεμαίου,			
k	τῶν ἐν Ιερουσαλημ.			

Addition F

APPENDIX 2: THE MANUSCRIPTS OF THE ALPHA–TEXT

The alpha–text of Esther is preserved only in four medieval manu–scripts:

Siglum		Manuscript	Date	Current Location
G.	C.[1]			
19	b	Chigi R.vi. 38	12th cent.	Vatican Library, Rome
93	e_2	Royal I.D.2	13th cent.	British Library, London
108	*b*	Vat. Gr. 330	13th cent.	Vatican Library, Rome
319	y	Vatop. 600	1021 A.D.	Mt. Athos, Greece

Manuscript 19, Chigi, 12th–century

Unlike Royal I.D.2 and Vat. Gr. 330 which contain both the LXX and AT of Esther, the Chigi ms. contains only the alpha-text of Esther. It is written on eleven pages, one column per page in a finely written hand in small but clear, well-formed characters. Of the three examined, the Chigi manuscript is the most aesthetically pleasing to the eye. In this manuscript the alpha–text of Esther is preceded by the Pentateuch, Joshua, Judges, 1–4 Kings, 1–2 Chronicles, 1 Esdras, and Judith; it is followed by 1–2 Maccabees.

A notable feature of the AT of Esther in this manuscript is that it has the colophon at the end referring to Ptolemy and Cleopatra which is otherwise found only on manuscripts of the LXX text of Esther.

---

[1] G. = Göttingen notation; C. = Cambridge notation

Manuscript 93, Royal, 13th–century

This manuscript of the alpha–text of Esther is written with a bold hand with well-formed letters on twelve pages in two columns per page. It contains two copies of Esther; the first is the alpha-text, the second the LXX text. This manuscript of the AT contains chapter numbers.

The AT of Esther is preceded by 1–4 Kings, 1–2 Chronicles, and Esdras; it is followed by 1–3 Maccabees, the LXX text of Esther and, in a different hand, Isaiah.

Of the three manuscripts examined, ms. 93 has the most interesting features. The title of both copies of Esther is spelled αισθηρ, even though Esther's name is clearly spelled εσθηρ within the text. The six letters of the title of the book are split in two, with the first three letters written over the first column and the last three over the second column on each page.

The manuscript has been extensively corrected intra–line; furthermore, its margins contain extensive notes written in Greek in a second hand and some notes written in Latin.

Of greater interest are nine lacunae deliberately indicated by the original hand. Apparently, the exemplar of the AT from which ms. 93 was copied was defective in nine places. The scribe copied the text until it broke off, left a few blank lines to indicate the lacuna, then picked up where the text resumed. Subsequently a second hand filled in the lacunae, using an ink which has faded much more than that used by the original scribe. Of the nine lacunae, six are filled with text from the LXX of Esther, two are filled with asterisks, apparently because the AT of Esther differs so greatly from the LXX in those sections that there is no corresponding text. One lacuna is filled with text which this writer could not identify. The lacunae are located and filled as follows:

Lacuna	Location	AT text stops	AT text resumes	Filled by
1	pg. 1, col. 1	A:9	A:11b	LXX A:11,12a
2	pg. 3, col. 4	1:20b	1:21b	unidentified text
3	pg. 4, col. 6	B:15	B:15b	LXX B:2 (ms. 130 = AT)
4	pg. 5, col. 9	C:13b	C:13c	LXX C:2b
5	pg. 7, col. 12	5(D):1	5:2c (D:3)	LXX D:2
6	pg. 8, col. 14	6:4a	6:4b	asterisks
7	pg. 9, col. 16	7:7	7:9	asterisks
8	pg. 10, col. 19	E:26	E:26	LXX E:14
9	pg. 11, col. 21	9:50 (10:1)	9:51	LXX 10:2

It is interesting that lacuna 3 was filled with a text which is identical in both the AT and LXX except that the AT reading includes a definite article which is lacking in all manuscripts of the LXX, except one, ms. 130. Therefore the exemplar from which this lacuna was filled was either a manuscript of the AT or, more likely, a LXX manuscript of the lineage of ms. 130. Where the text can be identified, all other lacunae in this manuscript were filled with a reading from the LXX. Clearly manuscripts of the AT of Esther were corrected using the LXX manuscripts of Esther. The mingling of the AT and LXX is further indicated by the appearance in ms. 19 of the AT of the colophon otherwise found only at the end of the LXX text of Esther.

Another distinctive feature of ms. 93 is that margin numbers divide the text into ten chapters. The beginning of chapters 2–10 are indicated by a number followed by a colon and ~ (e.g., 2:~). A square bracket ([) marks the first word of the chapter within the line of text. The divisions are located as follows:

chapter 2:~	ms. pg. 3, col. 4
3:~	3, col. 5
4:~	5, col. 8
5:~	6, col. 11
6:~	8, col. 14
7:~	8, col. 15
8:~	9, col. 17

9:~	11, col. 20
10:~	11, col. 21

In this manuscript the LXX text of Esther is annotated using text critical marks to indicate additions and deletions with respect to the Hebrew text.

Manuscript 108, Vat. Gr. 330, 13th–century

Ms. 108 is written in a neat, crisp hand. The AT of Esther comprises 17–1/2 pages, one column per page. Both the AT and LXX texts of Esther are contained in this manuscript. The AT of Esther is preceded by the Pentateuch, Joshua, Judges, Ruth, 1–4 Kings, 1–2 Chronicles, Esdras, and Judith; it is followed by the LXX of Esther and Tobit. The LXX text of Esther comprises 20–1/2 pages, one column per page, written in the same hand as the AT of Esther.The manuscript is characterized by large, ornate capital letters written in the left margin to indicate paragraph (or section) breaks.

Manuscript 319, Vatop. 600, A.D. 1021

A confusion in the Mt. Athos sigla prevented my examination of this manuscript. Hanhart's Göttingen edition of Esther (pg. 15) and Jellicoe (1989, 364) both list ms. 319 as Vatopedi 513 of the Mt. Athos library. However, 513 was apparently its number under and old system. The correct current sigla in the Athos catalogue is Vatopedi 600. Unfortunately, the correct current sigla was not identified until after this work was completed.

Appendix 3:

Tables of Data from Syntax Criticism

Syntactical Data for the Alpha–Text of Esther

AT Table 1: *Summary of Criteria*

Seventeen criteria used to determine if a text is translation or composition Greek have been applied to the AT of Esther. The value of each criterion indicates whether the text is exhibiting, for that syntactical feature, characteristics of translation Greek (T) or composition Greek (C). A value is deemed inconclusive (I) if either the syntactical feature does not occur within the given pericope or if the value of the criterion falls between translation and composition Greek.

Table 1. Summary of Martin's Criteria Applied to the Alpha–text of Esther

Chapter:	A	1	2	3	B	4	C	D	5	6	7	E	8	9	10	F	Proto– Total	Proto– AT	Proto– Fox[1]
1: διά gen.	I	T	I	I	C	I	I	I	I	I	I	C	I	I	I	I	T	T	C
2: διά total	I	T	I	C	C	I	I	I	I	I	I	C	I	C	I	I	T	T	T
3: εἰς	I	T	C	C	T	C	C	T	C	T	T	C	I	C	T	T	C	C	T
4: κατά ac.	T	C	C	C	I	I	C	C	C	C	C	C	I	I	I	C	I	I	I
5: tot. κατά	T	C	C	T	C	C	I	C	C	C	T	C	I	I	I	C	C	C	I
6: περί	C	T	I	C	C	C	I	I	I	T	T	I	I	I	I	I	T	T	T
7: πρός dt.	I	I	I	I	I	I	I	I	I	I	I	C	I	I	I	I	T	I	I
8: ὑπό gen.	I	I	I	I	C	I	I	I	I	I	I	C	I	I	C	I	T	T	I
9: καί cop.	T	T	T	T	C	T	T	T	T	T	T	T	T	T	I	T	T	T	T
10: sep.art.	I	T	I	C	C	I	I	I	T	I	T	C	I	I	I	I	I	I	T

continues ...

---

1 Fox's calculation from his analysis of 57 lines of the AT as published in M. V. Fox, *The Redaction of the Books of Esther*, (Atlanta: Scholars Press, 1991) 32–33.

AT Table 1: *Summary of Criteria, cont.*

Table 1. Summary of Martin's Criteria Applied to the Alpha-text of Esther, cont.

Chapter:	A	1	2	3	B	4	C	D	5	6	7	E	8	9	10	F	Proto— Total	AT	Fox 2
11: gen. pre.	I	I	I	I	C	I	I	I	I	I	I	C	C	I	I	I	I	T	T
12: gen. pronouns	T	T	T	T	C	T	T	T	T	T	T	C	T	C	T	T	T	T	T
13: gen. pro. an. s.	T	T	T	T	T	T	T	T	I	I	T	T	T	I	I	I	T	T	T
14: attrib. adj. prec.	I	I	I	I	T	I	I	I	T	I	I	C	C	I	I	I	I	I	I
15: attrib adj.	I	I	I	T	C	C	C	I	C	T	T	C	T	T	T	I	I	T	T
16: adv. ptc.	T	T	I	I	C	C	T	C	T	C	T	C	T	I	I	I	I	T	T
17: dative case	T	T	C	T	C	C	T	T	C	C	T	C	C	T	T	T	T	T	T
# trans.	7	10	4	7	3	5	5	5	5	5	11	1	5	3	3	4	9	11	11
# comp.	1	2	4	2	12	5	2	3	5	3	0	15	2	3	1	2	2	2	1
# inconcl.	9	5	9	8	2	7	10	9	7	9	6	1	10	11	13	11	6	4	5
Origin	I	T	I	I	C	I	I	I	I	I	T	C	I	I	I	I	T	T	T

2 Fox's calculation from his analysis of 57 lines of the AT as published in M. V. Fox, *The Redaction of the Books of Esther*, (Atlanta: Scholars Press, 1991) 32–33.

Martin's Criteria 1-8: The Relative Infrequency of Certain Prepositions with Respect to ἐν in Translation Greek.

Table a'. The Frequency of Occurrence by Chapter

chapter:	A	1	2	3	B	4	C	D	5	6	7	E	8	9	10	F	Total	Proto–AT
ἐν	5	14	1	6	4	3	12	5	3	5	6	5	2	5	2	5	83	47
1. διά with gen.	0	1	0	0	2	0	0	0	0	0	0	3	0	0	0	0	6	1
2. διά total	0	1	0	0	3	0	0	0	0	0	0	4	0	2	0	0	10	3
3. εἰς	0	4	1	5	2	4	9	1	5	2	2	5	0	4	1	2	47	28
4. κατά with acc.	1	4	3	1	1	0	0	2	1	0	1	3	0	0	0	2	19	10
5. κατά total	1	4	3	1	1	1	0	2	1	2	1	5	0	0	0	2	24	13
6. περί	6	1	0	2	0	1	0	0	0	1	1	0	0	0	0	0	12	6
7. πρός with dat.	0	0	0	0	0	0	0	0	0	0	0	2	0	0	0	0	2	0
8. ὑπό with gen.	0	0	0	0	1	0	0	0	0	0	0	4	0	0	1	0	6	1

AT Table a: *Criteria 1–8*

Martin's Criteria 1-8: The Relative Infrequency of Certain Prepositions with Respect to ἐν in Translation Greek.

The relative frequency is the ratio of the number of occurrences of the given preposition to the number of occurrences of ἐν. Translation Greek is indicated when the following relative frequencies occur:

1. διά with the genitive: .01–06	4. κατά with accusative: .01–18	7. πρός with dative: .01–02
2. διά in all occurrences: .01–18	5. κατά in all occurrences: .01–19	8. ὑπό with genitive: .01–07
3. εἰς in all occurrences: .01–49	6. περί in all occurrences: .01–27	

Table a. The Relative Frequency of Prepositions in Relation to the Frequency of ἐν.

chapter:	A	1	2	3	B	4	C	D	5	6	7	E	8	9	10	F	Total	Proto-AT	Fox [1]	LXX [2]
1. διά with gen.	—	.07	—	—	.5	—	—	—	—	—	—	.6	—	—	—	—	.07	.02	.14	.11
2. διά total	—	.07	—	—	.75	—	—	—	—	—	—	.8	—	.4	—	—	.12	.06	.14	.18
3. εἰς	.29	1	.83	.5	.5	1.3	.75	.2	1.6	.4	.33	1.0	—	.8	.5	.4	.57	.60	.21	.50
4. κατά with acc.	.2	.3	.16	.16	.25	—	.4	.4	.33	—	.17	.6	—	—	—	.4	.23	.21	.28	.18
5. κατά total	.2	.3	.16	.16	.25	.33	.4	.4	.33	.4	.17	1.0	—	—	—	.4	.29	.28	.35	.22
6. περί	1.2	.07	—	.33	—	.33	—	—	—	.2	.17	.4	—	—	—	—	.14	.13	.21	.11
7. πρός with dat.	—	—	—	—	—	—	—	—	—	—	—	.4	—	—	—	—	.02	—	.07	.015
8. ὑπό with gen.	—	—	—	—	.25	—	—	—	—	—	—	.8	—	—	.5	—	.07	.02	—	.097

(Dash, "—", indicates that the syntactical feature did not occur within the given pericope.)

---

[1] Fox's calculation from his analysis of 57 lines of AT as published in M. V. Fox, *The Redaction of the Books of Esther*, (Atlanta: Scholars Press, 1991) 32–33.

[2] Martin's calculation from his analysis of the LXX of Esther as published in R. A. Martin, *Syntactical Evidence of Semitic Sources in Greek Documents* (SBLSCS:Missoula: Scholars Press, 1974) 7.

AT Table b: *Criterion #9*

Martin's Criterion #9: The Relative Frequency of καί Copulative with Respect to δέ

Translation Greek is indicated if the ratio of the number of occurrences of καί copulative to the number of occurrences of δέ is ≥ 2.0. Composition Greek is indicated if the ratio is < 1.

Table b. Number of Occurrences of καί Copulative and δέ and their Ratios

chapter:	A	1	2	3	B	4	C	D	5	6	7	E	8	9	10	F	Total	Proto-AT	Fox[1]
καί	21	16	21	17	2	18	14	19	13	26	15	3	14	7	2	9	217	147	na
δέ	1	4	2	3	4	5	3	3	3	5	4	11	4	2	1	0	55	33	na
Ratio	21	4.0	10.5	5.6	0.5	3.6	4.7	6.3	4.3	5.2	3.75	0.3	3.5	3.5	2	—	3.9	4.5	3.86
Origin	T	T	T	T	C	T	T	T	T	T	T	C	T	T	I	I	T	T	T

(Dash, "—", indicates that the syntactical feature did not occur in the given pericope.)

T – Translation Greek indicated; C – Composition Greek indicated; I – Inconclusive (either the syntactical feature does not occur within the given pericope or the ratio is on the border between translation and composition Greek.)

---

[1] Fox's calculation from his analysis of 57 lines of the AT as published in M. V. Fox, *The Redaction of the Books of Esther*, (Atlanta: Scholars Press, 1991) 32. "na" indicates that Fox's data is not available (not published).

Martin's Criterion #10: Separation of the Definite Article from its Substantive Translation Greek is indicated if the ratio of the number of separated definite articles to the total number of definite articles is ≤ 0.05. Composition Greek is indicated if the ratio is > 0.18.

Table c. Frequency of Occurrences of the Definite Article and Ratios

Chapter:	A	1	2	3	B	4	C	D	5	6	7	E	8	9	10	F	Total	Proto-AT	Fox[1]
Separated articles	4	2	1	3	10	2	4	4	1	6	1	33	6	5	1	4	87	28	na
Total articles	52	81	37	48	42	36	64	42	45	72	59	80	47	38	10	35	788	473	na
Ratio	.07	.02	.02	.06	.23	.05	.06	.09	.02	.08	.02	.4	.13	.13	.10	.11	.11	.06	.006
Origin	I	T	T	T	C	T	I	I	T	I	T	C	C	I	I	I	I	I	T

T – Translation Greek; C – Composition Greek; I – Inconclusive (the ratio falls between the limits given by Martin.)

---

[1] Fox's calculation from his analysis of 57 lines of the AT as published in M. V. Fox, *The Redaction of the Books of Esther* (Atlanta: Scholars Press, 1991) 32. "na" indicates that Fox's data is not available (not published).

Martin's Criterion #11: Infrequency of Dependent Genitives Preceding the Word on Which They Depend

Translation Greek is indicated if the ratio of the number of dependent genitives following the word on which they depend to the number of dependent genitives preceding the word on which they depend is ≥ 22. Composition Greek is indicated if the ratio is ≤ 3.

Table d. Occurrence of Dependent Genitives

Chapter:	A	1	2	3	B	4	C	D	5	6	7	E	8	9	10	F	Total	Proto–AT	Fox[1]
Genitive Follows	19	29	15	19	5	9	53	29	19	17	28	10	6	3	7	8	276	152	na
Genitive Precedes	2	—	—	—	4	—	—	—	—	—	9	1	—	—	—	—	16	1	na
Ratio	9.5	—	—	—	1.25	—	—	—	—	—	1.1	6	—	—	—	—	17.25	152	65
Origin	I	I	I	I	C	I	I	I	I	I	C	C	I	I	I	I	I	T	T

(Dash, "___", indicates that the syntactical feature does not occur within the given pericope.)

T – Translation Greek; C – Composition Greek; I – Inconclusive (either the syntactical feature does not occur within the given pericope or the ratio is on the border between translation and composition Greek.)

---

1 Fox's calculation from his analysis of 57 lines of the AT as published in M. V. Fox, *The Redaction of the Books of Esther* (Atlanta: Scholars Press, 1991) 32. "na" indicates Fox's data is not available (not published).

Martin's Criterion #12: Greater Frequency of Genitive Personal Pronouns in Translation Greek

Translation Greek is indicated if the ratio of the number of lines of text to the number of genitive personal pronouns is ≤ 9. Composition Greek is indicated if the ratio is > 9.

Table e. Occurrence of Genitive Personal Pronouns

Chapter:	A	1	2	3	B	4	C	D	5	6	7	E	8	9	10	F	Total	Proto–AT	Fox[1]
# Lines of Text	32	41	20	30	27	26	55	25	27	43	32	47	26	19	6	16	472	270	na
Genitive Personal Pronouns	10	11	6	7	2	8	44	19	17	12	22	1	4	1	4	4	172	92	na
Ratio	3.2	3.7	3.3	4.3	13.5	3.25	1.25	1.3	1.6	3.6	1.6	47	6.5	19	1.5	4.0	2.7	2.9	2.95
Origin	T	T	T	T	C	T	T	T	T	T	T	C	T	C	T	T	T	T	T

T – Translation Greek; C – Composition Greek

---

[1] Fox's calculation from his analysis of 57 lines of the AT as published in M. V. Fox, *The Redaction of the Books of Esther* (Atlanta: Scholars Press, 1991) 32. "na" indicates that Fox's data is not available (not published).

AT Table f: *Criterion #13*

Martin's Criterion #13: Greater Frequency of Genitive Personal Pronouns Dependent on Anarthrous Substantives

Translation Greek is indicated if the ratio of the number of lines of text to the number of genitive personal pronouns dependent on anarthrous substantives is ≤ 77. Composition Greek is indicated if the ratio is > 100.

Table f. Occurrence of Genitive Personal Pronouns Dependent on Anarthrous Substantives

Chapter:	A	1	2	3	B	4	C	D	5	6	7	E	8	9	10	F	Total	Proto–AT	Fox[1]
# Lines of Text	32	41	20	30	27	26	55	25	27	43	32	47	26	19	6	16	472	270	na
Gen. Pronoun with anarth. substantive	2	1	3	3	1	1	11	3	—	—	3	1	1	—	—	—	30	12	na
Ratio	16	41	6.7	10.0	27	26	5	8.3	—	—	10.7	47	26	—	—	—	15.7	22.5	29.5
Origin	T	T	T	T	T	T	T	T	I	I	T	T	T	I	I	I	T	T	T

(Dashes, "—", indicate that the syntactical feature does not occur in the given pericope.)

T – Translation Greek; C – Composition Greek; I – Inconclusive (the syntactical feature does not occur in the given pericope.)

---

1 Fox's calculation from his analysis of 57 lines of the AT as published in M. V. Fox, *The Redaction of the Books of Esther* (Atlanta: Scholars Press, 1991) 32. "na" indicates that Fox's data is not available (not published).

AT Table g: *Criterion #14*

Martin's Criterion #14: Infrequency of Attributive Adjectives Preceding the Word They Qualify

Translation Greek is indicated if the ratio of the number of attributive adjectives preceding the word they qualify to the number of attributive adjectives following the word they qualify is ≤ 0.35.

Composition Greek is indicated by a ratio >1.

Table g. Occurrence of Attributive Adjectives

Chapter:	A	1	2	3	B	4	C	D	5	6	7	E	8	9	10	F	Total	Proto–AT	Fox[1]
Adjective Precedes	—	—	—	—	2	—	5	—	1	—	—	13	1	1	—	1	24	3	na
Adjective Follows	4	8	3	2	5	2	7	—	5	2	1	5	1	—	—	1	46	24	na
Ratio	—				.4		.7		.2			2.6					.5	.1	.5
Origin	I	I	I	I	T	I	I	I	T	I	I	C	C	I	I	I	I	I	I

(Dash, "—", indicates the syntactical feature does not occur in the given pericope.)

T – Translation Greek; C – Composition Greek; I – Inconclusive (either the syntactical feature does not occur in the given pericope or the ratio falls between the limits given by Martin.)

---

[1] Fox's calculation from his analysis of 57 lines of the AT as published in M. V. Fox, *The Redaction of the Books of Esther*, (Atlanta: Scholars Press, 1991) 32. "na" indicates Fox's data is not available (not published).

AT Table h: _Criterion #15_

Martin's Criterion #15: Relative Infrequency of Attributive Adjectives

Translation Greek is indicated if the ratio of the number of lines of text per attributive adjective is > 10. Composition Greek is indicated if the ratio is < 6.5.

Table h. Occurrence of Attributive Adjectives

Chapter:	A	1	2	3	B	4	C	D	5	6	7	E	8	9	10	F	Total	Proto–AT	Fox[1]
# Lines of Text	32	41	20	30	27	26	55	25	27	43	32	47	26	19	6	16	472	270	na
# of adjectives	4	8	3	2	7	2	12	—	6	2	1	18	2	1	—	2	70	27	na
Ratio	8	5	6.7	15	3.9	13	4.5	—	4.5	21.5	32	2.6	13	19	—	8	6.7	10	19.6
Origin	I	I	I	T	C	T	C	I	C	T	T	C	T	T	I	I	I	T	T

(Dash, "—", indicates the syntactical feature does not occur in the given pericope.)

T – Translation Greek; C – Composition Greek; I – Inconclusive (either the syntactical feature
does not occur in the given pericope or the ratio falls between the limits given by Martin.)

---

[1] Fox's calculation from his analysis of 57 lines of the AT as published in M. V. Fox, _The Redaction of the Books of Esther_
(Atlanta: Scholars Press, 1991) 33. "na" indicates Fox's data is not available (not published).

AT Table i: *Criterion #16*

Martin's Criterion #16: Infrequency of Adverbial Participles in Translation Greek

Translation Greek is indicated if the ratio of the number of lines of text to the number of adverbial participles is > 6. Composition Greek is indicated if the ratio is < 6.

Table i. Occurrence of Adverbial Participles

Chapter:	A	1	2	3	B	4	C	D	5	6	7	E	8	9	10	F	Total	Proto–AT	Fox[1]
# lines of text	32	41	20	30	27	26	55	25	27	43	32	47	26	19	6	16	472	270	na
# adverbial participles	3	3	—	5	8	6	3	10	3	10	5	18	3	—	1	—	78	36	na
Ratio	10.7	13.7	—	6.0	3.4	4.3	18.3	2.5	9.0	4.3	6.4	2.6	8.7	—	6.0	—	6.1	7.5	10.7
Origin	T	T	I	I	C	C	C	C	C	C	C	C	T	I	I	I	I	T	T

(Dashes, "—", indicate the syntactical feature does not occur in the given pericope.)

T – Translation Greek; C – Composition Greek; I – Inconclusive (either the syntactical feature does not occur in the given pericope or the ratio is between translation and composition Greek.)

---

[1] Fox's calculation from his analysis of 57 lines of the AT as published in M. V. Fox, *The Redaction of the Books of Esther*, (Atlanta: Scholars Press, 1991) 33. "na" indicates Fox's data not available (not published).

Martin's Criterion #17: Frequency of the Dative Case

Translation Greek is indicated if the ratio of the number of datives not used with $\dot{\epsilon}\nu$ to the number of datives used with $\dot{\epsilon}\nu$ is < 2. Composition Greek is indicated if the ratio is > 3.

Table j. Occurrence of Dative Case[1]

Chapter:	A	1	2	3	B	4	C	D	5	6	7	E	8	9	10	F	Total	Proto-AT	Fox 2
Dative without $\dot{\epsilon}\nu$	6	11	8	12	17	7	13	5	6	15	6	26	15	5	1	5	158	86	na
Dative with $\dot{\epsilon}\nu$	5	14	1	7	3	3	12	6	2	6	6	4	2	5	2	5	83	48	na
Ratio	1.2	0.8	8.0	1.7	5.7	2.3	1.1	0.8	3.0	2.5	1.0	6.5	7.5	1.0	0.5	1.0	1.9	1.8	2
Origin	T	T	C	T	C	C	T	T	C	C	T	C	C	T	T	T	T	T	T

T – Translation Greek; C – Composition Greek

[1] To conform to the counting used by Martin and Fox, datives used with forms of λέγω, εἶπον and δίδωμι have been excluded from this count.

[2] Fox's calculation from his analysis of 57 lines of the AT as published in M. V. Fox, *The Redaction of the Books of Esther*, (Atlanta: Scholars Press, 1991) 33. "na" indicates Fox's data not available (not published).

Syntactical Data for the LXX of Esther

LXX Table 1: *Summary of Criteria*

Seventeen criteria used to determine if a text is translation or composition Greek have been applied to the LXX of Esther. The value of each criterion indicates whether the text is exhibiting, for that syntactical feature, characteristics of translation Greek (T) or composition Greek (C). A value is deemed inconclusive (I) if either the syntactical feature does not occur within the given pericope or if the value of the criterion falls between the values given by Martin for translation and composition Greek.

Table 1. Summary of Martin's Criteria Applied to LXX-text of Esther

Chapter:	A	1	2	3	B	4	C	D	5	6	7	E	8	9	10	F	Total	Proto–LXX	Fox[1]
1: διά gen.	I	C	I	C	C	C	I	I	I	C	I	C	C	I	I	I	C	C	C
2: διά total	I	T	I	C	C	T	I	I	I	C	I	C	C	C	I	C	C	I	C
3: εἰς	I	T	C	C	C	C	C	T	C	T	C	C	T	T	T	C	I	I	C
4: κατά ac.	I	C	T	C	C	I	I	I	I	I	I	I	C	T	I	C	T	T	C
5: tot κατά	I	C	I	C	C	I	I	I	I	T	T	I	C	T	I	C	T	C	C
6: περί	C	T	C	I	I	C	I	I	I	C	T	T	I	I	I	C	T	T	C
7: πρός dt.	I	I	I	I	I	I	I	I	C	I	I	C	C	C	C	I	C	C	I
8: ὑπό gen.	I	C	T	C	C	I	I	I	I	I	I	C	C	C	I	I	C	C	C
9: καί cop.	T	T	I	T	C	T	T	T	T	T	C	C	I	T	C	C	T	T	I
10: sep. art.	I	T	T	C	C	I	I	I	I	T	I	C	I	I	I	I	I	I	T

continues ...

---

[1] Fox's calculation from his analysis of 57 lines of the LXX as published in M. V. Fox, *The Redaction of the Books of Esther* (Atlanta: Scholars Press, 1991) 32.

LXX Table 1: Summary of Criteria, cont.

Table 1. Summary of Martin's Criteria Applied to LXX–text of Esther, cont.

Chapter:	A	1	2	3	B	4	C	D	5	6	7	E	8	9	10	F	Total	Proto–LXX	Fox 2
11: gen.pre.	I	I	T	I	C	I	I	I	I	I	I	C	I	I	I	I	I	T	T
12: gen. pron.	T	T	T	T	C	T	T	T	T	C	T	C	T	T	T	T	T	T	T
13: gen.pron. anarth. sub.	T	I	T	I	T	T	T	T	T	T	I	T	I	T	I	I	T	T	I
14: attrib. adj. prec.	T	I	T	I	C	T	T	T	I	I	C	C	T	C	I	C	T	T	C
15: attrib.adj.	C	T	I	T	C	I	I	C	I	T	T	C	I	I	I	C	C	I	T
16: adv.ptc.	I	T	T	T	C	C	T	C	T	T	C	C	T	T	T	T	T	T	T
17: dat. case	T	I	T	I	I	C	T	T	T	I	I	C	T	T	T	T	T	T	C
# trans.	5	8	9	4	5	5	6	6	5	6	3	1	5	8	3	4	9	9	4
# comp.	2	4	2	7	13	5	1	2	2	4	4	13	6	4	1	7	5	4	9
# inconcl.	10	5	6	6	3	7	10	9	10	7	10	3	6	5	13	6	3	4	3
Origin	I	T	T	C	C	I	I	I	I	T	I	C	I	T	I	C	T	T	C

Fox's calculation from his analysis of 57 lines of the LXX as published in M. V. Fox, *The Redaction of the Books of Esther* (Atlanta: Scholars Press, 1991) 32–33.

Martin's Criteria 1-8: The Relative Infrequency of Certain Prepositions with Respect to ἐν in Translation Greek.

Table a'. The Frequency of Occurrence Distributed by Chapter

chapter:	A	1	2	3	B	4	C	D	5	6	7	E	8	9	10	F	Total	Proto-LXX
ἐν	6	9	11	7	5	6	17	4	4	8	4	4	10	15	2	4	116	76
1. διά with gen.	0	1	0	2	2	1	0	0	0	2	0	2	2	1	0	0	13	9
2. διά total	0	1	0	2	3	1	0	0	0	2	0	4	3	5	0	1	22	14
3. εἰς	2	2	6	4	4	5	9	1	7	2	3	4	2	6	1	3	61	38
4. κατά with acc.	0	6	1	2	2	0	0	0	0	0	0	0	4	1	0	1	17	14
5. κατά total	0	6	1	4	2	0	0	0	0	1	0	0	4	2	0	1	21	18
6. περί	3	1	0	0	0	2	0	0	0	3	1	0	0	0	0	2	12	7
7. πρός with dat.	0	0	1(?)	0	0	0	0	0	1(?)	0	0	1	1(?)	1(?)	0	0	5	4
8. ὑπό with gen.	0	2	0	1	1	0	0	0	0	0	0	3	3	2	0	0	12	8

LXX Table a: *Criteria 1-8*

Martin's Criteria 1-8: The Relative Infrequency of Certain Prepositions with Respect to ἐν in Translation Greek.

The relative frequency is the ratio of the number of occurrences of the given preposition to the number of occurrences of ἐν. Translation Greek is indicated when the following relative frequencies occur:

1. διά with the genitive: .01 – .06	4. κατά with accusative: .01 – .18	7. πρός with dative: .01 – .024
2. διά in all occurrences: .01 – .18	5. κατά in all occurrences: .01 – .19	8. ὑπό with genitive: .01 – .07
3. εἰς in all occurrences: .01 – .49	6. περί in all occurrences: .01 – .27	

Table a. The Relative Frequency of Prepositions in Relation to the Frequency of ἐν.

chapter:	A	1	2	3	B	4	C	D	5	6	7	E	8	9	10	F	Total	Proto-LXX	Fox 1	Martin 2
1. διά with gen.	—	.11	—	.29	.4	.17	—	—	—	.25	—	.50	.20	.07	—	—	.11	.12	1.16	.11
2. διά total	—	.11	—	.29	.6	.17	—	—	—	.25	—	1.0	.3	.27	—	.25	.19	.18	1.16	.18
3. εἰς	.33	.22	.55	.57	.8	.83	.53	.25	1.75	.25	.75	1.0	.20	.4	.50	.75	.53	.50	.83	.50
4. κατά with acc.	—	.66	.09	.29	.40	—	—	—	—	—	—	—	.40	.07	—	.25	.15	.18	.50	.18
5. κατά total	—	.66	.09	.57	.40	—	—	—	—	.13	—	—	.40	.13	—	.25	.18	.24	.66	.22
6. περί	0.5	.11	—	—	—	.33	—	—	—	.38	.25	—	—	—	—	.50	.10	.09	.33	.11
7. πρός with dat.	—	—	.09	—	—	—	—	—	.25	—	—	.25	.10	.07	—	—	.04	.05	—	.015
8. ὑπό with gen.	—	.22	—	.14	.20	—	—	—	—	—	—	.75	.30	.13	—	—	.10	.11	.66	.097

---

[1] Fox's calculation from his analysis of 57 lines of LXX as published in M. V. Fox, *The Redaction of the Books of Esther*, (Atlanta: Scholars Press, 1991) 32–33.

[2] Martin's calculation from his analysis of the LXX of Esther as published in R. A. Martin, *Syntactical Evidence of Semitic Sources in Greek Documents* (SBLSCS:Missoula: Scholars Press, 1974) 7.

Martin's Criterion #9: The Relative Frequency of καί Copulative with Respect to δέ

Translation Greek is indicated if the ratio of the number of occurrences of καί copulative to the number of occurrences of δέ is ≥ 2.0. Composition Greek is indicated if the ratio is < 1.

Table b. Number of Occurrences of καί Copulative and δέ and their Ratios

chapter:	A	1	2	3	B	4	C	D	5	6	7	E	8	9	10	F	Total	Proto-LXX	Fox[1]
καί	20	23	41	20	1	24	34	22	18	15	6	3	16	24	2	12	281	189	na
δέ	2	4	5	7	7	8	2	3	5	13	13	10	10	10	2	3	104	77	na
Ratio	10.0	5.75	5.86	4.0	.14	3.0	17.0	7.3	3.6	1.15	.46	.30	1.6	2.4	1	4.0	2.70	2.45	1.7
Origin	T	T	T	T	C	T	T	T	T	I	C	C	C	T	C	T	T	T	I

(Dash, "—", indicates that the syntactical feature did not occur in the given pericope.)

T – Translation Greek indicated; C – Composition Greek indicated; I – Inconclusive (either the syntactical feature does not occur within the given pericope or the ratio is on the border between translation and composition Greek.)

---

1 Fox's calculation from his analysis of 57 lines of the LXX as published in M. V. Fox, *The Redaction of the Books of Esther* (Atlanta: Scholars Press, 1991) 32. "na" indicates that Fox's data is not available (not published).

Martin's Criterion #10: Separation of the Definite Article from its Substantive

Translation Greek is indicated if the ratio of the number of separated definite articles to the total number of definite articles is ≤ 0.05. Composition Greek is indicated if the ratio is > 0.18.

Table c. Frequency of Occurrences of the Definite Article and Ratios

Chapter:	A	1	2	3	B	4	C	D	5	6	7	E	8	9	10	F	Total	Proto-LXX	Fox[1]
Separated articles	4	4	10	13	12	5	5	5	0	3	4	40	9	15	2	7	138	65	na
Total articles	44	91	101	60	39	56	59	38	42	64	46	82	66	108	12	41	949	646	na
Ratio	.09	.04	.099	.22	.31	.09	.08	.13	—	.05	.09	.49	.14	.14	.17	.17	.15	.10	.016
Origin	I	T	I	C	C	I	I	I	—	T	T	C	I	I	I	I	I	I	T

T – Translation Greek; C – Composition Greek; I – Inconclusive (the ratio falls between the limits given by Martin.)

---

[1] Fox's calculation from his analysis of 57 lines of the LXX as published in M. V. Fox, *The Redaction of the Books of Esther*, (Atlanta: Scholars Press, 1991) 32. "na" indicates that Fox's data is not available (not published).

LXX Table d: Criterion #11

Martin's Criterion #11: Infrequency of Dependent Genitives Preceding the Word on Which They Depend

Translation Greek is indicated if the ratio of the number of dependent genitives following the word on which they depend to the number of dependent genitives preceding the word on which they depend is ≥ 22. Composition Greek is indicated if the ratio is ≤ 3.

Table d. Occurrence of Dependent Genitives

Chapter:	A	1	2	3	B	4	C	D	5	6	7	E	8	9	10	F	Total	Proto–LXX	Fox 1
Genitive Follows	13	23	27	14	2	10	65	24	8	10	11	6	13	17	6	10	259	139	na
Genitive Precedes	4	—	1	1	5	1	—	—	1	1	—	14	1	—	—	—	29	6	na
Ratio	3.25	—	27	14	0.40	10	—	—	8.0	10.0	—	0.43	13.0	—	—	—	8.93	23.12	23
Origin	I	I	T	T	C	C	I	I	I	I	I	C	I	I	I	I	I	T	T

(Dash, "—", indicates that the syntactical feature does not occur within the given pericope.)

T – Translation Greek; C – Composition Greek; I – Inconclusive (either the syntactical feature does not occur within the given pericope or the ratio is on the border between translation and composition Greek.)

1Fox's calculation from his analysis of 57 lines of the LXX as published in M. V. Fox, *The Redaction of the Books of Esther*, (Atlanta: Scholars Press, 1991) 32. "na" indicates Fox's data is not available (not published).

LXX Table e: _Criterion #12_

Martin's Criterion #12: Greater Frequency of Genitive Personal Pronouns in Translation Greek
Translation Greek is indicated if the ratio of the number of lines of text to the number of genitive personal pronouns is ≤ 9. Composition Greek is indicated if the ratio is > 9.

Table e. Occurrence of Genitive Personal Pronouns

Chapter:	A	1	2	3	B	4	C	D	5	6	7	E	8	9	10	F	Total	Proto–LXX	Fox[1]
# Lines of Text	30	50	55	35	27	40	56	25	23	34	22	51	40	60	6	22	576	365	na
Genitive Personal Pronouns	7	11	11	5	2	7	51	18	7	3	8	4	12	8	3	5	162	75	na
Ratio	4.29	4.55	5.0	7.0	13.5	5.71	1.10	1.39	3.29	11.33	2.75	12.75	3.33	7.5	2.0	4.4	3.56	4.87	4.7
Origin	T	T	T	T	C	T	T	T	T	C	C	C	T	T	T	T	T	T	T

T – Translation Greek; C – Composition Greek

---

[1] Fox's calculation from his analysis of 57 lines of the LXX as published in M. V. Fox, *The Redaction of the Books of Esther*, (Atlanta: Scholars Press, 1991) 32. "na" indicates that Fox's data is not available (not published).

LXX Table f: *Criterion #13*

Martin's Criterion #13: Greater Frequency of Genitive Personal Pronouns Dependent on Anarthrous Substantives

Translation Greek is indicated if the ratio of the number of lines of text to the number of genitive personal pronouns dependent on anarthrous substantives is ≤ 77. Composition Greek is indicated if the ratio is > 100.

Table f. Occurrence of Genitive Personal Pronouns Dependent on Anarthrous Substantives

Chapter:	A	1	2	3	B	4	C	D	5	6	7	E	8	9	10	F	Total	Proto–LXX	Fox[1]
# Lines of Text	30	50	55	35	27	40	56	25	23	34	22	51	40	60	6	22	576	365	na
Gen.Pronoun with anarth. substantive	1	—	1	—	1	2	24	1	1	1	—	2	—	1	—	—	35	6	na
Ratio	30.0	—	55.0	—	27.0	20.0	2.33	25	23.0	34.0	—	25.5	—	60.0	—	—	16.46	60.83	0
Origin	T	I	T	I	T	T	T	T	T	T	T	I	T	I	I	I	T	T	T

(Dash, " — ", indicates that the syntactical feature does not occur in the given pericope.)

T – Translation Greek; C – Composition Greek; I – Inconclusive (the syntactical feature does not occur in the given pericope.)

---

[1] Fox's calculation from his analysis of 57 lines of the LXX as published in M. V. Fox, *The Redaction of the Books of Esther*, (Atlanta: Scholars Press, 1991) 32. "na" indicates that Fox's data is not available (not published).

Martin's Criterion #14: Infrequency of Attributive Adjectives Preceding the Word They Qualify

Translation Greek is indicated if the ratio of the number of attributive adjectives preceding the word they qualify to the number of attributive adjectives following the word they qualify is ≤ 0.35.
Composition Greek is indicated by a ratio >1.

Table g. Occurrence of Attributive Adjectives

Chapter:	A	1	2	3	B	4	C	D	5	6	7	E	8	9	10	F	Total	Proto-LXX	Fox[1]
Adjective Precedes	2	—	1	—	4	1	2	1	—	—	1	19	1	7	—	3	42	11	na
Adjective Follows	9	3	7	1	2	4	4	3	—	1	1	4	7	5	—	3	54	29	na
Ratio	0.22	—	0.14	—	2.0	0.25	0.50	0.33	—	—	1.0	4.75	0.14	1.4	—	1.0	0.77	0.38	1.0
Origin	T	I	T	I	C	T	T	T	I	I	C	C	T	C	I	C	T	T	C

(Dash, "—", indicates the syntactical feature does not occur in the given pericope.)

T – Translation Greek; C – Composition Greek; I – Inconclusive (either the syntactical feature does not occur in the given pericope or the ratio falls between the limits given by Martin.)

---

[1] Fox's calculation from his analysis of **57 lines** of the LXX as published in M. V. Fox, *The Redaction of the Books of Esther*, (Atlanta: Scholars Press, 1991) 32. "na" indicates Fox's data is not available (not published).

Martin's Criterion #15: Relative Infrequency of Attributive Adjectives

Translation Greek is indicated if the ratio of the number of lines of text per attributive adjective is > 10. Composition Greek is indicated if the ratio is < 6.5.

Table h. Occurrence of Attributive Adjectives

Chapter:	A	1	2	3	B	4	C	D	5	6	7	E	8	9	10	F	Total	Proto–LXX	Fox[1]
# Lines of Text	30	50	55	35	27	40	56	25	23	34	22	51	40	60	6	22	576	365	na
# of adjectives	11	3	8	1	6	5	6	4	—	1	2	23	8	12	—	6	96	40	na
Ratio	2.73	16.66	6.88	35.0	4.5	8.0	9.33	6.25	—	34.0	11.0	2.22	5.0	5.0	—	3.67	6.0	9.13	16.0
Origin	C	T	I	T	C	C	I	I	C	I	T	T	C	I	I	C	C	I	T

(Dash, "—", indicates the syntactical feature does not occur in the given pericope.)

T – Translation Greek; C – Composition Greek; I – Inconclusive (either the syntactical feature does not occur in the given pericope or the ratio falls between the limits given by Martin.)

---

1 Fox's calculation from his analysis of 57 lines of the LXX as published in M. V. Fox, *The Redaction of the Books of Esther*, (Atlanta: Scholars Press, 1991) 33. "na" indicates Fox's data is not available (not published).

LXX Table i: *Criterion #16*

Martin's Criterion #16: Infrequency of Adverbial Participles in Translation Greek

Translation Greek is indicated if the ratio of the number of lines of text to the number of adverbial participles is > 6. Composition Greek is indicated if the ratio is < 6.

Table i. Occurrence of Adverbial Participles

Chapter:	A	1	2	3	B	4	C	D	5	6	7	E	8	9	10	F	Total	Proto-LXX	Fox[1]
# lines of text	30	50	55	35	27	40	56	25	23	34	22	51	40	60	6	22	576	365	na
# adverbial participles	5	2	1	3	10	11	4	8	2	4	5	12	5	6	2	2	80	39	na
Ratio	6.0	25.0	55.0	11.67	2.7	3.64	14.0	3.13	11.5	8.5	4.4	4.25	8.0	10.0	3.0	11.0	7.2	9.40	6.6
Origin	I	T	T	T	C	C	T	C	C	T	C	C	T	T	T	T	T	T	T

(Dash, "—", indicates the syntactical feature does not occur in the given pericope.)

T – Translation Greek; C – Composition Greek; I – Inconclusive (either the syntactical feature does not occur in the given pericope or the ratio is between translation and composition Greek.)

---

[1] Fox's calculation from his analysis of 57 lines of the LXX as published in M. V. Fox, *The Redaction of the Books of Esther*, (Atlanta: Scholars Press, 1991) 33. "na" indicates Fox's data not available (not published).

Martin's Criterion #17: Frequency of the Dative Case

Translation Greek is indicated if the ratio of the number of datives not used with ἐν to the number of datives used with ἐν is less than 2. Composition Greek is indicated if the ratio is > 3.

Table j. Occurrence of Dative Case[1]

Chapter:	A	1	2	3	B	4	C	D	5	6	7	E	8	9	10	F	Total	Proto-LXX	Fox 2
Dative without ἐν	4	26	18	17	11	20	12	3	6	13	6	33	19	20	1	5	214	146	na
Dative with ἐν	6	9	10	7	5	5	13	3	4	6	3	2	12	16	2	5	108	74	na
Ratio	0.67	2.89	1.8	2.43	2.2	4.0	0.92	1.0	1.5	2.17	2.0	16.5	1.58	1.25	0.5	1.0	1.98	1.97	5
Origin	T	I	T	I	I	C	C	T	T	I	I	C	C	T	T	T	T	T	C

T – Translation Greek; C – Composition Greek

---

[1] To conform to the counting used by Martin and Fox, datives used with forms of λέγω, εἶπον and δίδωμι have been excluded from this count.

[2] Fox's calculation from his analysis of 57 lines of the LXX as published in M. V. Fox, *The Redaction of the Books of Esther*, (Atlanta: Scholars Press, 1991) 33. "na" indicates Fox's data not available (not published).

General Index

Index of Biblical & Apocryphal References

Index of Biblical & Apocryphal References